# TOWARD A SOUND ECOLOGY

# MUSIC, NATURE, PLACE
Sabine Feisst and Denise Von Glahn

# TOWARD A SOUND ECOLOGY

*New and Selected Essays*

Jeff Todd Titon

INDIANA UNIVERSITY PRESS

This book is a publication of

Indiana University Press
Office of Scholarly Publishing
Herman B Wells Library 350
1320 East 10th Street
Bloomington, Indiana 47405 USA

iupress.indiana.edu

© 2020 by Jeff Todd Titon

All rights reserved
No part of this book may be reproduced or utilized in any form or by any means, electronic or mechanical, including photocopying and recording, or by any information storage and retrieval system, without permission in writing from the publisher. The paper used in this publication meets the minimum requirements of the American National Standard for Information Sciences—Permanence of Paper for Printed Library Materials, ANSI Z39.48-1992.

Manufactured in the United States of America

Cataloging information is available from the Library of Congress.

ISBN 978-0-253-04967-4 (hardback)
ISBN 978-0-253-04968-1 (paperback)
ISBN 978-0-253-05236-0 (ebook)

1 2 3 4 5   25 24 23 22 21 20

# CONTENTS

*List of Illustrations* vii

*Acknowledgments* ix

Introduction   1

## I. Field Work: Folklore and Ethnomusicology

1. The Life Story   11
2. Ethnomusicology as the Study of People Making Music   27
3. Text   38
4. Knowing Fieldwork   66
5. Applied Ethnomusicology: A Descriptive and Historical Account   87

## II. Cultural and Musical Sustainability

6. "The Real Thing": Tourism, Authenticity, and Pilgrimage among the Old Regular Baptists at the 1997 Smithsonian Folklife Festival   123
7. Music and Sustainability: An Ecological Viewpoint   152
8. Sustainability, Resilience, and Adaptive Management for Applied Ethnomusicology   171

## III. Toward a Sound Ecology

    9  A Sound Commons for All Living Creatures  *219*

  10  The Nature of Ecomusicology  *223*

  11  Thoreau's Ear  *236*

  12  The Sound of Climate Change  *248*

  13  Sustainability and a Sound Ecology  *254*

*References*   *277*

*Selected List of Publications by Jeff Todd Titon*   *297*

*Index*   *303*

# ILLUSTRATIONS

Figure 1.1. Eddie "Son" House, Minneapolis, Minnesota, 1970 — 15

Figure 1.2. John Sherfey preaching, Stanley, Virginia, 1977 — 25

Figure 4.1. Lazy Bill Lucas, Minneapolis, Minnesota, 1969 — 68

Figure 6.1. Old Regular Baptist Cemetery, Kentucky, 1993 — 127

Figure 12.1. Hermit thrush — 251

Figure 13.1. Bumblebee pollinating arbutus flower by means of sonication — 257

Figure 13.2. Homo reciprocans — 264

Figure 13.3. Conference poster, Culture-Gene Interactions — 270

Figure 13.4. Interspecies cooperation between white-breasted nuthatch and black-capped chickadee — 272

# ACKNOWLEDGMENTS

IN WRITING THESE ESSAYS, I INCURRED MANY DEBTS along the way from friends, colleagues, and hosts to whom I'm very grateful: Aaron Allen, Samuel Araujo, Robert Baron, Greg Barz, Max-Peter Baumann, Cherice Bock, Mia Boynton, Michael Bull, Bob Callahan, Bill Clements, Bill Coles, Tim Cooley, Elwood Cornett, Kathy Cornett, Marta Daniels, Dan Dennett, Mark DeVoto, Mark DeWitt, Beverley Diamond, Barry Dornfeld, Anu Dudley, Salwa El-Shawan, Veit Erlmann, Burt Feintuch, Dosh Fields, Jim Fields, Linda Fujie, Leslie Gay, Ken George, Henry Glassie, Darrell Grant, Steve Green, Klisala Harrison, Bess Hawes, Meredith Holmgren, Mary Hufford, Susan Hurley-Glowa, Patrick Hutchinson, Lewis Hyde, Ken Irby, Sam Jenkins, Loyal Jones, Alan Kagan, Enrique Leff, Albert Lord, Bill Lucas, Leo Marx, Dave McAllester, Judy McCulloh, Kiri Miller, Larry Millman, Bruno Nettl, Cameron Nickels, Wayne Newell, Barry O'Connell, Marcia Ostashewski, Diana Parker, Dan Patterson, Mark Pedelty, Erkki Pekkila, Svanibor Pettan, Don Pratt, Shirley Pratt, Tom Rankin, Phil Rhodes, Jesper Rosenmeier, Suzanne Ryan, Oscar Schotté, Tony Seeger, John Sherfey, Christopher Smith, Bob Stange, Jeff Summit, Barbara Tedlock, Dennis Tedlock, Tom Turino, Rory Turner, Denise Von Glahn, Franziska von Rosen, Thomas Walker, John Wallhausser, Jernej Weiss, Maryanne Wolf, and Andy Woolf. Those I mentioned will know why; to those I've forgotten to name, my sincere apologies.

I owe an unrepayable debt to the educational institutions that have supported me over the years: my undergraduate alma mater, Amherst College; my graduate school alma mater, the University of Minnesota; Tufts University, where I taught from 1971 to 1986; and Brown University, where I directed the doctoral program in ethnomusicology from 1986 to 2013. I'm grateful to several organizations for fellowships supporting my research, among them the National Endowment for the Humanities, the National Endowment for the Arts, and the Hutchins Center (formerly W. E. B. DuBois Institute) at Harvard. A number of colleges and universities graciously hosted me as a visiting professor, including East Tennessee State University, Indiana University, Berea College, and Amherst College.

I thank the following publishers for permission to reprint essays that first appeared in their books and journals: the University of Illinois Press for "The Life Story," from the *Journal of American Folklore*, and for "Text," from

*Eight Words for the Study of Expressive Culture*, edited by Burt Feintuch; Oxford University Press for "Knowing Fieldwork," from *Shadows in the Field*, edited by Gregory Barz and Timothy Cooley, and for "Applied Ethnomusicology: A Descriptive and Historical Account" and "Sustainability, Resilience, Adaptive Management, and Applied Ethnomusicology," from *The Oxford Handbook of Applied Ethnomusicology*, edited by Svanibor Pettan and Jeff Todd Titon; *Muzikoloski Zbornik* (Musicological Annual, Slovenia) for "Ethnomusicology as the Study of People Making Music"; *the world of music* for "'The Real Thing': Tourism, Authenticity and Pilgrimage among the Old Regular Baptists at the 1997 Smithsonian Folklife Festival" and for "Music and Sustainability: An Ecological Viewpoint"; the Smithsonian Institution for "A Sound Commons for All Living Creatures," from *Smithsonian Folkways Magazine*; ABET (the Brazilian Ethnomusicology Society) for "The Nature of Ecomusicology," from *Música e Cultura*; Taylor and Francis for "Thoreau's Ear," from *Sound Studies*; and *Whole Terrain* for "The Sound of Climate Change." Full references to these essays may be found in the Selected List of Publications.

# TOWARD A SOUND ECOLOGY

# INTRODUCTION

Anyone who's been published and reviewed knows that feeling of bewilderment when critics tell you what you really said, or meant to say, or should have said but didn't. Decades ago, a writer made a reputation from "The Intentional Fallacy," an essay claiming that because authors never truly, deeply know what they intend, there isn't much point in reading for meaning in what they write about their own writing. The meanings, wrote William K. Wimsatt (1956, 3–20), lie hidden in the hieroglyph that the literary text itself makes; it is not in the author's life or beliefs nor how the author might interpret them. A few decades later, most critics were in agreement that a text's meaning varied depending on its interpretive communities, each operating according to its own rules, traditions, and consensus and each more or less valid in its own right. So readers are advised to take my interpretive remarks for what they may be worth, knowing they'll also discover their own patterns, like a "figure in a Persian carpet," in the words of Henry James (1897, 33).

The figure in the carpet can be a helpful metaphor to think through the problems of coherence, discovered and imposed. James aficionados will recall that in his short story of that title, a well-known novelist, one Hugh Vereker, tells the story's narrator, a literary critic trying to rise in the world, that encompassing Vereker's entire oeuvre there exists a pattern, a figure in the carpet, a "general intention," "the very string upon which the pearls are strung" (ibid.). Vereker won't say what the figure is, though, and the rest of the story details the narrator's failed quest to discover it, even though his good friend (another literary critic) and friend's wife have, after years of effort, puzzled it out. The trouble is, they won't—or can't—reveal it, and all three go to their graves with the secret, leaving the narrator as baffled in the end as he was at the beginning. This reader of James's story does not doubt the existence of a figure in the carpet but comes to wonder about it: When it comes to be known, can it be put into words? And more, if it can be put into words, could the words possibly do it justice without diminishing its effect?

With those forewarnings in mind, I avoided looking for a figure in the carpet of my teaching, research, and writings until I was required to do so, the occasion being an invitation in 2014 to address one of my professional societies in answer to some questions based on the American Council of Learned

Societies' "My Life in Learning" premise. One of their questions was "What are the key organizing concepts you have found consistently interesting in your progress and your career?" In response, I told them that only in the past dozen or so years had an organizing concept seemed to reveal itself. I named it: the affective and connecting powers of sound, music being one manifestation of it among many. The figure in my carpet is not just sound but the connections among beings that sounds make: physical, communicative, technological, social, economic, and metaphysical. In some of the writings, it is close to the surface; in others, it is in a deeper layer.

That said, I went on to remark that I had some reservations about progress and career. I recalled that when I was in my forties, a colleague remarked that I'd traveled an unusual academic pathway. What she meant was that curiosity had led me in several directions. I've done most of my teaching in national research universities, but I've also held visiting positions in regional universities and small colleges. I have graduate degrees in American studies and in English. I've taught in and either founded, cofounded, or directed programs in ethnomusicology and in American studies; and I've been appointed in departments of English, music, Appalachian studies, and religious studies. Since college and graduate school, I've also been deeply interested in cultural anthropology, ecological science, history, economics, and philosophy. My social conscience was formed in the counterculture of the sixties—in the civil rights, anti–Vietnam War, and environmental movements in particular—and directly or indirectly, that has always informed what I wrote about. I've also been a musician since I was a boy—my mother told me I sang before I talked—and an organic gardener for more than forty years; my experiences making music, growing food, and sustaining the musical and cultural soil that provides for them have deeply impacted my outlook.

Therefore, I went on to say, that curiosity had led me to cobble together procedures and methods from a variety of perspectives—and not only academic ones—to help me think through several related questions or problems. In my research and writing, besides the organizing principle of sound's affective and connecting powers, I can discern recurrent themes and topics, among them the following:

- a concern with the creative imagination and expressive culture: how people, in their daily lives, make and express themselves to themselves and others by making sounds, telling stories, and shaping materials within their environments; leading me to
  - an experiential, friendship-based approach to ethnographic fieldwork, documentation, and interpretation; leading me to

- a concern for reciprocity, equity, and justice; leading to
- partnership with communities, advocacy, and humanities in the public interest; leading me to
- developing strategies of stewardship, commons, sustainability, and resilience; leading me to
- theorizing a sonic orientation in the world as a way of being and thinking about nature and environment, social groups, economic exchanges, and ways of being in community—not only with other humans but also with all the creatures that inhabit Earth.

In the past dozen years or so, these themes and topics have come together in the project that I have been calling a sound ecology.

Like John Cage ([1973] 2010, 18), who wrote in his diary that "reading Thoreau's journal, I discover any idea I've ever had worth its salt" had been expressed earlier by Henry David Thoreau, I found much inspiration for a sound ecology in Thoreau's writings, especially his journals. In his journal for March 3, 1841, he wrote, "It is a strangely healthy sound for these disjointed times. It is a rare soundness when cow-bells and horns are heard from over the fields. And now I see the beauty and full meaning of that word 'sound.' Nature always possesses a certain sonorousness, as in the hum of insects, the booming of ice, the crowing of cocks in the morning, and the barking of dogs in the night, which indicates her sound state." In 2006, I began speaking and writing about an ecological approach to musical and cultural sustainability. Sustainability has become a key concept among folklorists and ethnomusicologists in the dozen years since then. In writing about a sustaining sound ecology, I expanded my scope to sound, social groups, and cultural theory more generally. The question I've been puzzling over, ever since I first formulated it (Titon 1994, 8) in a keynote address before the Finnish Ethnomusicological Society in 1993, is this: What would happen if we took music and sound, rather than text or material object, as the basis for our being in, understanding, and acting in the world? It is an ontological, epistemological, and action-oriented question. By a sound ecology, I refer not only to an acoustic connective tissue but also, following Thoreau, to a sound basis for a healthy economy and to a sound and just community of and for all beings.

When in 1969 I chose to write my doctoral dissertation in American Studies on blues music and culture, my program adviser wondered aloud to me about the professional consequences of such an odd choice. And if blues was a more obscure academic subject then than, say, military technology and foreign policy, or agrarianism and the American novel, it would be hard to find words to describe how recherché was my next project. After revising my dissertation for publication, I began ethnographic research on the sound and meaning of musical, or intoned, preaching in the black and white folk traditions and joined a tiny group of scholars in religious folklife, none of whom was investigating that, precisely, though all of us were working within a similar context involving ritual, belief, and performance. I recall that when we attended meetings of our professional societies, we invariably were made to present our research at 8:00 a.m. on Sunday in the smallest conference room of the hotel, until one among us became so annoyed that she suggested to the program committee that we might have had something else to do on a Sunday morning. In that same decade, the 1970s, collaborating with four other ethnomusicologists teaching at New England colleges and drawing on my education in ecology in college and graduate school, I wrote a textbook based on the idea that musical cultures could be understood as ecological systems, worlds within worlds of music (Titon 1984, 9). Then, in the 1980s, after more than a decade of ethnographic documentation and interpretation, as well as a not especially successful attempt to bring blues lyrics and traditional African American sermons into the American literary canon, my ethnographic research took a turn toward community partnerships in the service of musical and cultural conservation. I began to think more broadly about a methodological toolkit and started writing theoretical articles on ethnomusicology as the study of people making music; on fieldwork, collaboration, and friendship; on an applied ethnomusicology and its relation to the public good; on the nature of evidence and experience in the work we were engaged in—that sort of thing. Colleagues began soliciting more essays on these topics, and I was invited to direct a doctoral program in ethnomusicology. The president of the Society for Ethnomusicology asked me to edit their flagship journal, *Ethnomusicology*.

    In the midst of this flurry of professional activity, I cherished time when I could get away to a small summer house in the woods on an island off the Maine coast, where I could write and tend an organic garden. There, I read Thoreau's journals and compared his natural history observations with what I found on my daily walks in the forest and alongshore. Always interested in sound and meaning, in the 1990s I took a serious interest in birdsong and found to my delight that Thoreau had been a keen observer of birdsong as well as other environmental sounds: of frogs, crickets, wind, rain, the cries of children, the sounds of livestock, and the echoing church bells. I was drifting from music to sound. Like so many others before and since, I was looking for a resonant alternative to the epistemological stance that is often called Cartesian dualism, the separation between mind and body, subject and object, the thinking scholar interpreting the external text or, as Richard Rorty (1985) put it, the natural scientist analyzing the behavior of "lumps" (things). In the 1970s and 1980s, I was complicit with this epistemology in considering performance to be an ethnographic text comprised of referents—direct, metaphorical, and symbolic. Text was everywhere waiting to be interpreted; anything that could be interpreted was text. But where, then, was the interpreter in relation to the text? Experience suggested an intersubjective connection of some sort, but that connection had been severed by a hermeneutic of distance. In the early and mid-1990s, I was still writing about text but seeking a sound alternative, both in hypertext and multimedia and then in the conscious experience of making music, "doing things together" as sociologist Howard Becker (1986) insisted.

I might have realized how important doing things together—connected by sound—was to me around 1982, when I started offering a new course, an old-time string band ensemble, in our university ethnomusicology curriculum. Once a week, I convened a jam session; showed the students how to play fiddle, banjo, mandolin, and guitar by ear; and taught them some tunes, and for the rest of the time, we just enjoyed ourselves playing them. This instruction was new for me—all my previous university teaching had been in academic courses, not performance—and new to the field of ethnomusicology, for university ensembles in ethnomusicology featured non-Western music such as Ghanaian drumming or Javanese gamelan. I remember that our music department's chairperson asked me if I expected course relief or extra pay for it, and that I said I didn't, adding that just doing it gave me plenty of relief. Thirty-one years later, after I retired, a couple of former students took over the course, and as I write, it still attracts about thirty students and community members every semester.

In the spring of 2004, the program committee at the state of Maine's Common Ground Country Fair asked me if I'd bring some friends and neighbors to their annual organic farming and gardening event the following September to demonstrate an old-time string band jam session. They'd heard that we'd been playing at our local farmers' market—one of our group brought organic produce to sell at the market weekly, and word got back to the fair—and then they learned that for us music making chiefly meant getting together in each other's homes for tunes, sociality, and potlucks. It represented a kind of community music, said the fair sponsors (the Maine Organic Farming and Gardening Association), that was very much in the spirit of the fair, which was themed as a celebration of sustainable living.

Although I was familiar with the idea of sustainability in connection with economic development, agriculture, and energy resources, my operative concepts for music and culture were tradition and conservation, not sustainability. And I hadn't thought about any of those three in connection with a string band musical revival I'd been participating in personally for decades. The director informed me that as the fair had grown from a small, countercultural celebration to a three-day event that then attracted nearly forty thousand people each year, they now were rethinking the kind of music they wanted to showcase. Until then, they'd hired folksinger-songwriters, but now, in the spirit of sustainable living, they'd decided they wanted to showcase neighborhood music more than they wanted to provide entertainment. And so they began to invite community music groups, contra dance bands, and people like us. We began an annual appearance at the fair. In the dozen years since then, yearly fair attendance has doubled to eighty thousand, though surely not on account of us.

Fortunately, in 2004 I was in a sabbatical year away from teaching. I shelved my original project and instead researched sustainability. I started thinking about what it might mean for music and culture and what advantages sustainability offered over the then operative concepts: preservation, conservation, and safeguarding. When I was invited to give the Nettl Lecture at the University of Illinois in the spring of 2006, I decided that the time had come to begin speaking to my academic colleagues about musical and cultural sustainability. Bruno Nettl, in partial retirement after a distinguished career in ethnomusicology, came up to me after I spoke, smiling while exclaiming, "Well, we've never heard anything here like that before!" I wasn't sure if he was referring to the personal nature of the scholarship with its roots in organic farming, to the concept of sustainability as it might connect with music making, or to my advocating for an applied ethnomusicology. Possibly it was all of those.

In the fall of 2006, I spoke to the American Folklore Society about sustainability, and for the Society of Ethnomusicology I organized a panel on music and sustainability. Our presentations from that panel were published three years later in a special issue of a European ethnomusicology journal, *the world of music*. Musical and cultural sustainability caught a tailwind, and in the next few years I was invited to lecture on it at more than a dozen universities, including a series at the Central Conservatory of Music in Beijing. Under the guidance of Rory Turner, an MA program in cultural sustainability was established in 2010 at Goucher College; and in 2013, the American Folklore Society made it the overarching theme of their annual conference. As I write, a group of my colleagues' contemporary essays on the subject of sustainability, dedicated to my work in this area and edited by two professors whose dissertations I advised, is being prepared for the University of Illinois Press (Cooley 2019). For its foreword (Titon 2019, xi–xx), which may be of interest in conjunction with this introduction, I was asked to reflect on my intellectual development and how I came to bring sustainability to music and culture. In the collection you are reading now, several essays bear on musical and cultural sustainability. Indeed, the essays that follow were written over a forty-year period. Inevitably there is some recurrence of theme, concept, context, and reference. Yet I trust that in these essays, those ideas don't just repeat but develop and deepen.

In 2011, two events occurred that moved me further in the direction of a sound ecology. The first was an invitation to offer, as a representative of the humanities, a Sidore Lecture to a gathering of scientists and engineers involved with the Sustainability Academy (now the Sustainability Institute) at the University of New Hampshire; and the second was my growing interest in ecomusicology. To prepare for the lecture, I turned back to Thoreau, looking throughout his journals and other writings to find specifically what he wrote about preservation, conservation, and sustainability. Instead, I was captivated once again by his entries on sound, on the ear (the healthy ear, the innocent ear, listening from the side of the ear, and so on), and especially on the sounds of the natural world, including the "earth song," as he often called the sounds that insects and amphibians made. It became ever clearer to me, as it had been to Thoreau, that music was a special case of sound in the world; sound was the covering category while music, I knew, was made as sounds and constructed as a formal, cultural domain. As a result, my Sidore Lecture to the Sustainability Academy was about Thoreau and sound. In addition, I delivered a paper in 2012 on Thoreau and sound for the second ecomusicology conference (Titon 2016). My sustainable music research blog (Titon 2008–) began to fill with entries on Thoreau and sound, and topics in other directions where that was taking me: animal sounds, animal communication, animal rights, animal consciousness, and so forth.

Since 2012 the project on a sound ecology has occupied most of my attention. It starts from the premise that sound waves announce the presence of a being and connect one being to another through copresence. The copresence of sound communication is characteristic not only of humans but also nonhuman animals and, as scientists are gradually discovering, the plant world as well. Copresence encourages certain kinds of exchanges among beings while discouraging those in which the connections are distant or absent. Copresence has implications, therefore, not only in communication exchanges but also in other kinds, such as economic exchanges, favoring close relations over more formal and contractual arrangements. Copresence also encourages certain kinds of exchange-based communities while discouraging others. Animal sound communication, music psychology, behavioral ecology, ecological economics, environmental humanities, and sustainability and resilience studies all bear on this project, expanding it to consider all beings, within a posthuman context. The integration of materialist worldviews into traditional ecological knowledges and their relation to Western scientific, philosophical, religious, and social thought also contribute to this ongoing project whose purpose, as I wrote above, is to try to understand what would follow from taking music and sound, rather than text or object, as the basis for being in, knowing, and acting in the world.

# I.

# FIELD WORK: FOLKLORE AND ETHNOMUSICOLOGY

THIS SECTION'S ESSAYS ADDRESS SOME OF THE QUESTIONS that, for me, have constructed folklore studies and ethnomusicology during the last fifty years: What are the natures of oral narrative, and how are they experienced? What is the nature of fieldwork, and what kinds of knowledges arise from it? What are the meanings of text, how are they experienced in performance, how do they live in memory and community, and what will the texts of the future be? What definitions of ethnomusicology and of applied ethnomusicology are worth having, in light of the history and praxis in the field? I also address these questions in *Early Downhome Blues, Worlds of Music, Powerhouse for God, Give Me This Mountain*, and my other books, but the essay form offers an opportunity for more precise focus and, paradoxically, for more speculative conclusions.

# 1

## THE LIFE STORY

AUTOBIOGRAPHY BEGAN TO WHET MY CURIOSITY IN THE 1960s in connection with blues lyrics and the narratives blues singers told me about their lives. In the mid-1970s, I developed a seminar on oral and written narrative where, among other things, we explored the fictive aspects of nonfiction genres such as autobiography and ethnography. (I write about that seminar in "Text" and "Knowing Fieldwork," both reprinted in this volume.) "The Life Story" emerged after John Sherfey, the principal figure in my book Powerhouse for God, replied to my interview question "When and where were you born?" by telling me the story of his life, uninterrupted until my recorder ran out of tape a half hour later. Conversations with anthropologists Dennis and Barbara Tedlock about our fieldwork; about stories, oral poetry, and ethnopoetics; and about the rendering of oral performance in print helped me understand Sherfey's life story narrative further within a broader performance context. Around that time and then unbeknownst to me, folklorist Sandra Kay Dolby-Stahl was naming and defining a similar folkloric performance genre, the "personal experience narrative." Like life stories, personal experience stories were first-person oral narratives. As a folklore genre, the personal experience story had been neglected because of its allegedly nontraditional content; it was not a folktale, riddle, proverb, or other defined genre of verbal folklore but rather a true story. Yet, she and other folklorists contended, it could be examined for its performance characteristics and for the folklore themes and motifs it displayed, even when its content was nontraditional. Its status as a folklore genre did not trouble me. I was interested in the life story as oral autobiography, concerned with distinguishing it from life history, biography, and oral history, while emphasizing its fictive aspect and discussing the relation of life storytelling to meaning making and personal identity. Toward the end of this essay, I wrote about fieldwork and friendship, a theme I developed in several subsequent essays. An anti-instrumentalist bias ("the life story need not be 'used' for anything"), developed in my sound ecology project thirty years later, is also evident here.

*An earlier version of this essay was presented to the Graduate Colloquium in Folklore and Folklife at the University of Pennsylvania on October 1, 1979.*

A life story is, simply, a person's story of his or her life, or of what he or she thinks is a significant part of that life. It is therefore a personal narrative, a story of personal experience, and, as it emerges from conversation, its ontological status is the spoken word, even if the story is transcribed and edited for the printed page. The storyteller trusts the listener(s), and the listener respects the storyteller, not interrupting the train of thought until the story is finished. That is not to say the listener is passive as a doorknob: he or she nods assent, interposes a comment, frames a relevant question—indeed, his or her presence and reactions are essential to the story. The listener may coincidentally be a folklorist, but the role is mainly that of a sympathetic friend.

This essay is directed to folklorists whose fieldwork, like my own, involves talking to people and finding out about their lives. My intention is to define and develop an approach to the life story as a self-contained fiction and thus to distinguish it sharply from its historical kin: biography, oral history, and the personal history (or "life history," as it is called in anthropology).

Among the dimensions of folk culture that Richard Dorson observed during his 1968 field trip to Gary and East Chicago, Indiana, was something he called "personal history." He told folklorists to cast aside worries over whether the personal history is a traditional oral genre and urged them to collect the "thousands of sagas created from life experiences that deserve, indeed cry for, recording" (Dorson 1970, 67–68). Dorson caught the documentary spirit of the times. The following decade witnessed a rebirth of interest in the experiences of ordinary Americans, especially blue-collar workers, racial and ethnic minorities, and women. Not since the New Deal era was there such a burst of documentary energy. Studs Terkel's books became best sellers; Robert Coles's books influenced public policy; Theodore Rosengarten's life of black Alabama sharecropper Ned Cobb won the National Book Award; professional sociologists turned out monographs on the lives and opinions of the so-called silent majority; hundreds of oral history projects were born at the local level, thousands of people were interviewed, and millions of pages of typescript were produced (Terkel 1967; Coles 1967; Rosengarten 1974). Folklore's contribution to the documentation decade, in the popular mind, resides in the Foxfire concept of education and the resulting *Foxfire* book (Wigginton 1972) and the subsequent books in the series.[1]

In the midst of all the documentation, it is well to recall what Thoreau ([1854] 1985, 411) wrote: "Much is published, but little is printed." Most of the published documents appear to be life stories but are not. That is, they give the impression that a person is speaking about their life in their own voice, but in reality someone else has muffled and distorted it. What appears to be a person telling a life story is usually an informant answering a series of questions. Then by a common ruse, the interview comes to masquerade as a life story. The interviewer or an editor selects the relevant answers; arranges them according to editorial purposes, be they chronological, topical, or historical; smooths out the talk for the printed page; and then removes the questions. This false alchemy is clear enough when one compares Terkel's writings with his tapes. It is a brazen art in the hands of Coles (who does not use a tape recorder);[2] it is obvious in the two or three segments of each Foxfire book given over to personal narratives; and it is evident also in the relatively small number of personal documents that professional folklorists have published.

The reason we transform interviews into life stories on the printed page without much uneasiness is that we habitually fail to distinguish story from history when the medium is talk. Dorson's choice of the phrase "personal history" is illuminating, for he used it interchangeably with the phrase "life story" when recalling how he happened upon examples of them: "Several memorable life stories," he wrote, "came to my ears without prompting" (Dorson 1970, 67). As a good historian, Dorson knows that story is not the same as history. If he sometimes conflates the two, it may be because his concept of folk history relies on the transformation of oral traditions and personal documents, set in the structures of everyday life, into the history of the folk (Dorson 1972).

The difference between story and history is perhaps best understood through what Charles Olson, that most historical of poets, labeled "stance." Olson identified two complementary stances toward life: fiction (story, including poetry) and history. In its root sense, *facio*, fiction is not a lie but a "making," whereas history, *'istorin*, is "found out." To Herodotus, the Greek verb *poiein* (from which our "poet" derives) meant "to make," whereas the noun *histor* meant a "learned man," and the verb *'istorin* meant "to find out for oneself" (Olson 1970, 19–23). A story is made, but history is found out. Story is language at play; history is language at work. The language of story is charged with power: it creates. The language of history is charged with knowledge: it discovers. Story is a literature of the imagination; history, though it be imaginative, drives toward fact. The generation of historians who were my teachers believed, along with R. G. Collingwood, that history was a branch of the humanities. So long as history is humanistic, it is a complement of story; but they are not the same and certainly not interchangeable (Collingwood 1948).

"The real language of men in a state of vivid sensation" was how Wordsworth (1805, i) characterized the source of his own poetic diction, contrasting it with the language of artifice used by poets who had been long out of touch with genuine human sympathy. The romantic baggage that accompanied Wordsworth's revolutionary ideas placed a value on rustic life that few modern folklorists would publicly embrace. Nonetheless, his interest in the common man and woman of the countryside was chiefly an interest in the renewing power of a natural language that arose from deeply felt, personal experience. This, of course, is the language of the life story, not the language of history. It is particularly not the language of history today, for increasingly during the past twenty years the narrative mode of writing history has been attacked for its failure to meet adequate scientific standards of explanation. Many historians now believe that so-called covering-law explanations—that is, explanations of specific events by a general law that "covers" the specific conditions—are the only valid form of historical explanation. Whatever its value in historical writing, this scientific criterion is irrelevant to explanation in storytelling. Why it is irrelevant is best illustrated by an example, a life story. The following life story is the religious conversion narrative of blues singer Son House (fig. 1.1), which he told to me in response to my asking why he waited until adulthood to become a blues singer. I have transcribed it verbatim from my field tape:

> When I was a kid, a youngster, a teen—a young teenager and up like that I was more churchified. Then that's mostly all I could see into. 'Cause they'd had us go, we'd had to go to the Sabbath school every Sunday. We didn't miss goin' to no Sabbath school. We'd be into that and then in this church there, some of the ones a little larger than me and like that, and it come time of year for 'em to run revival meetin'. Some pastor come to open up the revival meetin', oh, for a week or more. [Coughs.] Well, we'd all be goin' to the thing they call the mourners' bench. Gettin' on your knees, you know, and lettin' the old folks pray for you. Yeah, and in a couple of days or weeks, somebody'd come up, holler out they had something. They had religion. They'd squall round man, go on. So they left me thataway I guess, oh about, near 'bout six or eight months sometime. I didn't fall for it because I, I figured they was puttin' on and I didn't want to be puttin' on. I wanted mine to be real and so I just kept on until finally, [clears throat] the next session, I said, "Is there—this one time I'm just gon see is—is any way to get this thing religion they goin' 'round here talkin' about, puttin' on and goin' on." I prayed and prayed, commenced prayin', man, every night, workin' in the field, and plowin' the mule and everything. Work all day hard, and go on home, whew, tryin' to pray, tryin' to pray, and work. So, finally, I kept on like that until they come back home that night, middle of the night after the pastor turned out. So I went on home. And I was livin' down in the lower part [of] the place from where my daddy an' them stayed, down to my cousin's. Went down there; I didn't

Figure 1.1. Eddie "Son" House, Minneapolis, Minnesota, 1970. Photo by Jeff Todd Titon.

want to be up there around the old folks. And man, I went out back of the house a little bit, in this old alfalfa field out there. I had been scared of snakes, 'cause snakes would be bad in the summertime, you know, crawlin' through them weeds and things. But I wasn't studyin' them snakes then. I'd say they better get out of the way if they don't want to get their heads mashed off! [Laughs.] I went on. I was there in that alfalfa field and I got down. Pray. Gettin' on my knees in that alfalfa. Dew was fallin'. And man, I prayed and I prayed and I prayed and for wait awhile, man I hollered out. Found out then. I said, "Yes, it is somethin' to be got, too, 'cause I got it now!" [Laughs.] Sure did. Went on back there to that house and told my cousin Robert and all them 'bout that and went, walked about two miles and a little better, and up to another white fellow's house, and woke him up and told him all about it. We was workin' for him, too. But I wouldn't care how tough he was or what not. "Get up out of that bed and listen to what I got to say." [Laughs.] He thought I was crazy! Yeah. Name was, we all called him Mister Keaton, T. F. Keaton. Yeah, I say, "Oh yeah!" Found out better now. (Titon 1976, 2–6; 1977, 21–22)[3]

On hearing this story, a doubting Thomas might object that it contains a hollow core—that the before and after of conversion is described but not the moment itself. Someone who had undergone a similar experience and was less of an empiricist would perhaps say such a demand was philistine. But proof is not at issue here. Nor is it a question of whether the religion Son House was converted to is a delusion. What is at issue is a human being recollecting, in a state of vivid sensation, a critical moment in his life and to a degree reexperiencing it by means of storytelling. Covering laws stating conditions under which conversion is probable operate in an entirely different dimension. A sophisticated religious critique might score Son House for confusing an intensely felt experience with the validation of a worldview, but no critic could rob him of the memory of his religious conversion. His life story is not a historical description, and it does not obey historical laws. It is a fiction, a making, and like all powerful fictions, it drives toward enactment.

## Biography, Oral History, and Personal History

Among the historical kin to the life story are biography, oral history, and the personal history (or anthropological life history). Any folklorist interested in the life story would do well to become familiar with the procedures of these historical genres, if only to avoid them. Folklorists practicing these historical genres, which of course *are* perfectly legitimate folkloristic interests, should, on the other hand, understand why they cannot pretend, to themselves or others, that their products are life stories.

The word "biography" came into English with Dryden, who in 1683 defined it as "the history of particular men's lives" (quoted in Holman 1972, 64). The biographical impulse is praise for an exemplary life, and so the public function of most biography is didactic, either implicitly or explicitly (Gittings 1978, 19–21).[4] Modern standards of professionalism in biographical writing, however, dictate that the biographer owe his allegiance not to his subject but the facts of his subject's life. In *Theory of Literature*, René Wellek explains why the biographer adopts historical methods: "The problems of a biographer are simply those of a historian. He has to interpret his documents, letters, accounts by eye-witnesses, reminiscences, autobiographical statements, and to decide questions of genuineness, trustworthiness of witnesses, and the like. In the actual writing of biography he encounters the problems of chronological presentation, of selection, of discretion or frankness. The rather extensive work which has been done on biography as a genre deals with such questions, questions in no way specifically literary" (Wellek and Warren 1956, 75–76). The biographer is thus a historian, a life writer aiming to describe and explain the circumstances of his subject's life, personality, and influence. Yet because his product is the record, sometimes even the story, of a life, the historical imagination will sometimes crawl out from the avalanche of data available to the modern biographer and turn its subject into a palpable human being, usually by giving him or her words to say. Boswell, the first modern biographer, catches Johnson's person through his conversation more than anything else. When we hear him, then we know him, or at least we think we do.

A biography that announces itself as the writer's account of someone else's life is not likely to be confused with the life story because there is no question about who is the author. The question of authorship is central to the problems of oral history and the personal history, but the lines are clearly drawn in biography. Biography per se has not had much of an appeal to folklorists, particularly in recent years, when the main lines of research and writing have concentrated in collection, annotation, and analysis of texts; in folkloristic theory; in material culture; and in the application of folklore to the concerns of local, tradition-bearing groups (but see E. Ives [1978] and his other biographical studies).

Oral history, like biography, proceeds from a historical rather than a fictive stance. Like biography, its overriding concern is with factual accuracy. Unlike biography, its focus is chiefly on events, processes, causes, and effects rather than on the individuals whose recollections furnish oral history with its raw data. A recent development, oral history dates from just after World War II, when Allan Nevins of Columbia University convinced his institution to become a repository for interviews with the men—and in most cases they *were* men—who had "made history." Historians were trained to ask lawyers' questions in an effort to get evidence from living witnesses. By 1974, more than three hundred institutions in the United States housed more than five hundred different oral history projects (Baum 1977; Davis, Back, and MacLean 1975).

Not all the projects in oral history are elitist. Possibly in response to the climate of the "new" social history, oral history projects now sometimes focus on the experiences of ordinary Americans. When Richard Dorson called for a folk history built up from the personal histories whose collection he urged, he could not have anticipated the local oral history projects that were springing up even as he was writing. Yet his assessment that professional historians would not be the ones to undertake folk history projects is still correct (Dorson 1972, 239–241). The new social history's emphasis on quantification and its distrust of literary evidence drive historians into harder and harder "scientific" lines in order to maintain professional respectability (Veysey 1979). Charts, graphs, tables, Greek symbols, and a variety of English sentences reduced to laws expressed by mathematical equations now stare out from the pages of the historical journals, while personal documents are left far behind in the quantitative analysis.

Scientism of this sort has not yet appeared among folk-culturally oriented oral histories, but they suffer from other problems. The Appalachian Oral History Project, for example, based at Alice Lloyd College in eastern Kentucky, began interviewing residents of central Appalachia in 1971. In 1977, it published *Our Appalachia: An Oral History* and introduced the book as a "social *history*" that "has provided the opportunity to let residents of the region tell their own *story*" (Shackelford and Weinberg 1977, 3, my italics). Here is another illustration of the confusion of history with story. This oral history is really the product of highly directed interviews, and we know this because the editors had the good sense to print some of the questions. When we come across a leading question in *Our Appalachia* such as, "What was it about John Wright that made his word law among the children?" (60), we know we are not listening to a story. Instead, we are reading the result of a collaborative venture between the historians and the informants. This collaboration is the nature of oral history, as Edward D. Ives recognizes in his introduction to *Argyle Boom*, an oral history of log transportation on the Penobscot River: "The descriptions men like Ernest Kennedy and Alphonse Martin gave came in response to the questions the students put to them, and new questions grew out of their responses. Oral history interviews are the joint creations of two people, interviewer and interviewee" (E. Ives 1976, 18). In oral history, the balance of power between the informants and historian is in the historian's favor, for he asks the questions, sorts through the accounts for the relevant information, and edits his way toward a coherent whole—as, for example, Ives quite properly did in *Argyle Boom*. But in the life story, the balance tips the other way, to the storyteller, while the listener is sympathetic and his responses are encouraging and nondirective. If the conversation is printed, it should ideally be printed verbatim, or if presented on film, it should ideally be unedited.

Folk-cultural oral histories often share a curious editing technique that is worth comment here. It may be observed in the aforementioned oral histories and the Foxfire books. The editors do not hesitate to splice together sections of one or more interviews outside the chronological order of the telling. They do not hesitate to delete sections of interviews or words from the informants' sentences. Yet they seem to believe that by bracketing words that they supply for continuity, thereby distinguishing them from words that the informants actually spoke, they are remaining faithful to their informants' language. This bracketing procedure seems to me to pretend to a degree of scrupulousness that is unjustified, given the editorial liberties taken in excision and rearrangement. The false claims that result—and I am aware of the problem because I have been one of the claimers—can sometimes even go so far as to convince the editor that what results is what the informant had in mind and would have said if he had been more articulate (Titon 1974a, 1).

Of the historical kin to the life story, the personal history is the most problematic, for it is a written account of a person's life based on spoken conversations and interviews. The anthropological literature is filled with hundreds of these personal histories, called life histories, while folklorists and ethnomusicologists have produced perhaps two dozen. In his 1965 treatise on the anthropological life history, L. L. Langness views the enterprise as essentially biographical rather than autobiographical, and in this he is surely correct. In his review of the literature, he acknowledges that anthropologists collect life histories primarily to obtain information about culture, not individuals. Given its orientation toward culture, it is no wonder that the typical life history strips the individual of his voice. Langness advises the would-be collector that "life history materials are seldom the product of the informant's clearly articulated, expressive, chronological account of his life," without stopping to ask whether that might be the fault of the collectors' close questioning and frequent interruptions, or perhaps the result of difficulties in translation from the native language. Langness continues: "This means that a certain amount of editing must be done . . . particularly when commercial publication is concerned" (Langness 1965, 1–12, 48). In other words, it is the pressure of the marketplace that forces the anthropologist to take the raw material from choppy interviews and turn it into a biography that pretends to be an autobiography. But it is just as likely that these pressures repose in his colleagues, his readers, and he himself, all of whom might find verbatim transcripts of the interviews tedious, unrewarding, and at times embarrassing.

My position with regard to life histories is similar to but not so radical as Linda Degh's. She writes that "the anthropological concept of life history collection is unacceptable to the folklorist, basically because of the lack of accurate and exacting methods of recording and publication which reflects the lack of interest in human creativity manifested in the formulation of the narrative" (Degh 1975, viii). That creativity cuts both ways, for the life history narrative is as much the creation of the anthropologist as of the informant (Frank 1979).[5] But the anthropological concept of life history collection cannot always be "unacceptable" to the folklorist. Sometimes it is impossible to obtain a life story, either because of poor rapport or because the informant is unwilling, taciturn by nature, or incapable of a sustained narrative. Yet the life history of an important tradition bearer whose life story cannot be obtained will surely contribute folk-cultural information. Moreover, the anthropological literature contains some life histories that are products of sympathetic conversations among friends; they usually can be told from the rest because, Langness notwithstanding, the informants are articulate and expressive in the context of friendship (Mintz 1960; Dyk [1938] 1967).

Folklorists have not published as large a proportion of their informants' personal histories as anthropologists have. But since the personal history is closer to the life story than biography or oral history is, folkloric publications in personal history, however small their number, merit attention here. I shall concentrate on easily accessible, English-language examples. In this genre, then, we may note the early influence of the Lomaxes. John Lomax was the guiding force behind the Works Progress Administration slave narrative collection and the life histories published in *These Are Our Lives* and *Such as Us*, while Alan Lomax recorded Jelly Roll Morton's life story for the Library of Congress in 1938 (Yetman [1937] 1975; Terrill and Hirsch 1978). The resulting life history, *Mister Jelly Roll*, exhibits unusually strong tension between story and history. Morton was a splendid narrator, and Lomax knew it: "To every query his responses were so instant and so vivid with time and place and who was there and what they said, that I knew Jelly was seeing it in fancy if not in actual recollection" (Lomax 1950, 241–242). But much of what Morton said was extravagant, and in writing his book, Lomax was torn between his interest in getting the facts about the birth of jazz and this incredible and bizarre relic who was desperate to tell his boastful story. Lomax finally decided it was personal history that he was hearing: "That hot May afternoon in the Library of Congress a new way of writing history began—history with music cues, the music evoking recollection and poignant feeling—history intoned out of the heart of one man, sparkling with dialogue and purple with ego" (xiii). *Mister Jelly Roll* is an extraordinary mix of fact and fiction, life story, personal history, and oral history, served up by a folklorist whose creative energies were a sympathetic match for his informant's.

The majority of folkloric personal histories have taken musicians for their subjects. My own published attempts in this genre have been no better than most. I miscalled the personal histories of Lazy Bill Lucas and Baby Doo Caston autobiographies, put their statements into chronological order, and then deleted my questions (Titon 1974a, 1974b). A few years ago when I had second thoughts about the standard editorial procedure, I decided to publish Son House's personal history as a verbatim transcript of our conversations

(Titon 1976). Robin Morton's life of John Maguire is similarly a personal history in the words of the informant and the product of a conversation among friends. Here is what he says about his nondirective interviewing method, and it is good advice:

> First of all I knew John very well before I ever started this project. I discussed with him what I wanted to do and he agreed to "have a go." So we sat down with an empty tape on the recorder and began. I first asked a very general question—"Tell me about your early life." I always asked general questions except when I wanted something explained in more detail. Once I had asked a question I sat quietly and let John talk. Even when he seemed to have finished I sat with an expectant look in the hope that he would continue, as he often did. Only when he seemed to have nothing more to say did I continue with a subsidiary query, or go on to a new area altogether. To the extent that I asked questions at all the "story" probably tells us much about me and my interests as it does about John. It is difficult to see how one sidesteps such a danger completely. (Morton 1973, xii)

One cannot sidestep such a danger so long as there is an audience for the story in the anticipatory mind of a storyteller who conceives of his task as communicating with that audience. But that only means that unless the informant is talking to himself, what seems a "danger" is inherent in any conversation, and the folklorist therefore should pay attention to how the talkers' ideas about who their audience is shapes their conversation. This aspect of the relation of text and context has of course been the focus of a great deal of recent theory from folklorists who conceive of folklore as "communication" based on "performance." But despite Morton's awareness of Maguire's story as a collaboration between the two of them, he followed the accepted historical editing practice and rearranged Maguire's answers according to topic, whereupon he deleted his questions and departed, ghostlike, from the text. The resulting personal history serves mainly as a vehicle for introducing the songs in Maguire's repertoire, whose texts and tunes are printed. In a similar vein is Roger Abrahams's *A Singer and Her Songs*, a book that contains important information about Almeda Riddle's song sources and her aesthetic criteria as well as the texts and tunes of a large portion of her repertoire. Although the book is in Riddle's own words, Abrahams (1970, 147) correctly claims that it centers on "the ways in which folklore has persisted, emphasizing the hows and whys of performance and transmission." We learn about Granny Riddle's personal history from time to time insofar as it bears on her songs, but the edited product is not meant to be a life history; at times, one feels in it the cumulative effect of Granny Riddle introducing her entire song repertoire at a folk festival.

Two folkloric personal histories that do not concern themselves with musicians are focused on work as a means of individual identity. *Me and*

*Fannie* is billed as the "oral autobiography" of Maine woodsman Ralph Thornton (Bean 1973). (Fannie, his wife, is seldom on center stage, but her presence is felt.) Resulting from tape-recorded conversations, it was edited by the interviewer, Wayne Reuel Bean, who chronologized and spliced, deleted his questions, and then supplied comments for continuity. If it deserves to be called an autobiography, it is because Thornton himself selected the material from the interviews, and this selection gave Thornton a greater degree of control than most personal history informants are allowed. Best regarded as a memoir, *Me and Fannie* is an unusually external account, with almost no reference to Thornton's inner life. Page after page goes by in which he recalls the adventures of his workaday life, mostly as a cook, and it comes as a surprise when, toward the end of his chronicle, he casually observes that he does not like cooking (73). Another personal history concerned mainly with work is Bruce Jackson's (1969) *A Thief's Primer*, but here the account is more introspective, and Jackson, who in editing did not delete all his interviewer's questions, shows himself responsive to the ironies of criminal pride and self-respect that permeate his informant's recollections.

Even when they are mistakenly presented as stories, biography, oral history, and the personal history share a historical rather than fictional base. The editing procedures, the data gathering, the research plans, and the resulting publications are oriented toward factual accuracy. The historical method is well suited to the folklorist seeking folk-cultural information. But it sometimes happens that in doing fieldwork, we folklorists find ourselves caught up with the lives of our informants, not so much because of what they can do or what they know, but who they are. In their stories of personal experience, they try to tell us.

## The Life Story as a Fiction

Folklorists have published few personal documents sensitive to the fictive aspects of the conversational situation in which a person tells the story of his or her life or a significant portion of it. I have argued that most personal documents in which the informant supposedly speaks in his or her own voice are historical in nature, the folklorist destroying by design or accident the fictive potential inherent in the original conversations. One exception is Linda Degh's (1975) *People in the Tobacco Belt: Four Lives*, a verbatim publication of four life stories, with brief analyses of the stories, storytellers, and their backgrounds. Although Degh uses the terms "life story" and "life history" interchangeably, her rejection of standard anthropological field and publication methods and her interest in the individual storytellers led her to publish the transcripts of conversations in which they told her, and usually a few friends and family members as well, about their experiences as Hungarian immigrants in Canada. Reviewing this book in *Folklore Forum*, Larry Danielson (1976, 172–173) pointed out that "on occasion . . . the informant's remarks indicate that a question has been asked, though not included in the transcription" and that probably "certain speaker's designations disappeared between transcription and publication. Such details may be trivial, but they assume importance if we are to rely on texts as unedited and authoritative." Now, of course, the mere transcription of the spoken word onto the printed page involves editing, for one must decide at the very least how to render it, in prose or ethnopoetic transcription, for example (D. Tedlock 1972).[6] And even if one chooses the conventional rendering in prose paragraphs, one must edit to the extent of inserting punctuation, which, as anyone who has ever done it knows, can lead to difficult decisions about emphasis and meaning. This aside, I take it that since there was no reason for them, the omissions in Degh's published transcript were editorial accidents, pure and simple.

How, then, is the dearth of unadulterated life stories in the folkloric literature to be explained? The most insidious reason, I have argued, is the conflation of story with history and the transformation of the one into the other. Kenneth Goldstein's *A Guide for Field Workers in Folklore* is an interesting case in point. Thorough and useful though it is, it exhibits the classic difficulties of approaching fiction as if it were, or ought to be, history. Using the framework of cultural anthropology to approach the "data" of folklore, Goldstein (1964, 121, my italics) writes, "One of the most important contributions which the field worker can make to folklore studies is the gathering of data for use in personal *history* documents. As they apply to the field of folklore, such documents may be defined as the *story* of the life (or some part of it) of an individual folklore informant. The data for these documents are obtained mainly by the use of interview methods." To be fair, Goldstein elsewhere is sensitive to the advantages of a fictional stance when he advocates verbatim publication of interviews when the informant describes in detail a topic or activity of interest to folklorists, and when he reveals his preference for the nondirective interview (123–124, 127). Still, the guide's folk-cultural orientation dominates, and the would-be fieldworker comes away with the clear impression that life stories of tradition bearers ought to be treated as historical documents.

Aside from the conflation of story and history, other causes may be cited to help explain the scarcity of folkloric life stories presented and interpreted as fictions. One is that folklorists are better read in contemporary anthropological verbal-art theory than in contemporary literary theory. Another is the debate over the folkloristic legitimacy of the personal experience story (Stahl 1977). Another is the hit-and-run approach to fieldwork, a method based on the assumption that folklore consists of items to be collected on field trips. Armed with finding aids and eager for data, the hit-and-run fieldworker is like the botanist who brings back a great variety of specimens for analysis and preservation. Under these conditions of efficiency, any life stories collected are likely to be mined for traditional elements, then stored on reels of tape until they are erased for future field trips. Fortunately, this type of field collecting is on the wane, though why some of us accept it from—even encourage it in—our students is beyond me. But as folklorists increasingly come to develop friendships with their informants over several months', even years', time, the word "informant" becomes inappropriately impersonal. As those friendships deepen, the opportunities for life story conversations increase. Seeking cultural information, the folklorist is likely to conceive of these conversations as life history. But if one is interested in a friend as a person, and what it is that makes him or her a tradition bearer, one will look to the life *story* as an expression of personality and self-conception—the who and why rather than just the what and how of one's friend's life.

Personality is the main ingredient in the life story (fig. 1.2). It is a fiction, just like the story; and even if the story is not factually true, it is always true evidence of the storyteller's personality (Pascal 1960, 1). The most interesting life stories expose the inner life, tell us about motives. Like all good autobiography, as opposed to mere chronicling, the life story's singular achievement is that it affirms the identity of the storyteller in the act of the telling (Spacks 1976, 1). The life story tells who one thinks one is and how one thinks one came to be that way.

The naive listener might assume a life story to be a truthful, factual account of the storyteller's life. The assumption is that the storyteller has only to penetrate the fog of the past and that once a life is honestly remembered, it can be sincerely recounted. But the more sophisticated listener understands that no matter how sincere the attempt, remembering the past cannot render it as it was, not only because memory is selective but because the life storyteller is a different person now than he or she was ten or thirty years ago; and he or she may not be able to, or even want to, imagine that he or she was different then. The problem of how much a person may change without losing his or her identity is the greatest difficulty facing the life storyteller, whose chief concern, after all, is to affirm his or her identity and account for it (Spacks

Figure 1.2. John Sherfey preaching, Stanley, Virginia, 1977. Photo by Jeff Todd Titon.

1976, 28). So life storytelling is a fiction, a making, an ordered past imposed by a present personality on a disordered life. Yeats (1915, vii) acknowledged in the preface to his *Autobiographies*, "I have changed nothing to my knowledge, and yet it must be that I have changed many things without my knowledge." We do not turn to Yeats's autobiographies if we want to know the facts of Yeats's life; we turn to them if we want to know Yeats.

We can learn much from life stories. We can learn how the tradition bearer thinks of himself or herself, and why he or she continues to make chairs or play the fiddle or preach as the Spirit moves. What is it about this person, we ask, that makes him or her an artist in the face of all the pressures to stop? What makes one an exceptional artist? Obviously one's self-conception, who one thinks one is, is greatly responsible for what one does. We get behind the mere facts of one's life, the historical data, when we let him or her tell the story. So conceived, the life story need not be "used" for folk-cultural information or as a "specimen" of oral performance or as "data" for oral history.

The life story need not be "used" for anything, because in the telling it is a self-sufficient and self-contained fiction. Fictions go on all the time, as Gertrude Stein (1935, 35) pointed out: "I do not cannot believe that anything is or can be more interesting than the fact that everybody is always telling everything and that anybody can in their way go on listening or not go on listening. But everybody can feel about telling and about listening like that. Anybody can." We are curious, and the life story is intrinsically interesting. If not, we do not listen. If it is interesting and we do listen, we are moved with pleasure. Stein also wrote that "if you live a daily life every minute of the day the description of that daily life every day must be moving, it must fill you with complete emotion, and it must at the same time be soothing" (4–5). The life story told to a sympathetic listener is a fiction complete in itself. The trouble with most poets, Wordsworth (1805, xix) wrote, was that they could not fix their gaze steadily on their subject, implying that he took his ideas from close observation of concrete experience, not literary convention. They jumped away too quickly, classified it, transformed it, used it. Let us not use the life story too quickly; let us know it first. Charles Olson (1966, 54) had this in mind when he wrote, "that a thing, any thing, impinges on us by a more important fact, its self-existence, without reference to any other thing, in short, the very character of it which calls our attention to it, which wants us to know more about it, its particularity. That is what we are confronted by, not the thing's 'class,' any hierarchy, of quality or quantity, but the thing itself, and its relevance to ourselves who are the experience of it (whatever it may mean to someone else, or whatever other relations it may have)." An approach to the life story that recognizes its validity as a fiction, quite apart from its value as a historical document, places it squarely in the human universe about which Olson was writing, a universe that is enlarged, even as we are enlarged, by the complementary stances of finding out and making, of history and fiction.

## Notes

1. Terkel published four books altogether from his interviews, Coles five; between 1972 and 1979, five Foxfire books were published.
2. Interviewed by Dick Cavett on a television program I saw in Boston in early 1978, Coles said the tape recorder made the people he spoke with nervous. He said he learned to catch language by watching William Carlos Williams emerge from house calls and jot down his patients' phrases.
3. Recorded in Minneapolis, Minnesota, 1971. [Author's note, 2020: for the audio recording of this narrative, see *Alcheringa: A Journal in Ethnopoetics*, n.s., 1, no. 2 (1975), http://writing.upenn.edu/pennsound/x/Alcheringa.php].
4. I suppose another impulse must be curiosity about an allegedly scandalous life.
5. I am grateful to Barbara Tedlock for pointing this out and for showing me Frank's essay.
6. The journal *Alcheringa: Ethnopoetics*, edited by Jerome Rothenberg and Dennis Tedlock, presented numerous ethnopoetic transcriptions during the journal's life (1970–1980). All the issues of the journal are available at https://jacket2.org/reissues/alcheringa/.

# 2

# ETHNOMUSICOLOGY AS THE STUDY OF PEOPLE MAKING MUSIC

*T*HIS DESCRIPTIVE DEFINITION OF ETHNOMUSICOLOGY GAINED ASSENT AMONG *my colleagues and may now be found, among other places, in* Worlds of Music *and in the* Wikipedia *entry for ethnomusicology. In 1988, preparing to teach a doctoral seminar in the history of ethnomusicological thought, I was disappointed that the histories and definitions of the field in the ethnomusicological literature failed to describe the work being done by our younger generation of ethnomusicologists who'd come of age in the 1960s and become professionals in the field in the 1970s. I believed that the "humanizing ethnomusicology" project Kenneth Gourlay (1982) had called for had been underway for at least fifteen years and that the praxis of my generation could be better understood by situating the field within the currents of poststructuralism and critical theory. In this philosophical paper, I attempted to theorize a constructivist reorientation: from studying music as an essentialized scientific object to studying music instead as a culturally contingent category in which the experiential acts that make music (as meaningful sounds and as a cultural domain) are primary. I hadn't yet articulated the connections between it and what in my graduate seminar on field research I was calling "the new fieldwork" (see Barz and Cooley [1997] 2008), nor had I yet concluded that ethnomusicology proper began in the 1950s, as an anthropological venture intended by the Society for Ethnomusicology's (SEM) founders to be significantly different from the comparative musicology and folk music research that had preceded it (see "Applied Ethnomusicology: A Descriptive and Historical Account," this volume).*

*Now, three decades later, some ethnomusicologists (myself included) are studying beings making sound, and SEM has a study group on ecomusicology—the study of music, sound, culture, nature, and the environment in a time of environmental crisis. Asked whether I still believe ethnomusicology ought to be regarded as the study of people making music, my answer is yes.* "Ethnomusicology" *is a coined word made from "musicology" (the study of music) and "ethnos," the Greek word for a people or an ethnic group. Ethnomusicologists who study beings making sound are doing ecomusicology. We are, as Jennifer Post calls us, ethno-ecomusicologists.*

*This essay was originally presented as a lecture to the annual conference of the Northeast Chapter of the Society for Ethnomusicology, Hartford, Connecticut, on April 22, 1989.*

The few within the discipline of ethnomusicology who have written its history date its beginnings to the 1880s and mark it not by any expansion of interest beyond the borders of Western art music but by the rise of scientific methodology in the study of music. Indeed, the question that until the 1970s almost single-handedly constructed the field of ethnomusicology was the following: How can the music of the world's peoples be studied scientifically? For all their differences, Hornbostel, Bartók, Brăiloiu, Sachs, Herzog, Hood, Seeger, Lomax, and Merriam—I have purposely left out McAllester—did not stray from the idea that ethnomusicology was the scientific study of world music. In the 1970s, a revolution that occurred in sociocultural anthropology—itself centered on ethnography and influenced by literary and philosophical theory, particularly from France and Germany, and bristling with ominous-sounding words like "phenomenology" and "hermeneutics"—began to be felt in ethnomusicology and threw up a great challenge. This challenge was not the call to study music in its cultural context; that gauntlet had been thrown down by McAllester and Merriam years earlier. Music in its cultural context could be studied scientifically; this was Merriam's great task, and it remains one of Lomax's.

Instead, the challenge was directed to the very conception of music itself. Henceforth, music was no longer to be construed as like an object to be analyzed, as science would dictate; instead, music was to be understood as like a cultural text to be interpreted, as the humanities would do. Beyond that, music was also to be understood as praxis—that is, as a productive activity in the social world with an economic basis and political implications. When I devised some themes for the 1989 Society for Ethnomusicology Conference, I summarized this challenge as "Analysis vs. Interpretation and Beyond." Because I am forbidden to read a paper at this conference for which I am program chair, for obvious reasons of conflict of interest, I have decided to try to present my thoughts at this regional chapter meeting. I must say that they remain at a preliminary stage and that I expect to be writing about them for some time.

In this presentation, I want to lead up to the proposition that it would be worthwhile to conceive of the field of ethnomusicology as "the study of people making music" and to define "making" in two ways: (1) making the sounds that peoples call music and (2) making or constructing the cultural domain that leads peoples to call those sounds music and to experience them both subjectively and objectively in the world. This notion of "making" has, of course, a great deal in common with the idea of "praxis," and it also rests on the premise that the world we experience is socially constructed. Although it may appear that this formulation privileges anthropology over musicology, it is not meant to do so. One student suggested that my phrase "people making music" privileges people over music because the word "people" comes first. Not so; I could just as easily, although less elegantly, phrase it as "the study of music as made by people." What I *do* mean to privilege is interpretation over analysis, meaning over explanation, understanding over law, and the humanities over science, and ultimately to show how music—indeed, music sound—may be studied from the point of view of the humanities. I will not get that far in this paper, of course.

It may be helpful at this point to say that I am not intending to privilege subjectivity over objectivity either. I want, perhaps foolishly, to have it both ways. After all, I experience music both ways, and I suppose you do, too. This is another way of saying that I want to deal with a music-specific version of a problem brilliantly formulated by the philosopher Thomas Nagel: "how to combine the perspective of a particular person inside the world with an objective view of that same world, the person and his viewpoint included. It is a problem that faces every creature with the impulse and capacity to transcend its particular point of view and to conceive of the world as a whole" (Nagel 1986, 3). I make and am moved by music inside the world, and at the same time as an ethnomusicologist, I transcend that standpoint to reflect on myself and others as participants in our worlds of music.

The solution, I am persuaded, is not to be found in a conventional scientific methodology, for it falsely objectifies the world and shuts off the move to reflexivity as it removes "the human element" of the observer from the world analyzed. In other words, it abandons the perspective of, as Nagel puts it, "a particular person in the world." Nor is a solution to be found in a conventional artistic paradigm, for it falsely subjectifies the world as an extension of one's particular experience and is hostile to transcending one's particular point of view. When I try to think of where a solution lies, I often feel as Nagel (1986, 12), who writes that "there is a persistent temptation to turn philosophy into something less difficult and more shallow than it is. It is an extremely difficult subject, and no exception to the general rule that creative efforts are rarely successful. I do not feel equal to the problems treated in this book. They seem to require an order of intelligence wholly different from mine."

Let me begin, then, by reviewing the scientific paradigm, the construction of ethnomusicology as the scientific study of world music. By a paradigm, I mean an overarching explanatory theory in which people frame their specific questions and answers, their hypotheses and conclusions. The term is usually applied to mathematics and science; examples include Euclidean geometry, Newtonian physics, and so forth. In the field of ethnomusicology, the scientific study of world music followed from the conceptions of science that underlay the great achievements of the nineteenth century, particularly the comparative taxonomic classification of living objects and Darwin's theory of evolution, particularly as applied to human societies in the form of cultural evolution or, as it is sometimes known, social Darwinism. The field was known at first, of course, not as ethnomusicology but as musical folklore or comparative musicology. Its methods are familiar to us all: observation, recording, transcription, analysis, classification, comparison, and the hazarding of explanatory theory, perhaps the grandest formulations being those of Sachs and Lomax. Most of its ideas were in place as early as 1905 and can be found in Hornbostel's ([1905] 1975) definitive article, "The Problems of Comparative Musicology."

It is instructive to go through the early work and see how optimistic everyone sounds. Science was able to be applied to the study of world music in part because of the invention of the recording phonograph. Consider Hornbostel ([1905] 1975, 252): "With the invention of the phonograph, musicology was presented with a device that can record the musical utterances of all the world's peoples in an irrefutably accurate manner, thereby allowing for a rigidly scientific approach.... Thus, all the conditions are now met for the collecting of musical and linguistic specimens on a large scale and for their preservation in phonographic museums or archives." Music was not so well constructed as an object until the phonograph made it possible to do so. Reading Hornbostel, Bartók, Sachs, Brăiloiu, and other pioneers in the field of comparative musicology or musical folklore, one is struck by their reliance on the phonograph as a means toward objectivity, something necessary if science was to operate on the object. Consider Brăiloiu ([1931] 1984b, 63): "Concern for objectivity imposes on us in the first place the mechanical recording of the melodies. Only the machine is objective beyond question, and only its reproduction is indubitable and complete.... Finally, it provides us with that means of control which no exact science can do without."[1] Bartók (1992, 14) held the same concern: "[The phonograph] is one of the very best means for achieving the ideal aim in our collecting and investigative work on folk songs: elimination of the subjective element."

It is also interesting to compare the statements of these early pioneers concerning the goals of the discipline. Each was convinced that the future lay in collecting, classifying, comparing, and generating explanatory theory. For Hornbostel, the model was comparative anatomy. We may note in passing that Haeckel's famous "ontogeny recapitulates phylogeny" came from studies in comparative anatomy. Applied to music, the insight yields the theory of music-culture evolutionism, and this theory informed—we would now say misinformed—one direction of comparative musicology from Hornbostel through Sachs to Lomax. The kinds of questions that constructed the field for Hornbostel and those who came after him were these: What was the origin of music, how did it develop over time and space, and what is the nature of the musically beautiful (Hornbostel [1905] 1975, 249)? The first two questions were the same ones philologists had been asking about language and that folklorists were asking about myths and folktales. Moreover, the methods of these two other disciplines were similar to those envisioned by Hornbostel—that is, largely historic and geographic to trace the origin and growth of music.

Everyone agreed that the first step was collecting, and it is interesting to compare Hornbostel, Bartók, and Sachs on these matters. Hornbostel wrote ([1905] 1975, 252), "Now all the conditions are met for the collecting of musical and linguistic specimens on a large scale and for their preservation in phonographic museums and archives." Bartók expounded thus in a comparison with natural history (1992, 19–20):

> Up to this point we have discussed the collection of melodies as if they were isolated items. This, however, is not an adequate approach; indeed, it would be like the entomologist or lepidopterist who would be satisfied with the assembly and preparation of the different species of insects or butterflies. If his satisfaction rests there, then his collection is an inanimate material. The genuine, scientific naturalist, therefore, not only collects and prepares but also studies and describes, as far as possible, the most hidden moments of animal life. Although we admit that the most minute description cannot restore to life that which is dead, it nevertheless recaptures some of the taste and fragrance of life and imparts it to the dead collection. Similar reasons direct the folk music collector to investigate in detail the conditions surrounding the real life of the melodies.

Yet with collectors, we must remind ourselves of their psychic impulse. As James Clifford (1988, 215) reveals, collections are efforts "to make the world one's own, to gather things around oneself tastefully, appropriately.... The self that must possess but cannot have it all learns to select, order, classify in hierarchies to make 'good' collections." As museums appropriated objects for preservation and display, these objects came to be authentic and authenticating cultural representations, to "stand for" a "school" of painting, say, or an extinct species, or a human group's former way of life. We need only look at the "good" collections of recordings by Hornbostel or Brăiloiu to see this procedure at work (Hornbostel 1963; Brăiloiu 1984c). Then, too, most of us are record collectors and we need look no further than to our own shelves. Collecting tends to reify music as a "thing." But there are good grounds for rejecting the concept of music as a "thing," as I shall shortly suggest.

In my view, the science of comparative musicology reaches its apotheosis in the work of Sachs and Lomax. Sachs proposed—with varying degrees of strictness over the course of his career—to reduce the music of the world's peoples to melodic types that correlate with stages of sociocultural evolution; he proposed that general theory at some length in his last book, *The Wellsprings of Music* (Sachs 1965). Alan Lomax's cantometrics theory correlates musical structure and behavior on the one hand with the sociocultural features of human groups noted by Murdock in his *Ethnographic Atlas* (Lomax 1968, 1972b, 1976; Murdock 1969). His findings rely greatly on the computer. But of course it is not the computer that makes Lomax's work scientific; it is his methodology.

Science offers explanations "[that] tell us why things are as they are, that is, how they came to be as they are now," according to Daniel M. Taylor (1970, 32), a philosopher of science. And certainly, the comparative musicologists were trying to tell us how world music came to be as it is now. The fact that they did not attempt to formulate theories of cause and effect only shows that they understood that science does not rely on discovering causes that precede and bring about effects. Rather, "a scientific explanation consists in a deduction from premises which comprise universal generalizations and statements of circumstances" (33). Note, of course, that an explanation may pass the test of being scientific without being true or even probably true.

The comparative musicologists were following conventional procedure in the natural sciences. What, after all, were the elements of music, the smallest properties of music comparable to atoms and molecules in matter, or to phonemes in language, or to motifs in folktales? The answer was clear: as Hornbostel ([1905] 1975, 254) put it, following Stumpf, "the fundamental material of all music" is "the tones" or musical sounds. From this arises one of comparative musicology's thorniest problems: how to represent "the tones" accurately in transcription. And within the scientific paradigm, we move to increasingly accurate measurement of the physical properties of tones, from the invention of the cents system through the monochord and eventually to the melograph and other automatic transcribers.

Collecting, transcribing, analyzing, describing, and comparing represent the application of powerful scientific tools and theories to the stuff of music. The challenges to this scientific paradigm came not because of logical difficulties in the model but because certain people interested in world music were not convinced that the fundamental basis of music was to be found in the tones themselves. In other words, they begin to ask additional questions. Two new important questions began to be asked that could not be answered by the prevailing model and methods. These questions began to reconstruct the field. The first question was asked by anthropologists and predictably was, what is the place of music in the science of man (*sic*), or what is the relation between music and culture? Although Bartók, even Hornbostel, and especially Brăiloiu had raised those questions and attempted to gather social data that would help place music in a cultural context, the thrust of their activity was on musical structures. McAllester indicates that he began to ask this question in the late 1940s in response to prodding from Margaret Mead (personal communication, 1989) and certainly his *Enemy Way Music* reflects this perspective. Moreover, it and its predecessor, *Peyote Music*, was based on participant observation (McAllester [1949] 1971, [1954] 1973). Most previous song collecting, on the contrary, had been done by asking the singer to sing for the collector, out of the natural sociomusical context. The most persistent attempts to answer this question came in the 1960s from Lomax (1968) and Merriam (1964, 1967). I have already referred to Lomax's work. Merriam devised a model that, as he himself oversimplified it in several articles, claims that the relation between music and culture may be studied scientifically if we understand that music sound is produced by human behavior, and human behavior is in turn produced by concepts or ideas. All of this was linked in a feedback system so that music produced in turn is understood to influence ideas about music. The implication was that it was a mistake for a science of music to view "the tones" as fundamental; rather, ideas, behavior, and music were all bound up with one another and should all be studied not only in themselves but in relation to one another. Lomax found that it was not necessary to separate ideas from behavior; his cantometrics theory assumes the unity of the two.

Lomax and Merriam did not oppose the people who wanted primarily to study "the tones" because they felt opposed to science. Quite the contrary, Merriam and Lomax held the banner of science high and often referred to what they were doing as a social science that was more appropriate to the study of world music than the outmoded and outdated methods of the comparative musicologists, many of whom, like Kolinski, continued their pursuits despite the field's name change in North America and parts of Europe to ethnomusicology. And so did Charles Seeger (1963) hold that music should be studied scientifically, repeatedly claiming that opposition between musicologists and anthropologists was silly because it was obvious that music should be studied both as a thing-in-itself and as a thing-in-context. To this formulation Merriam would have agreed, and in his major monograph, *Ethnomusicology of the Flathead*, he attempted just that; unfortunately, he segregated his book into two parts, concepts and behavior as one, and the most conventional and reductionist musical analysis as the other, never really integrating the two, going through the analysis almost as an exercise in futility (Merriam 1967). It was almost as if Merriam had divided his book into social science and natural science.

A second question challenged the dominant paradigm, to prove ultimately more difficult to those who regarded ethnomusicology as primarily a study of "the tones." The question was deceptively simple: What is it like for a person to experience music? This was not a question that the comparative musicologists were interested in answering. It would later be subjected to scientific research under the category of music cognition, but for the moment the question was posed in the more practical terms of musicality and musicianship. In this regard, it would be difficult to overestimate the influence of David McAllester and Mantle Hood. Hood, of course, is well known as a champion of the melograph, but it is his other side, the aesthetic side, that is under consideration here. Both Hood and McAllester advocated what Hood later termed "bimusicality"—that is, they wanted to experience, and wanted others to experience, directly competence in a music of a culture outside their own (Hood 1960, 1963). Although Hood meant this as an educational tool and a research strategy, the results, as we all know, were the incorporation of performance into the ethnomusicology curriculum and the incalculable humanizing effect that this has had on the discipline through the many whose study with master artists has changed their lives as well as their understanding of music.

At the same time, the question of what it is like to experience music was turned from the self to the other in the study of world music, and this partly constructed the "new musical ethnography" of researchers like Keil and Feld, as well as a new interest in biography and autobiography (Keil 1979; Feld [1982] 2012; Mitchell 1978; Vander 1988). Not long before his tragic death, Merriam (1977, 204) moved from a view of ethnomusicology as the study of music in culture to a view of the field as the study of music as culture. The same formulation soon appeared in an ethnomusicology textbook written by Marcia Herndon and Norma McLeod (1980). This, it seems to me, reflected the new trends in sociocultural anthropology I summarized at the outset of this paper: music as cultural text, and music as praxis.

We may recall that Seeger urged that music be studied both as a thing-in-itself and also a thing-in-context. Music, I believe, is not a thing-in-itself, and considering it so is the result of confusing science's objectified model of music with the real thing. There is nothing intrinsic to sound, not even human organization, that makes it music. In other words, just as there is no such "thing" as literature, nothing self-evident in language that marks it indisputably as literature, so there is nothing self-evident in sounds that mark them indisputably as music.[2] The great variety of scores, performances, and recordings that people call music do not share some common musical essence. This was the conclusion of Alexander Ellis (1885, 526) after his comparative studies of the musical scales of various nations: "The musical scale is not one, not 'natural,' nor even founded necessarily on the laws of the constitution of musical sound so beautifully worked out by Helmholtz, but very diverse, very artificial, and very capricious." What is music to one music culture is judged noise by another. Even within music cultures, one person's music may be another person's noise, organized or not. Certain music cultures have no word for music. As Henry Kingsbury (1987) points out, music is a cultural system, not an a priori phenomenon of the natural world. In other words, music is not an independent entity with its being in the world. Its nature is not as something "out there" as a separate object. Rather, music, like all other aspects of culture, is socially constructed (Berger and Luckmann 1966). We are born into a world of sound, and we learn from other people what sound is music and what sound is not. Response to many of John Cage's compositions, for example, and to much of contemporary music in the West, points out that "music" is not naturally occurring but rather is a human cultural invention.

Of course, the idea that music is not a phenomenon of the natural world does not preclude us from studying it scientifically. But it indicates that we should reject the notion that music has a priori fundamental units like tones in the same way that matter has molecules, with the implication that we should study tone structure like molecular structure and thereby get at the objective essence of music. Of course music has tones, but they are not to be understood as fundamental units of an objective musical matter. Music does not have fundamental units in this sense, and perhaps not in any sense. It is equally problematic to conceive of music as a thing-in-context. This formulation suggests that music is a "thing" (which it is not) surrounded by something else, or everything else, but fails to indicate the relationship between the thing and the context. It seems to me, on the contrary, that it is the context that constructs and experiences the thing, music, as a thing; and this suggests that the term "context" is too weak to describe what it is that brings music about and gives it meaning and significance.

In the past twenty years, much important work in ethnomusicology has been seemingly devoted, in one way or another, to solving the problem or bridging the gap between the music-culture dichotomy. I suggest that a more useful way of looking at it is to consider it a way of overcoming the limitations of applying a scientific model to the study of world music. What I am questioning here is Merriam's (1964, 25) notion that ethnomusicology should be a reconciliation of social science with the humanities and that what ethnomusicologists ought therefore to do is "science about music." Interest in linguistics and transformational grammars posits an analytical model meant to represent the human mind of the composer or performer; interest in film drives toward holistic representation of music in cultural context; new modes of performance of non-Western musics in Western settings explore the construction of music as cultural ritual; Marxist models, reflexive musical ethnographies, interest in the relation between myth and the conceptual soundscape, studies of the negotiated meaning of music in Western contexts, and the constant dialogue within the discipline about boundaries and definitions have taken the field in a new direction, which may best be summarized in the phrase "the study of people making music." Here I would mention the work of Hugo Zemp, Steve Feld, Marina Roseman, Henry Kingsbury, Charles Keil, David McAllester, David Locke, Mark Slobin, David Reck, Charlotte Heth, Charlotte Frisbie, and others. It is important, I believe, to view this not so much as a gap between music and culture—they are one—but as a gap between modes of scientific and humanistic constructions of music.

In this paper, I have proposed that it would be helpful if ethnomusicologists conceived of their field as "the study of people making music." This, of course, seems unexceptionable; of course people make music. But, to repeat myself, the definition turns on the meaning of the word "making." People make music in two senses: (1) by physical acts they construct music sound and (2) by mental and communicative acts, they socially construct a cultural domain called "music" to which they give meaning. Ethnomusicologists, therefore, study the acts that "make" music, including ethnomusicology itself (a second-order mental act that gives meaning to music). In this formulation, "music sound" conceived as pure object becomes a phantom of the positivistic imagination, and the dichotomy between "music" and "culture" collapses. I do not see how a scientific formulation such as comparative musicology can collapse the same dichotomy.

Such a "constructivist" formulation has the advantage, I think, of a better understanding of music and music making. I have already suggested that there are no grounds for believing that music is a "thing," evidence of recordings and scores to the contrary. I wish to suggest further that continued belief that music is a "thing" will permit an ongoing distortion: that music, reified into a "thing," invites the kinds of questions that ethnomusicologists ask of it. It has been assumed that the study of music in the world presents a set of questions in relation to which the procedures of ethnomusicology are found more or less adequate. But with some notable exceptions, ethnomusicologists have been unaware that the category music is contingent. For example, there is the problem of transcription, and our critical procedures address such questions as the purpose and reliability of transcription, alternative methods of transcription, and so forth. In other words, we assume that music stands ready to be questioned by procedures we have developed in response to our contemplation of its nature both as a thing-in-itself and as a thing in a sociocultural context. But to put it another way, I suggest that the field music is constituted by the questions we are able to ask because these questions presuppose the field. Thus, it becomes terribly important to construct those questions so that the field we get is the field we want, and in this case, it means bearing a relationship to music not as something that consists fundamentally as tones but as a human activity.

## Notes

1. Later in his career, he was not so sanguine: "A real idolatry of the machine soon seized some minds and still dominates many of them. The danger of excessive confidence in the automatic slave [lies in] the naive and all too stubborn conviction of certain scholars that once the detail of a music is presumed to be perfectly reproduced and irreproachably transcribed, we have nothing more to learn about it, when in reality it has revealed to us nothing of its true nature" (Brăiloiu [1931] 1984a, 95).

2. For the analogy with language and literature, I am indebted to Barry O'Connell.

# 3

## TEXT

*I*N 1993, BURT FEINTUCH, THEN EDITOR OF THE Journal of American Folklore, asked about a half dozen folklorists to write essays for a special issue on key ideas in folklore studies of expressive culture. Burt invited me to write on "text." By that time, my interest in the ontological nature of "text," especially oral text, was well known to my colleagues. It began with my mid-1970s ethnopoetic transcriptions in the journal Alcheringa; continued in "The Life Story," which had been widely circulated; and reached an apotheosis in Powerhouse for God, a mammoth ethnography of sacred speech, chant, and song that presented an enormous number of audio, visual, and verbal texts in a five-hundred-page interpretative monograph, one-hour documentary film, and two-LP recording. In "Text," after surveying the changing meanings of and attitudes toward the word "text" in folklore studies, I extended the argument I'd put forward in "The Life Story" concerning of the fictive nature of autobiographical texts, to the reflexive texts of contemporary ethnographic writing. I was suggesting that, as authors, ethnographers consider their fieldwork in terms of characters (themselves included), events, even plot and drama; and that to do these considerations justice, they take advantage of point of view to create what I called "knowing texts," ethnographic writing that is self-aware of the basis for and limits of its knowledge claims. Knowing texts depart from reflexive, first-person ethnographies, insofar as they take advantage of the necessarily fictive (that is, made) possibilities of ethnographic writing, because all narrators are to some degree unreliable. In that regard I was not advocating for experimental ethnography (Clifford and Marcus [1986] 2010); rather, I had been inspired by colleagues associated with Brown's Digital Humanities Group and by hypertext fictions such as Afternoon (Joyce 1987–1990).

Around 1990, I began making hypertextual computer representations of people performing narrative and music (Titon 1991). My Brown colleague Paul Kahn and I put together a hypertext/multimedia version of a chapter from

Worlds of Music, *then about to go into its second edition, to see if the publisher (Macmillan) would also bring out a full electronic version of the textbook (on DVD); however, in 1992, they were unwilling to pioneer in this area and make the financial commitment it would have required. (Today, ironically, Cengage, the conglomerate that swallowed Macmillan, offers the sixth edition in an electronic hypertext/multimedia version on the internet.) Disappointed in practice, I took to theorizing about hypertext instead, believing that its time would come sooner or later; and so I prophesied about hypertext/multimedia in this and other essays and created further representations for the computer, such as a "virtual folk festival" (a role-playing game that I demonstrated at a conference of the American Folklore Society) and a representation of bird species, their characteristics, and their calls and songs as I'd recorded them on an island off the Maine coast. "Text" appeared in 1995 in a special "keywords" issue of the JAF titled "Common Ground," at a time when it was becoming clear that the future of the World Wide Web was as a vast hypertext, with multimedia to follow as soon as internet transmission speeds would permit. By the time "Text" appeared in a revised version in 2003, with the added section "Ethnography and the 'Knowing Text'" (Feintuch [1995] 2003), hypertext/multimedia had become the lingua franca of the internet, and electronic publishing was growing apace. The revised 2003 version is printed here.*

Like the word "folklore," the word "text" is something folklorists can control only partially. I prefer to think of any object of interpretation as a text. But just as the general public has its own understanding of folklore, no matter how academic folklorists may define it, many constituencies are involved in constructing definitions of *text*. In this essay, I review what I consider to be the more important meanings of text, and then I consider the special contributions that folklorists can make to an understanding of text. Although text is an exceedingly important concept for folklorists, the folklore text by nature appears as a secondary document, a transformation or transcription of something more original—a performance. First, I explore the uses of transcribed texts, the folklorist's stock-in-trade. Second, I discuss the reconfigurations of the folklore text that emerged in the past three decades from the paradigm shift in folklore studies toward performance theory. Third, looking to the future, I propose what I call "knowing texts," fieldwork-based ethnographic writings that attend to critical issues of representation and authority through writing strategies involving point of view. Fourth, I discuss the use of texts in the age of computers and multimedia representations, particularly in terms of the theory and practice of *hypertext*. (In the context of hypertext, a text is any information that can be digitized, whether words, sounds, or pictures; hypertext may be regarded as linked, nonlinear text: postmodern text.)

In its oldest, narrowest, and still most common usage, *text* means written words, usually words given some kind of authority. Editors preparing literary editions or historical documents seek a text "most nearly representing the author's original work" (*Oxford English Dictionary*). For literary scholars, a text is a work of literature; for historians, a text is a historical document; for musicologists, a text is the words to a piece of music; for folklorists, a text is a transcription of a folklore performance: the words of a song or a tale, for example. But as we shall see, in recent years some folklorists have diminished the importance of text while concentrating more on performance and context. Other folklorists have taken an opposite path, expanding the meaning and significance of *text* so that now it also stands for any interpreted object, verbal or otherwise.

In the narrow sense, as a transcription, the folklore text is peculiar because it is a written representation of an original that is spoken, sung, gestured, or crafted from a larger oral and customary exchange among people. Whereas the original of a literary, historical, or legal text is writing (even if this writing is conventionally understood to represent speech), the original of a folklore text is not writing at all. An individual can produce writing alone, and it takes on a life of its own: newspapers, self-help books, novels, textbooks. These are not meant to be read aloud to others but to be absorbed alone, in a transaction between text and reader; the author is absent. Verbal folklore, on the other hand, lives in the intersubjective process that takes place when two or more people communicate face-to-face. The relationship between folklore and its written representation as text is not the simple equivalence of transcription. Nor is a folklore text a script or score meant for performance. Any written text arising from a communicative event that we recognize as folklore is clearly a transformation and a reduction.

Scholars usually make sense of literary texts using a combination of hermeneutic, phenomenological, and structuralist approaches. Hermeneutics, a method of interpreting meaning in written texts, arose as a means of explicating the Bible. While we still speak of a biblical text and a commentary attached to it, today hermeneutics covers the interpretation of any text, biblical or otherwise. The meaning of a literary text is usually a kind of paraphrase, using other words to express what is said and what is implied in the reader's confrontation with an author's text: what the text is "about." Most of what goes on in undergraduate literature classes, for example, is practical criticism of individual poems, short stories, and novels—what they mean, what they are about—and professors always are returning to the texts, the words on the page, for evidence. These days, individual texts are almost always considered in their historical contexts. The idea that literature inhabits an eternal realm of its own is no longer given credence when interpretive practice is brought to bear on texts. Phenomenological approaches emphasize the experience of the reader: what it feels like to read a particular text. Structuralist approaches, on the other hand, are not concerned with unique meanings in individual texts. Instead, structuralist strategies probe relations and patterns among a group of texts and particularly in "the conditions [of writing and reading] which make literature possible" (Culler 1975, viii). Structuralists not only discuss literary conventions, such as plot, but also theorize about communicative acts in general.

In his well-known essay "Is There a Text in This Class?," Stanley Fish reports the following conversation: A student asked a colleague that very question, and he replied with the name of the textbook anthology that he had ordered at the bookstore. "'No, no,' she said, 'I mean in this class do we believe in poems and things, or is it just us?'" (Fish 1980, 305). If it is "just us," then meaning is a matter ultimately to be determined by the reader, not by appeals to authorial intention or to evidence in "the text itself." Fish has defended this "just us" theory of reception. A number of literary critics have misread Fish, thinking that he has let loose an anarchy of interpretations, a world in which any interpretation of a given text carries as much weight as any other. Fish's answer is that interpretations carry more or less weight depending on the ideologies of the interpretive communities in which they reside. So, for example, a literal interpretation of the creation as recorded in Genesis carries weight within a fundamental Christian interpretive community but not outside it. Fish's point is that "right" interpretations of texts are right only within particular contexts; there is no universal or foundational or eternally correct interpretation of a text. Among folklorists today, one interpretive community is at home with texts and another is uneasy with them.

As a model of text, literature inhabits a visual realm—writing and reading, the words on the page—and that is text's narrowest construction. Broader constructions of text, as is true of any object of interpretation, include the tactile, the oral, the gestural, and so forth. Folklorists can contribute to the dialogue on text in part because so many of our objects of study are not written but oral (as a song or a story) or material (as a craft) or gestural (as a dance). For many years, folklorists transcribed and transformed them into written texts, and we inclined toward hermeneutic, structural, and analytical interpretation without examining alternatives. Until the 1960s, folklorists treated oral folklore as items of literature with a few peculiar features due to their orality. Analysis concentrated on various aspects of the texts but most importantly on the conditions of their existence, their evolution and the relations among similar texts, their social functions, and what they presumably indicated about the history and culture of the folk or peasant classes of society.

The narrow meaning of *text* as an inscription of an oral performance remains the most common usage of the term among folklorists today. It has a long and honorable history in folklore studies—some two hundred years. Texts in this sense are most often understood to be the written versions of orally delivered folklore, whether myth, legend, folktale, riddle, proverb, sermon, or something else spoken, chanted, or sung. The conventions of writing for a popular audience moved many folklorists to edit, or improve, the texts they collected; however, beginning in the nineteenth century, scientific standards required accurate transcription for scholarly purposes, whether deposit in archives or scholarly publication. Faithfully transcribed texts remain so authoritative nowadays that they are expected of students in folklore classes, can be found in many interpretive articles published in the leading folklore journals, and appear in most scholarly books written by folklorists.

Largely absent from those scholarly folklore journals, however, is the former practice of reporting undocumented texts, versions, or variants, without much accompanying theory or interpretation. Concomitant is a decline in the publication of anthologies of folklore texts. In the first half of the twentieth century, for example, anthologies containing regional ballad collections abounded, but few of these are published today (see, e.g., Brewster 1940; Gardner 1939; Henry 1938; Cox 1925; Hudson 1936; Barry 1939; A. Davis 1929). Folklorists collected and pored over texts, specializing in particular genres, seeking motifs and types, scrutinizing guides, indices, and bibliographies. These amateurs and professionals felt themselves engaged in a collective enterprise, tracking the movements of verbal folklore in textual variation through time and space. Today that activity has declined, while the ratio of interpretation to text in folklore publications has increased. This increase in interpretation is partly the result of a movement toward material culture and the ethnographic methods of cultural anthropology, and it reflects the professionalization of folklore and the increasing number of young folklorists trained in the academy, where for the past twenty-five years or so, in the face of a difficult job market, theorizing has been thought a better bet for an academic career.

Amid all the theorizing, academics risk forgetting that experiencing a representation of folklore affords pleasure. "Text of pleasure: the text that contents, fills, grants euphoria; the text that comes from culture and does not break with it, is linked to a *comfortable* practice of reading" (Barthes 1975, 14; italics in original). Many folklorists began their work with texts before they even thought of themselves as folklorists, simply by collecting and transcribing texts for their own contemplation or perhaps for performance: photographs of barns, for example, or transcriptions of song texts or tunes. Texts have a certain permanency. Transcription has the advantage of taking a performance out of the past and permitting the folklorist to experience it as an aesthetic object, bringing pleasure and knowledge more or less at will.

We like to think of transcribed texts as finite, bounded, and stable, as a novel is compassed between two covers. But a kind of indeterminacy principle is at work in any orally performed text, whether we think of text as words, event, or artifact, because its "motion"—that is, its unfolding process, considered in terms of its production and its reception—is anything but stable and replicable. Instability in the folkloric text derives from intertextuality, or the way texts exist in relation to other texts: there is no single authoritative text, but rather a folkloric text exists in multiple versions and variants, similar to one another and thereby referencing one another, generally exhibiting "major variation over space and minor variation through time" (Glassie 1968, 33).[1] And the instability of a folkloric text is the result of its emergent, processual character, stressing the dialectic of innovation and tradition within community-based expressive culture and the relations between the performer and audience.

The life of a particular verbal text clarifies what I mean by intertextuality and emergence in this context. More than twenty years ago, in an article titled "The Life Story" (reprinted in this volume), I used for illustration a story that blues singer Son House told me (Titon 1980). It was his conversion narrative, a story of how he experienced the presence of God and felt redeemed.[2] Although the story was deeply personal, it shares the same pattern and indeed some of the very same words and phrases as countless other Christian conversion narratives, whether written, as that of Saul/Paul on the road to Damascus, Augustine's *Confessions*, or Jonathan Edwards's *Personal Narrative*, to name a few; or oral, as one can see expressed every Sunday in religious broadcasts on television and in thousands of churches. Interpreting Son House's life story, I stressed the emergent qualities of its enactment, or its reenactment, as for the moment he and I were bound up imaginatively in re-creating this event.

Instability in texts presents difficult problems for representation and interpretation. "What is the text?" seems to be a wrongly formulated question in which the word "is" receives more pressure than it can bear. In "The Life Story" I represented Son House's story as an oral prose narrative on the printed page. Yet four years earlier, I had inscribed this same conversion narrative as a poem, in an ethnopoetic transcription—a different representation meant to show aspects of oral delivery, such as pauses and shifts in volume and tone of voice, that contributed to the meaning of the performance but would not normally have been notated (Titon 1976). The original tape recording is yet another, and an experientially more satisfying, representation. A reproduction of this representation on a plastic disc recording was bound into the journal that published the ethnopoetic transcription so that the reader could also hear the inflections of Son House's voice. Under other circumstances, House's conversion narrative would have been different. A former preacher, he surely varied the details of his narrative depending on his audience. Thus far, we have stability of neither text nor representation, and when we consider House's narratives as versions of countless other conversion narratives, we experience what might be called intertextual overload.

Today it is commonplace to speak of intertextuality as a quality of referencing among texts. Literary theorists Robert Scholes, Nancy R. Compley, and Gregory L. Ulmer (1988, 129) write, "Once you realize that all texts are reworkings of other texts, that writing comes out of reading, that writing is always rewriting, you can see that the desirable quality we call 'originality' does not mean creating something out of nothing but simply making an interesting change in what has been done before you." Folklorists understood intertextuality through versions and variants and genres of the folklore text long before literary critics began to see it as a feature of all texts. Oral tradition seems to "explain" intertextuality in folklore texts, but if intertextuality is also present in written texts, then orality cannot suffice as an explanation. Instead, intertextuality would appear to be a quality inherent in thought or consciousness.

And if intertextuality inhabits the way we think, it is not much of a leap to consider our minds not so much as socially constructed as textually constructed (see Culler 1982, 29). This "textualization" of the self has led to a new way of approaching people as loci of what Roland Barthes and Claude Levi-Strauss called mythology and Michel Foucault termed discourse. People are viewed as sites of ideological discourse—in other words, as bundles of text. These texts are equivalent to those beliefs and desires that lead to action in the world; indeed, they embody them. "Think of human minds as webs of beliefs and desires, of sentential attitudes—webs that continually reweave themselves so as to accommodate new sentential attitudes" (Rorty 1991, 93).

The relation of text to ideology has concerned Marxist critics. "The largely concealed structure of values which underlies our factual statements is part of what is meant by 'ideology'" writes Terry Eagleton. "By 'ideology' I mean, roughly, the ways in which what we say and believe connects with the power-structure and power-relations of the society we live in." Not all beliefs are ideology, but rather "those modes of feeling, valuing, perceiving and believing which have some kind of relation to the maintenance and reproduction of social power" (Eagleton 1983, 14–15). Texts are aesthetic cultural productions that provide "experiential access to ideology. . . . It is in [literary texts], above all, that we observe in a peculiarly complex, coherent, intensive and immediate fashion the workings of ideology in the textures of lived experience of class-societies" (Eagleton 1978, 101). Among folklorists, Jack Zipes's (1983) studies of fairy tales exemplify this approach. Antonio Gramsci's idea of hegemony was enlisted by Tony Bennett in a powerful formulation for cultural studies: that "hegemony specifies that relations between ruling and subordinate blocs are negotiated and that therefore the concept encompasses a theoretical reconciliation between the imposed structures of the dominant ideology and an active cultural expression by the dominated class" (as quoted in Easthope 1994, 178). This conception of hegemony provides both rationale and focus for studies of texts from "marginalized" peoples viewed as resistant to the ideology of the central or dominant class as promulgated by the state; an example is early African American hip-hop music and culture.

## Text and Performance

A difficulty with texted representations of folklore, then, is that because folklorists do so much trafficking in texts—we transcribe and interpret them, we publish them—texts have a nasty habit of reasserting equivalence; the text comes to stand for the folklore. Some folklorists have responded to the force of textual reification by accepting it, treating texts as the more or less unproblematic stuff of folklore, grist for the mill of analysis and interpretation. Others have diminished the importance of text while seeking other means to represent and interpret folklore. Diminishing means narrowing the definition of *text* as far as possible to written words, while saying that this written text represents but a small portion of the larger process called folklore and searching for alternative means of understanding folklore as human communication. This has led folklorists to ideas of folklore as process, as expressive culture, and most influentially, folklore as performance. Performing (acting and observing, gesturing, speaking, singing) thus replaces literature (reading and writing) as the key metaphor.

Still other folklorists have pursued a third strategy, the opposite of diminishing text—that is, expanding the definition of *text* to include not only words but also things. Expanding the definition, philosopher Richard Rorty (1991, 84) makes a useful distinction between texts and "lumps, a division which corresponds roughly to things made and things found." A lump is "something which you would bring for analysis to a natural scientist rather than to somebody in the humanities or social sciences—something which might turn out to be, say, a piece of gold or the fossilized stomach of a stegosaurus" (84–85). In this enlarged sense, a text is any humanly constructed object. It need not be words: it may be an artifact such as a painting or a building or a pot, or it may be an action or event such as a ritual, or it may even be a person or a group of people. Text in this view becomes a key metaphor for any humanly constructed sign system, and we inhabit a semiotic world of signifiers that are not limited to words but include the entire human universe.

While some folklorists have taken up this reconfigured and expanded notion of text, other schools of ethnographic and folkloristic thought emphasize the body, process, feeling, and persons, and they reject the idea that understanding expressive culture is like reading a text. Much in the recent history of folklore studies can be seen as an attempt to come to an understanding of folklore either as text or as something else. To paraphrase a philosopher friend of mine, folklorists have sought the varieties of text worth wanting. Is this literary metaphor, folklore as text, reading and writing as our means of representing and understanding the world, still appropriate to folklore? Today the functions of literature for most people in North America are filled by television, movies, and video and computer games, not to mention life stories in ordinary conversation. The school world is probably the last place that still acts as if literature exists mostly in print.

In the 1960s, folklorists began to problematize text. A few younger scholars proposed that folklore be conceived of and studied as an unfolding, living process, as performance, not as a product or literary text. Dan Ben-Amos's (1972, 13) influential and radical formulation of folklore as "artistic communication in small groups" sounded the battle cry, and Richard Bauman's (1977) "Verbal Art as Performance" solidified the gains against the older generation. Barre Toelken (1979, 147; emphasis in original) summarized: "If the active part of folklore can be called *performance*, then the actual total occurrence of that performance, including performer, audience, and context in a time-frame, can be called the *event*." Yet some folklorists resisted. Lamenting that "'text' is rapidly becoming a dirty word," in his 1972 presidential address before the American Folklore Society, D. K. Wilgus (1973, 244) defended the older, item-centered, structural approach: "Text . . . is the item, the artifact, or the record of a mentifact of folklore. . . . It is the manifestation of a folk idea, whether it be a song, a story, a dance, or a cooking pot. . . . There is certainly no reason that the making of a pot cannot be considered a 'performance,' even a kind of rhetoric in clay, but the concreteness of the pot calls attention to the artifact as survival, and 'survival' is another bad word these days."

For Wilgus, a text was a "thing," and as a thing it had its advantages: already objectified, it could be studied as a historical object, its path traced over time and space. He illustrated this in the balance of his address by performing a historical analysis of related song texts. Wilgus's defense of text was a defense of a structuralist method exemplified both in classic historical approaches (what Richard Dorson [1972a, 7–15] has called historical-geographic and historical-reconstructional) and also, by implication, in the pattern analyses of folklorists such as Vladimir Propp ([1928] 1968) and Albert Lord (1960).

Some "new folklorists" of the 1970s and 1980s continued to seek patterns and employ structuralist methods, now applying them to performances and to the "conditions which make [folklore] possible." Influenced by an interdisciplinary confluence of work in sociology (particularly that of Erving Goffman), ethnography of speaking (in sociolinguistics), and ethnoscience in cultural anthropology, Richard Bauman, Roger Abrahams, and several others took care to point out that performance events were signaled or marked as separate from ordinary goings-on and that they proceeded by rules understood, but largely unarticulated, by the participants. Deriving these rules from performance was one of the chief preoccupations of performance analysis (e.g., Glassie 1975b, a structural analysis of vernacular house types). But the new folklorists also applied hermeneutic approaches to performance; Henry Glassie's (1975a) *All Silver and No Brass* is an attempt at a cultural hermeneutics of Irish mumming and prefigures his holistic approach to Irish folklife in his widely admired *Passing the Time in Ballymenone* (1982).

The paradigm shift to performance created a movement away from the objectified text-as-folklore-item. Because text *was* a dirty word to some folklorists, they took care to avoid using it. Some writers took up the ritual metaphor implied by performance and found, in the anthropological work of Victor Turner and in the sociological analyses of Erving Goffman, frameworks that enabled them to interpret repetitive, ritual events. Others took very seriously the theatrical aspects of performance, thinking of a text as no more important to an event than a script is to a play or a film. The formal rigidity of a written text as a reader experienced it, its fixed nature on the page (despite variants and versions) seemed to ossify the living process of performance. And since the usual medium in which academic folklorists communicated was the world of the written scholarly text, many felt stymied. Some explored other media, such as film, but found that costs of production were substantial and academic rewards minimal. Others threw their energy into public sector (applied) folklore, working as cultural advocates and bringing about events such as festivals that featured performances directly. In one sense, the slow institutional decline of academic folklore since the 1970s reflects not only the diminished academic job market but also a declining interest in text-based research.

For those who gave up on text-in-itself and embraced performance, what was gained and what was lost? Gained was a more holistic enterprise and the possibility of doing justice to an intuitive sense of folklore as living process. Gained was an emphasis on persons as well as things, an emphasis on attitudes as well as acts. Gained, I think, was a sensitivity to the human exchanges involved in fieldwork, as folklorists did away with the notion that they were merely collecting data. Folklorists instead embraced reflexivity and intersubjectivity, becoming more aware of authority, power, reciprocity, and representation. Exchanged were one set of metaphors belonging to writing and reading for another belonging to the theater. To some, one of the more troubling implications of the theatrical metaphor, in a discipline that historically has placed such weight on sincerity and authenticity, is that performances imply inauthenticity—that is, staging, acting, and people playing roles different from their presumed real selves. Yet these implications do not trouble those postmodern folklorists who believe that there are no autonomous selves anyway, only a variety of roles available to a self that is constituted by ideology from without. A deeper dilemma turns on the practice of performance analysis, for insofar as analysis constitutes its object, it is forced to remove performance from living process and treat it as if it were a text. This dilemma appears to be inherent in our scholarly procedures, not only because we write our scholarship as text but also because analysis and interpretation are directed at objects; and if a text is anything that can be interpreted, then there is no interpretation without text. So even when performance theory has driven folkloristic analysis, transcribed texts remain in our work, embedded now in new interpretive contexts.

*Powerhouse for God*, a folklife ethnography about language in religious practice among a community of worshippers in Virginia's Blue Ridge

Mountains, is filled with textual transcriptions of songs, sermons, prayers, testimonies, and conversion narratives (Titon [1988] 2018). When I began this project in 1976, I deliberately turned to long-term fieldwork and contrived a text-heavy hermeneutic model involving affect, performance, community, and memory, as I recorded, transcribed, and interpreted texts from these performances of religious folklife. At the same time that I was recording and transcribing the texts for *Powerhouse for God*, I understood them within a performance framework—that is, I took texts like testimonies, sermons, and prayers to be products that people generated in performances. Conversations became occasions for generating metatexts—texts about texts—as we spoke about the meaning of the morning's sermon or a song that had a visibly powerful effect on someone in the congregation. From a theoretical point of view, I was interested in how language in religious performance brought about certain ideas, feelings, and actions and how it helped give meaning to the lives of people who had become my acquaintances and friends. But in order to gain any insight into their lives—how their lives worked—I had to try to understand who they were as persons.

Over and over, I learned that performances are intersubjective, emerging from personal relationships and to some extent shaped by them. Even though the texts were objects, I could not consider them objectively. My friends did not think of themselves as generating texts; they were talking to each other and to me. Always, there were persons behind texts. I became aware that my presence must have affected certain performances. For example, a number of people gently "witnessed" their experiences of God to me hoping that by example I might see how I could become born again. In so doing, they were not behaving unusually; they believe God requires them to witness and evangelize. Had I become born again, I would have been the recipient of performances that, as an outsider, they did not disclose to me.

We folklorists do not only study texts; we do not only study performances. We try to understand persons in performance generating texts and giving and finding meaning in their lives. That is what the film *Powerhouse for God* is meant to portray (Dornfeld, Rankin, and Titon 1989). In a different field project, the Reverend C. L. Franklin's life history emerged from our conversations, but it emphasized the kinds of things I asked to hear and the kinds of things he was interested in revealing to me. The text would have been significantly different had he been speaking with a person from a different background with different interests (see Franklin 1989). If we overlook the relations between individual people and the texts that they (we) generate, we never will understand texts—or people.

Recognizing these relations, many folklorists have embraced a newer sense of text as process. Rather than trade text for performance, we treat texts as performances and performances as texts, blurring the distinctions between them and extending the meaning of *text* to cover any object of interpretation. Metaphorically, then, artifacts, performances, events, and so forth are regarded as textual inscriptions to be read and interpreted: the performance, in this view, does not merely *have* a text (script) as a part of its totality. Rather, its totality *is* a text. Performances cannot be reduced to texts; rather, performances are texts. The movement away from the older concept of text-as-item can thus be understood as a broadening and reconfiguration of text. Evidence of scholarly movement in this direction has also appeared in American cultural anthropology where, at about the same time, there was an "interpretive turn," usually traced to Clifford Geertz, who wrote that just as words can be read, so events can be "read" as texts. Textual analysis of events attends to "how the inscription of action is brought about, what its vehicles are and how they work, and on what the fixation of meaning from the flow of events—history from what happened, thought from thinking, culture from behavior—implies for sociological interpretation. To see social institutions, social customs, and social changes as in some sense 'readable' is to alter our whole sense of what such interpretation is toward modes of thought rather more familiar to the translator" (Geertz 1980, 175–176). Geertz (1973, 448) demonstrated just such a "reading" in his famous article on the meaning of the Balinese cockfight, where he likened culture to "an assemblage of texts."

Although Geertz's formulation of a cultural hermeneutics greatly influenced the ethnographic enterprise in North America, he was operating within a European tradition of inquiry into the human sciences, emphasizing a humanistic approach to what Americans call social sciences. In "The Model of the Text: Meaningful Action Considered as Text," Paul Ricoeur (1981b, 197; italics in original) wrote, "the human sciences may be said to be hermeneutical (1) inasmuch as their *object* displays some of the features constitutive of a text as text, and (2) inasmuch as their *methodology* develops the same kind of procedures as those of *Auslegung* or text-interpretation." William Dilthey's insistence on the "humanness" of the nonnatural sciences and on the differences between explanation (the result of scientific method) and understanding (the result of interpretation in the human sciences) inaugurated this tradition. Dilthey stressed "the lived experience in cultural expressions rather than reducing experience to a system of semiotic exchange" (as quoted in Rajan 1994, 378). For Dilthey, the human sciences were hermeneutic, their constituents the objects of interpretive acts. Geertz (1980) had identified three competing social science paradigms in his "Blurred Genres" article: life is a game, life is a drama, life is a text. While happiest with the text metaphor, Geertz looked forward to the possibility of a reconciliation among them. Turner, arguing against Geertz, wrote that texts "are like the shucked-off husks of the living process" (Schechner and Appel 1990, 16). Turner's argument gave weight to those scholars in performance who felt that the word "text," like the word "folklore," was hopelessly outdated. Indeed, a new graduate field, performance studies, was established at New York University and Northwestern University; it drew on folklore, theater, and cultural anthropology.

## Ethnography and the "Knowing Text"

Within the discipline of folklore, text remains a problematized concept showing, among other things, that despite attempts to defeat it, the concept retains force. Among American academic folklorists, the performance-oriented theorists have succeeded in diminishing the older idea of text-as-item and the historical-geographical methods that accompanied it. But the attack on text resulted in a reconceptualization of text as any object of interpretation. This defense of text, if it is to be effective, does not merely return us to the older procedures of textual analysis; rather, the new text is open to the kinds of interpretations folklorists are interested in making, yielding to the new questions folklorists are interested in asking. Such questions, nowadays, involve postmodern critiques of scholarship, and they focus on ideas such as experience and belief and categories such as class, gender, ethnicity, region, and sexual orientation.

To make text responsive to current ideas in the discipline, folklorists will continue to make use of transcribed performances as objects of interpretation. But representations of these performances today enlarge to include far more than just objectified verbal discourse or artifact; wherever possible, they now include gestures, feelings, intentions, reception and resulting behaviors, and so forth: not so much text-and-context but text-in-process, text as experienced. This reflects a general shift of interest in experiential social science. The old questions involving origins, pattern, diffusion, and transmission of folklore never were answered satisfactorily and possibly never will be; whereas questions having to do with the uses of tradition, with tradition bearers' own ideas about folklore, with folklore as it is experienced in human consciousness are the more interesting questions today.

Those of us who broaden the meaning of text so that we may in effect read performance events also consider the interpretive books (and articles and films) we produce to be texts. We view ourselves as authors engaged in the cultural production of texts. Not only do we "collect" and transcribe texts in the field, not only do we interpret verbal and other texts, but we understand our scholarly productions themselves as texts because they too are objects of interpretation: we and our readers interpret them. I propose here that we write "knowing texts." By a knowing text, I mean a text that a reader will find to be self-knowing (reflexive), aware of the basis for and limits of its knowledge claims (authority). I mean a text skillfully crafted, particularly in terms of point of view, to establish an intersubjective relation among author, text, the "characters" (persons represented in the text), and reader. I mean a text written to take full advantage of the techniques available to authors. What follows is meant to be a preliminary discussion of the knowing text, not a definitive exposition.

In the 1970s, as performance theory was turning folklorists toward context, European folklife studies attracted folklorists toward ethnographies focused on expressive culture and the lived experiences of tradition bearers. Folklorists, after all, did fieldwork; and in an academic world grown sensitive to power relationships and exploitation of the marginalized groups folklorists traditionally studied, the image of the folklorist as collector, strip-mining folklore while traveling and surveying the field, was not a pleasant prospect. Some adopted Malinowski's fieldwork model in which rather than traveling, surveying, and collecting, the fieldworker takes up residence in the native village and tries to understand, through close observation over a relatively long period, the way of life of the natives—which, for folklorists, meant understanding the performance of expressive culture in its context. Just as cultural anthropologists in this tradition produced ethnographies—descriptions of aspects of native life that included texts, contexts, native points of view, and interpretations by the anthropologist—so did these folklorists produce studies of aspects of folklife among individuals in particular folk groups. With hindsight, it is now possible to see that ironically, just when American literary critics were abandoning certain tenets of the New Criticism in favor of a structuralist poetics (Culler 1975), folklorists gave up the text-centered structuralism that had constituted the issues (design, structure, and transmission over time and space) that they had sought to explore. While performance took center stage, some folklorists came to prefer the term "folklife" to describe their interests in a more holistic and affective approach to expressive culture. Insofar as a life-centered, rather than lore-centered, approach is an interpretive move in the direction of affect, it is also, ironically, a move toward the New Critics' emphasis on understanding not just how and what a literary work means but also how it feels to experience that work.

As American folklorists moved more toward anthropological research, some became involved in the anthropological reaction against older models of objectively reported text. Beginning with the essays collected in *Reinventing Anthropology*, a radical critique of the field based on the radical politics of the sixties generation, and later in *Anthropology as Cultural Critique* and *Writing Culture*, the two most widely read works of anthropological theory in the 1980s, a new kind of ethnographic text was called for, one appropriate to the "experimental moment" of cultural relativism when scientific objectivity no longer seemed adequate, epistemologically or ethically, in a postcolonial world (Hymes 1972; Clifford and Marcus [1986] 2010; Fischer and Marcus 1986). This new text would be experiential, self-reflexive, and it would recognize, as Geertz did, that ethnographies were made, not found, that they were rhetorical, not scientific. In a word, the new ethnographic text would be literary.

But would it succeed? Why produce a literary text when powerful currents pulled many toward feminist, Marxist, and other ideologically driven texts whose mark is an apparent outward sincerity, the writer speaking without artifice in his or her real voice? Why produce a literary text when contemporary reactions against political correctness pulled others back toward a purportedly objective stance? Isn't a literary text ambiguous when an ethnographer should be striving for clarity? How can we write fiction when our aim is truth? In answer, I claim that all interpretive texts are literary. All writing is artifice. The ethnographic text is a fiction in the root sense (*facio*) that it is a making, not in the sense that it is false. There is a difference between imaginative fiction and ethnographic fiction, of course. The novelist or short story writer is free to invent in ways that the ethnographer is not. The fieldwork-based claim of the ethnographer is "I was there," whereas the novelist's witness is chiefly in his or her imagination. Novels and short stories are made up, invented, whereas ethnographic fiction is made after experience is found out. But if we who author fieldwork-based ethnographic texts conceive of our work as rhetorical, literary, and self-reflexive, and so long as we continue to be concerned with issues of representation and authority, then we will write "knowing texts" whose epistemological ground is realized through self-conscious management of point of view to establish the nature of the author's authority and the relation between author, text, character, and reader.

My advocacy of knowing texts requires some background, particularly in an intellectual atmosphere in which the concepts of culture and fieldwork have been problematized to the point where, like text, there are those who would discard them entirely. It was with a shock of recognition that I read

Clifford, Tyler, Marcus, and others in the 1980s, for I had come to the same conclusions about the literariness of ethnographic texts independently and earlier. When I came to read popular ethnographies in the 1960s and 1970s, I responded to them as if they were literature. I am thinking especially of Colin Turnbull's (1961) *The Forest People* but also of Michael J. Harner's (1972) *The Jivaro*, Carlos Castaneda's (1968) *The Teachings of Don Juan*, and most influentially, *Tristes tropiques*, Levi-Strauss's (1974) brilliant travelogue of ethnography and memoir.

While teaching at Tufts in the 1970s I devised an English course and called it "Inventing Anthropology." In this course, typical of its time in that instructors taught by choosing subjects and readings centered on a particular theme, we read popular ethnographies and works of fiction, considering how each conformed to similar and different rhetorical and literary conventions. In addition to the above-mentioned anthropological works, we read Ursula Le Guin's (1969) *The Left Hand of Darkness* and discussed to what extent science fiction and ethnography employed similar devices, what they had in common, and how we understood their truth claims and authority claims. We read Thomas Pynchon's (1966) *The Crying of Lot 49* as (among other things) a work of detective fiction and asked how it differed from ethnography.

Thinking about ethnography, autobiography, and fiction led me to reconsider the assumptions connected with the autobiographical texts that fieldworkers obtain from the people they speak with. In "The Life Story," I claimed such talk was better understood as fiction, a making, rather than as something factual that the fieldworker discovered or found out (Titon 1980). I responded also by writing stories about the practice of public folklore, stories in which I established a fiction writer's point of view. To the amusement of a few, I delivered some of these as papers at folklore and ethnomusicology conferences. But the aim was more than to amuse myself; story and irony presented themselves as time-honored means toward truths. Besides, narrative, if done gracefully, can embed interpretation into the flow of ongoing events. One story, "Murder at the Folk Festival," permitted me, in the narrative voice of a detective who knew nothing about folk festivals and was impatient with their rhetoric, to explore some of the festivals' assumptions of representation (Titon 1979), which Robert Cantwell (1993) later questioned in *Ethnomimesis*. Another was cast in epistolary form, a series of letters from a putative fieldworker traveling through Maine in search of performers for a national folk festival (Titon 1983). This epistolary point of view encouraged me to pursue discrepancies between festival views of authenticity and those of tradition bearers and revivalist performers. I think of these as imaginative fiction, not as knowing texts.

I knew something about folk festivals because I had participated in them, but I invented these stories. On the other hand, the prologue, first chapter, and epilogue in *Powerhouse for God* are my renderings of events that did happen, "knowing texts" where I maintain narrative points of view (Titon [1988] 2019; see below) different from the general exposition in a book that has become known for careful textual procedures.

By point of view, I do not mean the author's personal opinions. Instead, I use the term in its conventional literary sense, to mean the author's relation to the text and reader. What options are open to authors of ethnographic texts? Typically, an ethnographer begins by writing narrative in the first person, in his or her own voice, not only to introduce the subject but also to establish authority. This authority is based on witness: the author did fieldwork, was there, was engaged long enough to understand something of what was going on. But once these credentials have been established, the "I" seems to be in the way, and so the author shifts to third-person exposition to describe those aspects of the culture that appear to be there for anyone to see. Those aspects often include verbal texts, artifacts, customary behavior, and so forth, along with native interpretations of them. From a literary standpoint, our ethnographer has moved from a position of limited, first-person authority to the position of omniscient author. Reading a work of fiction, one might find this shift in point of view puzzling. Reading ethnographic writing, one ought to be similarly skeptical. Claims to authority are undermined when authors move from their initial, limited, first-person points of view to omniscience because nowadays most are uncomfortable with the pretense of omniscience. In fiction, these claims can succeed only under a special set of circumstances: if the initial "I" is understood as a creation of the author, at best an alter ego, but not the author directly. Yet this strategy is unavailable to the ethnographic author who wishes to write directly of himself or herself in the first person. What other possibilities might there be? The knowing text offers one such.

A widely used book that teaches writing discusses point of view in terms of the following questions: Who speaks? To whom? In what form? At what distance? With what limitations (Burroway 1987)? (In what follows, we may take the "characters" in the story to be the fieldworker's consultants, informants, or colleagues who are written into the ethnographic text, sometimes given their own voice, edited or not.) Whatever the point of view, an author is admonished to stick to it throughout the text. The author may speak in the third person, omnisciently, or with partial omniscience (favoring the point of view of a single character, going into his or her mind and telling the reader what is passing there). The author conventionally speaks to the reader, but in a folklife ethnography the author is understood also to be speaking to the characters in his or her text, some of whom will read it. The author gives the story a form: it may be represented as something written or spoken; it may take the form of a report, a monologue, a dialogue, a diary, and so forth. The authorial point of view may be based on a close identification with the action of the story, as a central participant in it; or it may be the point of view of a peripheral participant or witness; or it may be removed in space or time. Finally, the narrator may be limited by who he or she is or by what he or she knows about the story, and those limitations may produce degrees of unreliability, as for instance when the narrator is ill, clearly biased, ignorant, unsympathetic, and so forth; and in those circumstances, the reader is meant to know more than the narrator.

In short, point of view permits the writer of an ethnographic text to begin experimenting with more solutions to the problems of representation and authority than omniscience, first-person confessional, or the conventional but awkward shift from the latter to the former. If in the course of our fieldwork we have recorded dialogue, we can present it verbatim or edited, from different points of view. An interview conversation need not be excerpted in the course of an expository argument (the conventional representation); it may be presented and interpreted as it goes along. Folklife performances may be represented evocatively, narrated as a story, with interpretation coming from the narrator's point of view. The narrator might be the folklorist but need not be. Or, as in the well-known 1950 film *Rashomon*, there might be multiple narrative voices, each with a different understanding of what was taking place (Kurosawa 1969).

*Powerhouse for God* is presented for the most part in the third person as text and interpretation, with the occasional presence of an "I" meant to represent me, the scholar in the process of thinking and writing it; but in three places I experimented with point of view. The prologue is *i* the story of an encounter and conversation between the book's chief tradition bearer (character) and a folklorist from Washington, Carl Fleischhauer. The conversation took place in a fast-food restaurant in Luray, Virginia, and I sat in the booth and witnessed it. Better, I made a tape recording of it, and when it came time to represent it, I could transcribe it and present the conversation verbatim. The words, at any rate, could be presented thus; but I told the story of the encounter, recalled and represented the setting, and gently put a few perceptions into the characters' minds based on my understanding of what transpired. I wrote the prologue entirely in the voice of a first-person narrator, an "I" who represented the author taking part in the action at a particular time and place when he did not know what he knew later on. This "I" was the "I" at the start of the project and at the start of the book. The first chapter of *Powerhouse*, on the other hand, is an evocative representation of a homecoming service—again, one that was tape-recorded and videotaped—but from the point of view of an omniscient author at the end of the project, ten years after he first witnessed it. That point of view was informed by years of observations and by hours and hours of conversations with the book's characters about the meaning of the events. At the same time, I kept in mind as audience for this chapter a thoughtful and well-educated adult who, nevertheless, had no experience with this kind of worship or language in religious practice. The epilogue, also a narration, revisited the town homecoming, a secular version of the most important annual occurrence in the church's calendar. The town homecoming was one of the very first events I had observed while doing fieldwork in that community, but it seemed appropriate to end the book with a story that took the reader out of the close confines of the church, congregation, and pastor's family who are its center, and into the larger world. Embedded in that story is the pastor's own story, a reminiscence how one year he appeared in the town homecoming on a float, preaching to the crowd, caught up in it so completely that he did not know when he passed by the judges' stand.

Clifford Geertz has defended a hermeneutics of observation, one in which the interpreter deliberately stands outside of and apart from the cultural production that is the object of interpretation. In this formulation, experience is the experience of others, conveyed in part insofar as these others are able to articulate it and in part as it is "caught" through cultural metaphor by an observer who occupies a privileged position to understand it. "Understanding the form and pressure of natives' inner lives is more like grasping a proverb, catching an allusion, seeing a joke—or, as I have suggested, reading a poem—than it is like achieving communion" (Geertz 1977, 49). In so saying, Geertz put himself in opposition to Dilthey and others who espoused a hermeneutics of empathy in which the interpreter claims to understand "Others" through friendship and by imaginatively changing places with them.

Geertz's objectivity is not a necessary component of hermeneutic approaches to text, however. Dennis Tedlock and Barbara Tedlock, for example, have both undertaken a hermeneutics of empathetic participation in which the hermeneutic circle extends to include the relationship between the interpreter and those people who are the subjects of an intersubjective interpretation. In the classic Malinowskian formulation of participant observation, "participation" meant living among one's informants but refraining from fully participating in that life. Yet for the Tedlocks, as for others, participation meant apprenticeship and adoption into the culture (B. Tedlock 1992). The resulting representations have included, for example, Dennis Tedlock's (1990) attempts to convey experience by writing poems. Ethnomusicologists nowadays participate in the musical life of the people they observe (see Titon 1995a). Of course, in some circumstances, full participation is impossible because one lacks ability or time to learn, or feels that to participate will be to change one's being and identity in an unwanted way. And in some situations, people being "studied" are suspicious, hostile, not very forthcoming, dissembling, or bored—reactions that occur more frequently in the postcolonial world.

Many fieldworkers understand that they have been, to some degree, transformed by their experiences. Until recently, most did not make personal transformation a part of their ethnographic text. It was not appropriate. Now that ethnographic writing has become more reflexive, and some ethnographers now choose to write in the first person, in their own voice, representing themselves, the urge to confess sometimes results in texts that foreground the author. Unfortunately, no matter how sincere the attempt, the products can be, and have been, dismissed as self-indulgent, displacing the reader's attention from the subject of the ethnography to the fieldworker, whose personal epiphanies are not rendered sufficiently compelling. The reader, who expected to learn of a particular people's way of life, feels short-changed, perhaps even a victim of bait-and-switch. And the ethnographic subject, in the words of a joke that has become commonplace among ethnographers, says to the author, "That's enough about you; now what about me?"

How, then, to handle the problem of the author in the text? Some readers simply will not accept ethnography as memoir or autobiography in any form. For the rest, if compelled to write about one's personal transformation, one may write a story that implicates the reader directly. One chooses a different point of view, one that best permits the reader to experience, through identification, the author's transformation. Let the reader experience the transformation as the author does but vicariously. The move toward this point of view and the reasons for it were discussed by the literary critic Percy Lubbock seventy-five years ago. Lubbock's ([1921] 1957, 252) subject was imaginative fiction writing, but what he wrote seems equally relevant in the case of transformational ethnography:

> If [the narrator] has nothing to do but relate what he has seen, what anyone might have seen in his position, his account will serve very well; there is no need for more. . . . But if he is himself the subject of his story, if the story involves a

searching exploration of his own consciousness, [then] an account in his own words, after the fact, is not by any means the best imaginable. Far better it would be to see him while his mind is actually at work in the agitation.... The matter would then be objective and visible to the reader, instead of reaching him in the form of a report at second hand.

Lubbock next asks how this can be managed through point of view. Rejecting the "account in his own words, after the fact," in the first person, he suggests that the author bypass the idea of the report and let the reader into the writer's consciousness as the action occurs, not in retrospect:

But how to manage this without falling back upon the author and his report, which has already been tried and for good reasons, as it seemed, abandoned? It is managed by ... a further shift of the point of view. The spectator, the listener, the reader, is now himself to be placed at the angle of vision,—not an account or a report, more or less convincing, is to be offered him, but a direct sight of the matter itself, while it is passing. Nobody expounds or explains; the story is enacted by its look and behaviour at particular moments.... Now ... the narrator is forestalled; he is watched while the story is in the making. (253)

This strategy suggests that authors of knowing texts deliberately create a character, a fieldworker-ethnographer who is meant to resemble the author during the stage of fieldwork. This character may write in the first person, as an unreliable narrator who becomes more reliable as the story moves along, understanding occurs, and the transformation is effected. Or the fieldworker character may be observed by yet another character, who writes in the first person—a narrator who observes the fieldworker-ethnographer's experiences. Or there may be no narrator but just an omniscient voice, writing in the third person, who chooses to limit the point of view to the consciousness of the fieldworker-ethnographer, and allows the reader to witness the transformation by seeing the ethnographer's mind "at work in the agitation," as Lubbock writes above.

Knowing texts are addressed to readers for whom the older ethnographic models no longer suffice. Readers today are skeptical; they are bored. "How can we take pleasure in a reported pleasure (boredom of all narratives of dreams, of parties)?" writes Barthes (1975, 17). "How can we read criticism? Only one way: since I am here a second-degree reader, I must shift my position: instead of agreeing to be the confidant of this critical pleasure—a sure way to miss it—I can make myself its voyeur." Because the reader already has shifted "position" and turned the ethnographic work into "a text, a fiction, a fissured envelope" (17), the author responds by shifting point of view and making a knowing text.

## Postmodern Representations in Hypertext and Multimedia

Ideology figures importantly in the theory of the "virtual class," technocrats (including professors and students) who spend many hours each day in front of a computer, viewing text on a screen. Arthur Kroker and Michael A. Weinstein (1994) suggest that in their eagerness to embrace virtual reality as a substitute for full sensory, face-to-face participation, the virtual class has found a way to interact in the world without bodies and without risk. Kroker is thinking primarily of those who search the internet for pleasurable interactions in cyberspace: examples are multiplayer game sites in which World Wide Web surfers take on the attributes of various characters and interact through role-playing. Channeling their energies into virtual reality, where cyberpunk ideology reigns, this virtual class challenges the hegemonic discourse without risk (unless behaving as a criminal, for example, hacking one's way into a corporation's presumably secure computer system).

But there are less dramatic and more powerful forces at work in the virtual world, forces that are reconfiguring our notions of text yet again. Variously described as hypertext, multimedia, and hypermedia, a new kind of computer representation models the world, one that combines words, sounds, and images (can touch and smell be far behind?). What is hypertext? The word suggests hyperactivity, and that is not a bad way to begin thinking about it. "Hypertexts are electronic documents, read on the screen of the computer rather than printed on paper" (Bolter, Joyce, and Smith 1993, 21). So states the instruction manual for Storyspace, one of the better computer programs that enable one to write hypertexts. "In a conventional book, one page follows another in a single, fixed sequence. In a hypertext, writing spaces are linked together. Frequently a writing space may offer several different links, each leading to different information" (25). Hypertexts are nonlinear. Several writing spaces can appear on the screen simultaneously. The reader of a hypertext often feels hyperactive, jumping around by means of links from one space to another in a sequence of his or her own choosing. In a hypertext, the reader is always offered multiple pathways through the information, and the reading will be different depending on which pathways are chosen and what is read and not read.

Hypertext offers, first of all, a superior environment for modeling intertextual relationships among texts traditionally considered as "things." Suppose one chose several performances of a Native American ballad such as "Poor Omie" (Laws F31, F4) as the subject of a hypertext. An imaginary hypertextual construction for folklorists might consist of the following writing spaces. Ten writing spaces could be given over to ten versions and variants of the words to the ballad, one space to each version. Each version could be linked to any number of the other versions, perhaps on the basis of similarities. Readers could activate the links by pressing on-screen virtual buttons with a mouse or set of keyboard commands: press the button and another writing space appears. Other linked writing spaces could contain contextual information. For example, one or more could contain newspaper reports and other chronicles of the murder of Naomi Wise by John Lewis (the event on which the ballad was based). One or more could contain musical transcriptions of performances of versions of the ballad, and these could be compared by means of links and on-screen juxtapositions. Singers' ideas about the ballad could occupy other spaces. An essay on balladry could occupy others. Performance analysis, still others. Links to other American murder ballads, still others. This hypertext is an open text with many possibilities.

Hypertexts may also contain multimedia presentations such as sounds. In our imaginary construction, there is no reason why one or more writing spaces could not contain buttons that, when activated, could "play" a digitized field recording containing one or more of the versions of "Poor Omie" under discussion. These sounds could be stored on the hard drive, CD-ROM, or DVD for that purpose. In fact, one could "play" a video clip in the same way. And these days, computers have the capability of recognizing sounds. So, for example, one could "practice" singing any of these versions of "Poor Omie," and the computer would not only tell how accurate the melody was but also suggest where and how one could improve it.[3] Finally, one can, in some hypertexts, add material and modify the whole. Reader additions may take the form of comments that can be seen by the next reader, new links to already-established writing spaces, and new writing spaces with reader-generated material (one's own version of the ballad, perhaps) linked to other writing spaces.

The possibilities of hypertext have not yet been fully realized. Many of the early hypertexts were little more than books on the computer screen, or versions of book-like activities made more convenient through the computer. *The In Memoriam Web* (Landow 1992b) centers on the text of Alfred Lord Tennyson's long poem. Links are provided not only to explain words in the poem but also to contextual essays having to do with aspects of Victorianism. Such a construction may be considered to have a central hub (the poem text) and several interlinked spokes (the contextual essays). The experience of reading this hypertext is meant to suggest the experience of a scholar in a library doing research. *The Clyde Davenport Web* (Titon 1991) is an early model of hypertext that takes the reader to visit with Kentucky old-time fiddler Clyde Davenport. Links are provided to members of his family, to various incidents in his life, to some of his fiddle tunes (which are given as sounds and as musical transcriptions), to his aesthetic preferences, and to brief essays on old-time fiddling and on bluegrass. One writing space discusses the relationship between Clyde and the author of the hypertext. In the original HyperCard version, every writing space offers readers an opportunity to comment and thereby alter the text for the next reader. An unusual feature of this hypertext is that it offers the reader opposite conclusions without resolving the difference, thereby modeling some of the ambiguity a researcher faces. For example, the reader hears Clyde play two tunes and is told that musical analysis suggests that they are quite similar. Transcriptions illustrate the similarities. But another path leads to Clyde saying that these same two tunes are different, then demonstrating the difference.

The centralized hypertext invokes a hierarchical structure in which there is always a core text and varying degrees of peripheral information and interpretation. This text evokes an impression of an omniscient point of view. In a second type of hypertext, a central text is absent or undermined in some way, and the experience of reading the hypertext is more like playing a game than doing a research assignment. Without a single central text the branching structure is nonhierarchical; instead, it is like a web or mosaic, with some nodes more central and important than others. *Afternoon* (Joyce 1990) is a work of hypertext fiction in which the narrative depends on the reader's choices. The narrator is unreliable. Readers learn more or less about the characters and events depending on the paths that they choose and the order in which they choose them. The reading is complicated in that certain links become available only after the reader has activated other links. *Uncle Buddy's Phantom Funhouse* (McDaid 1993) is also a work of fiction, but it has no narrative structure. In this hypertext, the reader enters the virtual house of "Uncle Buddy," a writer, who has disappeared, leaving only his artifacts: desk, file cabinets, screenplays, music, and so forth. The hypertext reader rummages around Uncle Buddy's effects and tries to understand who he was on the basis of various clues, some contradictory, others secret. In some ways, the reader is placed in the position of a detective; in other ways, a fieldworker.

Hypertexts are unlike conventional books in important ways. They do not have the same kind of closure; they do not end, but readers stop. J. Yellowlees Douglas (1991, n.p.) likens them to

> the elaborate memory palaces constructed by Greek and Roman speakers which once enabled them to memorize vast chunks of perfectly finished oratory. . . .

> Where ancient rhetoricians strolled through every room . . . you'll be wandering through this narrative edifice more or less as you would through a museum. You don't need to peer intently at every exhibit in every room of a museum to feel that you've "done" the museum. What prompts us to leave the museum is not the sense of having digested its every aspect, but the sense of having satisfied—or exhausted—something in ourselves.

People will increasingly experience text as hypertext in the twenty-first century. Text will be digitized, stored, and available online as information. Scholars will continue to write books, but more and more will work in hypertexts. It would seem that hypertext offers many advantages over linear text, and indeed I believe it does. For one thing, it offers grand opportunities for producing knowing texts and virtual realities. At the same time, there are reasons to be cautious and critical. Many hypertexts at present are dull and annoying, and hypertexts are never any better than their contents. Access to hypertexts is limited at present to the segment of the population that can afford it.[4] Issues regarding copyright of intellectual property are extremely difficult to resolve in this new medium because policing is much more problematic. And linear forms of text organization offer a kind of representation that for many is reassuring. Indeed, most of the information available on the World Wide Web today is organized with links designed to mimic the linear world insofar as possible. A case in point: the "back" and "forward" buttons on today's web browsers encourage movement back and forth in a straight line. Ambiguity, unreliable narrators, and lateral movement to another world are unsuitable and irritating when using the web to find, for example, the cheapest airfare to a travel destination. But although the web has now become the way most people experience linked text, for representations of lived experience the information retrieval model on the web cannot provide the richness of knowing texts. Fortunately, as I mentioned earlier, hypertexts that operate on a virtual reality model are also available in electronic form on the web and in CD-ROM and DVD format.

Virtual reality does not mirror reality any more than other "realist" representations do. It is a representation of its own: the experience of a person at a computer mentally confronting a text. Is a computer merely a channel through which minds communicate via texts? Can a computer offer a virtual performance? One of the lessons that performance-oriented folklorists learned is what Nathaniel Hawthorne taught over and over: that the life of the intellect, divorced from human contact and pursued single-mindedly, leads to madness. Ethan Brand and Roger Chillingworth would have been cybersurfers today—no doubt about it. The reason why the new folklorists were interested in performance was that they were interested in persons.

What kind of experience is the experience of a virtual world of text without risk, without responsibility?[5] How fulfilling are experiences of virtual reality? If our minds are but bundles of texts, sites of competing ideologies, how do we account for our minds becoming critically self-aware? Can a text become aware of itself? It would seem a logical impossibility. Critics of text who view the problem as one of disembodiment will be little comforted by the virtual reality of hypertext.

Despite this critique of text, it is clear that just as we are being led to understand text in new ways, we are being led to understand mind and self in new models. Rorty's notion of minds as self-reweaving webs is very close to the concept of interactivity in hypertext, particularly as readers become authors. Further, Rorty (1991, 93) emphasizes that "there is no self distinct from this self-reweaving web. All there is to the human self is just that web." And for Rorty, there is no mind-body problem either: the body is one with the mind and self, the web of desires continually reweaving as it acts and is acted upon in the world. Jacques Derrida's (1979, 83–84) view of the new and "transformed" text sounds very suspiciously like a hypertext version of the world:

> A "text" that is henceforth no longer a finished corpus of writing, some content enclosed in a book or its margins, but a differential network, a fabric of traces referring endlessly to something other than itself, to other differential traces. Thus the text overruns all the limits assigned to it so far (not submerging or drowning them in an undifferentiated homogeneity, but rather making them more complex, dividing and multiplying strokes and lines)—all the limits, everything that was to be set up in opposition to writing (speech, life, the world, the real, history, and what not, every field of reference).

The Indo-European root of text, *tek*, means to weave, to fabricate. Texts are not a given in the world; they are made. Even if we are inhabited by language and constructed by texts, if our selves are webs of beliefs and desires, I am not ready to believe our experience always comes to us already textualized, in language, bit by bit. Ecstasy or transcendent experience seems to me to be outside of textualization, at least initially, and language can only point to it, not model it, though occasionally it can induce it. Texts may make us, but we also make texts; we translate, we represent. Texts in this sense are always nostalgic, longing for experience. The pretexted world is a processual world. It is the flow that, for example, most people recognize when making or listening to music: an unfolding. Texts considered as digitized information are reproducible, exactly replicable; experiences (including experiences of texts) are not. Texted, language seems to be a reasonable translation; the stuff of thought, it represents thought. Notated, music is only a fair translation; its realization requires much more in the way of context. Experience ordinarily is texted as art: we tell stories about ourselves (often to ourselves), we write poems, we make films, we paint, we draw, we make music, we build houses, we cook, we arrange our lives, we express ourselves; this is our expressive culture. Texts about texts, metatexts, are representations of texts that already are representations. This is the textualized world that scholars inhabit. This world of text is an already virtual world. Hypertext representations encourage artful authoring and reading, and good hypertexts turn readers into authors. Like the best texts, the best hypertexts are not ends in themselves but means that return us refreshed and knowing to the world of people, performance, and community.

## Notes

1. A few folklorists have argued that multiple versions and variants are not a necessary condition of folklore and that other conditions, such as expressive quality, the folk community base, aesthetics, and so forth, are more fruitful avenues for interpretation. When text is understood as a representation of a process, rather than as an item, however, this problem disappears.

2. [Author's note, 2020: A transcription of this narrative may be found in "The Life Story," this volume. For the audio recording of this narrative, see *Alcheringa: A Journal in Ethnopoetics*, n.s., 1, no. 2 (1975), http://writing.upenn.edu/pennsound/x/Alcheringa.php.]

3. In 1995, when this essay was first published, Claire, the "personal music coach," was commercially available software that taught sight singing on any Macintosh computer. In this software, musical notation appears in exercises on the screen, the student "sings" into the computer's microphone, and the computer calculates the pitch accuracy. Unfortunately, the manufacturer abandoned the software about 1997.

4. Efforts have succeeded in making the internet free to the general public, however, through public library workstations.

5. *Per*, an Indo-European root of "experience," means to try, to risk, to lean forward.

# 4

# KNOWING FIELDWORK

*I* FIRST LEARNED ABOUT FIELDWORK IN GRADUATE SCHOOL *when I took courses in cultural anthropology in my first year and ethnomusicology in my second. In this essay, I discuss my early attempts at fieldwork, my growing ambivalence about it, and how it thrust me into thinking about myself and the relationships I had with the blues musicians I'd been hanging out with. My ontological turn, to use a phrase that's become fashionable in anthropological knowledge production (Holbrand and Pedersen 2017), thrust me into a self-reflexive posture as a participant-observer in the 1960s, one that was at odds with the scientific objectivity advocated in my graduate training. I've been intrigued with fieldwork in folklore and ethnomusicology ever since, certain that in many ways fieldwork is epistemologically constitutive of what we can know, how we can know it, and how our experiences and being in the world bear on and partially determine what we come to know and the knowledge we produce—and this all while we are being perceived by the people we encounter in the field in ways that differ from our ideas of who we are and what our roles are (Titon 1985). Fieldwork ethics in a postcolonial world; the fieldworker's role and stance; insiderness, outsiderness; engaged observer, participant observer, or initiated participant; visitor, guest, friend, collaborator; objective scientific observer, investigative reporter; along with the practical matters of fieldwork such as the art of the interview, the technique of sound recording, the skills of visual documentation, the crafting of field notes, the making of ethnography—all these seemed to me so important that I devoted an ongoing graduate seminar entirely to the subject of fieldwork, its ethical dimensions, and its production of knowledge and activity along with its transformative impact on the fieldworker and field partners. The experiential dimension of fieldwork led me, in the mid-1970s, to Ninian Smart's writings on phenomenology in comparative religious studies; these were formative in my own field research and also in my teaching. In "Knowing Fieldwork," I develop further the description of ethnomusicology and its history that I began in "Ethnomusicology as the Study of People Making Music" and the idea of generating knowing texts from "Text." In this essay discussing "the new fieldwork" of my generation, I emphasized phenomenological approaches to doing fieldwork and generating ethnographic knowledges. Phenomenology enabled my curiosity about the experience of flow and musical being, an ontological idea that has reappeared as sonic being twenty years later, now a cornerstone of the sound ecology project. The first version of this essay was the basis for the keynote address to the Annual Conference of Finland's Society for Ethnomusicology, at the Sibelius Academy, in Helsinki, on April 1, 1993. That Finnish version (originally a hypertext) was published as "Knowing People Making Music" (Titon 1994). The second version was published in* Shadows in the Field *(Barz and Cooley 1997). The version that follows appeared in the second edition of* Shadows in the Field *(Barz and Cooley 2008), with the added postscript.*

Epistemology is that field of inquiry whose subject is the origins, nature, and limits of human knowing (see Rorty 1979, 140). An epistemology for ethnomusicology is therefore concerned with the origins, nature, and limits of human knowledge concerning music in human life. An epistemology for ethnomusicology attempts to answer two basic questions: What can we know about music, and how can we know it?

Not long ago, musical transcription was the distinguishing mark of our discipline, not only as a passage rite (Hood [1971] 1982; McAllester 1989) but also as a generative practice. Transcription told us what we could know about music and how we could know it. Music was objectified, collected, and recorded in order to be transcribed, and transcription enabled analysis and comparison. Transcription—that is, listening to a piece of music and writing it down in Western notation—not only became a guild skill but also "wrote across" lived experience, eliminated the lifeworld, and transformed what was left (sound) into a representation that could be analyzed systematically and then compared with other transcriptions so as to generate and test hypotheses concerning music's origin and evolution. Today it is not transcription but fieldwork that constitutes ethnomusicology. Fieldwork is no longer viewed principally as observing and collecting (although it surely involves that) but as experiencing and understanding music (see Titon [1984] 1992b, xvi). The new fieldwork leads us to ask what it is like for a person (ourselves included) to make and to know music as lived experience.

As it did most, if not all, ethnomusicologists, music caught hold of me before ethnomusicology did. In the late 1960s, when I began formal study of

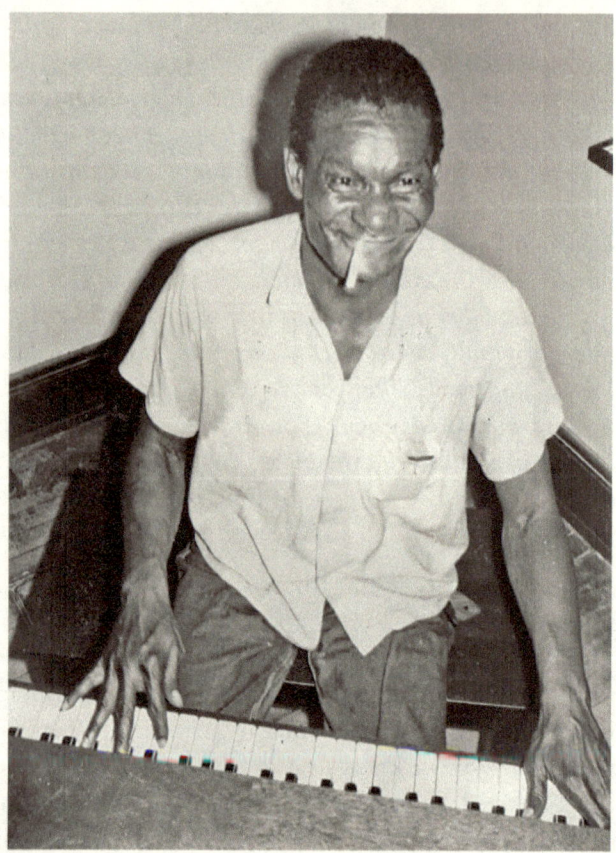

Figure 4.1. Lazy Bill Lucas, Minneapolis, Minnesota, 1969. Photo by Jeff Todd Titon.

ethnomusicology at the University of Minnesota, I was already part of a blues musical community centered on Lazy Bill Lucas (fig. 4.1), who was born in Arkansas and had a career as a blues singer in St. Louis and Chicago before moving to the Twin Cities in the early 1960s. Harmonica player Mojo Buford, who had been with Muddy Waters's band, bass player JoJo Williams, guitarist Sonny Boy Rogers, and pianist and singer Leonard "Baby Doo" Caston also visited Bill's apartment, the hub of this community. We played music together, ate Bill's fried chicken dinners (he was a superb cook), drank Fox Deluxe beer, and became friends. I got to know them, their wives, and their girlfriends, and we passed time together. Later, in Alan Kagan's seminar in ethnomusicology, I learned about fieldwork. Then, fieldwork relied on in-person observation and on data gathering through structured interviews, a method derived from the Trobriand Island practice of anthropologist Bronislaw Malinowski during World War I.

Thinking about my blues musician friends, I wondered whether to do fieldwork with them. *Why not?* I thought, and I proceeded to interview Bill for a class project. Of course, I had already "observed" him for a long time (and vice versa). I had no difficulty speaking with them about their lives and careers, particularly because they felt that it might result in useful publicity—and it did. The publication of Bill's interview, for example, led a French blues enthusiast to produce two LP recordings of Bill's music (Titon 1969; Lucas 1971, 1972). In those interviews, I asked questions such as when and where they were born, what kind of work their families did, when they first learned music, how their musical careers progressed, and so forth; and they answered them. I was doing oral history and was interested in obtaining facts of their lives. In a word, I was data gathering. As a result, my relationship with them added a dimension: I became someone who might be able to promote them, to help them in their careers, instead of just a young man hanging around older ones and trying to learn music from them. Besides friendship, I now had a tacit contract with them.

I had discovered that my fieldwork thrust me into thinking about relationships; it wasn't just about surveying and collecting. Later, I also realized that structured interviews did not always result in my best understanding. Blues singer-guitarist Son House had come to the Twin Cities to do a concert, and I was able to get an hour alone with him and a tape recorder. I had my oral history questions ready, but I had decided to begin by playing him a tape of a blues recording from the 1920s by his friend Charley Patton, hoping to enlist his help in deciphering Patton's lyrics. (House later told me that you could sit at Patton's feet and not understand a word he was singing.) House listened to the tape, and I was ready to start asking questions, but before I could do so, he began to speak and reminisce about "Papa Charley" and those days. I forgot about my questions and listened to what he wanted to say. He told me a long and detailed story about how he "got religion" when he lived in the Mississippi Delta. He also spoke about the old times and the bad whiskey they made and drank, and he acted out a story about how he got put in jail one night because he was so drunk he wouldn't let a Greyhound bus pass him while he was driving home. He told me how his white landlord had interceded with the sheriff and the judge to free him but added a fine of indebtedness to his sharecropping arrangement. In telling the story, he played the parts of the boss and sheriff.

BOSS (HOUSE WHISPERS): "You got to let him out of there; he's so good with the tractor. I need him Monday morning."

JUDGE (HOUSE WHISPERS): "Well, all right, we'll tell him he had to pay such and such a fine."

HOUSE (NORMAL VOICE): "See, that's how they stepped in with each other."
(Titon 1976)

I sat there raptly listening, wanting more. When House stopped telling stories from his life, I steered him through a series of oral history questions, hoping to get more stories; but now I was directing it by the questions I asked, and House no longer felt free to move in his own direction. And so began a long process in which I pondered the different kinds of knowing that arose from the structured interviews that were a part of the old fieldwork versus those life stories told to sympathetic listeners or friends in a "real life" situation that could not, then, be described as fieldwork but whose resultant texts I maintained ought to be valued, not as a form of data gathering but as a means toward understanding (Titon 1980).

Continental European philosophy since the nineteenth century regularly distinguishes between two kinds of knowledge: explanation and understanding (Dallmayr and McCarthy 1977). Explanation is typical in the sciences, and understanding typifies knowledge in the humanities. We are all familiar with the scientific method of inference, hypothesis, and experiment; scientific explanations in their strongest form are expressed as universal laws of nature, such as the law of gravitation. Explanation gives us the kind of knowledge that enables prediction and control (Carnap 1966). Understanding, on the other hand, represents a different kind of knowledge. If explanation is directed toward objects, understanding is directed toward people. If explanation drives toward law, understanding drives toward agreement, sometimes, though not always, through lived experience (Gadamer [1975] 1992; Schutz 1962). Explanation proceeds through analysis, understanding through interpretation. Explanation is a type of "knowledge that," whereas understanding is a type of "knowledge of." "Knowledge that" is a typical concern of British and American positivist philosophers in this century, because in their view all meaningful knowledge propositions can be expressed in prepositional form as "I know that." (Of course, not all "knowledge that" propositions are meaningful in a positivist sense.) Understanding's "knowledge of," on the other hand, is more characteristic of an earlier view: knowledge of subjects, expressed in statements like "I know my friend William" or "He knows plumbing" or "You know ethnomusicology" (Rorty 1979, 141).

Most writings about ethnomusicology as an academic discipline favor explanation theories of knowledge in which music is considered a type of language (see, e.g., Nettl 1964; Hood [1971] 1982; Kunst 1959; H. Myers 1992). Ethnomusicology is said to have begun in the 1880s when it became a scientific project. At the time, it was not called ethnomusicology but comparative musicology, reflecting its close kinship with similar disciplines such as philology (comparative linguistics). The person generally regarded as its founder, Alexander Ellis, set out to measure the musical intervals in selected non-Western musics. Most Europeans thought that these musics were more or less "out of tune." Ellis, representing the best tradition of ethnomusicological relativism, had another hypothesis: that the modes and scales of other nations had their own patterns, different from those of Western Europe, but coherent in their own terms. Measuring the intervals confirmed his hypothesis. Significantly, Ellis was tone-deaf and employed an assistant to make the measurements. That is, Ellis could not experience the musical intervals and had to rely on an external instrument to do so.

The most obvious application of explanation theories of knowledge to ethnomusicology came via linguistically based theories of music. Comparative musicology and musical folklore both rely on philology (comparative linguistics) for their methods. In this century, linguistics has changed, but whether in the systematic musicology of Charles Seeger, the transformational ethnomusicology of John Blacking, the cognitive ethnomusicology of many of our European colleagues, or the semiotic ethnomusicology of Jean-Jacques Nattiez (1990), the notion that music behaves and ought to be studied as a system like language continues to have a profound and shaping influence on our discipline, one that has affected my work as well as others'. Ethnomusicology, as a paradigm, owes a great deal to anthropology—after all, the Society for Ethnomusicology was originally planned at meetings of the American Anthropological Association—and anthropological linguistics is one of the four fields of traditional American anthropology. (Archaeology, physical anthropology, and cultural anthropology are the other three.)

Theories of knowledge based on understanding rather than explanation, on the other hand, find their philosophical defenders in a continental philosophical tradition that begins with Dilthey and includes Husserl, Sartre, Heidegger, Schutz, Merleau-Ponty, Gadamer, and Ricoeur. This tradition, an alternative both to Anglo-American positivism and to European structuralism, involves mainly two kinds of activities: phenomenology and hermeneutics. Phenomenology emphasizes the immediate, concrete, sensory lifeworld, and it attempts to ground knowledge in the world of lived experience (see Ihde [1977] 1986). Hermeneutics originated as a way of interpreting the Bible but has come to be a method for interpreting texts in general. In recent years, Paul Ricoeur has attempted to integrate the two into what he calls hermeneutic phenomenology. For Ricoeur (1981b), any meaningful action can be considered, or read, as a text; thus, a musical performance, for example, can be understood as the equivalent of a text. Clifford Geertz took up this formulation, likening cultures to "an assemblage of texts," and his work has been enormously influential in American ethnomusicology in the past fifteen years or so. Although much of my work from the 1980s is based in hermeneutic phenomenology, I have more recently become critical of the poststructuralist tendency to textualize everything, musical experience included, and I have proposed that we stand Ricoeur on his head, that meaningful actions be experienced as music, not read as text (Titon 1994, 1995a). In other words, I suggest that we change the metaphor we use for our interpretive acts. The world is not like a text to be read but like a musical performance to be experienced. But I must leave that for a future essay.

Ethnomusicology, in my view, has made use of four paradigms, or bedrock sets of assumptions, during the current century, of which comparative musicology was the first. The English translation of the second is musical folklore. It is typical in Eastern Europe, and was until recently in Britain. Although musical folklore involves collecting, transcribing, analyzing, and comparing, it adds four other features: an ideology of nationalism, an ethnographic emphasis on surveying social context, an ethical dimension that involves the preservation of music thought to be traditional and endangered throughout the world, and an educational aspect in which the music becomes part of the public school curriculum and is offered to adults as well. The collecting, classifying, and analytical works of Béla Bartók and of Constantin Brăiloiu are representative of musical folklore.

The third paradigm is ethnomusicology itself, associated with the birth of the Society for Ethnomusicology in the 1950s, which grafted in American anthropology, with its emphasis on fieldwork and cultural immersion, rather than survey work; in addition, ethnomusicologists tend to distrust broad comparative generalizations and produce, instead, monographs based on detailed studies of particular music cultures. Ethnomusicologists also distrust nationalism, rejecting it as ethnocentric, and they do not, by and large, emphasize preservation; rather, their focus is on acculturation and change. Nor do ethnomusicologists find much enthusiasm for public school music education; they think of themselves as scholars. (The late Alan Merriam used to dismiss the efforts of his world music colleagues in music education as "sandbox ethnomusicology.") The "native point of view" is important to ethnomusicologists, many of whom adopt in one form or another Merriam's (1964) three-part feedback model of music in culture: ideas, behavior, and sound. For Merriam, and most of the ethnomusicologists of his generation, ethnomusicology nevertheless was about data, while the personal experiences of the ethnomusicologist, including all the relations with others in the field that not merely affected but constituted the meaningfulness of the data, were absent; ethnomusicology was to be, in his memorable phrase, "sciencing about music" (Merriam 1964, 25).

The seeds of the fourth phase, for which we do not yet have a single name, were sown by those ethnomusicologists who brought master artists to American universities, where they led non-Western ensembles in which some graduate students found their most profound musical experiences. I have called this new paradigm the study of people making music (Titon 1989, [1984] 1992a),[1] but it might also be called the study of people experiencing music. In retrospect, it is also apparent that this fourth paradigm came from a generation transformed by the politics of the 1960s: the women's movement, the peace movement, and the civil rights movement. Because it is still emergent, this fourth phase is difficult to describe systematically, but some of its consequences are evident. An emphasis on understanding (rather than explaining) the lived experience of people making music (ourselves included) is paramount. Other emphases involve reflexivity and an increase in narrative representation that is descriptive, interpretive, and evocative (see, e.g., Kisliuk 1991); sharing authority and authorship with "informants" (who are now considered teachers, consultants, friends, or all three) (see von Rosen and Francis 1992; Guilbault 1993); a concern for history and with issues of power relationships, ethics, identity, and belief; a deconstructive approach to boundary concepts such as race and ethnicity; close attention to how class and gender operate within music cultures;[2] skepticism toward the culture of science and engagement with feminist and third world perspectives; a willingness to explore various media, such as museum exhibits, festivals, film, video, and hypertext, to represent people making music; and an active involvement as musical and cultural advocates trying to help people in the music cultures with whom we work have better lives in which their music can flourish (Sheehy 1992). All of these emphases are implicated in "the new fieldwork" and many are generated by its emphasis on human relationships rather than on collecting information. The new fieldwork does not abandon musical sounds and structures; it just repositions them as "texts" (subjects of interpretation) in a hermeneutic circle (Ricoeur 1981a). Musical sound is still documented, and if musical structure is an important aspect of the musical experience, as it so often is, then it is analyzed and interpreted as part of the matrix of meaning. Nor does the new fieldworker abandon documentation; if anything, documentation increases. But documentation, too, is repositioned and is now considered reflexively, as an intersubjective product, rather than as the report and analysis of a witness.

If we enlarge the history of our discipline to include understanding-type theories, then we will be sure to attend to some of the writings of the early world travelers and missionaries whose understanding of native music took the form of an encounter with it. Jean de Lery, for example, a sixteenth-century missionary, narrated an account in which he told how he was "captivated" by Native American music, and in doing so, he weighted his narrative toward experience (F. Harrison 1973). In the revised histories, we will emphasize "bimusicality" (Hood 1960, [1971] 1982) and ponder the nature of knowledge that comes through the human relationships developed through fieldwork. David McAllester's ([1954] 1973) early work with the Navajo and cultural values will take on profound importance (see also Mitchell 1978), and Kenneth Gourlay's (1978, 1982) articles on the ethnomusicological researcher become key early theoretical statements.

Our approach, whether we favor explanation or understanding, will obviously depend on what we think music is. In my view, music is a socially constructed, cultural phenomenon. The various cultural constructions enable people to experience it as patterned sounds, aesthetic objects, ritual substance, even as a thing-in-itself. But to say that music is a culturally constructed phenomenon does not mean that it has no existence in the world, for like everyone I know, I experience my world through my consciousness, and I experience music as a part of my lifeworld.

In the rest of this chapter, I offer phenomenological and reflexive answers to questions concerning what we can know about music and how we can know it. I begin by examining experiences of music as they are presented to my consciousness. I proceed by examining experiences of fieldwork. Finally, I discuss some interactive strategies for representing these experiences so as to enlarge our understanding of music. Of course, there is no single phenomenology. Husserl's transcendental phenomenology is significantly different from Heidegger's existential phenomenology, which is different from Ricoeur's hermeneutic phenomenology. Nevertheless, they constitute a tradition and have certain common assumptions and emphases. In what follows, I will draw from this tradition without attempting to represent any single version of phenomenology. Indeed, I do not find any single version of it wholly satisfactory.

"Phenomenology insists that phenomena be investigated as they present themselves to consciousness" (Stewart and Mickunas 1990, 91). Consciousness is always consciousness of something—in this case, music. How am I conscious of music? How am I "in the world" when my consciousness is consciousness of music? First, of course, my consciousness of music constitutes an experience of music, and this is culturally mediated; obviously, my experience of music is bound to be different from someone else's in another culture, not to mention others in my own. And I experience various musics differently over the course of my life. But for the moment, let me attend to my ordinary and current consciousness of music, both generally and in one particular case.

I take people making music as my paradigm case of musical "being-in-the-world." For me, making music is incomplete when I do it by myself; it is completed in a social group when I make music with others. You may or may not feel the same way, but I want to take making music with others for my paradigm case. I could have chosen making music in a string quartet, a gamelan, a blues band, an Old Regular Baptist church, or a Ghanaian drum ensemble, but for this exercise I choose making music in an old-time string band, with fiddle, banjo, and guitar—a peak experience that I consciously seek and find.

Here is how I would describe this experience phenomenologically. Desire compels me to make music. I feel this desire as an affective presence, a residue of pleasure built up from my previous experiences with music and dance that makes me seek it out in order to know it better. It is a curiosity of all my bodily senses and I feel it embodied in them: an embodied curiosity. Knowing people making music begins with my experience of music. Playing the fiddle, banjo, or guitar with others, I hear music; I feel its presence; I am moved, internally; I move, externally. Music overcomes me with longing. I feel its affective power within me. Now I have moved from what phenomenologists call the natural attitude, the normal everyday way of being in the world, not to an analytical way but to a self-aware way. I feel the music enter me and move me. And now the music grows louder, larger until everything else is impossible, shut out. My self disappears. No analysis; no longer any self-awareness. The shutting out is a phenomenological reduction, what Husserl called *epoché*. It is a radical form of suspension. I no longer feel myself as a separate self; rather, I feel myself to be "music-in-the-world." Eventually, music returns me through desiring to myself. That is, the being of desiring brings me to myself, re-presents myself to consciousness. The "I" returns; I am self-aware, I see that I and others are making the music that I hear.

When I see that I and others are making the music that I hear, I want to know these others. For us to understand one another, we must know one another. How may we know one another? Who are you? If you were an object, I might come to know you as I know other objects. But you are a person making music and I come to know you as a person (see Code 1991, 37). We seek to know one another through lived experience. Through common, intersubjective experience, we enter the world of interpretation. Interpretation turns sound into music, being into meaning.

When my consciousness is filled with music, I am in the world musically. My experiencing mind tells me that I have a musical way of "being-in-the-world" when I make music and when I listen and move to music so that it fills my body. I call this musical being, and it is a mode of being that presents itself as different from my normal, everyday modes of experiencing, from my self-conscious modes of experiencing, and from my objectivizing modes of experiencing.

I would like to ground musical *knowing*—that is, knowledge of or about music—in musical *being*. I look, in other words, for an epistemology of music that is grounded not in a detached or objectivizing way of "being-in-the-world," nor in a reflexive, self-conscious way of being in the world, nor either in what phenomenologists call the natural attitude or everyday way of being-in-the-world. Rather, I think that musical being is a special ontology and that knowing music requires that we start from musical being.

Another way of saying this is that I ground musical knowledge in the practice of music, not in the practice of science, or linguistics, or introspective analysis. In my paradigm case of musical being-in-the-world, I am bound up socially with others making music, and when that music is presented fully to my consciousness, it is the music of the whole group, not simply "my" music, although at peak moments I feel as if it is all coming through me.

This brings me to my experience of doing fieldwork, for it, too, is an experience of myself in relation to other people. For many ethnomusicologists, fieldwork is intersubjective and personally transformative. Like many of my colleagues, I experience fieldwork not primarily as a means to transcription, analysis, interpretation, and representation, although it surely is that, but as a reflexive opportunity and an ongoing dialogue with my friends, which among other things, continually reworks my "work" as "our" work (see also von Rosen and Francis 1992; Hutchinson 1994). Risking immodesty, I offer a recent example: a letter from one of my Old Regular Baptist friends in which he said, "Thank you for the way you have helped us look at ourselves" (Elwood Cornett, letter to Jeff Todd Titon, August 18, 1993). And I thank them reciprocally. My experiences of fieldwork have usually been intensely lived; in them, I have become acutely conscious of my roles, stances, and identities; I have felt love, camaraderie, and anxiety. Most representations of ethnomusicological knowledge, of course, exclude expression of the experience of fieldwork, but a phenomenological approach to these representations requires its inclusion and the inquiry into values that it generates.

A reflexive look at the types of relationships fieldwork engenders reveals that fieldworkers, and those who are the subjects of fieldwork, bring identities to the encounter and are cast in a variety of roles (Titon 1985). By role playing I do not mean to imply inauthenticity but rather to use the concept as the sociologist Erving Goffman (1959) developed it, to show how people behave socially in daily life. In the postcolonial world, when mere collecting is considered exploitive, and when some peoples simply will not cooperate with visiting ethnomusicologists, it is naive to think that the ideal field relationship will always result in friendship. Sometimes a kind of contractual relationship, implicit or explicit, in which each party helps the other, is more effective. Sometimes a combination of friendship and tacit contract is most effective. In another frequent role in the new fieldwork, the ethnomusicologist becomes student and the "informant" becomes teacher or wise elder. Infrequent and atypical roles include opposition, deception, lying, and spying—unethical under most circumstances but rationalized on the grounds that the music culture being understood and then exposed is illegitimate and corrupting (see Pillay 1994).

A phenomenological epistemology for ethnomusicology arises from our experiences of music and fieldwork, from knowing people making music. If we believe that knowledge is experiential and the intersubjective product of our social interactions, then what we can know arises out of our relations with others, both in the field and among our colleagues where we live and work; and these relations have an ineluctably personal aspect to them. The documents (texts) that we and our friends generate in the field have a certain immediacy to them—field notes, photographs, recordings—that remind us, when we are no longer in the field, of those relationships.

While we are with our friends, these documents appear—at best, and when they do not get in the way—not so much as objectifications but as extensions of our relationships. But when we are back from the field, in the university, in the library, or study, alone, particularly if our friends are far away, these field artifacts take on a very different cast. They substitute for experience by evoking our memories of it. Like a photograph taken or a brochure brought back from a holiday abroad, they are documentary and evocative at the same time. They traffic in nostalgia. In their presence, and the absence of the people I knew, I experience loneliness and longing. My task now is to represent the music culture where I have worked, not only to students and colleagues but also to the people in that music culture. I search for forms of representing that will keep my experiences before me, in memory, and evoke the people making music whom I have known. Thus, I represent them to myself as well. The conventional representation that presents itself to me is narrative musical ethnography; two other forms that I will discuss are ethnographic film and hypertext/multimedia.

Narrative, of course, is the way we habitually tell ourselves and others about our experiences, and so it emerges as a conventional form in phenomenologically weighted representations of people making music. At its best, a narrative weighting in the descriptive ethnography of a music culture invites the reader to share, imaginatively, in the experiences that are represented. Anthony Seeger's (1987b) *Why Suya Sing* derives much of its interpretive power and authority from narrative. Not that the book is entirely narrative, of course. For Seeger and others writing narrative ethnomusicology, ethnography becomes an experience-weighted genre in which narrative includes background information, interpretation and analysis, and above all, one in which insights emerge from experience: one shows how one comes to understand (see also Feld [1982] 2012; Rice 1994). Narrative is not new to ethnomusicology. Mantle Hood's ([1971] 1982) narrative passages in *The Ethnomusicologist* and Bruno Nettl's (1983) stories in *The Study of Ethnomusicology* are among their most telling. And experience-based narrative interpretation is increasing in cultural anthropology as well. Instances abound. Renato Rosaldo's *Culture and Truth*, for example, begins with his celebrated article "Grief and a Headhunter's Rage." Rosaldo could not understand how grief and rage "go together in a self-evident manner" for the Ilongot of the Philippines until his wife died as "she was walking along a trail with two Ifugao companions when she lost her footing and fell to her death some 65 feet down a sheer precipice into a swollen river below." He wrote, "Immediately on finding her body I became enraged. How could she abandon me? How could she have been so stupid as to fall? I tried to cry. I sobbed, but rage blocked the tears" (Rosaldo [1989] 1993, 9). Rosaldo had to experience a combination of grief and rage himself before he felt he could fully understand this aspect of Ilongot culture.

As Clifford Geertz (1988) has pointed out, writing good ethnography takes a great deal of rhetorical skill, and it forces us to face the fact that we are primarily authors, not reporters. But if we are authors, we risk displacing the reader's interest from the people making music whom we are writing about to ourselves. Autobiographical narrative ethnography has generated opposition from those who find it self-indulgent and unprofessional; indeed, the popular term for it, "confessional," indicates the problem of displacement. Yet narrative ethnography need not displace the attention from people making music to authors' consciousness. Instead, an author may skillfully work up a scene and cast herself or himself in the role of a bit player, someone whose participation isn't very important during the event but whose reflections on it afterward serve as a kind of interpretation. This, after all, is what Geertz does in his celebrated essay about a Balinese cockfight, although one may pause at Geertz's literary method of divining meaning and wish that it were more congruent with the Balinese people's own views. The prologue and first chapter of *Powerhouse for God* are also written as narrative ethnography, carefully utilizing tape recordings, photographs, field notes, and recollections of my experience to re-create and evoke the scenes of a luncheon conversation and a homecoming worship service (Titon [1988] 2019). Finally, narrative ethnography is well suited to showing an ethnomusicologist in dialogue with people making music.

Film's (and video's) images and synchronized sound are conventionally understood to portray people making music and to place the viewer in the position of observer. Film's evocative power is extraordinary: we feel as though we are watching something real. Of course, it is possible to defeat the experiential aspects of film by making films that imitate books or by making films that represent scientific experiments, as much ethnomusicological filmmaking attempts to do. But a phenomenological approach to filmmaking attempts to involve the viewer by evoking and reflecting on the experiences and relationships that obtain in a musical community. This relationship between the filmmaker and viewer can take one of three forms: the filmmaker can place himself or herself in a fully authoritative position, usually through an omniscient narrator; the filmmaker can depart, ghostlike, from the film, making it appear that the viewer is merely looking at the action and eavesdropping; or the filmmaker can in the film itself interact with the subjects and the viewer, and both can reflect on the meaning of the film. It should be plain that interactivity and reflexivity is best suited to the kind of experiential understanding that arises from fieldwork and music making (von Rosen and Francis 1992; von Rosen 1992).

Hypertext and multimedia are a third means of representation that seem to me to do justice to an experiential bias toward people making music. Whereas a narrative text is a linear read, hypertext can be a weblike structure that allows readers to choose their own paths through the assembled information (Landow 1992a). A computer is not required for hypertext, but a computer enables hypertext very efficiently. Interactive hypertext empowers readers ("authors-who-are-to-be," in hypertext fiction writer Michael Joyce's words) to comment on the information and thereby alter it for the next reader.

Multimedia is often allied with hypertext to represent sound recordings, images, and movies. A carefully assembled hypertext is capable of representing the insights as well as the ambiguities of the experience of acquiring knowledge through fieldwork. For example, in the Davenport HyperCard Stack, a reader hears fiddle tunes and is told that they seem similar (Titon 1991). One path leads to musical analysis, and transcriptions demonstrate the tunes' similarity, but another path leads toward the fiddler himself and his demonstration that the tunes are different. The representation leaves it to the reader to resolve the paradox, or not resolve it. A further development is hypertext fiction (see Coover 1993).

Not all hypermedia projects allow meaningful interactivity. Many "educational" hypertexts are nothing more than huge text-and-context assemblages with very efficient links, organized hierarchically rather than in a weblike fashion. The experience of such hypermedia "learning" environments is not much different from the experience of being in a library, where one seeks explanations. But the experience of a weblike hypertext is more like the initial stage of playing a game: one seeks to understand it.

In this essay, I have maintained that we have usually sought to explain musical sounds, concepts, and behavior rather than to understand musical experience. And yet our own most satisfying knowledge is often acquired through the experience of music making and the relationships that arise during fieldwork. It seems to me that in our ways of being musical, and in our ways of doing fieldwork, we, like the subjects (people) of our study, are open to transformations through experience. Furthermore, when we ask our musical friends for their "native" points of view or overhear what they say, they most often speak in terms of personal experience and understanding rather than offer systematic explanation.

If all of that is so, then an epistemology erected on the ethnomusicological practices of music making and fieldwork as the paradigm case of our being-in-the-world, rather than on collecting, transcription, and analysis as that paradigm case, will privilege knowledge arising through experience, ours and others'. And in our external representations of that knowledge, we seek those forms that best produce understanding. If we must rule out such unconventional representations as fiction or musical performances, because these are not available to scholars, at least not now, then narrative but not necessarily self-centered nonfiction writing, interactive and reflexive rather than authoritative or merely observational film, and weblike, interactive hypermedia are promising forms of representation that will convey understanding both in us, in the process of their formation, and in those with whom we seek to communicate. Yet I do not wish to dispense altogether with explanations as a form of knowledge, only to privilege understanding. I cheerfully admit that I continue to practice transcription and analysis and to be curious about issues involving musical structures, history, and geography. An epistemology of musical knowing that follows from our musical being-in-the-world privileges experience and understanding, but it cannot possibly do without explanations because, after all, we also experience knowing by means of explanations, and we put those to work in daily life.

What of the future of fieldwork? If, as I have claimed, contemporary ethnomusicology rests epistemologically on fieldwork, then the poststructuralist challenge to fieldwork must be answered if the discipline is to continue. Indeed, some have called for the abolition of ethnomusicology. This critique is mounted on several grounds, three of which are central. The first is the charge, familiar since the late 1960s, that fieldwork-based enterprises rest on asymmetries of power and therefore involve the illegitimate use of the fieldworker's authority. In other words, fieldworkers have no legitimate right to represent their informants, for their purposes are not neutral—after all, ethnomusicologists' careers ride on these representations. The informants are the ones with the proper claim to authority, and they should be the ones to write—or not write—the ethnomusicological texts. A second charge is that fieldworkers enact a version of the heroic quest, although they do not realize this. The consequence is that musical ethnographies fall into a single pattern—the quest narrative, implicit or explicit. The problem is that the quest pattern, rather than the musical life of the culture under study, governs the representation and interpretation of the data. Thus, for example, music cultures are viewed as utopian or dystopian, and ethnomusicologists become heroes, flawed heroes, or antiheroes (see, e.g., Hood [1971] 1982, where he writes of the importance of the ethnomusicologist's role in helping to build a large gong). Moreover, as a questing hero, the ethnographer can scarcely claim authority to represent another music culture: the hero has a different agenda. A third charge is leveled on epistemological grounds. Poststructuralist thought denies the existence of autonomous selves. The notion of fieldwork as an encounter between self and other is thought to be a delusion, just as the notion of the autonomous self is a delusion, whereas the notion of the other is a fictionalized objectification.

Neither the poststructuralist challenge nor a variety of answers can be considered here in the detail they deserve. But the beginnings of an epistemological answer may be found in the preceding phenomenological account of music making. Making music, I experience the disappearance of my separate self; I feel as though music fills me and I have become music in the world. But I also experience the return of the knowing self. The experience of music making is, in some circumstances in various cultures throughout the world, an experience of becoming a knowing self in the presence of other becoming, knowing selves. This is a profoundly communal experience, and I am willing to trust it. A representation grounded in this kind of experience would, I believe, begin to answer the poststructuralist challenge by reconfiguring the ethnomusicologist's idea of his or her own self, now emergent rather than autonomous. Autonomous selves enact heroic myths. Emergent selves, on the other hand, are connected selves, enmeshed in reciprocity. Connectedness is a value that challenges the postmodern critique of contemporary society. I am willing to assert this ecological value and its intimate relation with music making and fieldwork on the grounds that the survival of far more than ethnomusicology depends on it.

## Postscript: 2006

I recall a conversation over lunch one day more than a dozen years ago with my friend Patrick Hutchinson, an uilleann piper. I remarked to Patrick that in order to play music well with old-time musicians (that is, among those of us who play southern Appalachian string band music on fiddle, banjo, mandolin, and guitar), "you have to know how to visit." Visiting means treating others with respect, care, modesty, courtesy, exchange, and reciprocity. It means establishing a sound and hopeful relationship before "getting down to purpose," if there is any purpose to get down to. It means that "special kind of courtesy," as Michelle Kisliuk (1988) wrote about bluegrass jam sessions, that leads to good music—though it does not always do so; yet without it, good music (by which I mean group musical experiences felt to be good in a way that is surprisingly delightful, even magical, while they are happening) is difficult, if not impossible.

Hutchinson replied that it was the same thing with Irish traditional music: you have to know how to visit. And his dissertation (Hutchinson 1997), conceived well before he met me, is all about visiting (always in his teacher Chris Langan's kitchen, tea and talk first, piping after), friendship, and what Hutchinson, who eventually tied for first place in the all-Ireland uilleann piping competition, learned over the years about musical being-in-the-world from Chris. And not just from their making music together but also from Chris's talking of music; for Chris had been a blacksmith, and his ideas about setting a tune rose to art in crafting metaphors that enlarged understanding as he brought them effortlessly from blacksmithing into piping.

Visiting, friendship—these are the products of a music-making epistemology, and they ground fieldwork in a musical being-in-the-world. They implicate music, not language (talk, writing), as the basis for knowing people making music. Language, of course, is usually taken as the basis of communication. I continue to suggest that we remove it from the center and replace it with music. The inconsequentiality of signified meaning in musical sound, thought to be an impoverishment when compared with language, turns out to be an advantage when we consider grounding ethnomusicological fieldwork in the relationships that arise from musical being-in-the-world. Language is inherently unstable, signifying multiple meanings, subject to differing interpretations. The language of literature gives us the heroic quest myth, the basis of scientific distancing, manipulation of objects, investigative reporting, our spying on the world. But this is an unreliable intelligence when human beings are our subjects. Music, conceived not as a signifying language but as a collaborative relationship among the people making it, gives us at those magical moments of self-transcendence a connection among living beings leading to friendship and thus the basis for an epistemology of fieldwork based in musical, rather than linguistic, being-in-the-world.

Visiting, friendship—in theorizing this friendship model of collaborative fieldwork, it is useful to distinguish between two points on the spectrum of friendship. One might be called an instrumental friendship, in which there is a quid pro quo, an unwritten contract-like relationship in which each benefits from the other's continued presence and work. The usual relationship between the fieldworker and chief informant, translator, advocate, consultant, teacher, however the relationship is best described, is always to some extent instrumental in that regard. Each is useful to the other; they are perceived as partners, and to a degree, they are.

The other point on the spectrum is one in which the friendship does not depend on usefulness, quid pro quo, or partnership, but rather is founded on admiration and a desire for the other's well-being. Now, an interesting thing about the social musical experience I wrote about in the first edition of *Shadows in the Field* is that the disappearance of the self and the co-becoming of music in the world suggests that same desire for the other's well-being. In other words, this kind of musical experience is always moving us along the spectrum from quid pro quo toward that selfless desire. To be sure, there is a quid pro quo in the musical experience; each of us contributes our part, and if someone, something, isn't felt to be quite right, it puts the peak moment out of reach. Instead, one compartmentalizes and is very much aware of one's separate self and everyone else's separate self. But to come back to the point: if we want to ground fieldwork with people making music in the experience of making music with people, then we will be led to theorize our relationships in fieldwork on the very same grounds as our relationships in music making. And this leads to friendship, and that leads to visiting.

Visiting, ceilidh: In *Passing the Time in Ballymenone*, Henry Glassie (1982) describes the old Irish tradition of the ceilidh, or visit among friends, where modesty rules and life is sometimes coaxed into art. Singing and music and storytelling and *craic*, or good talk, conversation raised to art, are sought and found in these visits that connect and reconnect friends. That good talk, intersubjective, is always a part of good fieldwork, where again mutual discovery is a sought and found experience. Visiting, then, is the social basis for fieldwork.

Now, visiting does imply decorum, a degree of distance, a certain privacy, and decorum can get in the way of, or postpone, understanding. In the long term, though, friendship and visiting offer a more sustainable way of getting to know people making music than the usual conception of fieldwork as a quest for knowledge, for that quest is born in an archetypal heroic myth, and it is a quest both for knowledge and power.[3] If you balk at this and the earlier comparison of fieldwork with the heroic quest, consider these parallels: long preparation, instruction from presumably wise elders, and apprenticeship (i.e., graduate school); the journey to a strange land, accompanied by various devices (not magic swords or incantations but pens, paper, and instruments to record sounds and images); the struggle with alien ideas and forces (maintaining one's identity, difficulties in making sense of it all); and the triumphant return home to the kingdom (to write the book and share the knowledge inside the academy), with rewards bestowed (degree, job, promotion).

While the knowledge side of the quest myth may appear innocent, the power side remains implicated as an adjunct to colonialism, despite ethnomusicologists' frequent proclamations against ethnocentrism and on behalf of musical relativism.[4] As for the knowledge side, literary critics have pointed out the irony that while the heroic quest may impart knowledge, the hero often cannot communicate it on return to the kingdom; the monster may be slain, but as the knowledge was in the hero's experiencing, it is unavailable to the others: they have not lived it. Contrast the quest myth with the fieldworker as visitor, as guest, rising to friend. That is the model I support, and of course it has implications for human relationships well beyond ethnomusicology.

Ruth Hellier-Tinoco (2003) has questioned my "friendship model" for ethnomusicological fieldwork, pointing out that friendship, with its complications and long-term obligations, can be very difficult, perhaps too difficult, to maintain without some sense of guilt and failure (see also Cooley 2003 for a discussion of fieldwork and friendship). No doubt that is true, as in friendships generally, though often under more difficult circumstances. Does fieldwork imply distance? Does friendship dissolve fieldwork, make it into something else? I have written here and elsewhere about my ambivalence in conceiving of what I was doing as fieldwork, with blues musicians who were my friends long before I learned the term "fieldwork" (Titon [1977] 1995b, 264; 2003a). The small literature on the friendships that arise from fieldwork also includes Joseph Casagrande's (1960) pioneering collection of essays *In the Company of Man*, and the more recent *Bridges to Humanity*, edited by Bruce Grindal and Frank Salamone (1995), with discussions of postcolonial complexities and their implications for fieldwork and friendship. In the introduction to the latter volume, the authors caution that "at least a portion of some field friendships is based on mutual, even if unacknowledged, gain; and once that gain is no longer present, the friendship no longer has active value" (Grindal and Salamone 1995, 2–3). Indeed, Hellier-Tinoco questions my term "fieldwork model" on the basis that "model" sounds too calculating. I do not intend it to be calculating. I mean to describe a way of thinking about sustainable fieldwork relationships. In this essay, I have tried to theorize field relationships for ethnomusicologists based on musical being-in-the-world. Friendships typically involve both mutual gain and caring for the other. The act of bringing into the world expressive culture rising to art, as in music, story, or just good talk, renews the connection of friendship and grounds it in mutual, shared experience—which *is* a mutual gain.

## Notes

1. "Making" in two senses: (1) producing the sounds that we call music and (2) constructing the cultural domain that we demarcate as music. See also the essay "Ethnomusicology as the Study of People Making Music," a reprint of Titon (1989), in this volume.

2. These boundary concepts continue to be discussed in an electronic conference on multiculturalism, primarily among ethnomusicologists, hosted on a LISTSERV beginning in 1992 by Marc Perlman at Wesleyan University. (I am not sure when the conference stopped. The internet address was MC-Ethno@Eagle.Wesleyan.edu.)

3. Susan Sontag's "The Anthropologist as Hero" ([1963] 1994), a reading of Levi-Strauss's *Tristes tropiques* (1961), brought this idea to my attention years ago, and in the 1970s, I devised and for several years taught a course titled Inventing Anthropology in which the students and

I explored the quest myth in popular ethnography as well as literature, reading ethnography as literature.

4. Especially Bruno Nettl, who in explaining the discipline many times over for fifty years, seldom misses the opportunity to state that ethnocentrism has no place in ethnomusicology. Reacting against those who have claimed Western art music is the finest music that humankind has produced, we proclaim a degree of relativism in which every music culture is entitled to respect and serious study. Of course, we each have our personal preferences among the musics of the world, but we would not want to say that those we prefer are worthwhile and those we don't care for are not.

# 5

# APPLIED ETHNOMUSICOLOGY
## A Descriptive and Historical Account

APPLIED ETHNOMUSICOLOGY WAS A LATECOMER TO ACADEMIA, FOR reasons discussed in the following essay. Elsewhere, I've discussed my activism and the role I played as a consultant in the growing public folklore establishment during the 1970s and 1980s (Titon 1992a, 1999, 2003a). I became convinced that ethnomusicologists not only ought to aim their research at accumulating knowledge inside academic communities, but that we ought to be able to work inside and outside the academy on practical projects to advance music and the arts for the public good. After moving to Brown in 1986, I offered a seminar in which students partnered with local communities to undertake applied ethnomusicology projects for the benefit of those communities. As program chair, I organized two special sessions on applied ethnomusicology at the 1989 Society for Ethnomusicology conference. Three years later, after I'd become editor of Ethnomusicology, I solicited and published the special issue devoted to ethnomusicology in the public interest, discussed near the end of the following essay. Since then, I've been identified as someone who brought applied ethnomusicology into the mainstream, but it bears emphasizing that several other ethnomusicologists felt just as strongly about it as I did and also that public folklore had entered the mainstream of folklore practice in the United States about a decade earlier. By 2012, when I wrote the following definition, description, and historical introduction to the field, applied ethnomusicology had become well established in the Americas and Europe.

### Ethnomusicology and Applied Ethnomusicology

I like to think of *ethnomusicology* as the study of people making music (Titon 1989; 1992b, xxi–xxii). People make sounds they call music, and they also make ideas about music. Those ideas form the cultural domain called music.

They include what music is and is not; what it does and cannot do; how it is acquired and how it should be transmitted; what value it has; what it should and should not be used for; what it has been in the past and what it will be in the future; whether it should be encouraged and supported, or discouraged and repressed; and so forth. Just as music differs among individuals and social groups throughout the world, so do people's ideas about it differ, and this has been so throughout history.

*Applied ethnomusicology* puts ethnomusicological scholarship, knowledge, and understanding to practical use. That is a very broad definition. More specifically, as it has developed in North America and elsewhere, applied ethnomusicology is best regarded as a music-centered intervention in a particular community, whose purpose is to benefit that community—for example, a social improvement, a musical benefit, a cultural good, an economic advantage, or a combination of these and other benefits. It is music-centered, but above all the intervention is people-centered, for the understanding that drives it toward reciprocity is based in the collaborative partnerships that arise from ethnomusicological fieldwork. Applied ethnomusicology is guided by ethical principles of social responsibility, human rights, and cultural and musical equity. Although some ethnomusicologists regard applied ethnomusicology as a career alternative to academic work—and indeed, it can be—it's not always helpful to make that distinction, because ethnomusicologists who do applied work are employed both inside academic institutions, such as universities and museums, and outside them in government agencies, nongovernmental organizations (NGOs), and client organizations directly. In other words, the place of employment does not determine whether the ethnomusicology has any application outside the world of scholarship. What matters is the work itself: how, where, and why the intervention occurs, and the communities to whom we feel responsible (Titon 2003a; Dirksen 2012).

Putting ethnomusicological scholarship, knowledge, and understanding to practical use and terming it *applied* implies the usual distinction made in the sciences between pure research, or the pursuit of knowledge for its own sake (as it is often called), and applied research, or knowledge put to practical use. It is possible to minimize this distinction, claiming that the moment a researcher circulates knowledge within a scholarly community it is being put to beneficial use. Classroom teaching is of course another kind of use. Besides, the phrase "knowledge for its own sake" appears oxymoronic, for in what sense can knowledge possibly be for its own sake if knowledge cannot logically be an agent or a self? If all ethnomusicological knowledge is put to use in one way or another, then the term "applied ethnomusicology" is redundant. All of this may be so, but for strategic reasons, the editors of this volume (Pettan and Titon 2015) find the term useful, in order to highlight a certain kind of activity and distinguish an ethnomusicology based in social responsibility where knowledge is intended for beneficial use in communities outside the academic world from an ethnomusicology that is meant to increase and improve the storehouse of knowledge about music and circulate it among scholars. In the absence of this distinction, as I will argue later (see below, "Applied Ethnomusicology in the United States: A Brief History"), applied ethnomusicology has been marginalized or ignored in the definitions and histories of our field that circulate among ethnomusicologists. Indeed, examination of ethnomusicology curricula reveals very few, if any, courses devoted to applied work at the doctoral level. The PhD is a research degree, after all, and the chief criterion for career advancement in the university remains research that enjoys a high intellectual reputation among scholars. Fortunately, however, a sense of social responsibility motivates an increasing number of ethnomusicologists, employed inside and outside the academic world, who find ways to integrate it into their scholarly research, and to apply it in the public arena. Readers who wish to know more about my personal involvement with, and views on, applied ethnomusicology are invited to consult Titon (2003a) and various entries on applied ethnomusicology on my blog at http://sustainablemusic.blogspot.com (Titon 2008–).

## Applied Ethnomusicology in Contemporary North America: A Brief Overview

What kinds of activities are applied ethnomusicologists involved in? Where, typically, do we intervene in the public arena? The coeditors of this volume (Pettan and Titon 2015), one active in North America, the other in Europe, have determined to write about these activities in the areas they know best. As I am most familiar with activities in the United States and the professional organization based there (the *Society for Ethnomusicology* [SEM]), what follows highlights US-based applied ethnomusicology. I will discuss the history (and prehistory) of applied ethnomusicology and its reception in the United States since the late 1800s. However, before sketching that history, I shall describe applied ethnomusicology as it is practiced today. What are applied ethnomusicologists doing now? What are our goals, and how are we positioned within the larger world both within and outside the academy?

First, we are involved in promoting traditional music, dance, and other cultural expressions in order to benefit artists, traditions, and communities.

Whether undertaken by ethnomusicologists acting primarily on their own behalf or whether supported by cultural organizations, these *cultural policy interventions* are among the oldest types of applied ethnomusicology and remain one of the most common, particularly as directed toward minority, immigrant, and otherwise underserved populations within developed nations and among indigenous peoples throughout the world. Sometimes, but not always, these musics are considered threatened or even endangered. Lately, sustainability has become the generally accepted policy goal, whether the musics are endangered or not. Cultural trauma has often been an important motivating factor, particularly when cultural renewal appears important in the face of political and economic stress. Examples of these interventions include the settlement schools in the southern Appalachian mountains, begun more than a century ago to promote the arts and crafts of mountain folk culture; the immigrant folk music and dance programs for children and adults in large cities such as New York and Chicago, which involved settlement schools and included festivals as well as adult recreation groups and additions to the public school curriculum; national radio broadcasts undertaken by Alan Lomax shortly before World War II to bring the songs and stories of ordinary citizens into media circulation; regional and national festivals such as the Smithsonian Folklife Festival, begun in the 1960s; policymaking and granting agencies that promote community arts, such as historical societies, arts councils, and the National Endowments; and NGOs devoted to expanding the creative economy through musical heritage and cultural tourism, sometimes with a view to recovering from ecological disasters such as hurricanes, urban blight, and mountaintop removal. In the twenty-first century, the United Nations Educational, Scientific and Cultural Organization (UNESCO) has become the major international force in cultural policy, with its treaties encouraging the preservation of what it calls intangible cultural heritage. The United States has not signed these treaties, but outside the United States many ethnomusicologists are involved with UNESCO activities and indeed, some North American ethnomusicologists participated in the planning and ongoing review stages. Ethnomusicologists have worked as consultants, arts administrators, ethnographic fieldworkers, festival presenters, radio and television producers, podcasters and internet site developers, educators, facilitators, mediators, writers, expert witnesses, and in various other capacities formulating and administering cultural policies whose purpose is sociocultural, economic, and musical benefit. Ethnomusicologists also have been among those theorizing cultural policy interventions and have contributed to a growing critical literature evaluating these practices. Many of the chapters in this volume are a part of this ongoing scholarship concerning applied ethnomusicology.

Another area of practice is *advocacy*, either on behalf of particular music makers or a music community as a whole. Rather than adopting the role of the neutral, objective, scientific observer gathering information, the applied ethnomusicologist assumes the role of a partisan, working in partnership toward goals that are mutually understood and agreed upon. Indeed, the most successful advocacy usually arises after ethnomusicologists have visited and listened to the musicians articulate their concerns and what they would like to achieve. Seldom has partnership worked when the ethnomusicologist plays the role of expert and imposes solutions to problems perceived from a distance, or fails to understand the musical community's perspective. Advocacy includes grant writing on behalf of individuals and communities; writing promotional and press materials; acting as an agent to arrange performances; facilitating community self-documentation initiatives; repatriation of recordings and musical artifacts from museums and archives; political lobbying for arts spaces; facilitating community arts education projects; researching the history of musical traditions for the community; acting as an intermediary between cultural insiders and outsiders; long-term planning for the sustainability of community music cultures; and in general working in partnership and on behalf of musicians and their communities. Advocacy usually arises from relationships developed over time, when an ethnomusicologist is attracted to particular musicians or music cultures, visits them for research purposes and returns, and determines to make a commitment that goes beyond mere study. Academic ethnomusicologists undertaking long-term fieldwork in a community are well positioned for this; while an increasing number do become advocates, yet some prefer to remain neutral observers.

A third area of practice involves *education*. Often educators themselves, applied ethnomusicologists work with other educators designing curricula and to bring musicians into the schools to demonstrate, teach, and perform; they also facilitate visits to performance spaces where youngsters may observe and participate in music-making activities. Music education once prepared youth to participate mainly in the culture of classical music, or as US academics call it these days, Western art music. As cultural pluralism and multicultural initiatives in North American schools gained traction in the last third of the twentieth century, musical pluralism increased, introducing popular music, jazz, and the music and dance of ethnic communities to the school curricula. Ethnomusicologists have been active in making musical activities more inclusive, fostering interest in local musical artists and traditions, particularly from newly arrived cultural and ethnic groups. In this way, music is viewed as a way to increase intercultural understanding.

Other areas of contemporary practice include *peace and conflict resolution*; *medicine*; *law and the music industry*; *libraries, museums, and sound archives*; *journalism*; and *environmental sound activism and ecojustice*. Peace-related applications are more frequent outside North America, but work of this sort has been done in Canada in disputes between First Nations communities and the Canadian government, while music has been an important part of labor and civil rights movements in the United States since the nineteenth century. Among the projects of medical ethnomusicology are HIV-AIDS work in Africa, therapeutic work with posttraumatic stress survivors, and music within the autism community. Legal applications have involved ethnomusicologists testifying as expert witnesses, particularly in music copyright infringement cases, and work on copyright and intellectual property issues as the question "who owns culture" becomes increasingly important when money is to be made and cases of exploitation have been documented. Ethnomusicologists have served as advisers to the World Intellectual Property Organization (WIPO), a UNESCO-sponsored group attempting to arrive at laws for protecting intellectual property rights in the international arena. Ethnomusicologists are contributing to ecological studies of the soundscape and of the effects of environmental noise on physiological and psychological health. We are involved in political action opposing sound pollution, such as noise from ocean vessels and military activities that affects whales, dolphins, and other sea mammals. Applied ethnomusicologists are contributing to the new discipline of ecomusicology, which involves music and sound in a time of environmental crisis. Journalists educated in ethnomusicology bring to world music a broadly informed historical and geographical perspective. Some are writing for newspapers, magazines, and online publications, many are active in promoting music, and some are performing musicians ourselves. Ethnomusicologists working in the music industry serve as consultants, ethnographers, technical assistants, and producers. Many libraries, museums, universities, and other institutions maintain sound archives where archivists with ethnomusicological training offer expertise in acquisition, cataloging, grant writing, preservation, and outreach.

Since the 1990s, when applied ethnomusicology became a recognizable force within ethnomusicology, other names have been advanced to describe some of the work that applied ethnomusicologists do; however, they ought not to be confused with applied ethnomusicology, which is the covering term. *Public sector ethnomusicology* describes applied ethnomusicology that is practiced by people employed by public sector, taxpayer-funded (i.e., government) institutions such as (in the United States) the Library of Congress, the Smithsonian Institution, the National Endowment for the Arts (NEA), and state arts councils, and whose efforts are directed to the public at large while often targeted at particular communities within it. By definition, "public sector ethnomusicology" is unable to include applied ethnomusicology as practiced by those who work in the private sector, in NGOs such as museums, historical societies, foundations, and various nonprofit organizations, even when part of their funding comes from government grants; nor does it describe the work of applied ethnomusicologists in corporations and client organizations. *Public ethnomusicology* is a better name for this activity insofar as it focuses on applications in the public arena. However, both terms, public sector and public, neglect the private sphere and perpetuate an unhelpful distinction between academia and the world outside of colleges and universities. As I have pointed out, applied ethnomusicology is practiced by those employed inside the academic world as well as outside of it. Ethnomusicology appears to be in danger of replicating the same terminological virus that has infected American folklore studies since the 1980s, one that American Folklore Society president Barbara Kirshenblatt-Gimblett (1988) labeled a "mistaken dichotomy."

## Applied Ethnomusicology: Being, Knowing, and Doing

Some ethnomusicologists are attracted to applied work, and others not so much. Most ethnomusicologists do share certain characteristics, however. Sound and music are immensely important to the way we orient ourselves. As humans, we are beings "in the world" through all of our senses, but we are particularly aware of vibrations that come to us as sound. Epistemologically, we feel that knowing sound—and knowing by means of sound—is essential to being human in the world and is one of the most important avenues through which to understand the human condition. Certainly, it is our special avenue. Where we diverge somewhat is in what we *do* as a result of this ontological and epistemological orientation. Some of us are most interested in pursuing and increasing knowledge about sound and music in the world, the music of the world's peoples. This is the usual end of scholarship. Scholars feel a special responsibility to present, discuss, debate, and circulate this knowledge among colleagues and students in the institutional world of universities and professional associations of ethnomusicologists. Others, those of us who practice applied ethnomusicology, also feel a responsibility to help put this knowledge to practical use in the public arena; so either in addition to our research, scholarship, and teaching within the university world, or instead of it, we also involve ourselves in interventions into musical communities for public benefit.

Forty-five years ago, Mantle Hood (1971) wrote a textbook about the nature of ethnomusicology, but instead of titling it *Ethnomusicology*, he named it *The Ethnomusicologist*. In the introduction, he described an ideal ethnomusicologist's background, education, skills and aptitudes, and personality. It was an unusual emphasis for a graduate textbook in ethnomusicology, but then, this was an unusual book, often written in the first person and, to some extent reflecting, I think, the California social and intellectual atmosphere of the 1960s that had also produced public figures like Stewart Brand, Paul Hawken and Jerry Brown. Although the influence of personality on an ethnomusicologist's accomplishments is not often written about, it is sometimes discussed among ethnomusicologists, especially when we reflect on ethnographic fieldwork, that rite of passage in which ethnomusicologists (like their counterparts in cultural anthropology) traditionally travel to a different, and sometimes strange, culture and while there, try to learn something of the musical universe among that group of people. It is difficult, sometimes alienating, even psychologically traumatic, work (Wengle 1988). We ethnomusicologists tend to think that certain personality types are better able to accomplish it than others. Applied ethnomusicologists like to interact with our field subjects, not just observe them. We feel a desire to give something back in exchange for what we are learning, and this impulse leads us not only to research but to also work directly for the benefit of those we visit. Thus, although most ethnomusicologists are in the world ontologically and epistemologically in similar ways, we differ somewhat over what we should be doing with those ways of being and knowing. It should go without saying that applied ethnomusicologists engage in research and contribute to the growth of knowledge. Our PhDs are research degrees, after all, and many of us have made substantial scholarly contributions to the flow of knowledge inside academia. However, we also feel a social responsibility to put that knowledge to use in the public arena.

### Applied Ethnomusicology in the United States: A Brief History

As coeditors Pettan and I saw the *Oxford Handbook of Applied Ethnomusicology* (Pettan and Titon 2015) through its eight-year gestation period, we became increasingly aware that US authors thought of their work within a local and national context but knew relatively little about the history, ideas, and accomplishments of applied ethnomusicologists living outside the United States. Non-US authors were similarly knowledgeable about applied work in their spheres of activity outside the United States but generally were unaware of the history, projects, scholarship, and cultural policies generated by applied ethnomusicology in North America. Ideas that had been theorized, practiced, and thoroughly critiqued in some localities were being introduced in others as if they were newly discovered. More than once, contributors seemed to be reinventing wheels. Many whose work would benefit from an exchange of ideas with others involved in similar projects elsewhere were not taking advantage of that possibility. We believe that the reasons for this insularity have more to do with institutional histories and geography than with any serious divergence over assumptions, approach, and goals. A consequence of this insularity, however, was that it became impossible for us to sketch a unified history and description of applied ethnomusicology apart from those considerations. For that reason, I construct here a history of applied ethnomusicology in the United States, related to the growth of ethnomusicology and its professional organization, SEM, founded in 1955.[1] In doing so, I draw on a graduate seminar in the history of ethnomusicological thought that I led at Brown University from 1988 until 2013. Reflexivity, postcolonial ethnomusicology, efforts to sustain musical genres and cultures, collaborative ethnography and advocacy, tourism and the creative economy, archival stewardship and repatriation of field recordings, applications to medicine and to peace and conflict resolution, proper roles for government in the arts, the place of world music in education—these are not new themes in our field, but the timing of their entrances, their reception, and their use in applied work has not been uniform among the North American, European, Asian, African, Australian, and Latin American communities of applied ethnomusicologists.

Strictly speaking, the history of ethnomusicology began in 1950, when Jaap Kunst (1950) invented the term and it entered scholarly discourse. I now prefer to think of the pre-1950 period as ethnomusicology's prehistory, paying particular attention to the two disciplines, comparative musicology and cultural anthropology, that combined in the 1950s as ethnomusicology.[2] I find prototypes of US applied ethnomusicology among nineteenth-century ethnologists and folklorists whose field research in music exhibited both social responsibility and collaborative involvement with musical communities for their benefit. Music was an integral part of early folklore and anthropology, not an afterthought. From the very beginning, scholars writing for the *American Anthropologist* and the *Journal of American Folklore* showed much interest in people making music. The second issue of the former contained an essay by Washington Matthews (1843–1905) on a Navajo sung prayer (Matthews 1888), for example, while the inaugural issue of the latter featured an article on Kwakiutl music and dance by Franz Boas (1858–1942), the most influential North American anthropologist of his generation (Boas 1888). Boas's article described some of the group's music, stories, and their ideas and behavior in relation to them; it contained musical transcriptions, and mentioned his 1886 music collecting trip with the German comparative musicologist and music psychologist Carl Stumpf among the Bella Coola. Nothing in Boas's article might be considered applied ethnomusicology per se, but Boas undertook a public anthropology project of enormous import in the early twentieth century when he opposed so-called scientific racism and helped establish the idea that differences in human behavior result from learned cultural, rather than fixed biological, traits.

Matthews's work was aided by a deeply collaborative relationship in which he underwent Native rituals and may have married a Hidatsa woman. Collaborative relationships in which the parties work toward mutually agreed-upon goals became a hallmark of applied ethnomusicology, but their roots may be found in people like Matthews as well as Alice Cunningham Fletcher (1838–1923), whose collaborative work moved more clearly in the direction of social and economic benefits that would be recognized today as applied ethnomusicology. Fletcher, who became president of both the American Anthropological Association and the American Folklore Society, as well as vice president of the American Association for the Advancement of Science, lived with the Sioux in 1881, and collaborated with an Omaha, Frances La Flesche, whom she took into her household from 1890 onward. Falling ill with a severe case of rheumatoid arthritis in 1883, she was nursed back to health by her Native American friends, who sang to her while she lay recovering. Then, she wrote, "the sweetness, the beauty and meaning of these songs were revealed to me" (Fletcher 1994, 8). Like the others, Fletcher undertook ethnographic studies of Native music, but she also worked tirelessly on behalf of Native American education, integration, and advancement into mainstream culture.

"Giving back" is the usual term North American ethnomusicologists employ to identify this reciprocity, which has taken various forms over the decades. However, Fletcher's efforts at aiding Native Americans are characterized today as attempts to Americanize them, a "grievous error in the administration of Native American lands and peoples" according to a Smithsonian Institution author (Smithsonian: Fletcher). Ethnomusicologists consider it unfortunate that the Omaha songs she collected were published with Western harmonization, added to them by the musician John Comfort Fillmore, who convinced Fletcher that these harmonies were implicit in the Omaha melodies (Fletcher 1994). Nonetheless, Fletcher may be understood in her time as a progressive. The principal alternative for Native Americans to Americanization (or Christianization), after all, had for nearly three centuries been genocide. And prominent American composers such as Edward MacDowell were quoting, transforming, and harmonizing Native American melodies in their musical compositions.

Daniel Sheehy (1992) and Anthony Seeger (2006) trace the history of twentieth-century pioneers in applied ethnomusicology, such as Robert Winslow Gordon, Alan Lomax, and Charles Seeger. In terming them applied ethnomusicologists, Seeger, Sheehy, and others combine ethnomusicology's historical and prehistorical periods. Certainly, these ancestors would have been called applied ethnomusicologists if ethnomusicology proper had come into being before 1950. To some extent, their work was related to that of early anthropologists such as A. L. Kroeber and others on endangered Native American languages. The Lomaxes' folk music collections, which included songs by African Americans, European immigrants, Hispanics and other ethnic and regional groups besides Anglo-Americans, were meant for the general public, to supply a kind of people's alternative to the art music that was being taught in the public schools. Alan Lomax insisted that the treasure trove of folk music should be made accessible through media production, which in the 1940s and 1950s meant radio programs—he produced dozens of them for national broadcast. He issued an appeal for "cultural equity" that articulated many of the principles under which he had been operating for decades (Lomax 1972a). Lomax's "appeal" may be the single most often-cited document in the literature of US applied ethnomusicology. Charles Seeger, Anthony Seeger's grandfather, had issued a call in 1939 for an applied musicology that would follow from government involvement in the arts, a vision in some ways similar to the situation in China today (A. Seeger 2006, 227–228). Seeger and his wife, Ruth Crawford Seeger, John and Alan Lomax, Herbert Halpert, Zora Neale Hurston, and others were involved in efforts to encourage folk music (as the authentic popular music of a democratic society) during the Roosevelt administration. These activities, of course, diminished greatly as the United States concentrated during the 1940s on mobilization for World War II. But Sheehy (1992, 329) concludes that "there is a tradition of applied thought and purpose that should be included in the history of ethnomusicology," as well as "an evolving sense of strategy and techniques for action that has flowed through this thought and that demands our attention as ethnomusicologists."

Anthony Seeger (2006) titled his essay "Lost Lineages" in the history of ethnomusicology and, like Sheehy, called for a more inclusive history of the field.

The usual historical accounts of ethnomusicology in the United States are not so inclusive: applied ethnomusicology is treated either as a peripheral activity or, more often, ignored entirely. These mainstream accounts trace ethnomusicology's roots to comparative musicology, a scientific project of the European Enlightenment. They do not pay much attention to its roots in folklore and cultural anthropology. In 1885, Guido Adler defined comparative musicology as "the comparison of the musical works . . . of the various peoples of the earth for ethnographical purposes, and the classification of them according to their various forms" (Haydon 1941, 117). Comparative musicology began in the latter part of the nineteenth century with the systematization of music knowledge, which proceeded with the measurable, classificatory, and comparative procedures borrowed from philology, embryology, and other sciences, generating various hypotheses concerning origins, growth, diffusion, and function. Aided by the recording phonograph and efforts of various music collectors, it included the comparative work on the musical scales of various nations accomplished by the Englishman Alexander Ellis and the research of the German Carl Stumpf and others in music psychology (or psychophysical science, as it was then called). Comparative musicology was further developed as a research discipline in early twentieth-century Berlin by Stumpf's younger colleague Erich von Hornbostel, Curt Sachs, and others, with related scholarship accomplished by Béla Bartók in Hungary, Constantin Brăiloiu in Romania, and others in the fields of comparative musical folklore and the sociology of music.

Comparative musicology arrived in the United States in 1925 in the person of George Herzog, who had been von Hornbostel's assistant in Berlin. He went on to study anthropology with Franz Boas at Columbia University, specializing in "primitive music," as it was then called. Herzog received his doctorate in 1931 under Boas's supervision and pursued an academic career at Yale, Columbia, and Indiana University that lasted until the mid-1950s. He was recognized during this period as the leading authority on "primitive music." Among his students were two of the founders of SEM, David McAllester and Willard Rhodes. Bruno Nettl, who has written knowledgeably about Herzog's contributions to comparative musicology, was another of his students (Nettl and Bohlman 1991, 270–272; Nettl 2002, 90–92; 2010, 168). Herzog's writings exhibited an empirical, scientific method that required large amounts of reliable data, a high standard to which he held himself and others. "All evidence," he wrote, "points to the wisdom of dispensing with sweeping theoretical schemes and of inquiring in each case into the specific historical processes that have molded the culture and musical style of a nation or tribe.... So little is actually known ... that the main attention of this field [of comparative musicology] is devoted to increasing that little, and collecting more material before it all disappears under the impact of Western civilization" (Herzog 1936, 3). He had learned the importance of fieldwork and data gathering from his teacher Boas, and he insisted on that, as well as musical transcription and analysis, from his students. His methods added Boas-styled ethnographic research to the comparative analysis that characterized the work of Hornbostel and the Berlin school.

A useful summary of comparative musicology, with due attention to Herzog's prominence in the United States, appeared in Glen Haydon's (1941) graduate-level textbook, *Introduction to Musicology*. As outlined there, its purpose was to increase knowledge of the music of the world's peoples. Academic research was the means to that end. The work of numerous comparative musicologists, chiefly European, was described and their most important publications referenced. But comparative musicology soon underwent a facelift. Historical accounts date this to Jaap Kunst's (1950, and two subsequent editions) book *Ethno-Musicology*, which defined "ethnomusicology" as the study of "all tribal and folk music and every kind of non-Western art music. Besides, it studies as well the sociological aspects of music" (Kunst 1950, 1). Although he is usually credited with inventing the term "ethnomusicology," Kunst's argument for the name change rested chiefly on redundancy of the word "comparative" rather than the added prefix "ethno." All good science, he argued, is comparative in nature; disciplines like linguistics and embryology had, after all, dropped the adjective for the time being. His argument was persuasive, and some comparative musicologists began to adopt the new name, while others who wished to place more emphasis on the cultural study of music and less on musical analysis welcomed the name change and saw opportunity in it. However, comparative musicology remained the ancestral predecessor for Kunst and in later US historical accounts of the discipline, chiefly by Bruno Nettl (1956, 1964, 1983, 2002, 2005, 2010) as well as others. For nearly sixty years, these historical accounts have informed generations of ethnomusicology professors and graduate students in the United States and elsewhere. Despite increased theoretical sophistication and a growing recognition of historical relativism (e.g., Nettl and Bohlman 1991; Nettl 2010; Rice 2014), different subject emphases by other authors (e.g., Hood [1971] 1982; Merriam 1964), and an enlarged cast of characters (McLean 2006), these mainstream histories continue to construct ethnomusicology as a research discipline almost exclusively centered on the academic world. Applied ethnomusicology seldom appears; when it does, it usually is treated with some reservations. As long as comparative musicology remained ethnomusicology's central occupation, applied work would be marginal at best.

The founding of the SEM in 1955 not only provided an opportunity for a new emphasis on the cultural study of music but might also have moved applied ethnomusicology to a more central position. Why it did not do so, at a time when applied anthropology was becoming important within US cultural anthropology, is an interesting question. In large part, as this brief history will show, the answer has to do with the founding generation's desire to establish and expand ethnomusicology as an academic discipline, on a firm institutional footing, throughout the university world. In doing so, they missed an opportunity to integrate applied work into the agenda of the new society. It was left for the next generation to do so.

The early period of SEM was predictably taken up with debate over the direction of the discipline. In its first fifteen years or so, the SEM journal, *Ethnomusicology*, was filled with essays by many leading practitioners who attempted to define the discipline and influence its course. Research in ethnomusicology's first two decades (ca. 1950–1975) has been characterized as falling broadly into two approaches, one musicological and the other anthropological (Kerman 1986, 155–181). This is an oversimplification, but it is useful in highlighting the musicological legacies of Hornbostel and Herzog, which in SEM could be seen in the work of Herzog's former colleague Kolinski, William Malm, George List, Mantle Hood, and Herzog's student Nettl, among others. Their focus was on collecting, recording, transcribing, describing, classifying, analyzing, and comparing music in order to increase the music knowledge base and to test theories concerning musical distribution, diffusion, and acculturation. Like Herzog, most were also interested in the ethnographic study of cultural contexts for music ("music in culture") and in comparing and contrasting music's functions within cultures. Unless one thinks of the polymath Seeger as a comparativist, these comparative musicologists were not represented among the four SEM founders; however, their work was prominent in monographs and in *Ethnomusicology*, where they advanced their scholarship and their view of what ethnomusicology ought to be. They also played a major role in establishing ethnomusicology as an academic discipline at the graduate level in US universities during the first twenty years of SEM.

On the other side of the debate over the future of ethnomusicology were the anthropologists, dance ethnologists, folklorists, and various other scholars who shared an interest in music and had been attracted to the new field. Most prominent among these were the anthropologists Alan Merriam and David McAllester, both among the four founders of SEM. Herzog was noticeably absent from SEM's origins, and it is worth asking why. Nettl, who writes movingly and generously about Herzog, observed that Herzog already was behaving erratically in 1952 (he would be hospitalized from the mid-1950s onward, with occasional time off, until his death in 1983, for what we would now call a bipolar disorder) and attributes his absence to this (Nettl 2002, 90–92; 2010, 168; Nettl and Bohlman 1991, 271–272). No doubt this is correct; but it appears that the founders also wished to escape Herzog's dominance over the field. McAllester reported that as far as he knew, he was the only student ever to complete the doctorate under Herzog's supervision. "The campus was littered with the bodies of failed Herzog students," McAllester said. Herzog's habit was to demonstrate to them time after time that they could not meet his standards. "He never failed them in so many words," McAllester continued, "but they had a very hard time ever getting an appointment with him, and when they finally did, it was all at such a high level that they felt sort of defeated. If they brought in a transcription, it was so bad that he went over it note by note to show them and said, now see if you can't, now that you've had this practice, do better next time. Then a month or so later, when they caught up with him again, then the same thing would happen again." Rhodes was one of the dropouts, but he was already a full professor at Columbia and did not need the degree; yet it remained a sore point with both him and his friend McAllester. Even before Herzog moved from Columbia to Indiana University in 1948, he had been showing signs of the mental instability that would cause him to retire in 1956 and institutionalize him (A. Seeger and Gebhard 1984). Herzog was Nettl's dissertation supervisor at Indiana, but before Nettl could complete his doctorate, Herzog's erratic behavior forced him to move to a different supervisor. "Bruno studied with him [Herzog] when he went out to Indiana, and he [Nettl] had a professor for a father, and so he had a strong position," McAllester said. (Paul Nettl, Bruno's father, was a professor of musicology at Indiana University.) "And he [Nettl] demanded another teacher, and he finished his Ph.D. with Carl Voegelin, the linguist. He left Herzog, but most of us couldn't do that. We were with Herzog and it was do or die, and many died" (McAllester 1989).

No wonder, then, given McAllester's and Rhodes's opinion of him, that Herzog was not invited into the inner circle of SEM founders. At that time, they may have been less aware of Herzog's illness and decline than Nettl and the others who worked with Herzog at Indiana. But that must be only part of the answer. The other part is that McAllester, Merriam, Rhodes, and Seeger wanted to take a new direction, to move away from comparative musicology and Boasian ethnography, and toward an ethnomusicology that would make room not only for a greater variety of authoritative voices but also for more emphasis on the cultural study of music. Reaching out to scholars throughout the world, in 1953 the four founders initiated an ethnomusicology *Newsletter*, and two years later they founded SEM, designed to foster communication and research in the field. SEM immediately began publishing a journal, *Ethnomusicology*, which since its inception has served as the flagship research periodical for the discipline. It is worth pausing for a moment to examine what the founders themselves thought they were up to. Nettl, reminiscing about this early period, the name change from "comparative musicology" to "ethnomusicology," and the founding of SEM, recalls that he (and others, he thinks) regarded these events more as a "revival" of a great scholarly tradition (comparative musicology, which had been all but eliminated in Europe during the Nazi era) than as a revolution (Nettl 2010, 160–162). Inclined toward his teacher Herzog's understanding of that tradition, Nettl's subject position is understandable. Still a graduate student at the time and not directly involved as a founder, he had nevertheless set his course and was already a major stakeholder in the new field. His memoirs (Nettl 2002, 2010, 2013) of this transitional period are both charming and invaluable, filled with information unavailable elsewhere and required reading for anyone interested in the history of ethnomusicology. In these memoirs, he tries to deconstruct the "myth" of SEM's "grand entrance," as he puts it, arguing that its historical significance and the importance of the four founders has been overrated (Nettl 2010, 160–165). In retrospect, it is apparent that comparative musicology continued to exert a strong influence on ethnomusicology during its first few decades (ca. 1950–1980). But the new society, the new name, and its founders' orientation toward anthropology is a historical fact that signaled a significant and enduring new direction for the field.

Let me try to reconstruct something of that significance as I believe it to have appeared to the founders at the time. (In so doing, I rely in part on my conversations with Rhodes, Merriam, Seeger, and especially McAllester about that period.) McAllester recalled that after Herzog was finally confined to a mental hospital, he could no longer exercise his former control over degrees, grants, and publications in the field. "He became so ill that he had to be in an institution, and then the lid was off and the society [SEM] could be established" (McAllester 1989). For the four founders, SEM represented a move away from comparative musicology, not simply as an escape from Herzog's iron grip but also in establishing a new interdisciplinary field: ethnomusicology. The founders resisted efforts from other societies that tried to dissuade them from starting a new society. The American Musicological Society sent representatives to their early meetings and "announced that we should not be a splinter group, but that we should be part of the American Musicological Society.... And we said, if we joined them, the AMS, there were a whole bunch of people that would not be any longer members. We had folklorists, anthropologists, ethnologists, acousticians, physicists . . . and they would have dropped out if we had become a part of the American Musicological Society." These same scholars likewise would have left SEM had they allied themselves with the International Folk Music Council (IFMC), McAllester reported:

> Maud Karpeles came and pleaded with us to become a wing of the International Folk Music Council. . . . Alan Merriam particularly, well, Charlie Seeger, too, they were both very insistent that it not get into the hands of . . . the International Folk Music [Council]. So when we started the society, they [the IFMC] soon got wind of it, and they were very upset because they had their American branch and they were afraid we would simply split their society and draw membership away from them.... There were scholars among them, great scholars among them, but they were not anthropologically oriented. And it just happened by the way we operated, that the Society for Ethnomusicology began with an anthropological orientation. (McAllester 1989)

Nettl (2010, 143) agreed: "The beginning of the SEM was deeply rooted in the anthropological background of its most influential leaders."

McAllester recalled the excitement that accompanied the founding of SEM, along with the possibilities of new directions for the society. For Merriam even more than for McAllester, that direction was to be cultural anthropology. Eventually, he termed this direction "the anthropology of music" rather than "comparative musicology," and he lobbied hard for the study of music, not in culture but *as* culture, a phrase ("music as culture") that Merriam (1977, 204) referenced to his earlier "unpublished thoughts." According to Merriam, music was not something that existed within a cultural context; it *was* culture in the anthropological sense itself, with its own domain of ideas, behavior, and sonic dimension. Obtaining a full professorship in anthropology at Indiana University in 1962, Merriam was not only a founder but also a forceful presence in SEM from the very beginning until his untimely death in an airplane crash in 1980. His area interests were in indigenous musics primarily, Native American and African. A former jazz musician, he had little use for the study of folk music and even less for bimusicality, about which more shortly. When I taught a summer session in Indiana's Folklore Institute in 1977, he invited me to his home a number of times. He had just remarried and was in an expansive mood. Relevant for this historical sketch is the attitude he expressed toward the IFMC. He affirmed that the founders had refused Maud Karpeles's invitation to join the IFMC rather than form their own society. Nettl (2010, 143) attributed Merriam's reasons for objecting to the IFMC in the early 1950s to "his perception of the IFMC as specifically interested in music alone, the notion that folk-music scholars were interested in only a small segment of the music of any society; and the idea that the IFMC included a substantial practical component, that is, was in large measure a society of folksingers and dancers." Merriam's views had evolved since then, for in 1977 he told me the IFMC as a group was insufficiently objective and scientific about music as a human phenomenon. If they had been, they would have been concerned with all music, not mainly the oldest layers of music in what were then regarded as folk societies (Redfield 1947). And if they had been, they would not have been so concerned with authenticity and so worried about salvaging this music for archival preservation—or worse yet, reviving it for a sophisticated urban audience. Merriam took some pleasure in noting that Indiana University's Folklore Institute did not share this attitude toward musical revivalism; indeed, Richard Dorson, the head of the institute, had coined the term "fakelore" to describe it, and on the advice of George List, the senior ethnomusicologist in the Folklore Institute, Dorson would not permit amateur folk musicians in their doctoral program to undertake music research unless they had had sufficient formal training in Western music theory and history to be admitted to ethnomusicology courses. As Indiana was one of only a very few universities in the United States granting doctoral degrees in folklore, the amount of academic research in US folk music during the Dorson-List-Merriam era was severely diminished as a consequence. For Merriam, ethnomusicology was revolutionary insofar as it elevated anthropology to a position of equality with musicology in birthing the new offspring, ethnomusicology. The *ethno* prefix (derived from the Greek *ethnos* [= people with a common culture]) firmly established it as a new discipline that was properly part of "the scientific study of man," as anthropology had long been defined. Merriam (1964, 25 et passim) assiduously pursued this goal, which he called "sciencing about music."

With SEM established on the promise of interdisciplinarity and new directions, particularly from cultural anthropology, one might have expected that the new organization would have been hospitable to applied ethnomusicology. Anthropologists had by then started putting their knowledge to use in solving social problems. John van Willigen (2002) dates the rise of a socially committed applied or "action" anthropology to 1945, although he notes that anthropologists had for decades previously taken on community consultantship roles. But this exciting, albeit controversial, development in anthropology did not cross over into SEM with any success until decades later. The reasons, in retrospect, are not entirely surprising. To establish ethnomusicology within the most secure of institutional bases—that is, within universities—it was necessary to position it as a research science, aiming to increase knowledge of the music of the world's peoples. Musicological and anthropological ethnomusicologists might disagree over the discipline's emphasis, but they agreed that scholarship and the production of knowledge were its goals. Applications of that research in the public arena might be well and good, but the pursuit of knowledge for its own sake had always been valued most highly in university settings, where it could be protected from outside forces. In 1950, ethnomusicology itself was a fringe discipline in the United States, with only a few courses being offered (sometimes in anthropology departments, sometimes in music departments) and only a few professors available to advise doctoral dissertations. For ethnomusicology to expand inside the university world, professors must succeed in establishing courses, programs (especially graduate programs), tenure tracks, and recognition of the discipline as a legitimate academic pursuit. The proven strategy to advance the discipline in the university world would be through research, emphasizing that study of the music of the world's peoples would add to the store of knowledge about human behavior and achievement. Research "for its own sake" was then, and remains, regarded in the academy as more elegant, of higher and "purer" disinterested purpose than research driven by applications. In the arts and humanities, where contemplation of the pure aesthetic object was required for philosophy, literary criticism, and art history, disinterested acts of scholarship were experienced as pleasurable in themselves. Eventually, one could hope, every music department, every music school or conservatory, and every anthropology department would have at least one ethnomusicologist doing research and offering music courses with a worldwide scope; some places would have more than one and would establish graduate programs training future generations of ethnomusicologists as the discipline would expand. Professionalization of ethnomusicology as a research discipline, and with that a need to distance it from well-meaning amateurs who also engaged in music research, was a second reason. Applied work might be done by those who lacked the proper scientific attitude and scholarly training to conduct credible research: missionaries, for example, who had historically put music to use in attempting to convert indigenous peoples, or amateur collectors who became partisans on behalf of those whose music they recorded. I believe that a third reason was the distrust, among this generation of scholars who came of age during or soon after World War II, of social engineering, whether for political, cultural, or musical ends. Applied research put to practical use in musical or cultural interventions, despite intended benefits, was something Americans might well oppose, particularly given the uses to which music had been put during the Nazi regime and was still being put in the Soviet sphere. Many in the previous generation of US music scholars had been born in Europe and had fled to North America to escape Nazi persecution and establish musical scholarship inside a university world where they would be free from political interference. I do not mean to suggest that a cabal of ethnomusicology professors drew up such a plan but rather that they were inclined by personality and training to move in that direction. Partly as a result, in its first two decades, ethnomusicology became more firmly established as a scholarly discipline; however, applied ethnomusicology languished inside the US academic world.

Merriam was perhaps the first US ethnomusicologist to recognize an applied ethnomusicology by that name, although he did not favor it. The phase "applied ethnomusicology" did not appear in the SEM *Newsletter* or journal until Merriam's 1963 review of Henry Weman's *African Music and the Church in Africa*. Merriam (1963b, 135) wrote that this book is "perhaps most accurately described as a study in applied ethnomusicology, for his principal concern is how African music can be used . . . [in missionary work]." Merriam (1964, 42–43) expanded on his comments a year later in *The Anthropology of Music*, and it is worth looking at them in detail:

> The ultimate aim of the study of man . . . involves the question of whether one is searching for knowledge for its own sake, or is attempting to provide solutions for practical applied problems. Ethnomusicology has seldom been used in the same manner as applied or action anthropology, and ethnomusicologists have only rarely felt called upon to help solve problems in manipulating the destinies of people, but some such studies have been made [here he references Weman's book] and it is quite conceivable that this may in the future be of increased concern. The difficulty of an applied study is that it focuses the attention of the investigator upon a single problem which may cause or force him to ignore others of equal interest, and it is also difficult to avoid outside control over the research project. Although this problem is not yet of primary concern, it will surely shape the kinds of studies carried out if it does draw the increased attention of ethnomusicologists.

Here, as elsewhere, Merriam privileges "knowledge for its own sake." In criticizing applied work for its narrow focus, Merriam is appealing to the idea that ethnomusicology should be the study of music as a whole; however, "outside control" may be viewed as a threat to academic freedom, while the phrase "manipulating the destinies of people" expresses that distrust of and distaste for the political and cultural interventions of applied anthropology and, by extension, of applied ethnomusicology.

Several books and articles critique recent interventions, especially those resulting from UNESCO initiatives to preserve intangible cultural heritage (e.g., Weintraub and Yung 2009). But this tradition of critique may be traced to Merriam's (1963a, 207) "white knight" label for those ethnomusicologists who feel called to "function as knights in shining armor riding to the defense of non-Western music." Skepticism toward applied ethnomusicology is also evident in Bruno Nettl's histories and descriptions of the field. Nettl (2010), more than anyone else among the founding generation of SEM, shouldered the responsibility to construct a history of ethnomusicology, something that he has come to call his "elephant." The sole active survivor of his generation of ethnomusicologists, Nettl early on assumed the mantle of spokesperson for the discipline, and today he is recognized in the United States and elsewhere as its elder statesman. As intellectual history is his central concern, he devotes relatively little attention to applied ethnomusicology. His most influential book, *The Study of Ethnomusicology* (1983, 297), treats applied ethnomusicology within the context of applied anthropology: "In the course of the 1950s there developed a concept and a subdiscipline, 'applied anthropology,' whose task it was to use anthropological insight to help solve social problems, particularly those occasioned by rapid culture change in the wake of modernization and Westernization." Applied anthropologists also were consulted in attempts to solve economic problems such as third world poverty. They advised government organizations such as the United States Agency for International Development (USAID) on interventions involving democratization, agricultural modernization, and economic development. Rapid social change and cultural upheaval was the result of the intervention, not the original problem to be solved. No wonder, then, as Nettl continues, that although "anthropologists wanted to help [they] frequently ended up offending the local population and doing what was perceived as harmful. As a result, in the late 1960s and early 1970s they were widely attacked for doing work of no relevance to social problems, of mixing in local politics, of spying. Ethnomusicologists shared in this criticism" (ibid.). Here, applied ethnomusicologists' efforts to conserve traditional music and culture are conflated with applied anthropologists' efforts meant to aid in the modernization of traditional culture. The implication is that, like applied anthropologists, applied ethnomusicologists were criticized as offensive, harmful, and irrelevant and that they barged into local politics and were accused of being spies. But if this critique of anthrocolonialism is accurate about interventions meant to bring about modernization and development, it does not follow that it applies to interventions by applied ethnomusicologists meant to conserve traditional music. Nettl (1983, 297; repeated in the 2nd edition [2005, 206]) then balances the critique with a somewhat more positive view: "The picture [of applied anthropology and ethnomusicology] is not entirely negative. Some societies are happy to have outsiders come, appreciate their efforts, their respect for the traditions, and their help in restoring vigor to rapidly disappearing musics. Persian and Indian music masters are proud to have Western scholars as students, for it raises their prestige locally and legitimizes their traditional art in the face of modernizing doubters. Even so, there is often the feeling that members of the society itself, given the right training, equipment, and time, could do it better."

Nettl (1983, 297) points out that some ethnomusicologists "espouse fieldwork in which informants become collaborators, the members of a community being studied in effect becoming co-collaborators." Yet Nettl's deep unease with applied work as social engineering is embedded in the tone and weight of his discussion and in the examples he offers, and it is apparent where he thinks the majority of ethnomusicologists stand. For the first edition of this book (1983), this was a correct assessment, but by the second edition (2005), it was not. Indeed, in a recent interview, he acknowledged applied ethnomusicology's considerable appeal to a new generation (Nettl 2014, 1).[3]

A few ethnomusicologists in SEM's founding generation were involved in applied projects during the 1960s and 1970s, yet they did not call it applied ethnomusicology. No doubt they thought of these as proper activities for an ethnomusicologist, but to my knowledge, they did not think of them as part of a subfield where research was directed toward the public interest. Some, most prominently SEM founder David McAllester, took on an advocacy role on behalf of the Navajo and also in music education: to educate music teachers and broaden the kindergarten–through–high school curricula to include examples of the musics of the world's peoples. McAllester worked through the Music Educators National Conference to accomplish this goal, and he advised several graduate students in the Wesleyan University world music program who went in this direction, among them Patricia Shehan Campbell. Another prominent ethnomusicologist in the founding generation, Mantle Hood, undertook applied ethnomusicology projects in Indonesia. He related the story of his successful intervention to revive Javanese gamelan gong making (for the large gong *ageng*), which had nearly gone extinct. However, he also reported that his intervention resulted in some unintended, negative consequences. He offered another example, when he was called on for suggestions to improve gamelan educational practice—what innovations would he recommend? But here he stepped back from applied ethnomusicology and refused to interfere, thinking that Western influence would not be good for the tradition (Hood 1971, 358–371). His major work on ethnomusicology, *The Ethnomusicologist*, ends with a section on cultural exchange through music and the arts as a means to further international understanding—putting ethnomusicological knowledge to practical use for a clear and intended social benefit.

Thus, it could be fairly said that SEM's founding generation concentrated their US efforts in two areas: first, on research in order to increase knowledge about music and to circulate it among scholars, and second, to secure an institutional base for ethnomusicology within the academic world. In the latter, they were more successful in the music divisions of the universities and colleges (variously called music departments, schools of music, conservatories, or in some institutions combined with fine arts departments as departments of the arts) than in anthropology departments. Growth within music divisions allied the discipline more closely with musicology than anthropology, and although the SEM founders envisioned a broadly interdisciplinary field with a new emphasis on the cultural study of music—and achieved this at SEM conferences and to some extent in the SEM journal, *Ethnomusicology*—the institutional growth of ethnomusicology favored the musicologically oriented scholars.

Ironically, however, it was not by positioning ethnomusicology as a research science that institutional growth was achieved; rather, in the last half of the twentieth century, ethnomusicology benefited from a combination of external circumstances that the founding generation did not foresee. The most important of these were, first, the meteoric rise in the popularity of world music among the general public, and especially the young, which began in the 1960s. Second was the reversal, in US cultural mythology, from the idea that the nation was a melting pot that produced a single American type to the acceptance of cultural diversity and pluralism, which in the field of education broke the Eurocentric hold on curricula and opened it to a variety of minority and international voices in the humanities: literature, fine arts, music, and history. Youth cultures became deeply involved in alternative musics, including folk music, blues, and bluegrass. World music began to enjoy widespread popularity, as George Harrison of the Beatles studied sitar in India, and Hindustani musicians Ali Akbar Khan and Ravi Shankar went on extended annual tours throughout the United States. Recording companies such as Nonesuch released world music recordings that targeted both indigenous as well as Asian art musics to an appreciative public. Young men and women turned to world music as one of many paths toward personal growth. Fueled by the rising popularity of world music, master musicians from Ghana, north and south India, the Arab world, China, Japan, and Indonesia were soon in residence as world music performance ensemble directors at American colleges and universities where ethnomusicologists were already teaching. Performance was attracting students into the field. Mantle Hood, director of the Ethnomusicology Institute at UCLA, spearheaded this movement, advocating on behalf of what he called bimusicality. Just as serious study of a foreign language could turn a person bilingual, so serious study of a foreign music could make one bimusical and impart a knowledge of that music that was otherwise unavailable. Some senior ethnomusicologists tempered their enthusiasm for world music performance ensembles, however, and for decades they were conspicuously absent at the University of Illinois and Indiana University. Nonetheless, the possibility that world music might be learned intrigued many, and some went on to enroll in graduate programs in ethnomusicology, resulting in more degrees, professors, and programs. By 1970, it was possible to study ethnomusicology and obtain the doctorate by studying with Hood at UCLA, Fredric Lieberman at Brown, Alan Kagan at Minnesota, George List and Merriam at Indiana, Nettl at Illinois, Robert Garfias at Washington, William Malm at Michigan, and McAllester at Wesleyan, among other universities. Moreover, those with doctoral training in ethnomusicology had begun teaching at other colleges and universities, and SEM's US membership had increased.

 Diversification and expansion of the US college and university music curriculum created a demand for professors who could teach the new courses. Within music divisions, this meant the end of the near-complete domination of Western art music (or classical music, as the American public calls it). Now popular music, jazz, and the music of the world's peoples took their place among the course offerings. Gradually, ethnomusicologists began to realize that they could take a proactive role and convince university administrators that one way to accomplish their goal of affirmative action toward so-called American minority groups (something that ethnomusicologists by and large supported) was through greater diversity of music offerings, which would also mean more ethnomusicology hires.[4] As programs and departments were established in African American studies, Native American studies, Asian American studies, Hispanic American studies, and the like, it became apparent that the music of American minorities, along with world music, had an important role to play in the expanded curricula. Of course, ethnomusicologists were far from the only ones to benefit from diversity, cultural pluralism, and affirmative action in the academic world; however, while the popularity of world music has ebbed and flowed since the 1960s, the movement toward greater cultural diversity within US higher education has been persistent.

The folk music revival, rising popularity of world music, and the positive value now attached to ethnic roots and cultural pluralism brought about a renewed emphasis in applied ethnomusicology outside the academic world before it had much impact inside it. Because Alan Lomax embodied this public work in applied ethnomusicology—not only as a collector, writer, and promoter but also as an advocate for cultural democracy and musical pluralism—it is instructive to ponder his encounter with none other than George Herzog, who also believed in the value of musical diversity and had devoted his life to the study of folk and "primitive" music. Herzog, as noted, embodied comparative musicology in the United States during the 1930s and 1940s. After Lomax had been "Assistant in Charge" of the Archive of American Folk Song at the Library of Congress for several years—field collecting, acquiring from others, and curating recordings—he decided to move his base of operations, from February through June 1939, to Manhattan to obtain "more systematic academic training in anthropology and in the anthropological approach to primitive and folk music." He hoped to study with Herzog and other anthropologists at Columbia and also "to study music with private instructors" (R. Cohen 2010, 115). A recently published collection of Lomax's correspondence reveals the encounter with Herzog—from Lomax's viewpoint, of course—to have been less than successful. Herzog would not let Lomax into his course, insisting that he must take his two courses in prescribed sequence—primitive music (offered in the fall) followed by folk music (offered in the spring). Herzog would not budge from the requirement. To Harold Spivacke, his supervisor at the Library of Congress, Lomax then wrote, "I met a very much surprised Dr. Herzog at Columbia this morning, a Dr. Herzog who told me that I had made a great mistake in coming to school to take his course this term, that I should have come next term, should have come next year and for a whole year. Such a neurotic little academic man you never saw before" (121). Although Lomax had a marvelous ear, outstanding musical taste, and broad knowledge of folk music, along with considerable field-collecting experience, he had little formal musical education and could be regarded as a well-meaning amateur in search of professional training. In some scientific disciplines, such as ornithology and astronomy, serious work by amateur researchers is highly valued; in the early history of science, the majority of natural historians and natural philosophers were amateurs and proud of it. However, Herzog was wary of amateur music research. Their confrontation, exacerbated by their prickly personalities and strong convictions, can be understood as a sign of incompatibility between public and academic ethnomusicologies in an earlier era; today, as mentioned earlier, more practitioners of applied ethnomusicology are employed within academia than outside it.

Indeed, the growth of US applied ethnomusicology from the 1960s through the 1980s owed much to Alan Lomax's continuing influence, his call for cultural equity, the work of public folklorists, and the establishment of government institutions that supported cultural pluralism within the arts. At the federal level were the Office of Folklife Studies at the Smithsonian Institution, the Folk Arts Division of the NEA, and the Archive of Folk Culture at the Library of Congress, enlarged from the former Archive of American Folk Song, which Lomax had directed, and under the aegis of a new library unit, the American Folklife Center. Regional, state, and in some cases, city arts councils also were established, funded in part by the NEA, and by the end of the 1980s, most of the state arts councils employed at least one folklorist and a few employed ethnomusicologists. Folklore in the United States, while conservative in the academic world, enjoyed a tradition of populist activism outside it. Each of these government agencies employed scholars as consultants, and some employed them as arts and humanities administrators; thus, a large public outreach and concern for the health of expressive culture within various US communities was put in place, with a growing number of ethnomusicologists involved in public folklore, most often as consultants, but sometimes as advocates and collaborators, doing applied work. Several ethnomusicologists worked as presenters at folk festivals, their prior fieldwork having identified and documented some of the musicians who performed there. Music was the most prominent among the arts singled out by public folklorists for identification, documentation, and presentation. As arts administrators, ethnomusicologists were employed by the Smithsonian Institution (Thomas Vennum, Charlotte Heth) and by the Folk Arts Division of the NEA (Daniel Sheehy), which also hired numerous ethnomusicologists as consultants to sit on panels recommending funding for various community music projects as well as for apprenticeships and heritage awards (Titon 2015). Bess Lomax Hawes, director of the NEA's Folk Arts Division, held an informal session at the SEM conference most years during the 1980s to inform ethnomusicologists of the opportunities for submitting applied ethnomusicology project proposals to the NEA. This activity, known in the 1970s and 1980s as public sector folklore, in the 1990s became known simply as "public folklore" and influenced the course of applied ethnomusicology in the United States profoundly.

Academic ethnomusicologists involved in public folklore thus began to think of their work as applied ethnomusicology, but SEM remained chiefly an organization devoted to communicating research among scholars. It was not until most of the founding generation aged and gradually relinquished leadership that applied ethnomusicology was able to enter SEM in a significant way. However, it was not merely a changing of the generations. A significant change within academia resulted from the growing critique of science, fomented by poststructuralist and critical cultural theory, and culminating in the so-called science wars of the 1980s. North American graduate students in ethnomusicology during this period—beginning in the late 1960s—could not help being affected, as were cultural anthropologists and folklorists. The result, particularly among those attracted to the study of music as culture, was a turn in ethnomusicology from science toward cultural critique, from the musical object to the musical experience, from analysis to interpretation, from explanation to understanding. As a result, US ethnomusicology took a humanistic turn, and the cultural study of music moved to the forefront until, by the end of the 1980s, ethnomusicology had assimilated the humanistic cultural anthropology of Clifford Geertz, Dennis Tedlock, James Clifford, George Marcus, Vincent Crapanzano, Paul Rabinow, and others, a far cry from the empirical anthropology Herzog had championed. Much of this ethnomusicological humanism eventually achieved theoretical expression in the "new fieldwork" (Barz and Cooley 1996) of reflexivity, reciprocity, and advocacy. Meanwhile, the scientific ethnomusicologists were in gradual retreat. A review of the essays in *Ethnomusicology* since about 1976 shows the balance point moving in the direction of music as culture rather than as form and structure. In 2010, the musicological ethnomusicologists came together outside SEM to form their own scholarly association (Analytical Approaches to World Music) with its own journal.[5]

Ethnomusicology's humanistic turn led a growing number of North American ethnomusicologists toward applied ethnomusicology in one form or another—advocating on behalf of individual musicians, musical communities, and musical life in particular places. The new fieldwork had become experience-centered, with ethnomusicological monographs such as those by Berliner (1978) and Keil (1979) reflecting this first-person turn to reflexivity. Kenneth Gourlay's 1982 essay in SEM's journal, "Towards a Humanizing Ethnomusicology," offered a theoretical basis for the new direction, along with a strongly worded critique of Merriam's insistence on science. In that same issue of *Ethnomusicology*, Charles Keil's (1982, 407) essay, "Applied Ethnomusicology and a Rebirth of Music from the Spirit of Tragedy," charted a path toward work that "can make a difference" through "an insistence on putting music into play wherever people are resisting their oppression." Keil's essay caught the spirit of the postcolonialism that was central to cultural critique in the new anthropology, and to critical theory in cultural studies. And because applied ethnomusicology did not become a movement until the era of decolonization, it could (and did) oppose colonialism, orientalism, and other manifestations of the arrogance of Western power, while answering (if not avoiding) the critiques of colonialism that were being (and that continue to be) leveled at applied anthropology. Meanwhile, an ever-increasing number of US ethnomusicologists were becoming involved in public folklore and were realizing that there was much good work to be done for music in the public arena.

A humanized ethnomusicology thus made it possible for a resurgence of a postcolonial applied ethnomusicology, manifesting itself not only in a new fieldwork based in reciprocity leading to advocacy but also through institutional gains within SEM. Applied ethnomusicology went mainstream within SEM during the 1990s. As the program chair for the 1989 SEM conference, I invited colleagues from my years in the early 1980s as a consultant for the NEA Folk Arts Division to present papers on a preplanned panel. Titled "From Perspective to Practice in Applied Ethnomusicology," the panel included the following presenters and papers: Robert Garfias, "What an Ethnomusicologist Can Do in Public Sector Arts"; Daniel Sheehy, "Applied Ethnomusicology as a State of Mind"; Charlotte Heth, "Getting It Right and Passing It On: The Ethnomusicologist and Cultural Transmission"; and Bess Lomax Hawes, "Practice Makes Perfect: Lessons in Active Ethnomusicology." When in 1990 I became editor of *Ethnomusicology*, this panel formed the starting point for a special issue titled "Ethnomusicology and the Public Interest," which featured articles by Daniel Sheehy, Bess Lomax Hawes, Martha Ellen Davis, and Anthony Seeger. This was the first time that applied ethnomusicology was featured in the SEM journal. In my introductory article for that special issue, I wrote that ethnomusicology in the public interest, which I termed "public ethnomusicology," "is work whose immediate end is not research and the flow of knowledge inside intellectual communities but, rather, practical action in the world outside of archives and universities" and that "as a way of knowing and doing, fieldwork [which is constitutive of ethnomusicology] at its best is based on a model of friendship between people rather than on a model involving antagonism, surveillance, the observation of physical objects, or the contemplation of abstract ideas" (Titon 1992a, 315, 321). Sheehy's (1992) article there began the process of constructing an alternative history for ethnomusicology in the United States, one in which applied work was more central. Hawes was invited to give the plenary Seeger Lecture at the 1993 SEM conference, and this autobiographical talk, meant in part to attract listeners to applied work as a calling, was published two years later in *Ethnomusicology* (Hawes 1995). In 1998, Keil (1998, 304), continuing in the vein of postcolonial critique and ever prophetic, called in the SEM journal for an "applied sociomusicology" that, by reclaiming participatory music making "for the vast majority," would help engender a revolution in consciousness that would overturn the global corporate capitalist world order and reverse the coming ecocatastrophe as we move toward "sustainable futures."

At the 1998 SEM conference, Doris Dyen and Martha Ellen Davis convened a meeting to assess interest in proposing a standing committee on applied ethnomusicology to the SEM board. Until that meeting, a single name for this activity had not yet risen to the surface; among those in circulation were "applied," "active," "action," "practice," "public," and "public sector" (Titon 1992a, 320–321). As applied ethnomusicologists themselves, with experience in the public sector and in the academic world, Davis and Dyen felt the time was opportune for organizing something more formal to bring together those with common interests in working for the benefit of musical communities in the public arena. Thirty-eight hopeful founders (the author of this essay among them) attended, their proposal was accepted by the SEM board of directors, and the committee was established, with a variety of definitions of applied ethnomusicology. In 2000, Dyen and Davis, who had taken on the role of chairs of the committee, appointed a deputy chair, Tom Van Buren, and successfully petitioned the board to recognize the group as the Applied Ethnomusicology Section. Dyen and Davis stood aside in 2002 while appointing cochairs Ric Alviso and Miriam Gerberg to join Van Buren, who stepped down in 2004 in favor of Mark Puryear. Alviso was succeeded in 2008 by Jeff Todd Titon, Gerberg in 2009 by Kathleen Noss Van Buren, Puryear in 2010 by Maureen Loughran, Noss Van Buren in 2014 by Michael Bakan, Loughran in 2015 by Erica Haskell, and Haskell in 2018 by Klisala Harrison.

During the committee and section's first decade, the cochairs worked to make the group a comfortable space within SEM for ethnomusicologists employed outside of the academic world. To that end, they organized practical panels on nonacademic careers for ethnomusicologists, such as the "Ethnomusicologists at Work" series, organized by Gerberg, and on strategies for survival both inside and outside official institutions. Cochairs Gerberg, Puryear, and Alviso established section prizes for outstanding presentations at SEM and awards for travel grants to the conference. In the new millennium, as applied ethnomusicology has become increasingly popular among graduate students and welcomed inside academic institutions, the section has become an SEM meeting place and platform for applied ethnomusicologists based both within and outside academia. Most recently, the section has sponsored panels involving themes such as music and politics, community advocacy, activism and "giving back," conflict resolution, ethics, repatriation of artifacts from archives and museums, medicine, the environment, and social justice. It also sponsors presentations from guests who do not normally attend the SEM conferences but who have worked in applied ethnomusicology either independently or in extra-academic institutions. For example, at the 2011 conference, Debora Kodish, public folklorist and director of the Philadelphia Folklore Project, led a section-sponsored discussion among traditional music and dance activists and community scholar-practitioners from the African American and Asian American communities in Philadelphia, showcasing a model for ethnomusicologists seeking strategies for work in community-based institutions. With more than three hundred members, Applied Ethnomusicology is now one of the largest and most active among the SEM sections, exceeded in membership only by the Student and the Popular Music sections.

As might be expected of a practical endeavor, theorization of applied ethnomusicology lagged behind practice, but recent years have witnessed an increasing number of publications and events centered on applied ethnomusicology itself. These included an international conference on applied ethnomusicology organized by Erica Haskell and Maureen Loughran at Brown University (Invested in Community 2003), a special issue of *Folklore Forum* devoted to applied ethnomusicology (Fenn 2003), a section devoted to applied ethnomusicology in an issue of *Ethnomusicology Review* (2012), and a book of essays, *Applied Ethnomusicology: Historical and Contemporary Approaches* (K. Harrison, Mackinlay, and Pettan 2010). Rebecca Dirksen (2012) authored an excellent overview of contemporary practice, with an emphasis on work by US-based ethnomusicologists, while Timothy Rice's (2014) book-length "very short introduction" to the discipline devotes the last two of nine chapters to what is in effect applied ethnomusicology. The *Oxford Handbook of Ethnomusicology*, first published in a one-volume clothbound edition in 2015, continued in this vein, offering a cross-section of contemporary international work in the field (Pettan and Titon 2015). In 2017, one entire day's programming of the annual SEM conference was devoted to public, public sector, and applied ethnomusicology. In response to the continued use of those three terms (public, public sector, and applied), Klisala Harrison (2017) reiterated that "applied" was the most appropriate term, particularly in the international context, and that "public" and "public sector" were best understood as subareas of "applied" that made sense only in certain national contexts.

Concluding this sketch of applied ethnomusicology in the United States, I do not mean to dismiss entirely the critique that applied ethnomusicology may be used for undesirable ends. Knowledge is not innocent; cultural information has a long history of being put to use for military purposes and colonial conquest. Music used in the service of a social or musical benefit may turn out to have negative consequences, or what looks like a benefit to one political entity may be a harm to another. Merriam's charge that applied ethnomusicologists are engaged in "manipulating people's destinies" is one way of looking at missionary work, for example, and it is a fact that missionaries have put their knowledge of music to use for that purpose for many centuries. Today, faith-based organizations such as SIL International put ethnomusicological knowledge to use in aiding local artists in indigenous communities with the goal of a "better future: one of justice, peace, joy, physical safety, social continuity and spiritual wholeness" (SIL International, n.d.) Other forces are intervening: corporations, governments, technology, the law, and so forth. Social responsibility requires social justice, cultural equity, and decolonization. I believe there is no self-correcting "invisible hand" in the marketplace or anywhere else that would permit scholars the luxury of research without social responsibility. Nor would scholars be well advised to accumulate knowledge and then supply it to those who in their ignorance would put it to use.

SEM had been slow to adopt a more active role, but recognition of the need for the organization to enter the larger political sphere has gradually come. For many years, SEM took the position that while ethnomusicologists were of course free to express their personal political views, the organization itself must not take a public political stand. But in 1976, the SEM *Newsletter* editor refused to print an employment advertisement from a university representing a government that practiced apartheid, an early harbinger of change. Not long afterward, SEM began endorsing resolutions supporting the rights of scholars detained by governments for political reasons and the rights of musicians to travel freely internationally. It has passed position statements on rights and discrimination, copyright ownership and sound recordings, and ethical considerations. Finally, in 2007, in response to a request from the SEM Ethics Committee, the SEM board of directors approved a "Position Statement against the Use of Music as Torture."⁶ Arising in response to numerous reports of music as part of the torture arsenal employed by US military and intelligence agencies and their allies against suspected terrorist detainees, it reads in part that SEM "calls for full disclosure of US government-sanctioned and funded programs that design the means of delivering music as torture; condemns the use of music as an instrument of torture; and demands that the US government and its agencies cease using music as an instrument of physical and psychological torture" (SEM Torture, n.d.). The position statement on music as torture was a significant step in SEM's evolution. It recognizes that ethnomusicologists are citizens of the world with social responsibilities and that our professional organization has not only the right but also the duty to represent the profession's ethical beliefs and act on them.

During the second decade of the twenty-first century, the SEM leadership's recognition of the ethnomusicologist's social responsibility continued to grow, fueled by increased interest in applied ethnomusicology among graduate students, many of whom were contemplating careers outside the academic world. At the University of Limerick, Ireland, in the same year that the *Oxford Handbook of Applied Ethnomusicology* was published (Pettan and Titon 2015), SEM and the International Council on Traditional Music (ICTM) sponsored a joint, three-day forum on the subject of an activist, community-engaged ethnomusicology, attended by more than one hundred ethnomusicologists from all over the world, at which the coeditors of that handbook were among the keynote speakers.⁷ As of 2019, a book of essays from that forum remains in preparation under the editorship of forum conveners Beverley Diamond and Salwa El Shawan Castelo-Branco. On publication, it will move both SEM and ICTM yet further toward *Transforming Ethnomusicology* (its tentative title) in an applied direction.

## Notes

1. Elsewhere in that *Oxford Handbook*, Pettan constructed a history of applied ethnomusicology in Europe and elsewhere, related to the growth of the International Council on Traditional Music, which was founded in 1947 as the International Folk Music Council (Pettan and Titon 2015, 30–56).

2. In Kunst's definition, ethnomusicology was chiefly a new name for the discipline of comparative musicology. But as we shall soon see, US cultural anthropologists interested in music saw opportunity in the new name, founded the international Society for Ethnomusicology in 1955, and were prominent among its leaders. Thus, by 1955 ethnomusicology could be described as a new and interdisciplinary field, not just a new name for an older academic discipline.

3. In a 2013 interview, he characterized as one of four "new, or newish developments in ethnomusicology" a "widespread concern with the need to do things that benefit the peoples whose music and musical culture are studied" (Nettl 2014, 1).

4. It didn't always work out that way, however. More colleges and universities either asked current faculty to develop a few of these courses or hired part-time instructors to teach them rather than adding full-time ethnomusicologists to their faculties.

5. In the new millennium, science is making a small comeback as music theory and comparative studies are applied in these analytical approaches to structural features of world musics. Science is manifest also in a growing interest among ethnomusicologists in neuroscience and music psychology, and questions concerning music and human evolution.

6. The proposal was brought to the ethics committee in 2004 by this writer, whereupon it was improved by then-committee chairman Laurel Sercombe, received a unanimously positive committee vote, and was sent up to the SEM executive board with a recommendation that they approve it as a SEM position statement. The board improved it further, due in no small part to the efforts of SEM president Philip Bohlman, and after months of deliberation issued it publicly on the SEM website. A press release followed; it received some media attention, and Bohlman was interviewed about it by conservative political pundit Hugh Hewitt who was skeptical while Bohlman defended it.

7. The forum was titled "Transforming Ethnomusicological Practice through Activism and Community Engagement" and was held in Limerick City, Ireland, September 13–16, 2015. Further information about it may be found at https://www.ictmusic.org/Joint-sem-ictm-forum-2015.

# II.
# CULTURAL AND MUSICAL SUSTAINABILITY

THIS SECTION'S ESSAYS ADDRESS CULTURAL AND MUSICAL SUSTAINABILITY with special reference to traditional music and expressive culture. For the past half century, the dominant strategy in the United States was conservation by means of identification, documentation, heritage designation, and then exhibition to tourists in museums, festivals, and the like as a part of the arts economy. About fifteen years ago UNESCO adopted the same strategy, designating various traditional arts to be "intangible cultural heritage" and extending conservation to the global arena, as I explain in chapter 8. But marking traditional music and expressive culture as heritage and then marketing it for tourists brings about negative as well as positive consequences. Sustainability offers certain advantages over conservation as a means of conceptualizing cultural integrity and maintaining continuity in the face of inevitable cultural and musical change. The first essay in this section reflects my field research and partnership with Old Regular Baptists, a religious community that in many ways represents the traditional ideal of the folk society, and centers on what happened to them before, during, and after they and their music were exhibited at the largest folk festival in the United States, the Smithsonian Folklife Festival. The last two essays address sustainability directly, advocating an ecological approach to musical and cultural sustainability that is based in strategies of resilience and adaptive management.

# 6

## "THE REAL THING"

### Tourism, Authenticity, and Pilgrimage among the Old Regular Baptists at the 1997 Smithsonian Folklife Festival

*I*N 1976, WHILE WORKING FOR THE SMITHSONIAN FOLKLIFE *Festival, I began to think about exhibition and cultural tourism as a way to promote and preserve traditional cultural practices by means of their display at museums, festivals, and historical sites. The festival had the best of intentions and raised the profile of the folk arts in Washington, DC. It was an important catalyst in establishing the Folk Arts Division of the National Endowment for the Arts and the American Folklife Center at the Library of Congress. At the same time, the 1976 festival was challenging, and despite its many benefits for the performers honored to be chosen to demonstrate their skills, a few were misunderstood and not well treated (Titon 2015a). As public folklore in the 1980s became allied with arts councils and invested in supporting heritage tourism as an engine for the arts economy, I felt, as did several other folklorists, that folk arts funding would be more effective if aimed directly at the artists and into their communities, rather than in offering up a mediated authenticity in exhibits to individuals outside those communities (Titon 1979). Robert Cantwell (1991, 1993) wrote an article and then a book,* Ethnomimesis, *exploring this subject in depth. But my later experiences as a blues tourist in the Mississippi Delta in 1993 and as a participant in the 1997 Smithsonian Folk Festival were more positive than my earlier ones and different from Cantwell's. They deepened my understanding of the consequences of heritage tourism and the folk arts. I wrote about blues tourism in the afterword to the second edition of* Early Downhome Blues *(1995c) and elsewhere during the 1990s. A few months after the event, I received an unsolicited document from one of the Old Regular Baptists whom I'd presented at the*

*1997 festival, a write-up of her and the others' trip, which she titled "The Baptists Go to Washington." A remarkable statement about their experiences, it helped me put together a number of strands in thinking about the exhibition of culture. This essay was the result. I've continued writing about heritage tourism, the arts economy, and the substitution of economic value for cultural values now and again on my sustainable music blog (Titon 2008–). Lobley (2014) offers a thoughtful and accurate summary of my views. My most recent consideration of "the real thing" is an essay on authenticity and authentication (Titon 2012a).*

In 1997, six Old Regular Baptists from southeast Kentucky demonstrated their traditional lined-out hymnody at the Smithsonian's Festival of American Folklife. The group's appearance there, timed to coincide with the release of an album on Smithsonian Folkways, was successful because they shared a common purpose with the festival organizers: they were "the real thing," and the power of their singing created a human community where before there only was an idea of one. On returning home, a member of their group wrote about their trip in response to a request from a member of her church. She framed their experiences in terms of travel, tourism, and pilgrimage. In considering their experiences in light of the aims of the festival, this essay joins a growing literature on authenticity, authority, reflexivity, folklore, and festival policy and administration.

Henry James's ([1893] 2015) short story "The Real Thing" suggests one of the reasons why tourist sites hire actors and impersonators. The story's protagonist is a talented painter who seeks models. One day, an old couple enter his studio. They are not models but the real thing—an aristocratic British couple. Down on their luck, they decide to try modeling. The artist is ecstatic. Instead of painting actors, he has a chance to paint authentic aristocrats. But the experiment is a failure. After trial and error, the artist realizes he cannot use them. They don't know how to model. He is unable to do justice to his conception. In this situation, acting, not authenticity, is required. The artist goes back to models. What happens when a tourist site, in this case the Smithsonian Institution's Festival of American Folklife, traffics in authenticity, hires the real thing, and presents it on a stage is the subject of this essay.

In 1997, I helped arrange for six Old Regular Baptist singers from the coal-mining region of the southern Appalachian Mountains to spend a week at the Festival of American Folklife (hereafter FAF), the largest folk festival in the United States.[1] They were "the real thing." For part of each day, they demonstrated and spoke about their traditional music in front of tourists visiting the festival.[2] In my official role of FAF presenter, I acted as a liaison between the festival and them, introduced them before they sang, made sure they had a chance to speak for themselves, and facilitated their demonstrations. When they were not needed at the festival, they visited many of the popular DC tourist sites. In a dual role, they were both tourists experiencing heritage and employees demonstrating heritage to tourists. I begin this essay by providing background on the Old Regular Baptists, their music and the scholarly literature on it, and my involvement with them and with the festival. I next address that literature and discuss themes of music, tourism, heritage and the conservation (that is, preservation and encouragement) of folk culture, theatricality, authenticity, and reflexivity as they bear on the FAF experiences of this group. Finally, I consider these issues both in light of an extempore talk that their leader, Elwood Cornett, gave to the audience in their last demonstration, in which he articulated the vision of the festival, and in light of a narrative of their experiences, "The Baptists Go to Washington," written by one of the Old Regular Baptists shortly after their return to Kentucky from the festival (Fields 1997). Grethel (Dosh) Fields's narrative is a humorous and delightful account of the encounter between six Old Regular Baptists, Washington's tourist sites, and the Smithsonian's Festival of American Folklife. It was not written at the suggestion of a scholar wanting to study participants' views on folk festivals; rather, it was produced after a member of the writer's church asked about her trip to Washington. It shows that foremost on her mind were feelings about the people and places they encountered, not the abstract ideas of authenticity, contextualization, presentation, and cultural conservation that bedevil the proponents and critics of folk festivals.

## Music of the Old Regular Baptists

Old Regular Baptists are concentrated in the central portions of the southern Appalachian Mountains of the United States: southeastern Kentucky, southern West Virginia, and southwestern Virginia. Subsistence farming in the nineteenth century and coal mining in the twentieth century has characterized the regional economy. Some Old Regular Baptists are blue-collar workers, some are white-collar workers, some are housewives, some are bosses, and some are unemployed; some are well educated and others have a grade school education; some live in expensive homes and others do not. In their geographical region, they are the single largest religious denomination; they represent a cross-section of the population. Howard Dorgan estimated about fifteen thousand in nine associations of churches, each church with its own members and church house (Dorgan 1989). They separated from the United

Baptists early in the nineteenth century as part of the conservative antimission movement among Baptists (see Wallhausser in Cornett, Titon, and Wallhausser 1997). Their doctrine of election by grace descends from the Calvinist wing of the Reformation. God issues a call and the sinner is free to respond or not respond, but salvation rests entirely with the Lord, and the most assurance a person can hold in this walk of life is a "lively hope" of heaven. They practice foot washing as an ordinance of Christ, along with taking the bread and wine at an annual communion. Children and teenagers attend services with the adults; there are no Sunday schools or missions. Baptism is by total immersion in a nearby river, lake, or stream. An Old Regular Baptist Sunday morning worship service begins unofficially with a period of fellowship in the church sanctuary. Everyone greets one another, shaking hands and often embracing. From about 9:30 until 10:00 a.m., the congregation lifts its voice singing praise to God. Prayer and anywhere from four to six intoned sermons follow, most sermons preceded by a song and each based on texts from the Bible. A song, an invitation to join the church, and a closing prayer conclude the service at about 12:15 p.m. Church buildings, like cemeteries (fig. 6.1), are modest and located mainly in the countryside rather than in the towns throughout this predominantly rural region. Each church meets but once per month, on a designated weekend. Old Regular Baptists attend their home church—that is, the church where they have their membership—once per month, and on the other Sundays they visit neighboring Old Regular Baptist churches of their choice. In this way, they get to fellowship with many more people than if their home church met every Sunday. It is a close and caring community.

Old Regular Baptist lined-out hymnody is characterized by heterophonic unison singing; elaborated, melismatic melodies; free rhythm; and the British tune stock that was responsible for the old ballads, songs, and fiddle tunes collected in the southern Appalachian Mountains.[3] They permit neither choirs nor musical instruments in their worship. They sing at home, on the job occasionally, outdoors in the natural world, and of course in church. The entire congregation is invited to worship the Lord in song together, and most participate. They use the term "song" (as in songs of Zion) rather than "hymn." Their song books contain words only, without musical notation. Among the churches in the Indian Bottom Association that I visited, most of the song texts are taken from eighteenth- and nineteenth-century English devotional poets and hymn writers such as Isaac Watts. Although they have more modern song books available at the pulpit, their favorites are the *Sweet Songster* (1854), compiled by Edward Billups, and the *Thomas Hymnal* (1877), compiled

Figure 6.1. Old Regular Baptist Cemetery, Kentucky, 1993. Photo by Jeff Todd Titon.

by E. D. Thomas. The congregation does not use the books when singing in a worship service; they either catch the words from the song leader (who does look at the song book), or they have committed them to memory. The song leader, who must be male, sings a line, and then the congregation joins in singing and repeats the text but to a tune different from the leader's lining tune. The songs proceed line by line in this way. Men take turns leading the songs. The congregation recalls the tunes from memory; no one uses musical notation. The melodies exist in oral tradition only. Nicholas Temperley (1981) has traced their singing style from the sixteenth-century English parish church to colonial America, where it predominated. In fact, it was given sanction under Cromwell's government, as the 1644 Westminster Assembly of Divines recommended lining-out throughout Britain and its colonies. During the eighteenth and nineteenth centuries, this "old way of singing," as it was called, gave way to reform movements that brought musical instruments, note reading, polyphony, and eventually, gospel song into American Protestant churches. The old way of singing prevails among certain Baptist congregations in central Appalachia today. Of course, the repertoire shows the influence of postcolonial hymns, spirituals, camp meeting songs, and gospel hymnody; however, their techniques of lining out and heterophonic melodic elaboration are at least four hundred years old. African American Baptists carry a related tradition of lined-out hymnody, even more elaborate than that of the Old Regulars, which they call "surge singing" and "Dr. Watts hymns" after Isaac Watts. A related tradition, involving the lined-out singing of Gaelic psalms, continues among Scots on the Isle of Lewis (Macleod 1975).

In the central Appalachian region generally, lined-out hymnody appears in decline. When William Tallmadge made field recordings of lined-out hymnody in eastern Kentucky in the 1970s, he found that it was decreasing among the United Baptists and Primitive Baptists. Even among the Old Regulars, lined-out hymnody was clearly in competition with gospel song in certain associations, notably in the Thornton Union Association, where some people improvise harmonies within the lined-out style. The fact is that song writers exist among them and that some of their recently composed songs, on gospel song models, have come to be included in the modern song books that can be found in the churches along with the *Sweet Songster* and *Thomas Hymnal*. These and other gospel songs are sung solo, in duets, trios, or quartets, at special times within the worship service. It is not unusual to hear a preacher in the Indian Bottom Association take time before his sermon to sing a popular gospel song. In this way, lined-out hymnody coexists with gospel song in the region.

Yet it would be an oversimplification to say that lined-out hymnody among the Indian Bottom Association Old Regular Baptists is endangered. It can be heard in their churches every Sunday morning (and most Saturdays, when they have business meetings). Singing is an important activity, in church and at home. Overall, the active repertory of lined-out hymnody, as I recorded it, consists of at least a hundred tunes and a somewhat larger number of texts (as more than one text can be sung to the same tune). Among Old Regular Baptists, Primitive Baptists, and United Baptists, Tallmadge recorded 305 hymn texts altogether. Still, its preservation requires effort. Like the seeds of heirloom flowers and vegetables, these songs must be kept in use if they will survive. There is competition from gospel songs. Tellingly, though, when the Indian Bottom Association churches take gospel songs into their repertory, they adapt them to their practice—that is, they line them out. If the gospel song has a chorus, the chorus is lined and sung once, as if it were just another verse. They understand that the meaning or message is in the words of the song, rather than style of singing. Among group members, arguments that favor the preservation of Old Regular Baptist singing because these traditions help make their way of worship uniquely satisfying in spiritual terms can be persuasive, but such arguments are complicated.

## My Involvement

In 1979, William Tallmadge and Loyal Jones convened a conference at Berea College in south-central Kentucky on rural hymnody that, besides scholarly papers, included a performance by a group of Old Regular Baptist singers invited for the occasion and a field trip to a Sunday worship service. This was where I first encountered Old Regular Baptist singing, and I resolved to return. In 1990, I spent a semester as Goode Visiting Professor of Appalachian Studies at Berea and welcomed the opportunity to hear Old Regular Baptist singing in its church context. With the help of John Wallhausser, a professor of religion at Berea College, I was introduced to Elwood Cornett, the moderator (head) of the Indian Bottom Association of Old Regular Baptists, a group of about thirty churches and fifteen hundred people chiefly in Letcher, Knott, and Perry Counties, Kentucky. Cornett, who holds a master's degree in education, is retired from a career that included years of teaching school, twenty-five years as the head of an educational purchasing cooperative in southeastern Kentucky, and an appointment as one of Kentucky's twenty-five "distinguished educators" who were sent in to troubleshoot and upgrade the performance of students and teachers in school districts where test scores were low. A distinguished minister as well as an educator, he is well known in the region. Most Sundays during the spring semester of 1990, Wallhausser and I drove two to three hours each way into the mountains and visited with the Old Regulars, attending church services and some wonderful dinners afterward. I noticed that a few church members were capturing the services with inexpensive, battery-operated tape recorders that they rested on the seats unobtrusively. They enjoyed listening to these recordings and made copies for their friends and relatives who were unable to attend. When I asked, I was told that I, too, could make tape recordings in the churches, so long as it would not interfere with their worship activities. I held a small microphone and tape recorder at my seat in the congregation. Photography inside the Indian Bottom churches during worship was not allowed.

I continued to find the music profoundly attractive, and I wanted to join in. But singing this slow-paced music was challenging. The music defied Western notation. Tallmadge had transcribed some of it, but in so doing he regularized and misrepresented it by giving it a metrical signature. Not only did the music lack meter, but it also had no regular beat. Although I could hear tune contours and the general melodic outlines, it was hard to discern the melodies precisely. Each singer elaborated a slightly different melody. Some singers inserted more (and some fewer) melismatic tones between the principal melodic notes. (One of the singers, Ivan Amburgey, known for his melodic elaborations, laughingly told me that an outsider asked him whether, in order to produce those added tones, he did not have extra vocal cords.) Knowing when to move to the next note and what that note could be was something I learned, more or less, through much listening and trial and error. Fortunately, the melodic grammar was familiar to me from the tune stock. In my mind, I was gradually able to construct skeletal melodies from that ocean of sound. These I could sing with a bit more confidence (particularly when alone in my automobile, the volume on the cassette player turned up high). Eventually, I realized that when the singers were of one mind, or as the Old Regular Baptist minister I. D. Back put it, "tuned up with the grace of God," line lengths turned out to be regular; the differences among analogous lines from one verse to the next were only a few tenths of a second, in periods that lasted from fifteen to more than twenty seconds (Titon 2005). Sometimes during the worship services I turned off my tape recorder and sang along. I felt that I had both known and been searching for these melodies since I was a teenager. A few months along in trying to learn the melodies, I was joined at church one Sunday by two curious colleagues who had come to Berea for a conference. Although musically talented, they were at a loss. I encouraged them to sing along, but they could not find the melodies.[4]

## Recording for the Smithsonian Institution

Some older church members had told me they feared that not enough younger people were learning to lead the singing. Doing so requires more than just familiarity with the melodies of several songs. Recall that besides its melody, each song has a unique (and ornate) lining tune, which the leader must learn if he is to perform his role. That is, the leader gives out the line solo, using a tune that is both different from and more highly elaborated than the tune that the congregation sings when they join in to repeat the words. A good song leader not only knows several lining tunes (one for each song) but sings loudly and has the ability to pitch the songs in a comfortable range. (Occasionally the song leader may pitch a song too high or too low; after a line or two when this becomes apparent, the leader may stop the song and begin again at a more comfortable pitch.) A Sunday's song leading is ideally shared among a half dozen men, but in some churches the number of potential song leaders is smaller than that.

I was told that the future of their singing was a subject of discussion among the Indian Bottom Association and that an effort had been made to bring experienced song leaders together with younger church members who wanted to learn to line out. The resulting teaching workshops had not been effective. In this group of modest people, the pressure for students to perform publicly at a workshop made learning difficult. It occurred to me, particularly after thinking about the small tape recorders that some church members were bringing to the services, that high-quality tape recordings of Old Regular Baptist singing, circulated on cassettes through the community, might give some future song leaders an opportunity to practice alone. The quality of the boom box recordings was insufficient for this purpose.[5]

In June 1992, I proposed a digital recording project to Elwood Cornett. He liked the idea, and we discussed how it might be implemented. All of us would participate without being paid. He would ask all who would be interested in participating to join in a singing session, not a regular worship service, at one of their churches where the acoustics were reasonably good. We would invite John Wallhausser to attend. I would bring digital equipment and make the recording. I would make copies and give them to Cornett. One set of copies would be kept with other archival materials by the Indian Bottom Association and another set would circulate among the members of the association, who could freely copy it. Further, I would approach Anthony Seeger and Smithsonian Folkways to see if they would publish a documentary CD and cassette with selections from these field recordings. The publication would be available to scholars, the general public, and (at cost) to the Old Regulars. No one would make a profit from it. Against the possibility that some might charge the Indian Bottom Association with vanity, they could point to the nonprofit status of the Smithsonian, coupled with its mission as the national museum and its interest in selecting this music for publication.

Approximately seventy-five people attended the Defeated Creek church for the singing session on August 20, 1992. Prior to the singing, Cornett emphasized the preservation aspects of the project, telling the assembled group that it would not be wise if their generation lost a tradition that had been kept by their forebears for some four hundred years. After they sang fifteen songs, Cornett invited all who wished to speak into the microphone to say what singing meant to them. Cornett wanted these statements in the record also. Many spoke about how this way of singing affected them, and how they hoped it would continue for generations to come. Reviewing the recordings when I returned to New England, I was satisfied with their quality. I found the statements moving and was pleased that Cornett had thought to ask for them. I sent cassette copies to Cornett for his evaluation, and he gave his approval. We also agreed that if I could find a way to return in the following year, he would issue another invitation and I would record another session. We did that on June 10, 1993, and another twelve songs were recorded.

We moved ahead with Smithsonian Folkways. In the fall of 1992, at the annual conference of the Society for Ethnomusicology, I played excerpts from my 1992 digital recordings for Seeger. About six months later, we had his agreement that Folkways would bring out an album. I asked Cornett and Wallhausser to write essays for the accompanying notes. Those essays, and my own, took far longer than we hoped they would, but in March 1995, I forwarded to Seeger a DAT master tape along with the essays. We waited for Folkways to bring out the album. Early in 1997, I received a telephone call from Seeger's assistant, Amy Horowitz, who asked me whether I thought some Old Regulars would be willing to participate in the Smithsonian's Festival of American Folklife for a week or two in June of the same year. I said I didn't know but would be glad to ask them. I had worked at the festival as a presenter twice before, in 1976 and 1992, and I could explain to the Old Regulars what it would entail. The FAF planners were looking for participants in a Sacred Sounds area for which they had decided that one of the festival themes would be religious music and dance from various parts of the world.

If I thought the Old Regulars might be willing to come and if I could come along and present them, Horowitz would bring their music to the planners' attention; if they liked it and the possibility of the Old Regulars' appearing in the FAF, it would be a good idea to hurry the production of the album and time its release for the festival.

I got in touch with Cornett at once. I said that the festival would frame their singing as a demonstration, not as a theatrical performance. They would not, for example, be asked to perform in a churchlike building constructed for the purpose. Rather, they would demonstrate their singing to an audience and talk to them about it. I said that although their decision should be based on whether they wanted to appear at the festival, a side effect of their agreement would be that Smithsonian Folkways would put the album into production and try to have it ready for the festival. He was favorably disposed and wondered how many singers the FAF wanted to bring to the festival. I said I thought anywhere from a half dozen to a dozen. He said that it would be easier to find a half dozen, and he would try. With that, I took up the conversation with Horowitz once more and learned that the FAF planners wanted the Old Regulars at the festival. The album would go into production immediately, and plans for their appearance at the festival would proceed. Smithsonian Folkways was as good as its word. The album appeared just in time for the festival. Three couples—Elwood Cornett and his wife, Kathy, Jim Fields and his wife, Dosh (and their daughter Renée), and Don Pratt and his wife, Shirley—drove to Washington, where I met them. Two or three times a day for a half hour or so, they demonstrated their singing to an audience of tourists.

## The Smithsonian's Festival of American Folklife

The Smithsonian Institution's Festival of American Folklife is a multicultural, international event, since 1967 staged annually in the nation's capital on the Mall (a large public promenade taking up the equivalent of several city blocks) between the Lincoln Memorial and Washington Monument. It is the largest, by far the most expensive, and longest-lasting folk festival in the United States. Typically, it runs for two weeks during late June and early July and offers a few hundred singers, musicians, dancers, storytellers, crafters, and other folk artists to the public in an outdoor museum setting meant to celebrate the diverse folkways of the United States and other lands. S. Dillon Ripley, the head of the Smithsonian, in 1973 expressed the rationale for the festival: "We are a conservation organization, and it seems to us that conservation extends to human cultural practices. The possibility of a historical documentary museum as a theater of live performance where people actually show that the objects in cases were made by human hands, and are still being made, practiced on, worked with, is a very valuable asset for our role as a preserver and conservator of living cultural forms, and should be understood in those terms" (Festival of American Folklife 1973).

The festival presents these folk artists free of charge on stages, in tents, and open-air spots in a celebratory atmosphere, where they perform and demonstrate for an audience made up primarily of tourists and secondarily of Washington bureaucrats taking a break from work. The events are open to all; the festival is not highly publicized, and for many tourists, it is just one more stop along the way. A small minority of visitors, however, specifically return to the festival year after year. A tourist, after all, is a traveler looking for recreation, enjoyment, and perhaps education outside his or her ordinary environment. Tourist sites such as museums and folk festivals offer mediated, recontextualized experiences. A visitor or participant in a court of law would expect to experience a trial, not a mediated representation of one. But bring a lawyer to a folk festival, have her demonstrate her techniques of courtroom narrative from a stage, and the act requires contextualization.

The festival is operated by the Smithsonian's Center for Folklife Programs and Cultural Studies (CFPCS), formerly the Office of Folklife Programs.[6] During the more than thirty years that the FAF has run, the staff has implemented a cultural policy that involves more than merely a demonstration and preservation theater. Theirs is a vision of a multicultural world living in harmony, celebrating mutuality while learning from one another's different traditions. In line with their liberal, inclusionary ideological legacy from the civil rights movement of the 1960s, the CFPCS has emphasized Native American cultures (more than 130 tribes since 1970); African American cultures and their relation to the African diaspora; relations between American immigrant cultures and their counterparts in the Old World; and the cultures of working Americans and occupational folklife, such as construction workers, cowboys, farmers, truck drivers, and in a departure from their emphasis on working-class Americans, trial lawyers. The FAF regularly also features folklife from a single state of the union.[7] In 1987, for example, the featured state was Michigan; in 1997, the featured area was the Mississippi Delta.

The CFPCS staff plans the festival each year. Typically, the staff chooses three or four area and/or thematic emphases. Once the principal areas are selected, a curator for each area consults with folklorists, ethnomusicologists, anthropologists, local community leaders, government officials, corporations, and philanthropists to survey and determine whom to invite and how best to present them. In 1997, the Old Regular Baptists were part of a Sacred Sounds area, involving singers and instrumentalists from various parts of the world. (The two other areas were the Mississippi Delta and African immigrants in Washington, DC.)

The Old Regular Baptists are the kind of folk community that the FAF wishes to present. CFPCS definitions of folklife draw on definitions of the "folk" as a community with artistic practices that go back several generations, based on aesthetic standards that are widely shared and transmitted informally within the folk group. Their "Guidelines for Research," a statement meant to guide fieldworkers' decisions on what is and is not authentic, offers the following definition of folk cultural traditions: "community-based forms of knowledge, skill and expression learned through informal relationships and exhibiting intergenerational continuity. Typical genres include oral tradition, social custom, material culture and its supportive knowledge, and the folk arts. Forms of folk culture are traditional to the extent that they maintain standards or values which have continuity with, and are informed by, past practice. They are living traditions to the extent that they are practiced, and are socially integrated within community life and speak to its cognitive, normative, affective, and aesthetic concerns" (Office of Folklife Programs 1988).

This document distinguishes authentic folk cultural practice from the formal, schooled, academic "elite" traditions such as classical music and the fine arts. But the word "folk" has in recent decades taken on another connotation outside of official and academic culture. Today, most Americans picture a folk musician to be a singer-songwriter with an acoustic guitar. When tourist sites, such as old-time seaports, hire these musicians to sing sea chanteys for visitors, they are hiring actors, models (in the sense of James's short story) better suited to performances than, presumably, "the real thing" would be, if the real thing could be found. The FAF means to present the real thing, however. Their guidelines therefore take pains to distinguish authentic folk cultural practice from what the general public thinks of as "folk music": "Folk cultural forms may be appropriated by exogenous individuals and organizations and enter popular or elite culture in refracted ways. 'Folk' or 'folk-rock' music, for example, familiar to most Americans, is a genre of popular music rather than a form of authentic folk culture. Typically, folk traditions can be said to be non-authentic when they are mediated through exogenous agencies. Such a mediation disarticulates a particular folk form from its social, cultural, historical, aesthetic, biographical and ecological context" (Office of Folklife Programs 1988).

That the CFPCS is in fact an "exogenous agency" mediating folk traditions through the FAF, thereby "disarticulating" the various folk forms from their contexts, is only one of the ironies of their enterprise. A small but growing literature critical of the FAF has explored the festival from the points of view of the CFPCS organizers, festival presenters, fieldworkers, and folk artist participants. This literature turns on the concept of authenticity.

The CFPCS idea of authenticity, explained in the guidelines, has a lengthy history within folklore studies. Folklorists have frequently seen themselves as arbiters of the difference between genuine folklore and spurious "fakelore," traditions invented by nonfolk, often industrial corporations (the Paul Bunyan myth is a good example), or the popular culture (Pokémon is the current representative). But requirements that authentic folk artists learn their skills in the time-honored ways within folk communities preclude the possibility that community outsiders could ever be counted among the authentic practitioners of the folk arts. Practically, this prevents people without a birthright in folk communities from representing folk arts at the FAF. In a nation where people believe in equal opportunity, this requirement strikes some as arbitrary and elitist. The fact is, of course, that communities, like families, adopt people who were not born into them. But, again, from a practical viewpoint, the FAF has difficulty authenticating such practitioners.

A typical problem with FAF authentication is cited by Sommers (1994a, 184–185). An African American blues singer, Eddie Bums, had been touring with a young, white harmonica player. The festival was interested in hiring only Bums. Thus, the FAF has sometimes been rightly criticized for perpetuating outmoded stereotypes of folk communities. Cantwell (1993) has deflected this critique, exploring the positive aspects of stereotyping that take place in the festival. Put another way, by its nature the festival constructs a stereotype (folk culture) as its object of study to begin with. The festival also works hard to deconstruct, or transcend, or problematize, the simple stereotype of folk culture that the visitor may hold. The Bums example is also poignant in my experience, for during the late 1960s when I was in graduate school, I played rhythm guitar in a blues band led by Lazy Bill Lucas, an African American. I had come to this tradition only in high school, as a white child of the folk revival. We played in several local venues, and we appeared together at some blues festivals, notably the one at Ann Arbor, Michigan, in 1970. Would I have resented it if the FAF had wanted to hire Bill alone? No. In this context, I would have gone along to cheer him on. The CFPCS vision is not one of folk communities as little ethnic villages ready to battle one another but as citizens of a multicultural nation, accepting, sharing, and celebrating, while maintaining their traditions and identities.

The FAF has been criticized on a number of other grounds. I will examine them chiefly in light of the 1997 appearance of the Old Regular Baptists. One point is ideology: the festival's notion of folklore as the possession of marginalized, usually working-class groups is said to be a legacy of colonial liberalism that "other"-izes, exoticizes, and turns the festival participants into a "folk," whether the participants conceive of themselves that way or approve of the categorization. Burt Feintuch (1989, 12–13) writes, "In modem academic folklore theory and the work it inspires there has been a tendency to move away from the discipline's historical focus on minority and marginalized groups.... All groups have folklore, or so the reasoning goes.... But, for better or worse, in the public sector folklorists tend to focus on such groups." Because it exists only in an oral tradition, within a comparatively small geographic area, and it sounds so different from mainstream American music, Old Regular Baptist hymnody appears exotic to most Americans. Their music is marginal in comparison with the mass-mediated music popular throughout the nation. However, as I pointed out earlier, in their geographic region they are not marginalized people. In central Appalachia, they are numerous and a force to be reckoned with, economically and politically as well as spiritually. And musically: as Mark Slobin (1993) has noted, the world is filled with "micromusics" like theirs which, though they may seem marginal to the outside world, are in good health within their regions.

An oft-heard criticism of the FAF is that the festival planners are paternalistic and controlling. When they select folk artists, they are said to apply strict academic criteria of authenticity that sometimes differ from the standards that the community applies. The CFPCS, after all, chooses the participants, determines how they will be presented, and discourages them (if discouragement is needed) from representing nontraditional activities or repertoire, even though in their local communities they may well engage in them. The Old Regular Baptists who went to the festival met the strict criteria, however, and were representative of a community that holds to their musical traditions. To be sure, there are currents of change within the community; yet it is also true that in the Indian Bottom Association, change is very carefully considered, and if change is desired, it is very deliberately implemented.

The FAF has been blamed for presenting a romanticized view of a happy folk community that shares values as well as aesthetics. Of course no community is without stress and difficulty. But the critics point out that if the festival were to represent the community truly, it should also display their disagreements and dysfunctional aspects (see Feintuch 1989; Sommers 1994a). Now, it is true that Old Regular Baptists, like most groups, including university professors, argue among themselves over matters both trivial and profound. It might have been interesting to try to stage a debate over whether the churches should permit singers to harmonize. In some churches in at least one association, a few singers do keep harmony, and presumably the practice is condoned there. It might also have been interesting to engage in a debate over whether the churches should encourage gospel songs at the expense of the lined-out hymnody. No doubt there are some Old Regulars who believe that this is what they want. I would love to have seen them persuaded, in this case, that lined-out hymnody should be continued, not because it is a tradition worth keeping but because among Old Regular Baptists this music, sung in this way, best awakens them to worship the Lord in song. But why should a festival promote adversarial relations? Imagine including in a couple's wedding anniversary celebration the representation of some dysfunctional moments in their life together!

Another critique has to do more with the way the festival is run than with ideology. Although the CFPCS has a budget for fieldwork to identify folk traditions and artists, fieldworkers complain that they are underpaid, overworked, and that their recommendations often go unheeded (see Leary 1994). Others charge that in some areas the FAF functions as a "Rolodex festival"[8] that relies on recycling previously identified, well-known folk artists rather than discovering new ones. The result is that although balance is sought, the festival often has to take what has already been found, leavened by the concerns of local and national politics (Sommers 1994a, 193–194). Finally, in any event on the scale of the FAF requiring a hierarchical chain of command and almost military logistics, friction among festival staff and participants is inevitable, mistakes are made, and people are not always well served. To my knowledge, Old Regular Baptists never before had appeared at this, or any other, festival to demonstrate their singing; however, in this case, the field research had already been done and their music was sitting at the CFPCS across the hall, waiting to be heard. (Actually not—Smithsonian Folkways unaccountably had lost the master DAT tape. However, I kept a cloned backup and sent it to them once they realized they were not going to find the original.) As we shall see, they were impressed with the personal kindnesses of the CFPCS organizers and FAF staff many times over and felt they were very well served.

By the time of the 1997 festival, the CFPCS had responded to many of these criticisms and prepared a twenty-two-page *Participant Handbook*, attending not only to demonstration and performance on the festival grounds but to details of travel, food, and housing as well. "If you misplace your [airline] ticket on the day you are scheduled to travel, please call [here they give a phone number] and ask for Barbara Strickland. We will make arrangements for you to fly" (Center for Folklife Programs and Cultural Studies 1997a, 5). This shows not only the level of detail but the type of logistical problem that the FAF must deal with. Presenters were given a twenty-six-page, typewritten, double-spaced manuscript; this helpful "Presenter's Guide" clarified the presenter's role and the CFPCS's expectations (Center for Folklife Programs and Cultural Studies 1997b). I did not remember a presenter's guide from the 1976 festival. Perhaps the FAF staff had assumed that as good folklorists and ethnomusicologists, presenters would share the organizers' goals, obey their orders, and put theory into practice without much needing to be told how or why. The CFPCS's usual response to criticism has not been to argue but to explain themselves further (see, e.g., Kurin 1994). Their idealism was integral to the FAF from the beginning. The festival's critics have lost sight of, or patience with, the broad liberal vision on which the FAF is based.

Two aspects of the literature on the FAF are of particular relevance here. The first is an analogy in which the festival is understood as theater; the second concerns attempts to find out how participants felt about their experiences. Festival as ritual theater is scarcely a new concept; however, in the context of a museum where authentic representation is meant to take precedence over the staged, scripted, and acted, hence false, the theatrical metaphor is both critical and daring. Robert Cantwell (1993) has written about "ethnomimesis," the imitation and representation, the "conjuring" of folk culture in performance at the FAF, calling attention to those magical moments in which something new and brilliant is forged. The CFPCS, while it was at best ambivalent about Cantwell's work—he was hired to write a history of the FAF, and then after he showed some of his work, he was fired—does not wholly reject the theatrical metaphor. Some of their associates, notably Alan Lomax and Bess Lomax Hawes, consider the most important success of this type of event not to be its impact on the audience but rather on the cast of performers, whose energy and dedication to their folk arts are increased by the camaraderie and common purpose of their involvement with like-spirited people (see Hawes 1992). As Laurie Sommers (1994a, 197) characterizes this view, "Ultimately, festival culture creates a synergy of its own. Concern for authenticity is replaced by a hope that all the preparation will allow something far more powerful to occur." I do not agree with the view that FAF concern for authenticity is replaced, however. In my view, that "something far more powerful" occurs precisely when the power of authenticity is acknowledged and emotional bonds are forged among participants. This can happen when the audience is invited to participate.

I observed some powerful moments like this with the Old Regulars at the 1997 FAF. Always, the frame was demonstration and discussion. The idea that they should be presented as acting out a performance of worship in song was repugnant to them, to me, and to the FAF organizers. Yet many experienced spiritual feelings during their singing. In fact, at the end of each demonstration, Cornett asked the audience to join in singing "Amazing Grace." This was not something an FAF staff member had asked him to do; as far as I know, it was his idea, his response to the situation. I remember he discussed it with me beforehand and asked if I thought it would be all right. I said I thought it would. After some demonstrations, they were approached by people from the audience who said that they had felt something. This was not sought, but it was not an unwelcome response either. It showed that what was happening was not theater. Rather, it transcended the tourist frame to become real. Toward the end of their last demonstration, when the audience was very large and the CFPCS organizers were in attendance, Cornett extemporized a speech (I print excerpts from it below) that forged emotional bonds. The Old Regulars followed it with "Amazing Grace" and a period in which everyone present shook hands (following the practice of fellowship in Old Regular Baptist churches) that enacted those bonds in a moving and appropriate way.

### The Indiana Project: Ethnography of Participant Experience

What has been the impact of the festival on the participants? Anecdotal evidence over the years suggested a number of things, from the positives of rededication to the negatives of jealousy within the home community (see Sommers 1994b, 239–241; Leary 1994). Dissatisfied with the nature of this evidence and hoping to involve Indiana University graduate students from the Folklore Institute in a project that would combine public sector work with academic study, institute director Richard Bauman contacted the CFPCS staff and arranged for a team of folklorists to attend the 1987 FAF. Their job was to shadow the participants from the featured state of Michigan and interview them about their experiences before, during, and after the festival. The results were published in an article and a short book (Bauman and Sawin [1991] 2012; Bauman, Sawin, and Carpenter 1992).

Bauman et al. focused their evaluation of festival participant experience on the issues of representation and authority. If the participants had been mute objects on display in a museum, the festival would have assumed complete authority to interpret them as it saw fit. But because the folk artists step, as it were, out of museum cases to demonstrate their folk art and to talk to the audience and because they have their own ideas about what they are doing, multiple authorities are in operation at the festival: those of the CFPCS staff, of the presenters, and of the folk artists themselves. Sometimes these authorities are in harmony and sometimes they conflict. The way the folk artists experience the festival, according to Bauman et al., turns in large part on how they negotiate conflicts with the CFPCS staff and with presenters over authority in their presentations.

The CFPCS staff authority is, of course, built right into the festival structure. It is exercised in the criteria used to select the artists in the first place and in framing the settings for their presentations (with signs, maps, and interpretive material in the festival program book). Further, presenters go over repertoire with folk artists and reinforce CFPCS ideas of authenticity. In action before the public, presenters are instructed to claim a good deal of authority as they explain and contextualize what the audience is about to see. In his book on folk festivals, Joe Wilson (1982, 81–82), head of the National Council on the Traditional Arts and a veteran festival presenter himself, suggests that a presenter might say something like this when introducing a Mississippi fiddler: "Mr. A's fiddling is a good example of an important regional style of fiddling first recorded in the 1920s on hillbilly recordings by such Mississippi performers as Narmour and Smith, and Freeny's Bam Dance Band. During the 1930s, Library of Congress collectors found much the same style played by such excellent fiddlers as Stephen Hatcher. If you'll listen carefully, you'll hear some notable differences in this music—the use of high notes and high sharp slides and a quality which some students of this fiddle style have called 'wild.'"

The FAF presenters in this way attempt to educate the audience. What, then, ask Bauman et al., is the effect of all this festival-driven authority on the performers who, after all, are unused to being interpreted in a museum setting and who normally, in their home contexts, take on the authority to represent themselves as they see fit? The authors of this ethnographic study of festival folk artists' experience felt it was important to understand the participants not as passive museum objects but as "agents, reflexive, adaptive, and critical, crafting the representations in which they are involved, working to figure out what they should and could be doing within a folklife festival, negotiating their way through structures of power and authority" (Bauman and Sawin [1991] 2012, 312).

Bauman et al. thus attempted to understand the participants' experiences objectively, using ethnographic methods including observation and interview. As an advocate of public folklore and ethnomusicology (see Titon 1992a) and as someone implicated (albeit in a minor way) in the festival's history, I read their reports with great interest. Not unexpectedly, several participants were portrayed expressing various frustrations with the festival. They were confounded by logistical problems, sometimes puzzled by the FAF staff's control over their performances, and in certain cases uneasy at being presented as "folk." Overall, the reports were critical of the festival. Yet some folklorists thought the documents were not critical enough. One review scored the report because "the employer (CFPCS) is also a powerful player within the profession" and could be expected to harm the reputations of those who were critical of the FAF. "The published version gives the distinct impression that substantial revisions of [earlier] drafts were undertaken in order to assuage FAF staff concerns about their collective self- and public images. More important, the researchers consistently frame their inquiry and interpret their data in terms most compatible with the festival organizer's own measures of success" (Joseph 1994, 276).

My problems with the reports of Bauman and his colleagues were a little different. It occurred to me, first, that there was little evidence in this ethnographic study that was new; it confirmed certain ideas festival workers already had about how some participants experienced the festival, while its principal value was in grounding the debate over authority. Second, I was struck by the possibility that by asking the participants to be reflexive and critical, Bauman and his cohorts might have induced more criticism than would otherwise have occurred. Third, I was uncomfortable with the notion that although Bauman, Sawin, and Carpenter viewed the festival participants as agents, in their writing they seldom permitted them the agency of direct discourse. Instead of quoting them, the authors summarized the folk artists' points of view for them, framing the entire study and its significance, putting it in terms useful for academics but not, perhaps, for the participants themselves. In other words, the authors of the study assumed that their concerns about festival structure and authority were the participants' concerns, or ought to be their concerns. Inevitably, the authors took on, in the article and book, the very role that, in their writing, they critiqued: the role of the authoritative presenter.

As I thought about the upcoming appearances of Cornett and his friends—my friends—at the festival, I wondered what I would learn about how they were experiencing it. I was certain that they would tell me some of the things they were feeling, but I did not like the idea of doing ethnographic research on people whom I found hard to objectify. My role at the festival was to advocate for them, not to research them. Besides, I felt a large degree of Heisenbergian reluctance to engage in this kind of research. What, I wondered, would festival participants say about their feelings if they were simply left to their own devices, to define their own areas of concern and interest? Yet it seemed impossible to find out. One couldn't ask them without interfering and introducing one's own agenda, whereas I wanted to know *their* agenda. To be sure, festival workers sometimes overhear participants talking to each other about the festival as it takes place, in ways that reveal something of how they feel about it; however, this is the fragmentary stuff of anecdote that has long been available. A coherent account from a participant's point of view without academic solicitation seemed unattainable.

And then suddenly, I had it in my hands. A few weeks after our appearance at the festival, Elwood Cornett and his wife, Kathy, visited me in Maine while they vacationed in New England and Canada's Maritime Provinces, and they gave me a copy of the twenty-six-page, double-spaced, typed narrative of their Washington experiences that Dosh Fields had written. I had not asked for it; I did not even discuss the possibility with them, or they with me. I was dying to know how it had come about. Later that year in September, I saw them again, this time in their home state of Kentucky, and I asked the author how she came to write it. It turned out that shortly after she returned, one of the ladies in her church asked if she would tell her about their experiences, and she launched into an account so full that her friend suggested she write it up. Relying on her almost photographic memory and the help of the others when memory failed, she went to her computer and produced "The Baptists Go to Washington."

## The Baptists Go to Washington

"The Baptists Go to Washington" frames the Old Regular Baptists' trip in terms of travel, tourism, and pilgrimage. This perspective is crucial in understanding how these festival participants processed their experiences. Travel allows them to think of themselves as doing something they would not ordinarily do. Tourism (that is, performing for tourists) permits them to feel that they are demonstrating their singing rather than attempting to re-create a natural church or home context for it. Pilgrimage, though mostly implicit, provides the overarching theme: that they were invited to sing in the nation's capital was an honor for which they were humbly grateful, and they reciprocated by becoming tourists and paying homage to American history at various heritage sites.

Humor is the author's chief device to represent the Baptists as travelers in Washington. She presents them as fish out of water, often contrasting what they find in DC with what they know back home. Back home, "a mall is where you can go at ten in the morning, shop till ten at night in many different stores, and never go outside." In Washington, the Mall is the "very large park" where the festival is held, and it was "all quite overwhelming" (Fields 1997, 5). The author has a good deal to say about the ethnic food. At the hotel where the festival participants were fed, "fish was on the menu, among other things. Some things I didn't recognize but I am not a picky eater so I ate them anyway" (4). At the festival, they ate ethnic food. In the Mississippi Delta section, she ate at Catfish Corner and "had a five dollar sandwich very much like one I could get at McDonald's for two dollars" (7). A few days later, she ate in the Africa section at the "Feast of the Nile" and of her meal she wrote, "I ate it anyway. I know part of it was chicken. Some of it I'm not sure what it was." The author writes humorously about riding in a taxi (a first-time experience for her): "We decided that cab drivers and van drivers in D.C. only know how to use their horns and their accelerators. And they use them a lot" (16–17). She was wary of riding the escalator down to the subway: "I just hate those things. But I made it. Elwood said when the train stops, to move quickly, grab a pole and hold on tight. I took a seat with a stranger, as I had no desire to be standing while that train was moving" (15).

Here the author uses humor in a slightly different way but one that is typical of her narrative: she pokes fun at and undercuts male authority. Cornett suggests that she hang on to a pole, but she decides to sit down. Earlier, she had written that Cornett had mistaken the place where they were supposed to meet. "So goes our leader," she commented (2). James Early, the Smithsonian official who was in charge of the Sacred Sounds section of the festival where the Old Regulars were to sing, "was wearing what looked to me like red checked flannel pajamas" at the festival site during the welcoming orientation program (6).

Women using humor to undercut male authority is a notable tactic in the male-dominated community of Old Regular Baptists. However, it is also used by both men and women within the group to put the authority of outsiders in perspective (see below for an example in which Cornett pokes fun at my attempts to learn about their music). The author of "The Baptists Go to Washington" employs irony to show that the travelers were out of place, perhaps even in a dangerous place. "We imagined D.C. as a push, shove, screaming, and rude place—the crime capital of the world. Elwood assured us there would be no problem with that" (1). And later, when they arrived at the hotel, they met a rather profane Mississippi writer and storyteller who teased them. "After a bit he wanted to know if we were going 'Juking.' We had him repeat that several times as he really has a southern accent. We finally came to a consensus that we probably were not. Especially since we had no idea what he was talking about" (4). Later, she described this gentleman as a "blowhard."

Tourism permits the author to view their singing in front of the festival audience as a "demonstration" (12, 16, 18) rather than as an unmediated attempt to worship in song. The author calls the festival tourists an "audience" and relates her apprehensions and eventually her relief that the demonstrations went well. She noted that at home before she left, "being the modest people that we are it was hard telling people that we were going to sing for the Smithsonian Institution. I never thought of myself as a good singer, but I surely wanted to go [to Washington]" (1–2). At their first festival demonstration, she suddenly realized, "The six of us had never sung as a group before. Had not practiced one song. I'm sure at some point the six of us had been in church together, but had never sung with just the six of us. There were about three microphones in front of us. Of course we weren't used to that either" (11–12). The next day, at the narrative stage, someone familiar with Old Regular Baptist music requested that they sing "Poor Pilgrim of Sorrow." The author relates, "Elwood explained that we sing that song but he didn't know if [any] of them had ever lined it before. [That is, he was not sure any had ever led the song by lining it out for the group.] He said, 'Nothing like coming to Washington D.C. to try it'" (16). But like their other experiences, despite the initial apprehension, she said, "It went very well" (16). She wrote, "[I] was much more relaxed than I thought I would be. I just sang like I usually do and felt much more normal than I thought I would" (12). The whole demonstration was "much more relaxed than I ever thought it would be. The whole city was—at least the part of the city that I saw" (12).

Describing their experiences demonstrating their singing, the author does not write directly about any spiritual feelings she might have had. Whereas a fieldworker doing research might have asked point-blank about the possibilities of authentic spiritual experience in this festival setting, the author treats the issue with great skill and subtlety. Demonstrating their singing for tourists is what they were doing, and she measures their success by the singing's effects. She gives most weight to the personal relationships they established with members of the audience and with the festival staff. "There were always people who came up after the demonstrations and had questions and said how much they enjoyed the singing" (20). One person asked them where in Kentucky they lived, and it turned out he lived nearby. Another person from Mississippi State University had come to the festival because of the Mississippi presentation there, but he said he was most interested in the Old Regular Baptists and came up after the demonstration to shake their hands. "He said he was so glad he had come by that tent" (12). The author leaves it to the reader to determine why these people were so moved.

Personal relations with the festival staff are noted on several occasions. Staff members are named and singled out for praise. "Everybody was very friendly and our wish seemed their command. We were told where each staff member would be during the Festival and no concern was too small for them to hear" (6). During the last demonstration, "a lot of the Smithsonian staff was there. They all seemed impressed with our singing. Some people cried. Some people rejoiced when we were singing, especially at the end when we sang 'Amazing Grace.' . . . [After we had finished,] James Early gave a little talk out how we had impressed everyone there. They also had made big certificates of appreciation for us. . . . We were all very pleased. . . . Ivy Young was the Program Director for Sacred Sounds. She seemed so sad to see us go. It was hard to believe we had only known these people for a week. They acted like we were family going away. They seemed very sincere" (23–24).

The author omits the little extempore talk that Cornett gave, thanking the Smithsonian for the opportunity to demonstrate their music, saying that the Old Regular Baptists were pleased to contribute to the Sacred Sounds section of the festival. I recorded this whole last demonstration as a keepsake for them; I transcribe a portion of it here. Cornett began by both acknowledging and gently poking fun at my research with a humorous device reminiscent of the way Fields deflated his authority in "The Baptists Go to Washington," but soon he moved to more serious things:

> Jeff [Titon] got interested in the way we sing and learned more about us than we knew about ourselves. The Smithsonian got interested in it and recorded some and released a recording of our singing. You see, there's not many people that still sing this way. One of my great ambitions is to see this way of singing perpetuated in such a way that future generations will have this experience which means so much to me. And I hope it'll mean a lot to them. We're not performers, and we were only interested in this being recorded because the Smithsonian is a nonprofit institution. I would not be willing to be involved in a profit-making endeavor that would involve this. . . .
> 
> We came here very apprehensive a week ago and wondered what would it be like, what will the Smithsonian folks be like, what will the guests be like? Well, two years ago after working twenty-five years in the same place, I left there.

In the midst of that leaving, there were all kinds of empty feelings and yearnings within me that made me say at the time I left, "I don't know if I can do this without crying, or not." Last week, I told you that I completely retired from my wonderful career of working with young men and young women, boys and girls, which is a great career. And still the same thing: there was this yearning within me, there was this emptiness and it made me think, "I'm not going to cry."

Well, we came to the Smithsonian. . . . We have met all of these folks that have opened their arms to us in a way that just makes us have a real sad feeling when we talk about saying goodbye. I told you that we have a lot of handshaking and we have a lot of embracing in our churches in a genuine and sincere love, one for another. We're going to sing "Amazing Grace," a few verses, and after we get started, I will ask you, if you would, to stand with us, and we'll shake hands one with another, and we'd like to shake hands with you, if you would want to. We don't believe in pushing ourselves on anybody either. But we'd like you just to shake hands with those around you, and come up here and shake hands with us, too, if you would.

What he said was so true to the vision of the CFPCS that the festival director was moved to tears. Cornett had come to understand and articulate the communal power of the festival. Then the Old Regular Baptists facilitated its enactment. Dosh's husband, Jim Fields, lined out "Amazing Grace," not in their usual tune but in the one most people know, and many joined in. Afterward, people shook hands and embraced, and a long line formed to say goodbye. They were "the real thing."

Pilgrimage was the third metaphor with which the author framed "The Baptists Go to Washington." Between demonstration times at the festival, the group explored Washington tourist sites: the Arlington Cemetery, the Smithsonian Museum, the Vietnam War Memorial, Congress, and the White House. In fact, as much space in the author's narrative is given over to a description of these sites as to their festival demonstrations. It took considerable planning for them to fit in their trips to the tourist sites, but they were anxious to make the most of this opportunity to see some of the nation's most sacred places. At Arlington Cemetery, the author was struck by the contrast between the simplicity and elaboration in the graves of John and Robert Kennedy. At the Smithsonian, she was disappointed in the small size of the Hope diamond. In Congress, she was concerned that the activity on the floor of the Senate was as disorganized as it appeared on C-Span.[9] Her conclusions about the White House were that it "needed a coat of white paint as well as some repair. . . . Still, it was a great honor to be there" (Fields 1997, 26). The most meaningful aspect of their pilgrimage was the time they spent at the Vietnam War Memorial, where they looked up names of friends and relatives. "It was a moving experience for us because that was our era," she wrote. "That was our generation. And most of us feel that way too many people died and not much was accomplished for the United States. That is another story and has been told just about any way a story can be told" (13). When the author describes it as "another story," I can't help thinking she is aware that she, too, is telling a story: the Baptists go to Washington. Not to the Smithsonian festival but to Washington, where they tried to pay homage to their nation and found the cemeteries inspiring and the living monuments a little shabby.

Not only does "The Baptists Go to Washington" present the festival in a more positive light than Bauman, Sawin, and Carpenter's ethnographic study, but it also presents it as something of a sideshow, alongside the other purpose of their trip, pilgrimage to the nation's capital. Decentering the festival gives their participation an added sense of irony. Nowhere in this document does the author state that they felt any paradox in being tourists one moment and demonstrating their singing for tourists the next. The author's account dwells on the group of Baptists as a little family and community, together all the time in Washington, and it is to this sense of community at the festival that they responded the most. They genuinely liked the people whom they met, and they sensed that the people liked them. When she got back home, "the next day seemed very strange," she wrote. "I think we had some kind of post-vacation stress syndrome. I felt like I had returned from a fantasy. Of course when I unpacked all those dirty clothes and the grandbabies came, it didn't take long to snap back into reality" (26). So concludes the author's account of their trip, one designed not in response to a group of inquiring academics but rather for her family and community at home, that they might understand it in familiar terms.

Bauman, Sawin, and Carpenter's study of Michigan at the 1987 festival concluded that participants had difficulty negotiating the reframing that inevitably takes place in the festival context. With their egos and reputations on the line, some objected to being treated as "folksy" and developed various strategies for challenging festival authority and for representing themselves. The Michigan participants' usual tactic was to make fun of festival authority. What of the Old Regular Baptists? When Fields amuses her audience over the unrecognizable food, or the pajama-like pants worn by a festival curator, or when Cornett jokes that I came to learn more about their music than they knew about it themselves, they might appear to be engaging in a similar practice; however, I think they were accomplishing something more than that. First, a wit that punctures authority was not something they worked up just for the festival; it is a common tactic at home, which is understood and admired for what it is, and it has a long history in this country.[10] Second, although they were concerned and apprehensive at first, Cornett and the others were successful in negotiating the authority structures of the festival, and they did so without alienating anyone, making a fuss, or staking out a site of resistance.

The Old Regular Baptists did not challenge the festival; they embraced it from a common purpose, as Cornett's concluding extempore talk before the attentive audience and CFPCS organizers reveals. Secure in their identities, rooted in a culture that values modesty, they may have found Washington a little strange, but they did not permit the festival to be a test of their egos and reputations. Instead of perceiving the solicitous treatment by festival staff as paternalistic, they genuinely welcomed it as a sign of respect. If they objected to being treated as "folk," they did not say so, nor does the author of "The Baptists Go to Washington" discuss it. Her work portrays the event as a festival but not by using the term "folk" festival. Louis Armstrong is reported to have said, "I guess all music is folk music; I never heard a horse sing it." I imagine that in this sense, then, as "ordinary folks," the Old Regular Baptists interpreted the term. In his talk, Cornett brought the CFPCS organizers and FAF staff into the same category as the participants when he called them the "Smithsonian folks," a usage that even the academic critics of the festival would have applauded.

But more than that, the Old Regular Baptists present understood the purposes of celebration and demonstration in an atmosphere of cultural pluralism that may be said to express the CFPCS vision, and Cornett shared those goals as they applied to his group and their music. He feels, with good reason, that events such as singing at this festival, and publishing a CD and cassette of their singing on Smithsonian Folkways, demonstrate to members of Old Regular Baptist churches that their music is valued by outside authorities, is something special, and deserves efforts at preservation in the face of pressures to diminish or dilute it. Cornett's extemporized speech was aimed at the CFPCS organizers, the listening audience, and me. However, the author of "The Baptists Go to Washington" directed her narrative toward a different group: her friends who had not gone along to Washington. She represented their trip in terms of travel, tourism, and pilgrimage for a home audience who were curious about what they saw and what they did and how they felt in Washington, the heart of the nation.

In "The Real Thing," Henry James concluded that actors (models) were required if an artist was to paint true to life, because the art audience demanded stereotypes, not the real thing. Most tourist sites that present folk music seem to agree with James. The tourists are willing to suspend disbelief and be entertained—at least some of them are. The Smithsonian's Festival of American Folklife, on the other hand, an educational institution unswerving in its ideal to have the real thing represent itself, is not always successful. But sometimes, of course, it is, and in this instance, when the Baptists went to Washington and sang from their hearts, the real thing was so powerful that it created a human community where a moment before there had been only an idea of one.

## Notes

1. In 1998, the Smithsonian Institution dropped the name "American" from the festival title and it became the Smithsonian Folklife Festival. The old name is retained here because it was in effect at the time of the 1997 festival that provides the ground of this essay.

2. Their music may be heard on Cornett, Titon, and Wallhausser (1997), a CD accompanied by a booklet of essays about their beliefs, practices, history, and music. Making this CD is discussed later in this essay.

3. Published scholarship on the Old Regular Baptists includes Tallmadge (1975 and 1984), Jones (1977), Wallhausser (1985), Dorgan (1989), Ritchie (1955, 84–85), Wicks (1989), and Jones (1999). Published recordings include Ritchie (1959; one selection), J. Cohen (1960; one selection), Lomax (n.d.; two selections), Lomax (1977; one side, with flawed documentation), and Cornett, Titon, and Wallhausser (1997). The largest collection of unpublished recordings is William Tallmadge's, some two hundred hours of singing, preaching, and prayer among the United, Old Regular, and Primitive Baptists recorded from 1968 to 1979. It is on deposit in the Appalachian Collection, Hutchins Library, Berea College, Kentucky.

4. When I left Berea in June 1990, I deposited copies of my field tape recordings in their Appalachian Collection. Most were audio recordings of worship services, but they included audio- and videotaped interviews and video recordings of an Easter sunrise service, a Memorial Day service, and a baptism. I was not happy with their sound quality. Sufficient for documentary purposes, none fully conveyed the power and beauty of the music.

5. In addition to the recording project for the Smithsonian, described in the following paragraphs, I proposed that they undertake a self-documentation project using high-quality equipment to record their singing on cassettes and distribute copies to those who wanted to learn the songs by practicing privately at home, in their automobiles, and so on. The Folk Arts Division of the National Endowment for the Arts awarded a small grant for this purpose, and I purchased some equipment for them and taught them how to use it.

6. In 1999, the Smithsonian's Center for Folklife Programs and Cultural Studies (CFPCS) became the Center for Folklife and Cultural Heritage. The old name is retained throughout this essay, however.

7. Examples of folklife presented at the FAF include preindustrial crafts such as quilting, weaving, boatbuilding, trap-making, basket weaving, local cooking traditions and foodways and, of course, all kinds of traditional music making.

8. Readers of a certain age will recall that Rolodex was the brand name of a once-popular card-filing system for contact names, addresses, and phone numbers.

9. C-Span is a cable television channel that shows the US Congress in session.

10. Royall Tyler's play *The Contrast*, written after the American Revolution, uses a frontiersman to poke fun at the sophisticated ways and implicit authority of a city gentleman—and in doing so inaugurates an American character different from his British counterpart. This same device was also a favorite of nineteenth-century American humorists such as Mark Twain. Loyal Jones (1989) asserts that this kind of humor is characteristic of the people of Appalachia when dealing with any kind of pretense.

# 7

## MUSIC AND SUSTAINABILITY
### An Ecological Viewpoint

*I*N 2004, I BEGAN TO RESEARCH THE SUSTAINABILITY *discourses in economics, developmental anthropology, and ecology and to think about how they might offer a different and perhaps better way than conservation for folklorists and ethnomusicologists to think about the goals and methods of our applied work. In the introduction to this volume, I discuss the events that led up to my sustainability epiphany. This essay, first presented in a panel on music and sustainability I organized for the Society for Ethnomusicology's 2006 annual conference, was one result. I began a blog on music and sustainability (Titon 2008–) and have continued speaking and writing about it while also enlarging its scope in my sound ecology project (section III) from music to sound and the expressive culture of all beings.*

### Introduction

The word "sustainable" has been doing some pretty heavy lifting lately. An internet search reveals sustainable aligned with food, development, packaging, future, forestry, education, business, energy, architecture, health, fashion (eco-chic clothing), water, technology, conservation, tourism, investing, and even furniture and flooring. Websites guide individuals and communities toward responsible, sustainable living, chiefly in response to threats posed by growing world population, diminishing natural resources, and now global warming. What about sustainable music? In this essay, I argue that cultural policy toward music should be informed by four principles from the new conservation ecology: diversity, limits to growth, connectedness, and stewardship. I also question the usefulness of the cultural heritage concept, arguing that its discourse puts cultural managers into a defensive posture of safeguarding property assets, and that by supporting the conservation of those assets with tourist commerce, heritage management is doomed to the paradox of constructing staged authenticities.[1]

It is a commonplace that human beings socialize their young in music as in other aspects of culture, instructing them formally or informally. In Western Europe, when music was thought to model the harmony of the universe and education in music was accorded far more importance than today, alarms sounded periodically about the tendencies of common, vulgar, or bad music to drive out the good. Such alarms are still with us, as educators, critics, and historians wonder if Western art, or classical, music has any future (Rosen 2001). Although a broad consideration of sustainability and music would include an assessment of classical music education in the schools and elsewhere, my focus in this essay is on music outside the Western art music tradition. This, after all, is the music that ethnomusicologists are granted some authority in dealing with, whether in musical and ethnographic description, interpretation, and comparison, or in matters of cultural policy.

Sustainability is directed today at resources thought to be endangered, on the road to extinction, and music is no exception. In a single generation—mine—government agencies and nongovernmental organizations have developed a new field: cultural heritage management. Here, culture workers or brokers (Kurin 1997) implement policies meant to protect and preserve outstanding musical (and other cultural) traditions considered to be threatened. Additionally, university ethnomusicologists and folklorists, independent scholars, music industry workers, and community scholars and activists intervene to help music cultures maintain and promote their music, whether considered endangered or not.

Speaking broadly, three kinds of public policy practices characterize cultural heritage management in regard to music. The first is the proclamation, in a way designed to add value, that a particular musical tradition (or musician, or musical group, or musical institution) is a masterpiece of human endeavor, a monument requiring special treatment. These proclamations almost always come from institutions carrying high cultural authority, thus offering a top-down validation of the tradition or tradition bearer. Examples are UNESCO designations of cultural heritage masterpieces, and arts council heritage awards to individual artists. The second, and currently most favored, is the creation of heritage spaces, theater-like sanctuaries such as festivals, heritage trails, interpretive centers, and living history museums, where music is mediated—that is, explained to—then performed for an audience. The third, and one that I endorse, decenters the top-down discourse of resource management by cultural heritage experts and instead it repositions culture workers collaboratively, both as students of community scholars and music practitioners and simultaneously as teachers who share their skills and networking abilities to help the musical community maintain and improve the conditions under which their expressive culture may flourish.

I will discuss chiefly the first and third types of these interventions, leaving the second (heritage spaces) for a future treatment. These quasi-sacred spaces have a lengthy history, a vibrant present, and effects that are too complex and varied to be examined in this short essay. Readers interested in my views on the hells and benefits of such heritage spaces as festivals may find an earlier essay of interest (Titon 1999, reprinted in this volume). There is a growing critical literature on that subject: for example, Baron and Spitzer (2007), Seitel (2001), Kirshenblatt-Gimblett (1998), Hufford (1994), Cantwell (1993), Feintuch (1988), and Loomis (1983). Suffice it to point out that these spaces embody a paradox: what is presented there as authentic cannot possibly be so, because it is staged.

Cultural heritage management has thus far drawn its theoretical base from the historical preservation and nature conservation movements. But just as nature conservation has sometimes gone awry, cultural conservation has not always succeeded. In some cases, protection efforts have stifled the ordinary kinds of changes vital to continuity in musical traditions. In others, preservation efforts have had the opposite of their intended effects, promoting the growth of musical "weeds," as it were, thus crowding out the music meant to be preserved. In yet other cases, conservation has foundered on the shoals of cultural politics and economic policies pitting national, regional, and local authorities against one another. While cultural heritage managers can point to some successes, the overall record (as it is in most human interventions) is mixed. Must cultural heritage management be abandoned or can we do better? My hope is that we will move beyond traditional preservation and conservation models, based as they are on the application of expert knowledge administered by heritage management agencies, with a limited view and the goal of controlling targeted resources so as to prevent their extinction. We should move toward newer participatory models, based on knowledge developed in collaborations seeking consensus among cultural heritage managers and community members, with a broader ecological view and the goal of adaptive management that relinquishes control, accepts uncertainty, understands the dynamic and person-centered nature of expressive culture, and that instead of looking toward a golden age in the past, develops flexible policies that enable a sustainable future.

Ethnomusicologists use the term "music culture" to refer to a group of people's total involvement with music: ideas, behavior, artifacts and material culture, institutions, and musical product. If we are willing to entertain the idea that music cultures behave as ecosystems, then from ecology we can discern four broad principles. The first, a familiar one, is the adaptive value of diversity. The second is that continuously expanding growth is unsustainable. The third principle is connectedness, with the corollary that interventions in one part of the musical ecosystem will have outcomes in other parts of it. The fourth is stewardship, or the idea that humans are caretakers, not owners, of resources. Considering these will help understand why cultural heritage policy is succeeding in some areas and failing in others, and help formulate and implement better practices in cultural management for sustainability.

Diversity underlies the philosophy of musical conservation with the view that all musics contribute, actually and potentially, to the adaptational capabilities of humankind (see Lomax 1972a on cultural equity). Proclamations of masterpieces by remote agencies, the creation of heritage spaces, and work within musical communities represent different kinds and degrees of culture worker involvement. Experience, as well as the ecological principle of connectedness, shows that proclamations alone, however well-intentioned, may have unintended consequences that work against safeguarding musical masterpieces. Experience, as well as the principle of stewardship, shows that policies aimed at encouraging local, grassroots, participatory (Faux 2009), often amateur, music making directly inside musical communities help to revitalize musical traditions and thus to ensure their continuation.

Insofar as the creation of heritage spaces encourages this kind of participatory music making, positive effects will be directed inside these musical communities. On the other hand, when heritage spaces emphasize music in presentational forms (Turino 2009) from the stage, packaged for tourists, with the value-added mechanisms of commerce, the effect will be to encourage thinking of music as a commodity, with consequences for the professionalization, commercialization, and a media-driven revival of music both within and outside these communities. To use an ecological analogy, representations of music at cultural heritage sites managed for tourists run the risk of being like chemical fertilizers, artificial stimuli that feed the plant but starve the soil. On the contrary, partnerships aimed at encouraging a balanced, healthy, life-supporting soil at the community level bring about musical continuity through adaptation, which is to say growth and change. Music is conceived, then, not as something directed from a stage at an audience by a master artist but as something we may all make in our quotidian lives, an activity that connects people, a way of being human. Persons sustain music, and music sustains people.

## An Ecology of Music

The dominant paradigm in twentieth-century ecology is the ecosystem, defined by its originator, Arthur Tansley (1935, 299), as "including not only the organism-complex, but also the whole complex of physical factors forming what we call the environment of the biome—the habitat factors in the widest sense [and that] range from the universe as a whole down to the atom." The "organism-complex" consists of individual organisms, populations of organisms (species), and communities (one or more populations). Organism, population, and community represent three hierarchical levels. The community and its surrounding habitat compose an interacting unit or ecosystem (Brewer 1994, 11). We speak of the ecosystem of a contiguous geographical area, such as a particular pond, or forest, or intertidal zone; we also speak of the ecosystem of a particular village or a city. We can also speak of pond, forest, or village ecosystems in general.

The idea of a world of music, which governs the book *Worlds of Music*, is of a music culture that is at once social and ecological (Titon 1984, 8–9). Although worlds of music exist at more levels than three, worlds of music do correspond to the organism, population, and community levels in ecological thought. A world of music exists at the level of the individual person who interacts with other people concerning music. Another world of music consists of the population or group of people who interact with one another over a particular kind of music. We speak of the world of classical music, or jazz, or hip-hop, and we note that there are divisions within these worlds just as there are divisions within populations. Of course, persons may participate in more than one world of music, whereas we do not usually think of organisms as members of multiple populations. A higher, community level involves the interactions among the various worlds of music, today often in competition in the global musical marketplace. The musical habitat includes both physical and cultural factors of the musical environment such as ideas about music, sound and sound-producing instruments, recording studios, media, venues, musical education and transmission, and the economics of music—indeed, music as cultural production and a cultural domain—which relate to the health of musical individuals, populations, and communities.

The first lesson that ecology teaches is the adaptational advantage of diversity. In the competition for resources, the more diverse the organisms, populations, and communities, the greater the chances of survival in, and of, the ecosystem. Thus, the argument in favor of diversity is not merely grounded in justice as fairness but also in adaptation for survival. The basis for multiculturalism, diversity informed the call for "cultural equity," associated with applied anthropologists, known to ethnomusicologists through the work and writings of Alan Lomax on behalf of conserving music cultures globally. Lomax (1972b) based his appeal on ecological grounds.

A second ecological principle concerns limits to growth. At the heart of the ecosystem concept is the cycle, production and consumption, increase and decrease, birth, growth, death, decay, and recycling back into life. Individuals, populations, and communities have their natural limits beyond which, due to finite resources, increase is unsustainable. Echoing Malthus, the widely discussed 1972 Club of Rome report *The Limits to Growth* (Meadows et al. 1972) postulated a collision between the earth's diminishing natural resources and increasing human population, industrialization, pollution, and food production. Sustainability thinking, therefore, is informed by the cluster of ideas surrounding resources and their renewability, knowing that continuous growth, whether among populations, economies, or music cultures, is unattainable.

A third ecological principle is interconnectivity. Twenty-five years ago, I wrote that "like all of expressive culture, music is a peculiarly human adaptation to life on planet earth. Each music-culture is a particular adaptation to particular circumstances. . . . Each world [of music] can be regarded as an ecological system, with the forces that combine to make up the music culture . . . in a dynamic equilibrium. A change in any part of the ecosystem affects the whole of it" (Titon 1984, 9). In the past twenty-five years, ecologists have revised their views on equilibria even further in the direction of dynamism, feeling now that change and disturbance is the normal state of affairs, to the point that flow and flux appears to describe the behavior of the natural world better than does equilibrium or balance. Interconnectivity means that sustainability interventions are shortsighted when directed at organisms, populations, or communities without considering how they interact with one another and with Tansley's "overall biome" or habitat. They run into the so-called law of unintended consequences. For example, US government scientists introduced Ethiopian buffel grass to feed cattle and prevent soil erosion in the American Southwest in 1938 during the dustbowl era, but today buffel grass is invasive, chokes out other plants such as saguaro, and poses a serious fire threat in the Tucson, Arizona, area (US Geological Survey 2002). Sustainability interventions in worlds of music are no different: efforts to maintain intangible cultural heritage embodied in individuals will have fewer unforeseen (and potentially harmful) consequences as interconnections with populations, communities, and habitat are better understood.

The fourth principle is stewardship, which properly belongs to the field of conservation ecology, a name that is coming to replace the older field name, conservation biology. In its original sense, a steward was a servant who cared for something not owned; thus, humans, conscious of Earth's bounty as no other species are, care for the biosphere. Musical stewardship involves a responsibility to care for musicians, musical institutions, musical resources—the global music culture. The organic farming movement exemplifies stewardship in agriculture. The story is well known: organic farmers oppose modern agricultural techniques based on chemical fertilizers and pesticides that temporarily increase crop yields while they destroy the life of the soil. Extractive harvesting methods, whether in coal (mountaintop removal), forestry (clear cutting), or agriculture are based in an ownership mentality (I own it so I can do what I want with it) rather than an attitude of stewardship. Organic farmers maintain the soil ecosystem, which feeds the crops and produces a sustainable yield. The analogy with heritage is that living heritage "masterpieces" are best maintained by managing the cultural soil surrounding them. Managing the cultural soil means partnering with the musical culture bearers and community scholars to help them care for their musical traditions in their community contexts.

## Safeguarding Musical Heritage

The most wide-ranging global efforts at sustaining music through cultural heritage management today emanate from UNESCO. A commitment to biocultural diversity, equity, and interconnectedness underlies the United Nations' activities aimed at advancing international peace and universal respect by promoting collaboration among nations. Because of its remoteness, however, UNESCO has had setbacks with the unforeseen and thus unintended consequences of interconnectedness, and it has had difficulties encouraging the kinds of stewardship that cultural heritage maintenance requires. Practically, this difficulty stems from attempts to add value to cultural activities by proclamations from remote agencies, without sufficient ongoing, on-the-ground connections (partnerships) between the agencies, cultural heritage workers, and the culture-bearing communities themselves. The root problem lies in the concept of cultural heritage itself.

Protecting rights and safeguarding heritage generate policies in related institutional arenas (Seitel 2001). Some of the resulting proclamations have the force of law. The discussions over protecting rights arose from outcry over exploitation, by global pharmaceutical corporations, of native plants and indigenous medical knowledge; and also over exploitation of indigenous music in recordings marketed globally, without just compensation to or permission from the social groups whose knowledge and products were thus used to earn considerable sums, both for multinational drug companies and also for musicians and recording companies. The chief international rights institution is the World Intellectual Property Organization (WIPO), allied with UNESCO to work toward an international copyright law that would protect group (i.e., collective) as well as individual rights.

Discussions about heritage, on the other hand, led gradually to the UNESCO Convention for the Safeguarding of Intangible Cultural Heritage (ICH). UNESCO's 2003 ICH Convention (a treaty with the force of law for those nations that sign on) models "intangible" heritage after their 1972 World Heritage Convention, which was meant to preserve "tangible" natural sites and cultural monuments, such as Stonehenge, the Statue of Liberty, the Mount Nimba Strict Nature Reserve in Guinea, and the Great Wall of China. The tangible cultural monuments are regarded as "masterpieces . . . of human creative genius," while the natural sites are discussed in terms that address sustainability issues directly: those that "contain the most important and significant natural habitats for *in-situ* conservation of biological diversity, including those containing threatened species of outstanding universal value from the point of view of science or conservation" (http://whc.unesco.org/en/criteria/). A 2008 World Heritage and Sustainable Development Conference announced by UNESCO makes the connection to sustainability explicit: "In a more globalized world, Heritage should be addressed in innovative and sustainable ways, underlining the role of human and natural heritage as a contra-hegemonic trend. By understanding cultural differences, different peoples may find opportunities to enhance their contribution to a more sustainable world" (UNESCO 2008b).

The 2003 ICH Convention applies the principles of the World Heritage Convention, as they have developed since 1972, to the "intangible" arena of tradition, which Article 2 defines as

> practices, representations, expressions, knowledge, skills—as well as the instruments, objects, artefacts and cultural spaces associated therewith—that communities, groups and, in some cases, individuals recognize as part of their cultural heritage. This intangible cultural heritage, transmitted from generation

to generation, is constantly recreated by communities and groups in response to their environment, their interaction with nature and their history, and provides them with a sense of identity and continuity, thus promoting respect for cultural diversity and human creativity. For the purposes of this Convention, consideration will be given solely to such intangible cultural heritage as is compatible with existing international human rights instruments, as well as with the requirements of mutual respect among communities, groups and individuals, and of sustainable development. (https://ich.unesco.org/en/convention)

It is a laudable definition of the way tradition sustains biocultural diversity and vice versa. However, the phrase "sustainable development," which ends the definition, has a troubled history, as I have noted in the introduction to this volume.[2]

The goal of the 2003 ICH Convention is explicit: safeguarding. Indeed, the conceptual terms changed during the convention planning stage. UNESCO had been using the word "folklore," but too many thought it carried colonialist baggage; it was replaced by "intangible cultural heritage." Protecting and preserving gave way to "safeguarding," which in the convention is defined as "measures aimed at ensuring the viability of the intangible cultural heritage, including the identification, documentation, research, preservation, protection, promotion, enhancement, transmission, particularly through formal and non-formal education, as well as the revitalization of the various aspects of such heritage" (Article 3, https://ich.unesco.org/en/convention). These goals recognize process as well as product, and they comprehend that safeguarding involves not only preservation and protection but also promotion and revitalization, measures aimed at the health of the musical cultures that sustain the ICH. It is a catch-all definition.

So far, however, achieving these goals has been difficult, in part because the convention's primary mechanism has thus far been limited chiefly to proclamations, by a remote international agency (UNESCO), that certain traditions are intangible cultural monuments or "masterpieces." Largely empty proclamations reinforce the notion that heritage is more of an invention, a cultural construction intended to add value, than it is a discovery of something that has value. These ICH monuments are represented chiefly by the performing arts, the "popular and traditional cultural expressions" as well as the "cultural spaces" where they occur (https://ich.unesco.org/en/proclamation-of-masterpieces-00103). The expressions and spaces must "be at risk" in order to be selected for safeguarding. Examples of the ninety named masterpieces involving music thus far include Albanian folk isopolyphony, the *duduk* and its music (Armenia), Baul songs (Bangladesh), the mask dance of the drums from Drametse (Bhutan), the Royal Ballet of Cambodia, the *guqin* and its music (China), Georgian polyphonic singing, the tradition of Vedic chanting (India), and many more.[3] And although it is only five years since the convention, and although not all nations have signed on (the United States is conspicuously absent), it is apparent that UNESCO's strategy of proclaiming ICH "masterpieces" has at times foundered on the principle of interconnectedness—that is, it has had unintended consequences, in some cases directly opposed to the convention's goals. I shall examine two instances.

UNESCO's 2003 proclamation of the Royal Ballet of Cambodia as a "masterpiece of the oral and intangible heritage of humanity" (UNESCO 2008c) provided powerful ammunition in ongoing local cultural debates for Cambodian arts traditionalists who opposed the Royal Ballet's composition and performance of new works. According to UNESCO's proclamation, the ballet "has been closely associated with the Khmer court for over one thousand years. Performances would traditionally accompany royal ceremonies and observances such as coronations, marriages, funerals or Khmer holidays. This art form, which narrowly escaped annihilation in the 1970s, is cherished by Cambodians. Infused with a sacred and symbolic role, the dance embodies the traditional values of refinement, respect and spirituality. Its repertory perpetuates the legends associated with the origins of the Khmer people. Consequently, Cambodians have long esteemed this tradition as the emblem of Khmer culture." UNESCO further claimed that the Royal Ballet "faces numerous difficulties, such as a lack of funding and suitable performance spaces, competition from modern media and the risk of becoming a mere tourist attraction." Such language appears to have had the unintended consequence of representing the ballet as a fixed-repertory performance company, doomed to the constructed authenticity of historical reenactment.

According to folklorist Toni Shapiro-Phim, the UNESCO proclamation discouraged the presentation and touring of new works, specifically one titled *Pamina Devi* that was nontraditional in many respects (Shapiro-Phim 2006). For example, the choreographer Sophiline Cheam Shapiro (related by marriage to folklorist Shapiro-Phim) claimed authorship for the piece, while the ballet itself was an adaptation of Mozart's *The Magic Flute* and used male dancers in traditional female roles. Although the Western press praised *Pamina Devi*, many in the Royal Ballet community have resisted it. UNESCO's proclamation entered local politics and worked against innovation, originality, and development of new repertoire within the ballet company. The defenders of the new work, which include some members of the Royal Ballet community, argue that it is appropriate and necessary for the company to stage new works instead of continuing the imperial dances that are unsuited for a new, democratic nation. Those who oppose the work argue that UNESCO's proclamation warned of the dangers of modernity and earmarked the Royal Ballet not because of innovation but because it represented a tradition that requires safeguarding. The controversy expanded from the ballet community into national discourse. UNESCO was consulted and replied that while it was not opposed to new works in general, decisions should of course be up to Cambodians. The issue remains unresolved, but the point to be taken is that UNESCO's proclamation entered into local and then national cultural politics in a partisan way, one that may not have been foreseen or intended by UNESCO itself because it may not have considered the interconnections among individuals, the ballet company population as a group, the Cambodian arts community, and the discourse taking place in the cultural and political habitat of the new nation as a whole.

In conceiving of ICH as a monument requiring protection and preservation, UNESCO implies that its authenticity rests in its past glory; yet in conceiving of ICH as a living tradition deserving safeguarding, UNESCO implies that its sustainability rests in its ability to adapt for the future. In proclaiming the Royal Ballet of Cambodia an ICH masterpiece, UNESCO found itself used in unintended ways as a weapon in local cultural politics. In proclaiming the music of the Chinese *guqin* an ICH masterpiece, UNESCO ushered in a series of events that pushed aside the very tradition it wished to support, unwittingly helping to establish the music in a virtuosic, professional, presentational performance form for the concert hall, which was contrary to the UNESCO proclamation's characterization of the music's heritage as an endangered, contemplative, amateur chamber music for the home.

The Chinese *guqin* is a seven-stringed zither whose name often is shortened to *qin* and was formerly written in English as *ch'in*. (*Guqin* translates into English as "antique *qin*.") UNESCO proclaimed it an ICH masterpiece in 2003: "Described in early literary sources and corroborated by archaeological finds, this ancient instrument is inseparable from Chinese intellectual history. Guqin playing developed as an elite art form, practiced by noblemen and scholars in intimate settings, and was therefore never intended for public performance." UNESCO went on to claim that "there are fewer than one thousand well-trained guqin players and perhaps no more than fifty surviving masters. The original repertory of several thousand compositions has drastically dwindled to a mere hundred works that are regularly performed today" (UNESCO 2008a).

According to the Chinese music scholar Bell Yung, however, the *qin* is heir to two traditions, one virtuoso and the other contemplative. Until the sixth century, the *qin* music culture was populated with literati and scholars, amateur musicians playing principally for their own edification in their homes. Between the sixth and tenth centuries, a presentational music culture of *qin* performers arose alongside the amateur one, centered on virtuoso performance in front of an audience. During the tenth to twelfth centuries, the two music cultures competed, while from the twelfth until the twentieth centuries they gradually merged, becoming two strains in a single music culture, gradually declining in popularity until, in the postrevolution era, *qin* music was condemned as elitist and nearly disappeared entirely. But after 1976, the virtuoso, professional *qin* music culture emerged in a concert hall setting to please a popular audience, where it was considered appropriate for the communist nation and a music "of the people." New compositions commemorating political events appeared, the old silk strings were replaced with ringing metallic ones, while the contemplative, amateur style of *qin* performance continued in disfavor.

With China's new emphasis on its cultural heritage, the 2003 UNESCO proclamation was greeted with great jubilation among *qin* music lovers. The Chinese public concluded that the *qin* was a symbol of the best of Chinese music, something that could be held up against the achievements of Western music. The result was a new resurgence in *qin* music, not merely of the virtuoso, presentational kind. The amateur tradition also made something of a comeback. The old arguments between the amateurs and professionals, literati and artists, resurfaced. According to Yung, while each side has now constructed its own history, each in an effort to win out over the other, it is clear that the concert hall has triumphed over the study, the virtuoso, professional performance tradition over the amateur, contemplative one. Although *qin* has never been more popular, both inside China and abroad, with many beginners taking up the instrument, it is virtuosity to which most aspire. If the original music culture had diminished when the traditions went underground after the Chinese Revolution in 1949, it has spawned a great many new works and performers in the past thirty years. Thus, the effect of the UNESCO proclamation was the opposite of its intention; what has been safeguarded is not the "elite art form, practiced by noblemen and scholars in intimate settings" but what appears to those who support that aspect of the *qin* tradition as a vulgarization (Yung 2009).

UNESCO's intervention in the Cambodian Royal Ballet and Chinese *guqin* ran afoul of their aims for at least two reasons. In the first place, their proclamations were without implementation mechanisms, as if a national government had proclaimed a species to be endangered without an endangered species law in place or any way to enforce one if there were. In the second, they mistakenly focused on the health of individual masterpieces without taking into sufficient account the particular persons who produce and maintain them and the musicultural ecosystems containing them. One ecologist summed up failures in management of single species (akin to masterpieces) as follows:

> The emphasis by traditional management on single species . . . is obviously misplaced. These species are members of ecosystems and an approach that manipulates the landscape to maximize the [production of] one species is apt to distort it to the detriment of many other species. Similarly, the emphasis on the management of a few endangered and threatened species is misplaced, and few conservation biologists would claim otherwise. We can apply heroic efforts and spend millions of dollars to restore the black-footed ferret in the wild, and that is good. But there are too many endangered species for each to receive similar treatment. In the long run, the black-footed ferret will live or die based on the presence of healthy Great Plains grasslands supporting a healthy biota. . . . Those grasslands will save other at-risk species—including many that are so poorly known that we have not yet recognized their risk. In the same way, maintaining and restoring large blocks of other ecosystems is the eventual route of choice to saving their endangered and threatened species. (Brewer 1994, 621)

Rather than looking at biological resources as commodities in nature's economy, which was the view of an earlier generation of conservationists, contemporary conservation biologists and ecologists preserve biological diversity, not simply by preventing species extinctions but also by maintaining communities and whole ecosystems (Soulé 1986). This is the kind of holistic thinking that, translated to the arena of musical sustainability, would attempt to safeguard music, not by focusing support on individual masterpieces but by enhancing habitat conditions under which people are able to continue to make diverse musics in different ways and for various reasons. In a healthy music-cultural habitat, there would be a place for new and old works, perhaps in two branches of the Royal Cambodian Ballet, and both the amateur and professional *guqin* traditions would flourish as they once did without needing to compete.

## Community Music

Habitat-level thinking leads to partnerships among culture agencies, culture workers, community scholars, and music practitioners to enhance the conditions under which music is able to be made. To take a nonmusical example,

Ted Ames, of Stonington, Maine, first went to sea at the age of six with his grandfather, a retired lighthouse keeper. As an adult, he made his living dragging for scallops, but when the fishery diminished, he started stirring things up on shore, getting a degree in biochemistry and setting up a water lab at home. The US government fish and wildlife management agencies' policy is intended to aid the fish population in recovery by keeping the fishing pressure off most of the year. The policy may help the fish, but it puts the fishermen out of business. Ames believed there was a way to help both fish and fishermen. Having identified the historic spawning grounds, Ames advocated a different approach, one that would permit fishing as long as it was kept away from those spawning grounds. The agencies would not listen. Then in 2005, he received a MacArthur Fellowship (genius grant). Ames said that the MacArthur "has given me a bully pulpit. I've rattled the cage at every corner on the same issue, which is for fishermen to get smaller without paying a terrible price. . . . If things go well it ought to look once again like it did back then [when fish were plentiful] but we'll have to do a little fishing for something other than fish to get there" (Clark 2006). Now the agencies have their ears open. Today his work involves partnerships with the state agencies, and with the fishermen, so that they have a stake in husbanding their own resources.

Ames's story is not unique. It happens to be about fishing, but it could be about music. Most communities have their own amateur historians, scholars, and conservationists. Local historical societies attract them. Applied ethnomusicologists are effective when directly partnering with community scholars and activists within music cultures, focusing on work directly inside those communities. This approach arises from long-term relationships among applied ethnomusicologists and local community members after they become acquainted and learn how each can contribute to common goals, goals that may not become apparent until after friendships and trust develop. Often, but by no means always, these common goals include preservation and conservation, safeguarding and adapting living traditional musics for a practical future. I will discuss two examples.

Ralph Rinzler's partnership with the Cajun fiddler Dewey Balfa ushered in a revitalization and revival of Cajun music beginning in the late 1960s within French Louisiana and elsewhere. Rinzler saw his role extending beyond producing the Newport and Smithsonian Folk Festivals, designed chiefly for an audience of urban aficionados of folk music. In addition, he wanted to encourage, promote, revitalize, and renew traditional music within its home communities. In Balfa, Rinzler found a partner with whom to develop this vision. Balfa had grown up in a family of traditional musicians. After World War II, the Balfa family band was in demand for local dances and house parties. But by the 1960s, Dewey's brothers Will and Rodney were playing with other, more contemporary Cajun bands that had been influenced by country music and rock. Rinzler went to Louisiana and made some field recordings of the family group, attracted to their ability to play in a more old-fashioned, acoustic Cajun style. To represent this older style, the festival consulted Mamou, Louisiana community folklorists Revon Reed and Paul Tate, and they recommended musicians Gladius Thibodeaux and Louis Vinesse LeJeune for the 1964 festival. A last-minute substitution, Dewey Balfa came along with them to play guitar. The story goes that the Cajun musicians' hometown newspaper had editorialized its dismay that a more contemporary Cajun group had not been selected. They predicted that the old-fashioned "chanky-chank" music (fiddle, accordion, guitar, and triangle) would be ridiculed and they would be laughed off the stage. But the opposite happened and the audience wouldn't let them off the stage. Dewey was so pleased by their reception that Rinzler was able to persuade him and his brothers to form a band and perform traditional Cajun music at the 1966 Newport Festival.

Although he must have already been inclined toward promoting his community's traditional music, Balfa said playing at Newport was a transforming experience. Taking on the role of spokesman and interpreter, Balfa explained Cajun musical traditions from the stage as the Balfa Brothers performed on the folk music circuit at colleges, coffeehouses, and in more festivals. Rhode Island's fascination with Cajun music led to the founding of an annual Cajun and bluegrass festival that nearly forty years later is still in existence. The partnership with Rinzler and Newport led to recordings, some for the folk revival audience and others for a newly interested audience in Louisiana. Dewey became involved in community revitalization, founding local and regional Cajun music festivals and joining with the Council for the Development of French in Louisiana (CODOFIL), to help reestablish French in the local schools. He was a cultural ambassador both outside and inside the Cajun community, and he and other older musicians inspired a new generation of Cajun musicians such as Mark Savoy who have been active since the 1970s in sustaining Cajun music in south Louisiana. Rinzler came to understand the far-reaching effects of this kind of partnership and modeled his later work at the Smithsonian Folk Festival in a similar direction. The Folk Arts Program of the National Endowment for the Arts, which has been in operation since 1978, gives grants to community folk cultural organizations under the same partnership philosophy, based both on a belief in cultural equity and the adaptational values of diversity. In the 1990s, public folklore moved in the direction of cultural heritage management, partly in an effort to position itself effectively within a more conservative political climate.

A second example comes from my own experience with Old Regular Baptists, a religious community of about fifteen thousand people living primarily in the coal-mining country of the southern Appalachian Mountains. Their oral traditional lined hymnody combines tunes from the English and Scots-Irish stock with lyrics written chiefly by eighteenth-century English devotional poets. The Old Regular Baptists sing them in their church services every weekend, at weddings, baptisms, funerals and memorial meetings in cemeteries (see fig. 6.1), and other public occasions; they also sing them at home, for devotion, or when traveling in their automobiles. Although this way of singing was common in the American colonies, it is outside of the experience of most Americans today. The music is not encountered on the radio, television, or on any but a few recordings; some is available on the internet now, but it has not caught the ear of the general public.

I visited a group of Old Regular Baptists in the Indian Bottom Association in southeastern Kentucky every weekend during a five-month period in 1990 when I was teaching at Berea College. I explained that I was an ethnomusicologist interested in learning about their music. It is their way to be modest and sometimes indirect in their dealings with strangers. A few weeks after I started attending their worship services, their moderator (elected leader), Elder Elwood Cornett, told me about a request he had from a Japanese documentary filmmaker who wanted to bring a film crew into eastern Kentucky. Cornett went on to say that he did not want to refuse but that he felt the filming could be too disruptive. His solution was to tell the documentarian he could film but only through a closed glass window that separated the church sanctuary from the dining area where the congregation gathered on special occasions for a meal. Under those conditions, the filmmaker declined.

Cornett had permitted me to see how he solved a problem, but he was also telling me something about visitors. Several weeks later, after we had gotten to know each other better, Cornett told me,

> I don't know that we're anxious to be studied. We certainly haven't sought out you or anybody else and said, "Come look at us." And we're not going to do that and don't believe in that. But if somebody does want to know what we are and what we're about, I'm certainly not ashamed of that. And to answer your question more exactly, I think the important thing for someone to know is that we're just what we are.... Over the years, many years, a lot of people have flown in and

looked at us and flown out and wrote, and it's been, I hope, a bigger embarrassment to them than it was to us. . . . But then when somebody comes and really looks at us, we don't mind that. (Interview, Blackey, Kentucky, April 1, 1990)

Cornett has always felt that the only songs that are appropriate for the congregations in worship are the old lined-out songs, and he opposes all attempts to bring in the newer gospel music or "radio songs" as he called them. He had been concerned that the younger men in the church were not learning the lining tunes needed to lead the songs. Without a lining tune, a song would disappear from the active repertory. On seeing one of my attempts to transcribe their free rhythmic singing into musical notation, he asked whether it might be used as a teaching tool. He said they'd made a few attempts to have a "school" in which the older song leaders tried to get the younger people to imitate their singing, but the younger ones were shy and unsure of themselves in front of the more experienced ones, and it didn't work. I said I'd noticed people bringing boom boxes into church to record the singing; tapes could be very helpful, and the younger men could practice singing along with the tapes in the privacy of their homes or their cars. A partnership had begun among us after some months of getting to know each other and discovering common goals.

When I visited southeastern Kentucky again in 1991, I noted that "cassette school" was operating in an informal way. That led Cornett to raise a related subject with me. Some of the singers in the oldest generation were the only ones who knew the correct lining tunes for some of the songs. If they could be recorded, the lining tunes would be preserved. Boom boxes didn't always make very good recordings, though. Could I teach them to make better ones? Indeed I could, and I obtained a small grant for them to buy good recording equipment so they could collect and preserve the tunes themselves. This recording activity stirred further interest among them in their musical tradition, and I suggested to Elwood the possibility of using this new equipment to produce a high-quality cassette tape of congregational singing that could be widely circulated among Old Regular Baptists. He thought it an excellent idea but required that the company that produced and distributed it would not make a profit from it. I proposed Smithsonian Folkways, and Cornett agreed. I made the field recordings for this purpose when I visited again in 1992 and 1993. Folkways was interested, but instead of a custom pressing they decided on an arrangement that would deliver, at cost, cassettes (and later, CDs) to the Old Regular Baptists while at the same time making the recording available in a regular CD issue to the general public. Cornett, John Wallhausser, and

I cowrote the accompanying documentation, and Folkways timed its release to coincide with an appearance of a group of Old Regular Baptists at the 1997 Smithsonian Folklife Festival, where they demonstrated their singing (Cornett, Titon, and Wallhausser 1997; see also Titon 1999, this volume).

Their final demonstration was so affecting that it brought the festival director to tears, but the effect on them of their trip to Washington, DC, a second Folkways album (Cornett et al. 2003), and appearances at two conferences at Yale on lined singing (2005 and 2007) not only helped to revitalize the tradition but also to secure the Old Regulars' support for their unique congregational singing style and repertory. As Cornett reported in an interview for Appalshop (an institution located in Whitesburg, Kentucky, devoted to promoting Appalachian traditional culture and its values),

> It would appear to me that this way of singing is probably much more accepted right now than it was a few years ago. . . . Our people have begun to say, "Hey, we've got something here pretty special." And I think you know already that the Smithsonian recorded a couple of CDs of our singing, and all of that has caused our people to say, "Hey, we need to, we want to hang on to this way of singing." Some of the younger folks, we have asked, "What do you think about some of these things?" And I was a bit surprised. They like that tradition; they want to see it perpetuated. (Appalshop 2007)

These two examples show how collaborative partnerships can lead communities to take on stewardship, whether in the case of Balfa and the Cajun diaspora, or Cornett and the Old Regular Baptists. In both cases, national institutions' acknowledgment of the music as a "masterpiece" helped the musicians think about their traditions in a way that they had not done beforehand. The two cases are different because revitalization in the Cajun community was accompanied by a full-scale folk revival that involves both participatory and presentational music, musical and cultural tourism, heritage, and an expansion well beyond the boundaries of the Cajun communities in south Louisiana, Texas, and California (DeWitt 2009). Revitalization among the Old Regular Baptists has not led to a folk revival or much in the way of presentational venues for their music, which is by nature participatory. They have demonstrated their music at a few folk festivals, where it is contextualized as both cultural heritage and religious practice; however, to them, the music is most significant not as heritage but because it helps them worship God. They would, I am sure, block any efforts to turn their churches into heritage sites for tourists. Although they welcome guests, they do so on their own terms. No one is beating a path to their door, at least not yet, to try to start a revival of this singing in New England, where it originated, as occurred decades ago with Sacred Harp Singing.

## Conclusion

The four principles of conservation ecology point culture workers toward fewer top-down, heritage organization proclamations of masterpieces and more partnerships among community scholars, practitioners, and culture workers; fewer preservation sanctuaries where music and other forms of expressive culture, mediated for tourists, becomes a commercial product, and more bottom-up, community-based efforts to promote participatory music making in local venues.

One of the more frequently posed questions in cultural heritage discourse is "Who owns culture?" and this has led culture workers to ethics and international property law, hoping to find a solution to vexing problems of relativism (different societies have different answers to that question) and of individual versus collective ownership. But asking "who owns culture" puts us into a universe of ownership. If we move the discourse from heritage to sustainability, we step outside of ownership and ask instead "Who are the stewards of culture?" Emerson's poem "Hamatreya" names the New England farmers who lived and died thinking they owned their land; however, the poem shows that the land owned them. They were, at best, stewards. If we think of music as heritage, primarily a thing of the past, we are immediately in a defensive posture of collecting, preserving, safeguarding, protecting, and mediating music, through proclamations and set-asides, special spaces and sanctuaries. But if we think of a music culture as something here, living, a renewable daily resource among us, we move into a discourse of sustainability, people in partnership, taking on the privilege and excitement and reaping the rewards of stewardship.

## Notes

1. For more on staged cultural performances, see "The Paradox of Authenticity" (Titon 2008), an entry on my blog on music, sound, and sustainability.
2. [Author's note, 2020: My most detailed discussion of sustainable development and its problems in the intangible heritage domain can be found in "Sustainability, Resilience, and Adaptive Management for Applied Ethnomusicology," chap. 8 of this volume.]
3. [Author's note, 2020: The full list may be found at https://ich.unesco.org/en/lists].

# 8

# SUSTAINABILITY, RESILIENCE, AND ADAPTIVE MANAGEMENT FOR APPLIED ETHNOMUSICOLOGY

*I*N THIS ESSAY, I SUMMED UP TEN YEARS *of reflections, blog entries, public lectures, and prior articles on musical and cultural sustainability, tracing sustainability's history and usage and contrasting it with the earlier concepts of preservation, conservation, and safeguarding. I introduce resilience and adaptive management as strategies for achieving sustainability. Sustainability requires a holistic, ecological approach because a community's expressive cultures exhibit uncertainty and other characteristics of complex systems.*

## Introduction

Sustainability is a hard concept to avoid these days, and resilience is not far behind. We are urged to conserve energy, carpool, turn down the thermostat, use renewables, recycle our waste, lower our carbon footprint, and live sustainable lives to maintain a sustainable planet. Conservation ecologists and environmentalists manage ecosystems to prevent species extinction and maintain biodiversity. Developmental economists promote modernization and sustainable development, while ecological economists remind us about environmental constraints on trade, markets, corporations, and governments. Some business economists have argued that corporations will be better able to profit and sustain themselves if they think of their activities as taking place within an ecosystem consisting not only of predators and prey but also allies and competitors.

In applied ethnomusicology, sustainability does not directly reference green energy or developmental economics, although it may involve them. Rather, it refers to a music culture's capacity to maintain and develop its music now and in the foreseeable future. Applied ethnomusicologists today, as in the past, often try to aid musicians and their communities in sustaining their musical activities. Many of us have considered it an ethical imperative to do so, a giving back to individuals and communities we consider to be our colleagues, friends, and teachers in exchange for what they have given us—information, music, friendship and social life, pleasure, and in many cases, the basis for the research that not only advances knowledge but also helps us advance our careers.

*Sustainability* is a relatively new term for ethnomusicologists, but many ideas related to sustainability have been with us for decades: documentation, archiving, and preservation; conservation, safeguarding, revitalization, and renewal. *Resilience* is an even newer term, not yet in common use among us, but it has many advantages and, I believe, deserves to enter the discussion surrounding applied ethnomusicology. One of the difficulties with sustainability and its related ideas is that they are ends, not means; they are goals, not strategies. Resilience, on the other hand, offers a strategy, a means toward the goal of sustainability. Resilience refers to a system's capacity to recover and maintain its integrity, identity, and continuity when subjected to forces of disturbance and change. Insofar as music cultures are systems, they too exhibit resilience to a greater or lesser degree. Resilient systems share certain characteristics. Identifying what makes a music culture vulnerable, what makes it resilient, and ameliorating the former while strengthening the latter becomes, therefore, a practical strategy for enhancing a music culture's sustainability. Resilience does not simply mean "learning to live with it," as people new to the term mistakenly think. Nor does it mean hunkering down in a defensive stance. Rather, resilience implies a way to manage disturbance and change and guide the outcome toward a desirable end.

This chapter is written to begin theorizing resilience as a sustainability strategy for applied ethnomusicologists. Just as conservation biologists intervene in the environment to restore, maintain, and develop ecosystems, so applied ethnomusicologists intervene in music cultures. Like it or not, we are committed to putting ethnomusicological knowledge and insight to practical use in order to improve musical life. We are guided by values. We are meddlers. We are experimenters, we live with uncertainty, we expect sometimes to fail, and we hope to learn from our failures. The strategy I am theorizing here for applied ethnomusicology has been called *adaptive management* by those who have been working with resilience strategies for a variety of systems, not just environmental ecosystems. Adaptive management is succeeding in strengthening resilience and decreasing vulnerability in social groups facing undesirable change and in individuals facing stress and trauma. Applied to organizations, adaptive management not only enhances resilience but remodels behavior based on a new understanding: that organizations are not merely competitors but rather exist interdependently with allies and competitors within larger ecosystems—think of the complex relations among Apple, Google, and Microsoft, for example.

Sustainability is current, while resilience and adaptive management point toward the future of applied ethnomusicology. Much of it represents new thinking, while drawing lessons from applied ethnomusicology's prior interventions, the decades-old ideas that have animated them, and the relationships between applied work in ethnomusicology and that of two of our sister, fieldwork-based disciplines, applied anthropology and public folklore. (I might also have considered applied sociology, but this sprawling chapter is already broad enough in scope.) Therefore, I treat the historical background of the ideas—preservation, conservation, and safeguarding—that both preceded and contribute to sustainability and resilience. As these ideas originated elsewhere—the conservation of natural resources, for example, and the historic preservation of material objects—I discuss them in their original contexts in addition to their later adoption in applied ethnomusicology and public folklore. Finally, I turn to sustainability and then to resilience, again with reference to their origins elsewhere, in this case economics (sustainable development) as well as environmentalism, before moving to their applications in applied ethnomusicology I concentrate on the United States because I am most knowledgeable about these policy concepts, strategies, and their histories in my homeland. Nevertheless, these ideas and their applications flow globally, and they move in different directions and at different rates outside the United States. The most prominent contemporary music sustainability project is based not in the United States but in Australia (Schippers 2015). UNESCO is the major player in the international arena, but its conservation rhetoric remains wedded to older concepts involving preservation and safeguarding heritage, while for it, sustainability operates in the realm of economic development, not musical and cultural continuity.

## Conservation: Natural, Cultural, and Musical

Ethnomusicologists are conservationists, whether preserving and transmitting knowledge of music or, in the case of applied ethnomusicologists, conserving musical practice itself. In addition to documenting and preserving the music of the world's peoples for research purposes, applied ethnomusicologists have sometimes intervened on behalf of music cultures to help them conserve music thought to be threatened and endangered, usually by modernization and development. In many ways, these musical and cultural conservation efforts have been modeled on those that preceded them in nature conservation, or the conservation of natural resources.

Ever since the early Enlightenment, preservation and conservation have been closely related. Taken as near synonyms, their meaning is to maintain an object or system insofar as possible in its present state, to protect it from change, usually for contemplation, research, display, and perhaps for use. Conservationists who distinguish their activities from preservation emphasize conservation's restorative aspects—restoring a historical musical instrument, for example, or a painting, or a dinosaur, or an ecosystem. Conservationists acknowledge change but try to manage it in order to prolong a desired state. Preservationists (who may nonetheless call themselves conservationists) think of themselves more as protectors. They sometimes criticize conservationists for setting an additional priority on yield or harvest or use, rather than interfering as minimally as possible in order to preserve the original object or system, as they would do. Preservationists would, for example, prefer to keep a historical musical instrument "as found" in a deteriorated state, for study, rather than to restore or repair it for display or use (Barclay 2004). Although the debate between preservationists and conservationists is most prominent in the environmental movement (deep ecologists versus "wise use" conservationists), in this chapter I use *conservation* as the cover term for both preservation and conservation, distinguishing the two when desirable.

Nature conservation, or conservation of natural resources (they are not the same thing, for nature need not be regarded as a resource), is surely as old as the earliest hunters who realized they must not slaughter the entire herd, or the first growers who saved seeds. There is evidence of Italian violin makers during the time of Stradivarius and afterward conserving the forest trees producing violin-tone wood, and of a plea from the Englishman John Evelyn before the Royal Society in 1662, advocating that trees be replanted to preserve the forests, which were being harvested at an alarming rate (A. Allen 2012; Evelyn 1664). German, French, and British conservationists during the eighteenth and nineteenth centuries similarly worked for forest preservation based on scientific principles, and much was accomplished, particularly in British India throughout the nineteenth century (Barton 2002). The origins of the US conservation movement may be found in the writings of naturalists such as John Bartram (1699–1777), William Bartram (1739–1823), and Henry

David Thoreau (1817–1862), while novelists such as James Fenimore Cooper (1789–1851) expressed a preservationist philosophy through characters such as Natty Bumppo, who, like the Native Americans, used only enough natural resources to provide for basic needs (Cooper 1823). In the later nineteenth and early twentieth centuries, the writings of John Burroughs (1837–1921) and John Muir (1838–1914) were especially influential. Muir not only founded the Sierra Club, which became an important nature advocacy group, but also successfully lobbied the US Congress for the establishment of the first national park, Yosemite, in 1890, the first in a succession of national parks, which came to embody the US conservation movement, and led to the establishment in 1905 of the US Forest Service, the state fish and game conservation departments, and so on.

However, the split between preservationists and conservationists was already underway, as Muir (the preservationist) spoke out against the national Forest Service's efforts to manage the US-owned parks and forests for timber harvesting. Gifford Pinchot, the Forest Service director, termed his scientifically guided conservation policies "wise use," a phrase that has endured. A pragmatist, Pinchot's idea of wise use was based in government management for the public good, which meant protecting the forests as a renewable resource so that the public would continually enjoy its benefits, including tree harvesting and mining as well as recreation (C. Miller 2001). His successor, William Greeley, transformed the Forest Service into an agency whose principal function was to prevent forest fires, while enabling the timber companies to make enormous profits by clear-cutting huge tracts. The Sierra Club and other preservationists were outraged, as was Pinchot. As the twentieth century wore on, the preservationist wing of the conservation movement was criticized on the grounds that purchasing natural areas in the eastern states, or seizing them through eminent domain, forced removal of populations living on those lands, while their recreational use was limited chiefly to those wealthy enough to travel and vacation there. Today, when conservation heritage trusts buy up and set aside farmland and seashore, critics charge that this is accomplished at the expense of economic development and jobs.

Conservation of cultural resources may be traced, among Europeans, to those Renaissance aristocrats of an antiquarian bent who traveled to observe ruins and kept objects in private *kunstkammer*, wonder rooms or "cabinets of curiosity." These little theaters were the precursors of museums and contained cultural relics of all kinds, as well as natural history specimens from the plant and animal world. Museums followed, and eventually a historic preservation movement (to use US terminology) arose to safeguard historically important buildings and monuments on their original sites. An example is Stonehenge in the United Kingdom, where such activities are termed "heritage preservation." Artifacts of music cultures (e.g., ancient musical instruments) have been preserved over the years in cabinets of curiosity, museums, libraries, or repositories dedicated to instruments and, since the early twentieth century, to recordings and other media. Most ethnomusicologists maintain personal archives for research purposes, gradually passing them along to archival institutions. Museum collections may be found at the Musée de l'Homme, the Smithsonian Institution, and elsewhere. Examples of dedicated sound archives include the Berlin Phonogramm-Archiv (begun in 1900), the Archive of American Folk Song (1928) at the Library of Congress, and the British Library Sound Archive (1955). Repatriation, or returning recordings and other musical artifacts to the indigenous peoples from whom they were collected and taken, has underlined a third purpose: safeguarding (Newell 2003). "Digital preservation" is yet another contemporary preservation activity, saving space and converting the printed or recorded artifact to a more easily maintained, perhaps more permanent, medium. However, digital preservation transforms the original medium; it does not protect it.

Conservation, of course, has a strong preservation component, sometimes with additional elements such as restoration. Archives and museums practice conservation when they restore deteriorating artifacts closer to a presumably original state, as they do with dinosaur bones, paintings, and musical instruments. Conservation places less emphasis on protection and setting aside, and more emphasis on continuing utility, than does preservation. Demonstrating and exhibiting collections may also inspire conservation in music cultures. The director of the Smithsonian Institution, S. Dillon Ripley, conceived of performances at the museum in which the artifacts would be demonstrated in use for the public. "Take the objects out of their cases and make them sing," he wrote (Smithsonian Center for Folklife and Cultural Heritage n.d.). Although some of these demonstrations involved crafts and the application of traditional cultural knowledge, music was the most common kind of performance. The Smithsonian Festival of American Folklife, which began in 1967, is an example. Until then, most folk festivals exhibited marginal, dying, remnant traditions. But the Smithsonian festivals underlined a conservation element that encouraged the participants to maintain those traditions within their own cultural groups.

"Cultural conservation" entered the US public folklore discourse in the late 1970s, partly in response to a change in the idea of American identity, from a "melting pot" in which immigrant cultures and ethnicities would forge a single new type of American to a "mosaic" that recognized, honored, and thereby meant to conserve elements of American ethnic diversity and cultural pluralism. In that same decade, three federal folklore agencies were established that greatly influenced traditional arts policy, including music. Their mandate was to support the folk and traditional arts, which were viewed as the expression of a culturally, ethnically, religiously, racially, occupationally, and regionally diverse set of communities that, taken together, made up the mosaic society of the United States. Music was an important community folk art, perhaps the most evident, along with foodways, dress, religious practice, language, and so forth. The three federal agencies were the Office of Folklife Studies at the Smithsonian Institution (the national museum for American history), the Folk Arts Division of the National Endowment for the Arts (NEA), and the American Folklife Center of the Library of Congress. Each played a crucial role in developing cultural conservation, an early version of sustainability for the traditional arts.

The Smithsonian's involvement was the earliest of the three and remained the most visible. The Smithsonian's folk festival (1967–present) led to the establishment of a separate folklife division in 1980, now called the Center for Folklife and Cultural Heritage. Held in the nation's capital, at first the Smithsonian's festival followed the model of the Newport (Rhode Island) Folk Festival, which since 1959 had presented a majority of professional folksingers, making careers from their music in the folk revival, with other, lesser-known musicians who came to be known as tradition bearers or source musicians. The former were later termed revivalists, which meant that they had not been born and raised within the musical communities that carried the music they performed now from a stage for an audience. They had learned it from recordings, from other revivalists, or in some cases directly from source musicians. Source musicians, on the other hand, had known the music they performed from childhood, when it prevailed in their communities, and although they may have had professional careers at one time, most were not earning their living as performers at present. Many of these were from American minority groups, or from regions where modernization came late and the older folk traditions had lingered. Among the professional folksingers were Joan Baez, Oscar Brand, Peter, Paul, and Mary, and Bob Dylan; among the tradition bearers were African American musicians such as Mississippi John Hurt, Cajun musicians such as the Balfa Brothers, and those from the Appalachian Mountain region of the American South, such as Clarence Ashley. In the early 1970s, the Smithsonian festival stopped presenting the revivalists and in doing so unintentionally ghettoized authenticity in the folk arts by means of ethnic, class, and regional criteria. Those who produced the folk festivals began to hope that the national attention gained from the festival might enhance the prestige of these source musicians in their home communities and help to preserve the musical traditions they represented.

This notion of conservation differed, of course, from archival preservation, as interventions could be targeted to aid particular traditions. This goal was realized by the Folk Arts Division of the NEA, which was (and is) a funds-granting agency. Monies were (and still are) granted to folk artists in the form of fellowships and to organizations involved in preserving and conserving the folk arts in various regional and ethnic communities throughout the United States. The Folk Arts Division guidelines articulated the program's goal: to help folk artists and their communities value their traditional expressive culture and move into their futures, steadied by continuity with the past. In other words, the guidelines were meant to help folk artists and communities conserve their traditional cultural beliefs and practices while becoming more modern. When I served on the Folk Arts Divisions grant decision-making panel in the early 1980s, for example, I realized that recent immigrants from Southeast Asia were a targeted group. Folk Arts staff told us that their abrupt removals to the United States following the war in that region had caused cultural trauma and that in this crisis their folk traditions were liable to disappear within a single generation if nothing was done to help them.

The American Folklife Center, established in 1976, was neither a festival-producing agency nor a granting organization. It combined the Library of Congress's folk music archive, which had been established in the 1920s, with a series of public initiatives that involved partnerships with cultural organizations in various regions of the United States and that served to identify, document, and present the results back to the region in an effort to strengthen regional and occupational folklife. Typically, these initiatives began with surveys and culminated in a series of recommendations, along with a traveling exhibit. Today the center defines its mission as to "preserve and present American folklife through programs of research, documentation, archival preservation, reference service, live performance, exhibitions, publications, and training" (American Folklife Center n.d.). Surveys characterized their efforts in the 1970s and 1980s, while in the 1990s partnerships with other agencies, including the National Park Service, were undertaken for cultural conservation.

In the 1980s, the Folk Arts Division of the NEA built an infrastructure of folklorists, employed chiefly in the state arts agencies. By the end of the decade, almost every state of the union had at least one. They undertook state-based surveys to identify and document folk artists and mounted exhibits and festivals to present them to the general public. The state folklorists' functions also included grant giving to local folk and traditional arts organizations. They hired contract fieldworkers to carry out some of the documentation and presentation activities. Where possible, they used the same authenticity criteria as the Smithsonian festival, seeking out tradition-bearing folk artists who had been born and raised with their community's traditions, rather than revivalists who had come to them later in life. The result was a folk artist inventory that also served the Smithsonian's folklife office, which had decided to give over one section of the festival to a different state of the union each year. Fieldworkers who had documented state folklife were often involved in presenting it in the nation's capital. They also were available to the American Folklife Center for its various regional initiatives.

As these efforts bore fruit, and not coincidentally employed hundreds of folklorists and some ethnomusicologists with graduate degrees, the leaders in this burgeoning field of public folklore began to reflect on what it was they were doing. Each agency articulated its goals with increasing precision, whether in terms of cultural equity, cultural pluralism, or—in what came to be the term almost everyone eventually settled on—cultural conservation. In doing so, they increasingly defined cultural conservation in terms of heritage.

In 1982, the American Folklife Center produced a book, coordinated by Ormond Loomis, titled *Cultural Conservation*. They had been tasked with compiling a report for the US Secretary of the Interior "on preserving and conserving the intangible elements of our cultural heritage such as arts, skills, folklife, and folkways" (Loomis 1983, 1). The Department of the Interior was the appropriate government agency because it was responsible for conservation of public resources. For the distinction between tangible and intangible cultural elements, the document drew on the practice of Asian societies, particularly Japan, which identified "intangible properties" as resources to be under government protection, folk artists among them (13). This identification of exceptional traditional artists as "national treasures" had already been the impetus behind Bess Lomax Hawes's successful 1980 proposal to the NEA to establish and permit the Folk Arts Division to select the National Heritage fellows, identifying a dozen outstanding American folk artists each year and offering them a cash honorarium of $5,000 and a ceremonial recognition in Washington, DC. This tangible/intangible distinction became much better known in its UNESCO incarnations. US folklorists ultimately came to critique it on the grounds that in the practice of folklife, tangible and intangible were inseparable (Hufford 1994, 2). The Loomis document identified two components of cultural conservation: preservation and what it called encouragement. By preservation was meant activities involving planning, documentation, and maintenance; by encouragement was meant publication, public events, and education in order that a healthy traditional expressive folklife culture would enable a community's sense of integrity and enhanced identity to flourish. In this way, cultural conservation was to be more than simply preservation and maintenance. Encouragement looked to a cultural future in which folklife played an important role. Cultural conservation was more effective than preservation, for "preservation plans can divert undertakings that would disrupt normal cultural development" (Loomis 1982, 10), and "to endure a group must pass on its distinguishing attributes from one generation to the next. Such attributes are the essence of cultural heritage" (3), and "it is possible, however, to temper change so that it proceeds in accordance with the will of the people, and not in response to the pressures of faddish trends or insensitive public or private projects. Conservation denotes efforts which ... ensure natural cultural growth" (29). Leaving aside for the moment what "natural" cultural growth might be, this rhetoric reflects an antimodernist agenda, opposed to materialism and consumer society and the cultural homogenization allegedly resulting from mass media and national brands. The Loomis document criticized identifying heritage items on a list, as UNESCO later was to do in compiling an inventory of world masterpieces of intangible cultural heritage (ICH) (16). Finally, cultural conservation drew the analogy between biological diversity and cultural diversity—if the one was good, so was the other (11). Thus many, if not most, of the arguments that would later surface in the cultural sustainability discourse in the new millennium had already been anticipated in this document. It became a working document for public folklore agencies in the 1980s.

In the 1980s and 1990s, the NEA's Folk Arts Division continued to support organizations, projects, and artists and to grow the network of state folklorists, who in turn initiated projects within their states and regions. These projects were aimed primarily at increasing opportunities for traditional folk artists to continue practicing their art. One of the most successful of these was the apprenticeship program in which tradition bearers were paid to teach younger members of their families and communities (and, in some instances, revivalists) their music, crafts, and so forth in an effort to transmit the folk arts to the next generations. Its only problem was that it was chronically underfunded, which diminished its overall impact. Concerts and festivals not only showcased traditional music but also gave the tradition bearers and source musicians recognition, acknowledgment, and prestige within their communities. The Smithsonian's was the largest of these festivals. Another was the National Folk Festival, a Washington, DC–based festival since 1969, which also came to be advised chiefly by folklorists and which in the late 1980s embarked on a new strategy of moving its venue to a new city every three years in hopes that the city would continue supporting the festival after they moved on to the next site. A few cities did: Lowell, Massachusetts, has sponsored its festival for more than twenty years, while Bangor, Maine, has kept its festival going for more than ten years. In the 1990s, the Smithsonian festivals took on an increasing international flavor, when one section of the festival was devoted to presenting the folklife of a nation other than the United States, resulting also in international cooperation among folklorists.

In 1990, the American Folklife Center held a conference on "Cultural Conservation: Rethinking the Cultural Mission." From that conference emerged the book *Conserving Culture: A New Discourse on Heritage* (Hufford 1994). New was the emphasis on heritage, along with the realization that cultural conservation worked best when folklorists, applied ethnomusicologists, and other cultural specialists partnered with community leaders and organizations to work toward mutually approved and understood goals. In her introduction, Hufford acknowledged that the cultural conservation movement places a value on both tangible and intangible culture marked for conservation, terming it heritage, something from the past that is both "ours" and worth preserving. Yet when folklife specialists began working with various constituencies to conserve heritage, it became clear that the separation of tangible and intangible heritage was misleading, particularly in those areas where the two were intimately bound up, such as intangible folk knowledge derived from interactions with the tangible environment. A second problem arose when folklife specialists attempted to "impose external standards on local communities" (2). A top-down approach could easily overlook or even discredit local knowledge, while outside experts imposed policies that proved unhelpful. A third problem arose in the "tendency of heritage planning to authenticate past cultures and environments [which] effectively reduced the power of present-day communities to manage the environments on which their dynamic cultures depend" (3). On the other hand, Hufford affirmed the term "conservation," writing that it acknowledged the dynamic aspects of culture, whereas "preservation" implied constancy. In other words, heritage need not be a thing of the past. Hufford argued forcefully for cultural partnerships between folklife specialists and community members whose local knowledge was essential so that the goals were mutual and the policies reflected broad agreement among all stakeholders.

Yet cultural conservation had its critics. Most prominent among these was folklorist Nicholas Spitzer, whose background included cultural conservation work for the Smithsonian Institution and a term as Louisiana state folklorist. Best known as the host of the public radio program *American Routes* and now also a professor at Tulane University, Spitzer argued in a series of presentations beginning in 1987 that conservation bound public folklore to an "ethically problematic" organic metaphor in which cultures follow a natural cycle of birth, growth, and decay. At its worst, this analogy smacked of Spencerian cultural evolutionism. Rather than work as conservationists to rescue cultures from threat and endangerment, Spitzer ([1992] 2007, 95–96) wrote, it would be better to think in terms of conversations with cultures to further "continuity, equity and diversity." Had Spitzer looked more closely at the environmental movement, he might have mentioned that nature conservationists were aiming to further continuity, equity, and diversity within ecosystems; and he must have known that public folklorists engaged in cultural conservation work had those ends in view as well. Nonetheless, Spitzer reminded folklorists to consider the limitations of the ecological trope: that culture does not necessarily behave like nature. Nor does nature necessarily behave like culture (Titon 2008–, 2013). Cultural conservation was also critiqued by several on the grounds that it proceeded from a romantic and nostalgic bias toward the past, one that was ill-equipped to analyze correctly the contemporary forces propelling cultures forward. Nevertheless, for nearly thirty years cultural conservation remained the dominant paradigm within public folklore, while it also guided applied ethnomusicologists in their work on behalf of music cultures. If cultural conservation has given way in the new millennium to cultural sustainability, the two paradigms nonetheless have much in common. Applied ethnomusicologists and public folklorists today are beholden to the history of cultural conservation, whether they know it or not.

## Safeguarding

UNESCO is the major international force on behalf of cultural conservation today; but the word UNESCO chose for it is "safeguarding." In the English language, safeguarding connotes preservation, not conservation. UNESCO had early in its history enacted conventions (treaties that are binding only on nations that sign them) protecting historic sites, monuments, and architecture throughout the world, particularly against the ravages of war; however, in the 1970s and 1980s their discussion turned to protecting traditional culture itself, usually termed *folkways, folklife,* and *folklore.* Eventually, in 1989, after years of international consultation, debate, and discussion, UNESCO issued a "Recommendation on the Safeguarding of Traditional Culture and Folklore" (UNESCO 1989). Many of the safeguarding ideas embodied in that cultural conservation document, and in its later implementation through two conventions (in 2003 and 2005), could also be found in cultural conservation discourse that was occurring in the United States (see https://ich.unesco.org/en/what-is-intangible-heritage-00003 and https://ich.unesco.org/en/convention). Indeed, the word "safeguard" had appeared in the American Folklife Center's 1982 report on *Cultural Conservation*: "The ultimate aim of documentation and of the other strategies that combine in cultural conservation must be to *safeguard* and promote the community life and values of ethnic, occupational, religious, and regional groups by recognizing and protecting the treasured patterns that arise from their ways of life" (Loomis 1983, 17–19, my italics).

Significantly, however, in its 1989 recommendation, UNESCO defined *preservation* and *conservation* exactly opposite to the common US understanding of the two terms. For UNESCO in 1989, conservation was what those in the United States understand as archival preservation. It was "concerned with documentation regarding folk traditions and its object is, in the event of the non-utilization or evolution of such traditions, to give researchers and tradition-bearers access to data enabling them to understand the process through which traditions change." Meanwhile, for UNESCO preservation involved what we in the United States think of as conservation of living traditions. It was "concerned with protection of folk traditions and those who are the transmitters, having regard to the fact that each people has a right to its own culture and that [its culture] is often eroded by . . . the industrialized culture purveyed by the mass media. Measures must be taken to guarantee the status of and economic support for folk traditions both in the communities that produce them and beyond" (UNESCO 1989).

The 1989 UNESCO recommendation fell on deaf international ears, as only a half dozen nations responded (Aikawa 2001, 13–14). As a result, throughout the 1990s UNESCO discussed ways of galvanizing international support, culminating in a 1999 conference sponsored by UNESCO and the Smithsonian Institution and leading to the 2003 Convention for the Safeguarding of the Intangible Cultural Heritage, which generated a mechanism for identifying outstanding examples of ICH ("world masterpieces").

In this document, the term "folklore" was replaced by "intangible cultural heritage," and "conservation" was dropped while "preservation" and a host of other activities were subsumed under the cover term "safeguarding," defined as a combination of "identification, documentation, research, preservation, protection, promotion, enhancement, transmission . . . and revitalization" of ICH (https://ich.unesco.org/en/convention). UN members were asked to sign the treaty and then to begin nominating outstanding examples of their ICH for inclusion on a list of "world masterpieces." If UNESCO approved the nomination, then the nation was obligated to undertake various actions to safeguard the ICH masterpiece, which they had promised in their nominating application. These usually included further documentation and interpretation, stimulus and promotion, and dissemination, which often resulted in cultural heritage tourism. Despite UNESCO's good intentions, in the United States safeguarding carried the unfortunate additional purifying connotation of cleansing and deodorizing, derived from the name of a popular soap sold in the United States and marketed under the brand name Safeguard. For political reasons, the United States has not signed either of the 2003 or 2005 UNESCO ICH conventions. US folklorists and ethnomusicologists have, of course, discussed the UNESCO ICH initiatives, but in general they have been critical of the results (Weintraub and Yung 2009).

## Sustainability

### In Theory

Sustainability, as I have noted, has much in common with preservation, conservation, and safeguarding. Some advocates of sustainability emphasize that their attitude toward development is progressive. Conservationists, they say, would prefer to manage things to maintain present conditions or restore earlier ones; sustainability advocates recognize that change is both natural and inevitable and seek to manage change in order to guarantee continuity, integrity, and resource availability for the future. The predominant sustainability discourses take place in economics, ecology, and environmental studies. Sustainability in economics means *sustainable development*; in ecology, it refers to the stability of ecosystems; in environmental studies, it centers on energy conservation and carbon emission reduction. Although the idea long preceded the use of the term, *sustainable development* appears to have entered public discourse first in the *World Conservation Strategy* of the International Union for the Conservation of Nature and Natural Resources (IUCN 1980). *Sustainable development* also occupied a prominent place in *Gaia: An Atlas of Planet Management* (N. Myers [1984] 1992). But it was with *Our Common Future* (World Commission on Environment and Development 1987), usually referred to as the Brundtland Report, for the UN, where the term "sustainability," coupled with "development," captured the imagination of the public policymakers. Particularly in the arena of developmental economics, where the chief problems were identified as third world population growth, poverty, outmoded and inefficient agriculture, lack of industry, poor infrastructure, and so forth, sustainable development was viewed as a reasonable solution, famously defined in the Brundtland Report as "development that meets the needs of the present, without compromising the ability of future generations to meet their own needs." Environmentalists interpreted the sustainability mandate as confirming their agenda: limits to growth, conservation of resources, safeguarding biodiversity, transitioning energy from fossil fuels to renewable sources, and so forth. Most economists, on the other hand, thought that sustainable development confirmed their belief that advances in science and technology would increase efficiency and solve third world problems. The environmentalists placed their emphasis on sustainable, while the economists took comfort in development. In retrospect, of course, it can be seen that for economics, sustainable development is not a new concept but rather a reinterpretation of the conservation concept of wise use and sustainable yield, which I have already traced to Renaissance Europe. For environmentalists, sustainability evoked the old idea of the "balance of nature" or, as it was expressed by natural historians including Gilbert White, Henry David Thoreau, and even by Charles Darwin, "nature's economy"—the idea that left to its own devices, nature tended toward efficiency as its parts worked together for the benefit of the whole (Worster 1994a).[1] For ecologists, sustainability evoked the scientific version of natural balance, expressed in the idea that an ecosystem tended "naturally" to move toward a state of stability, or dynamic equilibrium, except when disturbed.

Among applied ethnomusicologists and public folklorists, the ecologists' understanding of sustainability has been the most influential. As pointed out earlier, in the new millennium cultural conservation has become cultural sustainability while musical conservation has become musical sustainability, in both cases continuing the eco-trope. However, developmental economics is not without influence. For example, UNESCO views safeguarding ICH as a part of the UN's economic development mandate. Culture must be safeguarded not merely because it is part of our human heritage, but because culture is "the mainspring of sustainable development" (https://en.unesco.org/themes/education-sustainable-development/cultural-diversity). In addition, in the contemporary field of arts advocacy, one of the most powerful arguments advanced is that the arts are an economic engine (Throsby 2010). In this vein, applied ethnomusicologists and public folklorists sometimes advocate heritage tourism (festivals, living history museums, historic tours, and so forth) to fuel local and regional economies, believing that this will also give a boost to traditional music cultures and other arts.

Sustainability carries with it the notion of finite resources that are in danger of exhaustion. Given infinite abundance, there would be no need to think in terms of using resources in a sustainable way. If it is acceptable to speak of music as a human resource, then plainly it is a renewable one. As long as people can sing, they are not in danger of using up the resources required to make music. But just as language itself is not endangered whereas individual languages have gone extinct and others are going extinct, certain musics—that is, music cultures—and genres and instruments are endangered. Of course, those engaged in salvage folklore and ethnomusicology were well aware of these threats; indeed, it could be said that the impulse to preserve music arises at least partly from sadness over impending loss. Among US folklorists, as we have seen, conservation moved out of the museums and into living (or rather, supposedly dying) cultures with the object of renewal and revitalization. As I wrote above, only a small number of US ethnomusicologists took part in the cultural conservation movement led by US public folklorists. Most US ethnomusicologists continued to do their research outside North America, where their experiences with musical and cultural conservation were various and diffuse.

Although sustainability did not make an impact in ethnomusicology or folklore until the new millennium, it is helpful to see how the concept was implemented in late-twentieth-century developmental economics and the environmental movement, the two areas where it remains most deeply embedded today. Sustainability comes to ethnomusicologists with baggage from economics and environmentalism. Critics pointed out that sustainable development that reduced overall short-term resource yield would only exacerbate third world poverty in the face of population growth, but proponents argued that a combination of smart market regulation, wise political policies, and advances in technology would greatly increase efficiency, productivity, and ultimate yield and that the rising tide would lift all boats. The results of sustainable development initiatives are mixed. Economic successes have occurred in some areas, failures in others. Cultural anthropologists working in indigenous societies critique sustainable development on the grounds that it is a new form of Western colonialism that destroys traditional knowledge, lifeways, and cultural integrity. Meanwhile, resource exploitation and environmental degradation continue, though perhaps at a lesser rate, while living standards rise in some nations and stagnate elsewhere, and while income inequality also is on the rise. Nonetheless, sustainability brought environmental considerations into economics as never before.

The work of ecological economist Herman E. Daly has been notable within sustainable development. Daly was important not only as a theorist but also as an actor on this stage, for from 1988 to 1994 he was the senior economist at the World Bank. Daly began his career in the 1970s by opposing the possibility of continuous economic growth. He maintained that in their models, economists ignored the environment at their peril. Constrained by the environment, the world economy was better viewed as a steady-state, dynamic equilibrium (Daly [1977] 1991). After the Brundtland Report, Daly endorsed sustainable development. He defined it in terms borrowed from "wise use" conservation practice—that is, as sustainable yield in which the renewed resource is able to exceed the amount harvested or lost to disasters such as disease or fire. Alarmed at the way *sustainable development* was being used synonymously with *sustainable growth*, Daly argued that development need not imply growth. "When something grows it gets bigger. When something develops it gets different," he wrote. "The earth ecosystem develops but it does not grow. Its subsystem, the economy must eventually stop growing but continue to develop. The term 'sustainable development' therefore makes sense for the economy but only if it is understood as 'development without growth'" (Daly 1993, 267–268). Unfortunately, Daly's sensible distinction failed to influence most developmental economists. Not surprisingly, the business world also adopted the idea of sustainable development, but in their hands, it became a synonym for sustainable growth. To corporations intent on global competition, growth seemed necessary for survival. Many corporations adopted "green" practices, such as recycling waste, at the same time that they continued using up finite resources while researching technology for more efficient productivity and wiser use.

Daly was not the only economist to make use of ecology when discussing economy. In the 1990s, around the same time that Daly was proclaiming sustainable growth an oxymoron, James F. Moore argued that corporate leaders should understand their firms to be actors within ecosystems where they must not only compete but also cooperate in order to ensure the sustainability of the entire system and themselves within it. Just as predators and prey are interdependent in a natural ecosystem, so are corporations interdependent in a business ecosystem, even when they are rivals. His classic case in point was the cooperation and competition between Apple and Microsoft (Moore 1993). Whereas Daly's distinction between development and growth was ignored by those economists, business leaders, and government policymakers who maintained a bias toward growth, Moore's idea of business ecosystems caught on, augmented by Paul Hawken's (1994) popular writing on the subject. Today it is a commonplace to speak of the Apple ecosystem or the Google ecosystem. Daly and Moore believed that ecosystems were self-regulating and moved toward a stable, though dynamic, equilibrium.

Ecological thought had little impact on folklore and ethnomusicology until the new millennium, but its effect on cultural anthropology in the past century was significant.[2] In fact, the subdiscipline of cultural ecology gathered momentum in the 1950s and was well established a decade later (Netting 1977). It treated human groups and their behavior from an ecological perspective (Rappaport 1979). Modernization and progress in so-called underdeveloped nations in the post–World War II era had been a concern of developmental anthropologists all along, with some applied anthropologists working to further it, others critiquing it, yet others undermining it through action anthropology and by privileging local knowledge over a modern worldview. Sustainable development, as defined in the Brundtland Report, was useful to economic anthropologists concerned with the impact of modernization and progress on the environment. Cultural anthropologists used the sustainable development concept to probe the interface between the environment and economic equity as well as political ecology. John van Willigen (2002, 74) concluded in *Applied Anthropology* that "sustainability has come to be expressed in a wide range of [anthropological] themes in addition to economic development. These include biodiversity, climate change, soil and water conservation, efficient and renewable energy use, air qualify, solid waste, population planning, forestation, and alternative agriculture." Yet, as I mentioned earlier, applied anthropology is the target of a stinging contemporary critique coming from anthropologists specializing in indigenous studies, because of its historical alliance with developmental economics. The bad odor attached to it might threaten applied ethnomusicology, but it must be noted that applied ethnomusicology arose well after applied anthropology, during the period of postcolonial critique and that applied ethnomusicology's ideological stance is anticolonialism.[3]

Concerns with sustainability and the environment were also, of course, central in the environmental movement, represented within the science of ecology by a growing sustainability discourse in conservation biology, which also came to be known as *conservation ecology*. Michael Soulé, the founder of conservation biology, defined its "proper objective" as the "protection and continuity of entire communities and ecosystems." Conservation biologists are concerned less with "maximum yields, and profitability, and more [with] the long-range viability of whole systems and species. . . . Long-term viability of natural communities usually implies the persistence of diversity" and, because of human-made disturbances to these communities, requires redress through active management (Soulé 1985, 728–729). In emphasizing continuity and viability, Soulé is speaking of sustainability but not of sustainable development. His deemphasis on yields underlines the major difference between sustainable development, which has an economic end, and conservation biology's idea of sustainability, which concerns long-term endurance of ecosystems and maximizes biodiversity over yield. As conservation biology grew into an applied "crisis discipline," some wished to adapt it for sustainable development; yet Soulé's original vision of biodiversity remained central, while it impacted environmental activists and ecologists alike. Already in 1993, ecohistorian Donald Worster (1994b, 148) could write, "There is a widespread implication . . . that sustainability at bottom is an ecological concept: the goal of environmentalism should be to achieve ecological sustainability."[4] Worster worried that sustainability carried economic yield connotations of conservation's "wise use" back into the discussion, albeit under a new name. Furthermore, he pointed out the problems with the idea of ecosystem sustainability in the face of the changed ecological paradigm, which had abandoned ideas of stability and a balance of nature (149–150). Nonetheless, the contemporary environmental movement embraces sustainability to the point that it has become a vogue word for various eco-conscious activities.

### *In Applied Ethnomusicology*

As I mentioned at the outset of this chapter, US ethnomusicologists and other culture workers helped to sustain musicians, musical traditions, and music cultures long before the term "sustainability" became operative in the late 1980s, and before it entered ethnomusicological discourse in the 2000s. In the 1890s, a privileged, antimodernist wing within the Progressive movement established settlement schools for the poor in New York and Chicago, as well as remote rural areas such as the southern Appalachian Mountains, where immigrant and native traditions were collected from elders and taught to youngsters. The well-known Appalachian singer Jean Ritchie (1922–2015) grew up near the Hindman Settlement School in southeastern Kentucky, where many of her sisters attended; after she left Kentucky for New York, she took a job at a settlement school, where her singing came to the attention of Alan Lomax and others in the folk revival scene, and her career as a tradition bearer was soon launched (Ritchie 1955). While it suffered from noblesse oblige, the Progressives' uplift agenda for the poor favored the conservation of folk traditions, both rural and immigrant. Music and dance were prominent among those singled out for preservation and revival. Generations of American children learned them in school. This was not archival preservation but sustainability within living cultural groups in an effort to restore and maintain personal and cultural identity and integrity under the psychologically dislocating pressures of modernization.

Other twentieth-century efforts at sustainability before the term gained currency were directed at individual musicians rather than cultural groups. Although most folklorists and ethnomusicologists believed that folk traditions were endangered and would diminish and eventually disappear, it might be possible to help outstanding musicians revive and maintain their careers, even if it meant bringing their music to a different audience, the urban middle class, whose ethnic and regional traditions had vanished into the melting pot. Alan and John Lomax's work in this vein with the African American folksinger Huddie Ledbetter (Lead Belly) is a case in point (Porterfield 2001). In certain parts of the United States, folk festivals became occasions to reintroduce traditional musicians to their own cultures and bring them to the attention of a wider public, thereby stimulating them to maintain their musical skills and repertoires. Festivals such as the one started in Asheville, North Carolina (1928–present) by Bascom Lamar Lunsford are examples. In the 1950s and 1960s, rediscovered traditional blues singers and old-time string band musicians, as well as tradition-bearing folksingers were promoted on the newly reinvigorated folk music revival circuit. Musicians such as the aforementioned Jean Ritchie, Son House, Clarence "Tom" Ashley, Bill Monroe, and Almeda Riddle—regarded as authentic representatives of their regions and musical traditions because they had grown up learning them—mingled with folk music revivalists in widely promoted folk music concerts, as well as festivals that drew many thousands of spectators.

Many of those who promoted the sustainability of musical genres such as blues and bluegrass in the 1960s were themselves young, folk revival musicians, and some later became folklorists and ethnomusicologists. These included William Ferris, whose efforts to sustain blues in Mississippi included cultural tourism (especially for Europeans), a boost to the career of B. B. King, and promotion of the career of country blues singer Son Thomas. Ferris brought King to be an artist in residence at Yale, where Ferris taught as a professor of American Studies for a few years before returning to his native Mississippi to found the University of Mississippi's Center for the Study of Southern Culture. From 1997 to 2001, Ferris was director of the National Endowment for the Humanities, the first and only time that a folklorist has held this position, the most powerful cultural post in the United States. Kenneth Goldstein and Roger Abrahams both collected, recorded, and promoted folk musicians in the 1950s and 1960s folk music revival; they became professors of folklore at the University of Pennsylvania. My own trajectory was similar. While a graduate student, I joined Lazy Bill Lucas's blues band in Minneapolis in the late 1960s out of a desire to learn more about a music I had already been playing for several years. Soon, wanting to give something back, I saw that I could promote my new friend's solo career by publishing my interviews with him in fan magazines devoted to African American blues music, which led to a recording contract for him as well as an appearance at the 1970 Ann Arbor Blues Festival. David Evans's path was similar to mine. He researched blues while in graduate degree programs in folklore, promoted some of the blues singers' careers, and eventually became a professor of ethnomusicology at the University of Memphis.

The most significant relationship for what would become sustainability was what developed in the 1960s between folklorist and bluegrass musician Ralph Rinzler (1934–1994) and Cajun fiddler Dewey Balfa (1927–1992). Their partnership ushered in a revitalization and revival of Cajun music beginning in the late 1960s within French Louisiana and elsewhere. Although the sustainability concept was not available to describe it then, it remains one of the most effective instances of a US vernacular musical and cultural sustainability intervention. I have written about this elsewhere, so a summary here will suffice (Titon 2009c, 130–131). One of the promoters of the Newport Folk Festival, Rinzler had invited Balfa, among others, to perform at the festival. Balfa's local newspaper had questioned whether that old-fashioned, "chanky-chank" music ought to represent the region at such an important festival. Surely, Balfa and the others would be laughed off the stage, the paper had editorialized. But instead, the Newport audience would not let them leave the stage, calling for encores. Balfa returned to Cajun country so energized that he became a cultural ambassador and took his family band on tour throughout the world. But more than that, he led a cultural revival movement within his Cajun community that eventually extended even to a renewal of the Cajun French language. Whether Rinzler was responsible for doing anything more than galvanizing Balfa's latent sustainability talents, he understood what could be accomplished by a partnership between culture workers like himself and community leaders like Balfa. When, a few years later, Rinzler founded the Smithsonian Festival of American Folklife, he spread this idea among the festival workers and the group of folklorists and ethnomusicologists who came to join him in Washington, DC, in the 1970s, one that included Bess Lomax Hawes (1921–2009) and her brother Alan Lomax (1915–2002), as well as ethnomusicologists Daniel Sheehy and Thomas Vennum, along with folklorist Alan Jabbour, all of whom were to become deeply involved with the formation and early years of the NEA's Folk Arts Division, the American Folklife Center at the Library of Congress, and the Smithsonian's Center for Folklife and Cultural Heritage. To a greater or lesser degree, all of this work was animated by this vision of the possibilities of cultural renewal and sustainability as a result of various interventions: grants from the NEA, the Smithsonian's festivals, and the American Folklife Center's surveys and exhibitions. However, *sustainability* was not the operative term at the time, and as I discussed earlier, when in the early 1980s they began to theorize about what they had done and were doing and wanted to do better, they called it *cultural conservation*. But in defining it as "encouragement" along with preservation, they were thinking about sustainability.

The founding generation of the Society for Ethnomusicology was interested primarily in basic research and scholarship, not applied work. However, David McAllester and Mantle Hood undertook some interventions that could be considered applied, even though they never discussed them in those terms. McAllester was active in the field of precollege music education, working with the Music Educators National Conference to include world music in the curriculum for youngsters aged six to eighteen. His own research was with the Navajo, and although he was adopted by a Navajo family, he did not actively seek to influence the future of Navajo music, preferring to leave that to the Navajo themselves. Hood, on the other hand, intervened in Bali, both as a patron of the arts and in encouraging the revival of gamelan gong making and performance. A section near the conclusion of his book *The Ethnomusicologist* is titled "The Impact of the Ethnomusicologist" and concludes by reporting on the way his work and appreciation of their artistry raised the status of traditional musicians, and music and dance in their community, and gave them impetus to continue (Hood 1971, 358–371).

Only a few US ethnomusicologists were involved in these musical and cultural conservation efforts, as noted earlier. At the Smithsonian Institution and associated in one way or another with the folklife office were Thomas

Vennum and, in the late 1980s, Charlotte Heth, who had become director of their Native American museum initiative. A few ethnomusicologists worked as presenters at the Smithsonian's folklife festival—I had done so in 1976, for example—and in 1988, ethnomusicologist Anthony Seeger became the director of the Smithsonian's newly acquired operation, Folkways Records. Judith Gray, who had studied ethnomusicology at Wesleyan University, was hired as an archivist by the American Folklife Center. The Folk Arts Division of the NEA involved the most ethnomusicologists. Daniel Sheehy, who received his PhD in ethnomusicology from the University of California, Los Angeles, was the assistant director throughout the decade, while the Folk Arts panelists who met four times per year to advise the agency and recommend grant and heritage awards included ethnomusicologists Charlotte Heth (serving 1981–1982, 1987), myself (1981–1983), Robert Garfias (1982–1983), Jacqueline DjeDje (1983–1985), Ralph Samuelson (1984–1985), Hector Vega (1984–1986), Lorraine Sakata (1986–1989), Ric Trimillos (1987–1988), Adelaide Schramm (1988–1989), and Thomas Vennum (1989). A few more worked in state agencies such as arts councils, either doing contract fieldwork and festival and exhibit production, or as arts administrators. Each of us had a commitment to applied ethnomusicology and to musical and cultural conservation in our own academic and public work, but altogether we were only about 5 percent of the ethnomusicologists working in the United States at that time. The fact that most US ethnomusicologists researched music cultures outside the United States severely limited the percentage that might have participated, however. In short, while in the 1980s public (sector) folklore developed a strong US infrastructure, employing folklorists at the national and state government levels, there was nothing comparable in scope for US ethnomusicologists. The vast majority remained scholars aiming their research at colleagues while teaching students in the academic world. Some, however, developed a commitment to applied ethnomusicology.

Ethnomusicology's involvement in sustainability during the 1980s came chiefly from commitments to musical individuals and communities that were resulting from fieldwork, not from alliances with public folklore. While it was true even then that almost all fieldwork conducted by US academic ethnomusicologists was accomplished for the purposes of scholarship and contributions to knowledge about the music of the world's peoples, many ethnomusicologists were forming friendships with their principal informants (some of which led to marriage) and began asking how "giving back" might also be extended to communities. This was the same generation that had begun reciprocity of this kind in the 1960s as graduate students. Also, at this time, the "crisis" in US cultural anthropology was leading to a new reflexivity among North American ethnomusicologists who, in questioning their own subject positions and their rights to claim knowledge and authority, of necessity were considering the impact of their research on the communities studied, in addition to the impact of their studies on themselves. Notable in terms of their movement in the direction of applied ethnomusicology and sustainability were second-generation US ethnomusicologists Paul Berliner, Steven Feld, and Anthony Seeger. Berliner's (1978) work with Shona *mbira* music and musicians was unusually reflexive for its time, concerned as it was with the ethnomusicologist subject position vis-à-vis the people whose music he was learning. Feld and Seeger undertook ethnographic fieldwork among tropical rain forest peoples, with scientific research as their principal goal; however, each scholar gradually developed a sense of responsibility to help their subjects maintain their music and culture in the face of modernization. Feld's ([1982] 2012) efforts with the Kaluli in Papua New Guinea included a reflexive postscript to the second edition of *Sound and Sentiment*. Seeger (1991) began to investigate legal means of protecting Suya culture, including copyright for their music. Some ethnomusicologists undertaking graduate study in the 1980s were strongly affected by the currents of experimental ethnography and applied ethnomusicology; among them, Michelle Kisliuk (1998) wrote a reflexive ethnography of another tropical rain forest people, the BaAka. Alan Lomax should also be considered in this light. Although Lomax (1972a) meant cantometrics to be scientific, aimed it at anthropologists and folklorists, and seldom was reflexive, his work on behalf of musical and cultural equity was implicit in this research, and explicit in his strongly felt influence on the cultural conservation movement in US folklore.

It was conservation ecology's notion of diversity, coupled with equity and ecojustice, that provided the basis for sustainability thinking in folklore (cultural sustainability) and ethnomusicology (music culture sustainability and the persistence of musical traditions) in the twenty-first century. Within ethnomusicology, "Music and Sustainability" was the title of a panel presentation for the 2006 annual conference of the Society for Ethnomusicology. A special journal issue on music and sustainability published three years later included the papers from that panel plus two others (Titon 2009b). The essay introducing the special issue proposed that music is "a biocultural resource, a sound-producing activity natural to humans that comes into being as music through sociocultural processes. . . . Efforts to sustain music are best directed at, and regarded as, sustaining selected sociocultural activities that encourage music's production and maintenance. In short, sustaining music means sustaining people making music. Then if one grants that sustaining music is a legitimate public policy pursuit, a number of further questions arise: what are the wisest policies, how may they be achieved, and what role might ethnomusicologists play in defining them?" (Titon 2009a, 6).

The essays in that issue addressed music and sustainability from different vantage points, but all were concerned with music cultures in a state of revitalization. In the United States, these music cultures, particularly when regarded as expressions of ethnic identity, are cultural policy targets. Applied ethnomusicologists ask how healthy these musical cultures are and what can be done to help them survive and flourish, while at the same time honoring their traditional practices. Repatriation of archival recordings has been an enormous help to a number of them. In her essay for the special journal issue on music and sustainability, Janet Topp Fargion mentioned the Passamaquoddy recordings made more than a hundred years ago by Jesse Walter Fewkes (Topp Fargion 2009, 78). Wayne Newell, an educator and Passamaquoddy community scholar helping his nation to revitalize traditional music and language, uses these recordings and finds them invaluable (Newell 2003). This way of thinking about preservation is critical to Topp Fargion's holistic redefinition of field recordings. Recordings have always held a central place in ethnomusicological research. Yet among ethnomusicologists today, field recording itself may be becoming endangered. For one thing, it is increasingly difficult to keep pace with changing technological developments. For another, as social texts become more central to ethnomusicology, documentary field recordings recede in importance, along with musical transcription and analysis. Topp Fargion's essay showed how a more inclusive approach to research, particularly for sustainability purposes, enables the field recorded document.

In that same special journal issue on music and sustainability, Mark DeWitt and Tom Faux both presented case studies of particular musical cultures in a state of revitalization. DeWitt portrayed a Creole music-and-dance scene in Northern California that is largely self-supporting, based not only on a core of Creole (and to a lesser extent Cajun) out-migrants from Louisiana but also on a group of folk music and dance revivalists who, although not growing up in Creole or Cajun culture, have joined it. Although some of the Bay Area musicians have received recognition and support from arts councils and other agencies, most have received little or none. The health of this scene does not depend on stimuli from external agencies. But as it is competing with an ever-compelling musical marketplace, its vitality can be lost in a generation (DeWitt 2009).

For that reason, "passing it on" is a major concern of arts policy. Apprenticeship, funded by arts agencies, in which younger members of an arts community learn from respected elders, is one of the most widely praised forms of intervention. And in those instances where the master artists are, or become, community scholar-practitioners, "passing it on" becomes an important internal consideration. The experiences of Don Roy as discussed by Tom Faux are a case in point. Unlike the Creole music and dance in Northern California, Franco-American music in New England has received support from cultural agencies, particularly for festivals and tours; however, as Faux pointed out, Roy understood that these tourist-oriented expressions usually failed to foster the long-term, community social capital that sustains a music-and-dance scene. And so Roy teaches group lessons, and the teaching not only facilitates music but also encourages community building. One of the reasons, perhaps, that Don Roy is uneasy at cultural agencies labeling him a Franco-American musician is that he understands that this music transcends ethnic boundaries and attracts contemporary contra dance musicians in New England who are identified with "Yankee" (traditional British) rather than French culture (Faux 2009).

The ecosystem analogy that enabled the application of these principles to cultural management on behalf of musical sustainability has recently been subjected to a critique by Brent Keogh. In a wide-ranging review of the ecological trope in ethnomusicological theory, Keogh concludes that in considering musical cultures as ecosystems and in following the principles of natural management (that is, by "following nature" in privileging diversity, interdependence, and so on), we would be mistakenly attributing good intentions to nature, whereas "Nature does not care whether a particular species thrives or perishes and no one species is more important than any other.... Nature does not care about diversity, it does not manage its economy because Nature is not an agent" (Keogh 2013, 6). Keogh confuses agency (action) with intention, because common language does in fact assign agency to nature, as in statements such as "canals carved by the agency of the river." Granted, the Christian worldview that gave rise to the widespread Enlightenment idea of nature as the great economist saw a divine hand behind nature. And, indeed, certain conservation ecologists do attribute good outcomes to natural processes; for example, two of Soulé's (1985, 730–731) value statements for conservation biology are that "diversity of organisms is good" and that "evolution is good."

But there is a difference between good outcomes and intentions. Wetlands, for example, provide flood control, wildlife habitat, and so forth. One can say without violating scientific principles that flood control is the result of the agency of wetlands. Those of us working with the ecosystem analogy in applied ethnomusicology are not attributing good intentions to nature, pleasant as it is to entertain the fancy that nature "cares" when good outcomes occur. Of course, nature also acts destructively. Nor is nature indifferent. In the tradition of scientific realism, nature simply "is" as an external reality. Where sustainability is a desired outcome, it does not require belief in agency within nature. It is neither necessary nor desirable for conservation ecologists to anthropomorphize nature when harmonizing human interventions in the natural world with ecological principles in order to maximize desired outcomes. Nor is it necessary for applied ethnomusicologists to attribute agency to nature when working with that ecological analogy in cultural policy. It would be difficult to conclude that applied ethnomusicologists who base management of musical cultures on an ecosystem resilience paradigm attribute agency to nature or, for that matter, to culture. Keogh's critique of the eco-trope, like Spitzer's critique of conservation, points to the limitations they believe arise from employing analogies between culture and nature. The relationship between the two is, however, complex, as is the history of that relationship (Titon 2013).

When back in the late 1970s I began exploring music cultures as ecological systems, the analogy I had in mind was between music and energy—that is, as energy flowed in a natural ecosystem in a feedback loop among so-called producer organisms and consumers, so in a music culture music flowed in a feedback loop among producers and consumers (Titon 1984, 9). The analogy I have borne in mind is thus not merely at the system attribute level but a more basic analogy between the driving forces in these two systems—namely, energy and music. Indeed, ecological principles are derived from human constructions of the natural world to begin with. As we shall see in the next section, ecologists who favor the resilience paradigm not only deny agency to nature but also are skeptical of equilibratory constructions of nature.

## Resilience

Within the larger discourse of sustainability among ecologists, a related term, "resilience," has provided a different and, many think, more promising direction for ecosystem management. Advocates of resilience emphasize that whereas sustainability is a goal, resilience is a strategy. Like sustainability, resilience thinking has been taken up by economists, including business economists, and by psychologists and social workers, who recommend resilience to their clients as a response to disruptive change in their lives. To date, resilience has not had much, if any, impact in ethnomusicology, applied or otherwise. In this chapter, I begin exploring how applied ethnomusicologists might employ resilience as a strategy. Nonetheless, resilience has already entered public discourse, where its use is becoming more frequent.

Like sustainability, resilience has been used to mean two different, but related, ideas. In popular usage, resilience sometimes means resistance; but more precisely, resilience means the ability to bounce back. Consider a system such as a forest, a pond, a music culture, a computer, or a human being. To use a homely example, imagine a person on the verge of catching a cold. Persons may increase their resistance by boosting their immune system with echinacea, vitamin C, and so on. Resilience, on the other hand, refers to a person's ability to recover after catching a cold. Going from not having a cold to having one represents a change in state or, as ecologists call it, a regime shift from one state to another—in this case, from a more desirable equilibrium (health) to a less desirable one (having a cold). The more resilient a system, the more quickly it recovers and the more fully it returns toward its previous state. Ecologists stress that a resilient system need not bounce back entirely to its previous state. In the face of disturbance, it may—indeed probably will—change; but a resilient system recovers to the point where it is able to retain sufficient integrity to keep performing its core functions (Gunderson, Allen, and Holling 2009, xiv–xvi). Summarizing ecological thought about resilience, Philip S. Lake (2013, 20) writes, "The capacity to weather a disturbance without loss is defined as resistance, whereas resilience is the capacity to recover from a disturbance after incurring losses, which many be considerable."

Resilience strategies are meant to exhibit resilience themselves—that is, managing for resilience means living with a degree of uncertainty (although trying to minimize it). It means to experiment, sometimes to fail, and to adapt management techniques so as to learn from successes and failures. In the current phraseology, resilience thinking requires adaptive management. Adaptive management anticipates, and reacts to, changing circumstances, changes in values, and changes in knowledge. Resilience is meant to be pragmatic and realistic (Norton 2005). Environmental studies professor Lance Gunderson explains that

> adaptive management is an approach to natural resource management that was developed from theories of resilience. Adaptive management acknowledges the deep uncertainties of resource management and attempts to winnow those uncertainties over time by using management actions as experiments to test policy. Management must confront various sources of complexity in systems, including the ecological, economic, social, political, and organizational components of

> these systems as well as the interactions among system components.... Adaptive management attempts to bring together disciplinary approaches for analysis and assessment and then integrate those ideas with policy and government in the social arenas in a framework some describe as adaptive governance ... [which is] a framework for managing complex environmental issues ... the social and human context. (Gunderson, Allen, and Holling 2009, xx)

Resilience thinking is implemented through adaptive management. Restoration ecology is one area of application. Here, adaptive management attempts to increase an ecosystem's resilience and tip it back to a more desirable state.

Interestingly, many resilience advocates contrast resilience with sustainability not only by regarding the former as a strategy and the latter as merely a goal but also by linking sustainability to the old "balance of nature" equilibrium paradigm, which has been abandoned by most ecologists, even though many conservationists, cultural and otherwise, still believe in it. In other words, the majority of contemporary ecologists no longer believe that ecosystems exhibit periods of prolonged stability as well as an overall tendency to move toward a single, balanced equilibrium, a climax state. Rather, they accept that in complex systems, disturbances and changes are the norm and that there is no natural balance at a climax equilibrium point but rather any number of tipping points that, when passed, bring about regime shifts to different states of temporary equilibria, some more desirable than others (Pickett and White 1985, 155–156). Resilience strategies are meant to achieve and maintain the most desirable states whenever possible.

For some resilience advocates, abandoning the idea of stability in ecosystems also means abandoning a cornerstone of "wise use" conservation and sustainability thinking: that endangered renewable resources would "naturally" recover when harvest rates were reduced to a more sustainable level, as in a forest or fishery. Such recovery was predictable under the balance-of-nature paradigm, but it could not be anticipated after a regime shift to a less desirable state. The abrupt collapse of fisheries, without any real prospect of return, lends credence to the newer paradigm involving regime shifts and indicates a need for a change in strategy and policy (Gunderson, Allen, and Holling 2009, xiii–xiv). Gunderson concludes, "A resilience approach opposes the preoccupation with increased production/yields/returns through increased efficiency ... and control of natural variation. In contrast resilience thinking captures, and in fact embraces, the dynamic nature of the world. It recognizes the perils of optimizing for particular products. It leads to an understanding of the critical thresholds in the systems we depend upon, and, once a system has crossed such a threshold into an undesirable regime, resilience thinking explains why it can be so difficult to move out of that condition, and what might be done about it" (Walker and Salt 2006, 140).

Resilience strategies also are employed in current economic practice, and they are not new. Diversification, a common resilience strategy for sustainability, is proverbial; most languages contain wise old sayings such as "Don't keep all your eggs in one basket." Farmers understand that monoculture is vulnerable to predators, disease, and erratic weather. Organic farmers work to improve the soil, which boosts resilience in the face of disturbance. Investors are urged to allocate funds to more than a single type of asset. Business corporations employ similar resilience strategies, diversifying products, sources, and distribution channels. If they consider themselves part of larger ecosystems, they understand that alliances, even with competitors, build resilience. Insofar as applied ethnomusicologists follow business models, particularly when advocating for heritage tourism and the creative economy, they may choose to adopt resilience strategies similar to these. Diversification is an adaptive risk management technique.

In putting ethnomusicology to practical use, then, applied ethnomusicologists would be wise to consider resilience strategies and adaptive management when partnering with cultural organizations where sustainability is a policy goal. Whether working directly with music cultures in participatory action research, sometimes as members of those music cultures ourselves, or whether working for, or with, government agencies, arts councils, museums, historical societies, and other nonprofit organizations with an agenda that includes sustaining, or restoring, particular music cultures, we would do well to recognize regime changes and implement resilience strategies. As usual in such cases, questions arise over what is to be sustained or restored in a music culture—repertoire, style, performance practice, function and context, feelings and experiences, careers, and so forth—and how best to sustain what is to be sustained. Many of these are questions of value as well as management strategy, and they involve trade-offs.

Moreover, it is crucial to consider a sustainable music culture not as a stable, climaxed ecosystem but as a desired regime. In other words, strategies should not be aimed chiefly at removing supposedly "unnatural" distortions, as outlined in *Cultural Conservation* and quoted earlier in this essay ("it is possible, however, to temper change so that it proceeds in accordance with the will of the people, and not in response to the pressures of faddish trends or insensitive public or private projects. Conservation denotes efforts which . . . ensure natural cultural growth" [Loomis 1982, 29]). "Natural cultural growth" is a fiction; there is no reason to believe it any more than to believe in the balance of nature. Instead, resilience strategies of adaptive management respond to forces of disturbance and change, some good and some not so good, in an attempt to establish or restore, and then maintain, desired regimes.

As directed at traditional music within ethnic communities, the cultural conservation and safeguarding movements discussed earlier usually claimed that their interventions were being done on behalf of music cultures that were threatened and were headed toward a regime change. "Safeguarding" assumes that the regime change has not yet taken place, that the heritage remains to be preserved. Sustainability, while more flexible in concept, also assumes that the tipping point has not yet been reached and therefore that major aspects of the current regime are worth sustaining. In reality, many traditional musics had already undergone regime change to an undesirable state. The traditional aspects were at best a remnant, and therefore the desired end was restoration to a former state, rather than conservation or safeguarding of a present one, even if this could not be articulated or admitted as such. In other words, culture workers, particularly those dealing with heritage, are sometimes trapped in a preservation discourse that magnifies the presence, and importance, of a threatened tradition. If the tradition already has largely succumbed, for political reasons the discourse may have to emphasize sustainability; however, the strategies ought to be aimed at restoration and resilience.

I turn now to ask what general characteristics of complex systems make certain ones resilient in the face of disturbance and what make others vulnerable? After identifying some, I consider resilience in two contrasting amateur music cultures and see what kinds of strategies are likely to work and what may fail.

Andrew Zolli and Ann Marie Healy point out five characteristics of resilient systems. These overlap to some degree. They are (1) feedback mechanisms to alert a system to an impending change; (2) built-in mechanisms for dynamic reorganization in the face of disturbance; (3) a structure consisting of modular components that can be repaired or replaced individually, thus preventing the necessity to repair or replace the system as a whole; (4) an ability to detach parts and diversify, thus localizing operations and reducing dependencies without undermining the whole; and (5) clustering, or the ability to aggregate under favorable conditions and grow. We may add (6) social capital, when the resilient system is a cohesive social group. "Resilient communities frequently [rely on] informal networks, rooted in deep trust, to contend with and heal disruption. Efforts undertaken to impose resilience from above often fail, but when those same efforts are embedded authentically in the relationships that mediate peoples everyday lives, resilience can flourish" (Zolli and Healy 2012, 9–13). Other characteristics of resilient systems are (7) diversity and (8) innovation (Walker and Salt 2006, 145–148).

Consider resilience and adaptive management in two contrasting music cultures, the Old Regular Baptists in the coal-mining country of the US southern Appalachian Mountains, and the old-time string band revival, dispersed in communities throughout the United States with some smaller groups elsewhere, such as Ireland. In more than two hundred years, the music of the Old Regulars has not undergone a significant regime change. Old-time string band music has done so, although most revivalists persist in believing otherwise. Conditions within the two music cultures are significantly different, particularly in terms of geographical distribution, economic dependence, and social organization. Resilience strategies will reflect these differences and others.

The Old Regular Baptists are a regional music culture, living in an area that includes the mountainous, coal-mining portions of a few contiguous southeastern states, chiefly in southeastern Kentucky, southern West Virginia, and southwestern Virginia. Although a small number of out-migrated Old Regular Baptists have established churches in Ohio and Florida, 95 percent exist within this mountainous, coal-mining region. They are organized into seventeen associations. Each association consists of anywhere from about five to thirty churches, each church with its own congregation and ministers. Altogether, they number about ten thousand people. They possess the oldest English-language singing tradition in the United States, lined-out hymnody. This music proceeds without congregational song books and without musical notation. The tunes are in oral tradition. One of the men with the ability to lead songs sings out the words one line at a time, singing them to a special lining tune for each hymn. The congregation joins the leader to sing back the words one line at a time to a tune that is related to but more elaborate than the lining tune. The hymnody is unaccompanied and in free rhythm and is characterized by melismatic melodic elaboration, each singer being free to "curve" the basic melody with more or fewer passing tones. The result is a thrilling heterophonic unison for the singers, in step but out of phase. To nonparticipants, it may sound mournful and disorganized. This music has been described in more detail elsewhere, while field recordings are also available. It descends from the practice of the sixteenth-century English parish church and was the "old way of singing" characteristic of the Massachusetts Puritans and their descendants until it was eclipsed by the reform efforts of music educators in the eighteenth century. Scholars of American hymnody thought it had gone extinct, but it was discovered in the middle of the twentieth century to have survived among groups of old-fashioned Baptists in the southern Appalachian Mountains, where it persists most strongly among the Old Regular Baptist denomination (Dorgan 1989; Cornett, Titon, and Wallhausser 1997; Titon 1999).[5]

For resilience, the Old Regulars have great strengths in many of the characteristics identified by Zolli and Healy. Feedback is one. They are self-consciously old-fashioned and safeguard their religious beliefs and practices closely. For at least 150 years, they have carefully monitored possible intrusions from other religions, including such things as foreign missions, Sunday school, and the use of musical instruments in worship. They have resisted newer musical styles and repertoires, most notably gospel songs and harmony singing. These remain tempting for some, but in fact the church leaders do not permit the congregations to sing gospel songs or to sing in parts. Modular structure is another resilience characteristic of this group. Their feedback mechanisms are reinforced by a hierarchically organized, modular structure in which each church functions as a single module. Their number rises and falls as some join the association and others occasionally fall away, or go "out of correspondence," as they say—usually over disputes in doctrine. The Indian Bottom Association, in southeastern Kentucky, has in fact gained churches and members during the twenty-five years that I have known them. Informal networks in a community of deep respect is another resilience characteristic of this group. Communication and trust among the Old Regular Baptists is facilitated by the habit of visiting: each church holds its worship service and a business meeting only one weekend per month. This means that Old Regular Baptists attend their home churches but once a month while visiting other churches three or four times each month. Ministers do the same, as do persons with the knowledge and ability to lead the songs. All of these aspects of church governance and organization, coupled with a close and caring social life, make the Old Regular Baptists resilient and have kept them so for more than 150 years.

However, in some ways the Old Regular Baptist music culture is vulnerable. Their total population is relatively small, and new church members must reside within a narrow geographic region. This region sees little in-migration and is gradually losing population. One does not join the music culture easily by volunteering to do so; one must join a church, and the churches have membership requirements based on religious belief and how one lives one's life. The songs are difficult to learn and sing until one has been immersed in the music for a while. Other church denominations in the region, with different, easier, and more modern-sounding ways of singing, compete with Old Regular Baptists for members. But their greatest vulnerability, I believe, is economic dependence. They are concentrated in a region dominated by a single industry: coal mining. Since the 1930s, automation in the mines has gradually diminished the overall number of workers, but in the past few decades, strip mining and then mountaintop removal, which require many fewer laborers, have greatly accelerated this trend, increasing unemployment and poverty in the region. Low-paying jobs in fast-food restaurants and shopping centers are available, but they provide only supplemental income and cannot support a family, whereas coal mining, although dangerous, does not require much formal education and pays a living wage. The future of coal mining itself is also uncertain, given increasing environmental regulation, and the decreasing proportion of coal in the US energy mix. Meanwhile, strip mining and mountaintop removal greatly disturb the mountain ecosystems, increasing flooding, earthquakes, and pollution in the land and water, causing illness and death. Black-lung disease from coal dust had been an ever-present threat, but with mountaintop removal, the environment itself is endangered, along with all life in the region. How long the population can remain viable in that area is an open question; if they had to disperse, it is not known whether Old Regular Baptists would out-migrate to areas in sufficient numbers to reestablish their churches and associations.

Resilience strategy for adaptive management would suggest addressing the economic and environmental problems of coal-mining dependence first and foremost. To help alleviate poverty and modernize the region, the federal government has undertaken economic projects ever since the War on Poverty in the 1960s. These efforts have improved roads, consolidated schools, and built hospitals; however, the economic problems remain. In 2014, the federal government announced a fresh initiative and couched it in the rhetoric of sustainability and resilience. In January of that year, President Obama announced that southeastern Kentucky had been targeted as one of the first "promise zones" for economic development. Details remain sketchy as I am writing this, but among the goals are job creation, growing small businesses, job training and retraining, all to implement a "sustainable economic effort across eight counties . . . focused on diversifying southeastern Kentucky's economy to make it more resilient" (White House Fact Sheet 2014). The outcome of this initiative will not be known for some years.[6]

Tourism, including ecotourism, may be one industry targeted for expansion; the region has many lovely natural sites, but it also suffers from a reputation for poverty and violence that is unattractive to tourists. Heritage tourism, based on the region's rich heritage of crafts and music (ballads, old-time and bluegrass string band music, the roots of country music, and so forth) would also be a possibility; however, despite some efforts in that direction, it has not proved an economic panacea. And even if it did, Old Regular Baptists would not wish to participate as the regular objects of heritage tourism. As the moderator (elected head) of the Indian Bottom Association told me many years ago, "We're not anxious to be studied." Over the years, he said, a number of visitors had "flown in, taken a shallow look, and flown out," and their impressions had been predictably shallow as well (Cornett 1990). I believe that performing their music and worship (for to them, music is worship) regularly at heritage sites within the region could transform their worship experience and degrade it into something other than worship: an object for a tourist gaze that would be unacceptable to them. And of course, the idea of turning it into an economic engine for profit is contrary to their religious beliefs.

Ironically, the feedback mechanisms within the Old Regular Baptist communities are very sensitive to musical and cultural threats; but the threat of changing economic conditions is not within the domain of church governance. Outsiders who advocate today for economic alternatives tend to be dismissed as untrustworthy environmentalists who would eliminate coal mining entirely, thereby bringing the economy to an abrupt and disastrous halt.

Applied ethnomusicologists seeking to apply adaptive management strategies to help Old Regular Baptists sustain their music—which, by the way, they are eager to maintain—would not serve them well, then, by attempting to make them the objects of heritage tourism and the creative economy, even though that is the predominant strategy for cultural sustainability in the US traditional arts today and an important strategy elsewhere in the world, particularly in Europe (Throsby 2010). It might also occur to an applied ethnomusicologist to consider whether Old Regular Baptist music could be sustained in a revival mode, similar to the way a related traditional American music, Sacred Harp (or shape-note) singing, is currently being enjoyed and propagated. Old Regular Baptist music has, in fact, undergone a kind of revitalization and renewal within the Old Regular Baptist communities, partly as a result of attention from scholars and cultural specialists. But their music is not in a revival stage in the sense that people from outside their communities are joining in and spreading and developing the music elsewhere. There are no folk music revivalists gathering to sing Old Regular Baptist songs, nor are there likely to be. A full comparison with the Sacred Harp revival is beyond my scope, but it may be useful to draw certain contrasts here.

Sacred Harp (or shape-note) singing developed as part of a musical reform movement involving written notation in shaped notes (diamonds, triangles, squares, and circles) that made it easier for people to learn to read and sing from staff notation. In fact, this music literacy movement was meant to overcome the perceived problems in the "old way of singing," which is to say the heterophonic, lined-out hymnody of the Puritans and their descendants (such as Old Regular Baptists) who, according to the reformers, were making an awful noise, not a joyful one. Although this movement to sing from notation gradually succeeded in New England beginning in the late eighteenth century, where it was put to use for part singing in standard Western choral harmonies, a grassroots shape-note movement arose in the South during the mid-nineteenth century, and soon local amateur musicians were harmonizing traditional melodies (including many in the Old Regular Baptist repertory) for part singing in shape notes, but in unconventional harmonies (employing parallel fifths, for example) and voicings. This way of singing and the songbooks associated with it, such as *The Sacred Harp*, became very popular among Baptist and Methodist denominations in the South, and eventually among gospel hymnodists, whose books later in the nineteenth century also were printed in shape notation. Although this music was sung in churches, it also became popular among community singing groups, and in particular Sacred Harp singing groups arose, chiefly associated with Baptists but not as a formal part of worship or church activities. Eventually Sacred Harp singing became a community activity, with singing conventions of its own; partisans traveled considerable distances to participate in regional and state Sacred Harp singing conventions. Although these Sacred Harp sings gradually diminished in the first half of the twentieth century, during the waves of folk music revival that have occurred in the United States since the 1950s, Sacred Harp singing became a popular choral activity, to the point that there now are Sacred Harp singing gatherings in every state of the union, and most of them are not associated in any formal way with religious practice, although the repertory is based in the Sacred Harp song book, and the revivalists mingle with traditional singing groups that remain in the South (Bealle, 1997; K. Miller, 2008).

Could Old Regular Baptist music undergo such an exogamous revival? To me, it seems highly unlikely. Although the music is attractive to a small number of outsiders, including some Sacred Harp singers, it does not exist in community sings outside church worship, in any formal sense. Old Regular Baptist families sing when they get together, but it is quite informal and different from a community singing event. Such "sings," in other words, and singing conventions that became normal for Sacred Harp singers and provided a ready-made structure for revivalists, are absent in Old Regular Baptist practice. Of course, that could change. But whereas beginners rely on Sacred Harp songbooks for lyrics and music notation, they would be unable to use their music-reading skills to sing Old Regular Baptist music, because Old Regular Baptist song books lack music notation. Recordings could provide a model, but very few recordings are available. The melodies, particularly the lining tunes, would have to be learned by imitation and memorized. Unlike Sacred Harp music, which has a leader who swings his arms to mark a steady meter, Old Regular Baptist songs do not have a conductor or exhibit a pulse beat. Nor is there a single melody, and although a skeletal tune does exist, a proper realization involves individual elaboration. Indeed, one learns to "curve" the melody appropriately only through experience in singing it within an Old Regular Baptist community. An anecdote from my personal experience will illustrate.

In the spring 1990 semester, I was a visiting professor at Berea College, in Kentucky, about a two-hour drive from a cluster of Old Regular Baptist churches in the southeastern part of the state. While visiting with Old Regular Baptists there on most weekends from February through May of that year, I gradually learned to sing their songs, to the point that I began to sing along with them in church. I could follow the melodies and even sing a few of them by myself, however tentatively. Of course, they observed and heard me doing so. One Sunday late in April after the church meeting was over, the minister who was their moderator (elected head) asked me if I would accompany him and his wife to a funeral where he'd been called to preach the eulogy. He said that the deceased had joined the Old Regular Baptist church, and therefore it would be right to sing a few Old Regular Baptist songs on the occasion. The problem was that the rest of his family were not Old Regulars and therefore they would not know how to sing along in the Old Regular Baptist way—and so most likely they would not sing at all. It would not be right if only he and his wife sang. Normally on such an occasion a few other Old Regular Baptist ministers and their wives would travel with them and join in singing those few songs in honor of the deceased, but on that Sunday only one of those couples was able to go. He wondered if I would go along and help out by singing with them. I said I would try, and when the time came I raised my voice with theirs as best I could. In the years since, I have heard this minister more than once relate this story in the company of other Old Regulars, with a twinkle in his eye, always concluding by saying, "And he did fairly well." In mid-May of

1990 I invited two friends to come with me to an Old Regular Baptist worship service. Although they both were skilled musically, they told me they could not find the melodies in the sea of sound that the group made. Of course, after several visits they would have been able to distinguish them, but their experience reveals how inaccessible the music is for a beginner.

The other music culture that here provides an example for resilience and adaptive management is the old-time string band music revival. The repertoire consists primarily of tunes played in the rural American South for dancing during the period from the Civil War to the period between the World Wars. Folklorists began recording this music in the 1930s, but the collecting accelerated in the urban folk revival movement that began in the 1950s. Now not only folklorists but also musicians who wanted to learn this music were recording it from the older musicians, most born before 1900, who remembered the repertoire. Some of this same repertoire had also been recorded on commercial 78 rpm discs in the 1920s and 1930s aimed at a Southern audience. In its heyday, this old-time string band music was performed, and the repertoire shared, by both white Southerners and African Americans. It developed primarily as an oral tradition over the course of 150 years, as more and more tunes were brought into the repertoire, others underwent modification, and all circulated locally and regionally. Starting around World War I, the music fell into decline with the older square and round dances it had accompanied, replaced by ballroom dancing and the music that was appropriate for that style. During the same post-1950 folk music revival that strengthened Sacred Harp singing, old-time string band music also staged a comeback, as the older tradition-bearing musicians performed at festivals and college campuses and other venues and attracted a cadre of young musicians who had not heard this music before but who soon made it their own. Some of them moved to the South to live and work in the areas where remnants of the musical tradition remained, and beginning in the late 1950s, they gathered in various old-time string band "festivals" at places such as Galax, Virginia, Union Grove and Mt. Airy, North Carolina, and more recently Clifftop, West Virginia. Although the musicians call these gatherings "festivals," they are unlike the folk festivals, where music is performed exclusively from a stage and for an audience. Instead, at an old-time string band festival, thousands of musicians gather chiefly to mingle and participate in hundreds of small, spontaneous jam sessions throughout the festival grounds. Sometimes, as at Galax, bluegrass jams are also part of the festival. It is a participatory, not a presentational, music. Summer instructional camps also arose beginning in the 1980s, and as the revival has grown, their number has increased. At the beginning, they employed some of the older, tradition-bearing musicians as teachers, who showed how they played by demonstrating the music, sometimes slowly. As they passed away, some of the most skilled revivalist musicians took their places, leading jams and workshops and teaching classes.

Although the string bands of the nineteenth and twentieth centuries had included various nonstringed instruments, such as harmonicas, organs, and whatever else was popular or handy, the revival string band musicians settled on fiddle, banjo, and guitar as the primary instruments, to which sometimes a string (double) bass and/or a mandolin was added. Indeed, by the time the music began to be recorded in the 1920s, fiddles, banjos, and guitars were the most popular; however, the guitar was relatively new to the music, having entered late in the nineteenth century, long after fiddle and banjo had delineated it. In addition to this concentration of instruments, other changes resulted from the revival. Banjo players have narrowed the variety of picking styles that were prevalent before the revival to one dominant style, the so-called clawhammer (a down-picking) style, while the rhythms of the tunes have taken on a more modern syncopation and drive, sometimes referred to as "festival style." Tunes played at festivals, aided by a combination of conviviality and stimulants, can put musicians into a quasitrance during performance, as the tune may repeat twenty or thirty times and continue for as long as a half an hour, the groove shared by all players. And whereas the music's primary function until the end of World War II was for accompanying the dance, today the occasion for the music is the jams. The word "jam," borrowed from jazz, connotes the informal and fluid membership in any old-time string band session. The music is not improvisational in the way that jazz is; the melody is prominent at all times, with slight though meaningful variations introduced primarily by fiddlers. Jams have an informal, laissez-faire atmosphere, though an implicit etiquette prevails. Although the fiddle is the lead instrument, no single leader decides which tunes will be played; instead, different musicians, usually fiddlers, start tunes, and when others recognize them, they join in—or if they don't recognize them, they learn them as they play them. The jam as I have described it, particularly as it occurs at festivals and in people's homes (often with potluck meals) or, increasingly, in public venues where it may be overheard by nonmusicians, is an informal gathering of whichever musicians are invited (or not) and show up. It is a musician's music, done for the pleasure of the musical experience and the sociability of the occasion.

The old-time string band revival exhibits resilience in certain areas but not others. New members are joining the music culture every year, coming from all US regions and walks of life. The number involved with old-time music fluctuates and is probably uncountable, but anecdotal evidence would place it around fifteen thousand, not much larger than the total of Old Regular Baptists. The group is welcoming, and there are few, if any, requirements, other than an interest in playing this music. By contrast, to join the Old Regular Baptist music culture, one must live within a small region and profess and practice particular religious beliefs. In terms of accessibility, then, the old-time string band revival is much more resilient. Its structure is also very different. The music culture centers on a "scene," or subculture, not a membership organization (Pfadenhauer 2005). Unlike Old Regular Baptists, the old-time string band music revival has little formal organization and no hierarchical structure. It is an affinity scene, a loose collection of small, informal groups anywhere in size from two to about a dozen persons who gather to socialize and play music together. At the festivals, of course, people from many of the smaller groups travel to take part and roam from one group to another, looking for old friends and acquaintances, and for peak musical experiences in jams. The informal aspects of the music, and the high value placed on spontaneity and serendipity, make hierarchical social organization even more difficult. Such egalitarianism extends even to the food supplied at these gatherings, which inevitably results in a potluck in which everyone brings some food and all share. To be sure, organizations produce the festivals and the instructional camps, but insofar as the festivals are chiefly spaces set aside for informal gatherings and a great many spontaneous jam sessions throughout the festival grounds, the production does not extend much beyond planning activities, keeping order, and running contests, which many feel are peripheral and do not participate in. For the vast majority, the participatory jam sessions and the socializing are the reasons for festival attendance. The instructional camps exhibit a good deal more organization, with reservations, accommodations, wages for instructors and staff, food catering, lessons, and workshops, along with evening jams. Participants pay money to attend and expect to improve their musical skills.

Although old-time string band revivalists are conscious of changes in the music culture, and some are concerned that these are not for the better, the scene has no hierarchy, no leaders to counter threats to its sustainability, no way in which individuals can manage more than a small part of the scene. In this voluntary association, leading by example is the principal means of influence. Any musician who fears that the music scene may be changing in ways not to his or her liking seeks out other musicians who share his or her preferences and usually finds them, rather than attempting to influence the course of the music's development. The musicians are dispersed across the United States and may be found almost anywhere—old-time string band jams are popular in Ireland, for example. For that reason, the jams exhibit an almost perfect modularity, except that aside from sharing repertoire, instruments, playing techniques, and to some degree musical style and social rules, there is no whole system, only a scene with various parts. The parts are not like cells integrated into an organism, as Old Regular Baptist churches are integrated into associations. Those parts—the social structures that come together for the jams, in home neighborhoods and at distant festivals—are by nature able to detach themselves, dissolve, reform or not, and also to cluster, a feature of resilient systems. Such a system, without a hierarchically organized whole, exhibits a certain kind of resilience. It almost automatically self-reorganizes in response to change and disturbance. However, this flexibility also means that it can more easily change state, as it did when it entered the revival stage, significantly in those aspects mentioned earlier. The musicians themselves do not think of this as a regime change, because the repertoire, instruments, and playing styles exhibit continuity. The participants believe they are continuing a tradition, and many think that by playing the old tunes and keeping them alive, they are preserving it. But at the same time, in the past fifty years they have modified the social aspects of the scene considerably. Jam sessions as well as festivals are the most important of these, but they are inventions of the revival, and without them the scene would not exist. Prior to the revival, the music was played principally for dances and in contests. Another, more recent innovation is the instructional camps.

An applied ethnomusicologist seeking to help the music culture sustain itself through adaptive management would not encounter the main problem facing Old Regular Baptists—namely, dependence on a single, regional industry that is itself under threat and in turn threatens the environment sustaining the population in the region as a whole. But in attempting to aid the scene, applied ethnomusicologists would encounter difficulties not present among Old Regular Baptists. For example, an applied ethnomusicologist might conceive of the revival as a regime change and imagine that the participants would prefer to return to the older social forms; however, most would not. The applied worker would need to bear in mind that the revival has its own way of carrying on a musical tradition but with newer social formations. Furthermore, whereas adaptive management could operate among Old Regular Baptists through their organizational hierarchy, there is in fact no way to "manage" the old-time string band music revival because it lacks the institutional structures and leaders to carry out such management. The self-organizing aspects of the revival are so strong that an applied ethnomusicologist might wonder whether aid and advice is desirable, let alone whether it is administratively possible.

On the other hand, an applied ethnomusicologist might, in partnership with certain musicians, come to realize that threats to the ethos of spontaneity and serendipity do exist, particularly in the instructional camps. In the 1950s and 1960s, the early decades of the old-time string band revival, learning the music took place chiefly by informal imitation, whether of other musicians or of recordings, as it had done before the revival stage. Although a more experienced musician might demonstrate a technique to a learner, teaching in the form of lessons did not exist. This began to change in the 1970s, first through class lessons held at musical instrument shops and not long after that, in classes held at the instructional camps. These teachers usually instructed by ear, going over a tune phrase by phrase, demonstrating techniques, without any musical notation to guide the students. Nonetheless, because the students pay money for this instruction, an atmosphere of middle-class expectation increasingly surrounds these camp activities, which now can include evaluation and critique and resemble art music pedagogy in certain aspects that exert pressure toward formalization. Under these conditions, the remaining old-timers who grew up in the pre-revival music culture usually do not make the most effective teachers, even though their playing exhibits the characteristics thought to be most authentic to the tradition and, for advanced musicians who can learn by imitation, they are the most desired teachers. Private lessons are becoming increasingly available, almost always taught by revivalists. Music camps now offer instruction in several different musical traditions more formal than old-time string band music. Some of these, like Scottish fiddling, have depended on tune books and music notation for more than a century. In others, such as contra dance music, notation has always existed alongside oral tradition but for instruction notation has become standard. Some in the old-time music community resist notation as they would resist an infection, thinking it works against the spontaneity they prize. Given that the instructional camps exhibit more structure than the jams or festivals and given that the musical instruction influences the scene's future, adaptive management to maintain the spontaneity and serendipity of the old-time string band revival scene might be appropriate.

Ironically, public folklorists' and applied ethnomusicologists' efforts to manage and sustain old-time music, including string band music, have by and large confused and upset the revivalists. The culture workers did so in the

1970s by dividing the folk revival scene into tradition bearers and revivalists, and the division persists. In making that distinction, they ascribe authenticity to the tradition bearers and grant them funding support, while they deny both to revivalists. Revivalists seldom are hired to perform at the folk festivals or are funded in other ways. Given the cultural conservationists' views that equate authentic traditional music cultures with ethnic minorities and working-class communities, it seems unlikely that the revival movement will be targeted for funding. Nor does it need such interventions, because among other things, it is not endangered. Nonetheless, some of the revivalist musicians would like the honor of being selected to perform at these festivals. When they bother to consider it, they resent being categorized as inauthentic. They argue that because the tradition-bearing source musicians have adopted them into their communities, they have already been authenticated by those whose authentication matters most. In contrast, Old Regular Baptist communities, which fit the cultural conservationists' criteria as tradition bearers perfectly well, have gained much from partnerships with applied ethnomusicologists and public folklorists. They have become stewards of their music, and they understand that it is not only valuable to them for worship but also valuable to others who prize outstanding musical traditions as part of the cultural matrix of the nation. Yet the greatest threat to their musical and cultural future is economic and environmental, and here the role, if any, for applied ethnomusicologists and other culture workers is not yet well defined.

## Conclusion

Resilience refers to a system's capacity to recover its integrity, identity, and continuity when subjected to forces of disturbance. Insofar as music cultures are systems, they too exhibit resilience to a greater or lesser degree. Resilience and adaptive management have had a life within ecological thought and the environmental movement, psychology (not treated here), and economics. They offer promising sustainability and restoration strategies for applied ethnomusicologists, as for public folklorists. However, they must be understood with reference to the baggage they bring. "Yield" and "development" are not appealing concepts to many culture workers. And while "management" is an appropriate strategy for conservation biologists, it is not without its problems when human beings are subjected to it. Among those is the negative connotation that management has acquired when applied to ways in which entities such as nation-states or corporations attempt to control their citizens or workers. I have already alluded to the critique leveled at modernization and developmental applied anthropology as a new form of colonial management, from radical anthropologists working in indigenous studies. However, indigenous knowledge forms the basis for a bottom-up applied anthropology, just as in applied ethnomusicology (Sillitoe 1998).

Foucault coined the term "biopower" to describe the way in which modern nation-states regulate their citizenry, particularly in reference to controls over excesses of the body (and body politic). Their disciplinary power is even more effective because the regulations become internalized as culture. Foucault is working in a tradition pioneered by Karl Marx, who wrote about the Protestant religion's emphasis on bodily discipline (e.g., drunkenness as a sin), effectively providing efficient, submissive factory workers for the capitalists. George Orwell's prophetic *1984* portrayed such a society as a police state. These, of course, are forms of management, and a quick response to this apparent problem is to say that the kind of cultural management I've been advocating (and practicing) for nearly five decades is not and never has been top-down but rather grows out of a partnership between the culture worker and the community leaders and tradition bearers. In an ideal case, the culture worker learns the music culture's sustainability goals and helps its people plan and then implement a sustainability strategy in which they self-manage, relying on the culture worker as a collaborator and consultant, perhaps more in the role of coach than manager. In baseball, we call them managers, but in American football and basketball, they are called coaches. Of course, both manage the games, employing short- and long-term strategies and by putting the players in positions where they have the best chance to succeed. Both coach their players, teaching them better techniques. Interestingly, coaches appear in contemporary Euro-American cultures in "the game of life": people hire coaches for public speaking, for dress and appearance, for health, for social relationships, for business negotiations, and so forth. Many do not seem to mind being coached. Some want it, thinking it will advantage them. Why, then, the resistance to being managed, when one is willing to be coached? Perhaps the manager is thought to be impartial, whereas the coach is empathetic.

Marx, Orwell, and Foucault shared that resistance to management. It impinged on autonomy and freedom; it abrogated natural rights. Being managed meant being told what to do, what to say, even what to think, when one didn't want to be told—and then being coerced to do it. The difference, with coaching, is the willing partnership: presumably we want to be coached, even if we don't want to be managed, because we conceive of the goal as our own.

Adaptive managing may be regarded as coaching, then, when applied ethnomusicologists partner for sustainability.

Resilience and adaptive management abandon the questionable assumption that music exhibits "natural cultural growth" that proceeds to desired ends when freed from the fashionable and faddish trends that distort its true direction. Instead, resilience recognizes that perturbation, disturbance, and flux are constant characteristics of any complex system. Resilience theory and adaptive management practice therefore attempt to identify what makes a music culture vulnerable to regime shift and what makes one resilient, and to ameliorate the former and strengthen the latter. Resilience theory and adaptive management offer promising directions for applied ethnomusicologists working toward sustainability in music cultures.

## Notes

1. Adam Smith's "invisible hand" that efficiently adjusts exchanges in the free market is an analogous concept in economics.

2. Environmentalism, on the other hand, did impact ethnomusicology. Ethnomusicologists studying people making music attend to the relations between social groups, their music making, and their connections with the environment—for example, songs to influence weather, songs to ensure a successful hunt, and so on. With a few notable exceptions, they did not frame these inquiries as ecological.

3. In the years since this essay was originally published, ethnomusicologists have made decolonization an overriding theme.

4. Worster means environmental or ecosystem sustainability. Writers sometimes use "ecology" incorrectly as a synonym for "environment." Ecology is a science, defined as the study of organisms, their relations with one another, and with their environment. Environment is therefore not the equivalent of ecology but rather one area of the science of ecology.

5. [Author's note, 2020: Cornett, Titon, and Wallhausser (1997) provides the best recordings of Old Regular Baptist hymnody.]

6. [Author's note, 2020: In the period since this essay was written, the Trump administration has deregulated and encouraged a comeback in the coal industry, while eliminating Obama's initiatives for economic diversity; however, to date coal has not made a recovery, and the regional economy continues to suffer.]

# III.

# TOWARD A SOUND ECOLOGY

This section's essays reflect the development of my sound ecology project from an ecological approach to musical sustainability to an ecological rationality of sustainability and justice for all communities of living beings on planet Earth. A sound ecology starts from the premise that sound announces presence and connects beings who are copresent to one another. Copresence becomes a means for acknowledging not only relationship but also the possibility of kinship, and thus a basis for establishing sound (healthy) communities, sound economies, and ultimately a sound ecology. The essays in this section reflect, also, my growing engagement with the field of ecomusicology, the study of music, sound, culture, nature, and the environment in a time of environmental crisis.

# 9

## A SOUND COMMONS FOR ALL LIVING CREATURES

*THE IDEA OF A SOUND COMMONS CAME TO me in 2011 as a number of my interests were combining while I read about the effects of habitat loss on animal sound communication and its impacts on indigenous peoples whose cultural ecology traditionally was dependent on animals. I began to write about sound and commons in my blog,* Sustainable Music *(Titon 2008–), and began to look at the literature on animal communication, animal rights, animal language, and animal culture. By then the blog had gained many readers, and soon I was getting invitations to speak and write about music, sound, sustainability, and the environment for popular as well as academic audiences. I accepted an invitation from Meredith Holmgren to write about sound for* Smithsonian Folkways Magazine *and decided to issue an appeal for a sound commons. "A sound commons," I wrote in what follows, "where all living beings enjoy a commonwealth of sound, embodies the principle of sound equity, encouraging free and open sound communication, and playing its important part in environmental, musical, and cultural sustainability."*

Today the air is filled with discussion of commons as a democratic principle of access, sharing, and use, particularly the so-called cultural commons (Hyde 2010) and the digital commons. I believe that it is helpful to also think in terms of a sound commons and that we ought to be managing it instead of damaging it. Why? So that all creatures (ourselves included) may communicate in our acoustic niches in the soundscape. It isn't just because all creatures have the right to life (and they—we—cannot live if we're prevented from communicating in our sound worlds). A utilitarian argument from ecology supports the beneficial consequences of sound communication to (1) biodiversity in ecosystems and to (2) ecosystem resilience in the face of disturbance, such as human noise.

In the far northern Canadian wilderness, noise from helicopters flown by mineral explorers and from mining company construction confuses caribou, upsets their communication, and has caused them to change their migration routes. Not only does the soundscape pollution impact the caribou but also human groups such as the Innu, whose traditional lifeways (food, clothing, shelter) were fully dependent on caribou hunting—a practice they attempt to continue still to maintain their culture, even though these former nomads are now settled in villages. And yes, the Innu have songs about caribou hunting. One of them translates roughly as follows: "You [caribou] are so far away, I cannot reach you. I'll catch up with you and call my friends" (Titon 2012b).

It's all connected: music to sound, human to animal, culture to nature. Just as sound is enveloped by environment, so is culture, by both the human-built and natural environments. When, back in the 1950s and 1960s, Moses Asch published sound recordings of New York City sound environments alongside recordings of sounds of sea creatures singing in the ocean, sounds of the office and sounds of steam locomotives, sounds of birds in the forest and frogs in the desert, he must have also understood this. Work in cultural sustainability—which Folkways and the Smithsonian's Office of Folklife and Cultural Heritage has always supported on the grounds of musical and cultural equity—is intimately related to work in environmental sustainability and cannot proceed successfully without it. A sound commons, where all living beings enjoy a commonwealth of sound, embodies the principle of sound equity, encouraging free and open sound communication and playing its important part in environmental, musical, and cultural sustainability.

Soundscape studies in one form or another have proliferated since the mid-twentieth century, when Moses Asch was most active in publishing Folkways recordings of environmental sounds. Composers, sensitive to whole soundscapes, mixed environmental and electronically generated sounds into twentieth-century musique concrète well before the rise of ambient music and environmental sound art.[1] Many of these composers, such as Hildegard Westerkamp and John Luther Adams, have not only composed music in direct relation to nature but have also been very articulate in advocating for a kind of sound activism in response to human degradation of the environment.

Pioneering sound collector Bernie Krause, whose early musical career included a stint with the Weavers, and who time spent as a composer-performer of electronic music, has traveled to the remotest parts of the world recording vanishing soundscapes and theorizing about biophony (sounds made by animals), geophony (nonbiological sounds made by the earth, wind, thunder, rain, and so on), and anthrophony (sounds made by humans). His revamped website (Krause, n.d.) is noteworthy, while his book *The Great Animal Orchestra* (Krause 2012) is required reading for anyone interested in the way human environmental impact has affected animal sound communication and contributed to the extinction of species.

Rachel Carson (1962) titled her well-known book about DDT, the flow of chemicals in the environment, and the extinction of animal species *Silent Spring*. R. Murray Schafer, a Canadian composer, was concerned to reorient humans away from a sight-centered universe so as to have them attend to sounds and to managing the soundscape. Pollution, he argued in *The Tuning of the World* (Schafer 1980), was not only in the air we breathe but also in the sounds we hear. Acoustic ecology, the branch of soundscape studies that followed from Schafer's work, centers on managing noise pollution in the human environment.

However, much more than noise pollution is involved in soundscape ecology. I like to think of soundscape ecology as the study of the flow of sound in the environment. Zoosemiotics, the multidisciplinary science of animal communication, arose in the mid-twentieth century, with sound as one of the three primary animal communicative pathways (smell and sight are the others). Scientific study of birdsong, of course, has been underway ever since the advent of sound recording; the Cornell University Laboratory of Ornithology (Cornell Lab, n.d.) encourages study of bird sounds, and one can find amateur nature recordists in the field with their parabolic reflectors to concentrate the sounds into their mics—and also chatting in online LISTSERVs.

Long before the rise of soundscape ecology and its many tributaries, Henry David Thoreau was paying careful attention to sound in the environment. Human music, he thought, was but an echo of the music of nature, which was primary. Music, he wrote, was the sound of circulation in nature's veins. Unlike word-bound speech and writing, sounds communicate directly, in a language "without metaphor" (Thoreau [1854] 1985, 411). He understood and wrote about echolocation (orienting yourself by sound, as Native Americans did in the forests, or as bats do with their sonar); he understood how sound signals presence; he developed a proto-theory of ambient sound; and he paid very close attention to animal communication, writing volumes in his *Journal* about what he heard on his daily walks as the seasons progressed.

One of Thoreau's most prescient observations concerned what today we call acoustic niche theory: that species not only occupy ecological niches but communicate with one another in their own particular acoustic niches, according to sound frequency (some outside the range of human hearing), time of day, timbre, and so forth, in order to avoid noise interference. Can sounds lie? He also understood how animals could give false or misleading signals (prey to predators). Thoreau sought sound ecstasies and vibrated with the universe; he built an aeolian harp and kept it in his partially opened window. Sound was the source of Thoreau's deepest veneration of the natural world and a chief motivator in his desire to preserve and protect it.

The Smithsonian Folkways catalog has since the 1950s included recordings of urban soundscapes, animal communication, and other sound phenomena not normally considered music. Thoreau, who noticed and wrote about the sounds children made when playing games outdoors, would have been interested to hear *Sounds of Camp: A Documentary Study of a Children's Camp* (Folkways FW06105, 1959). Fascinated by animal communication, he would have been intrigued by *Sounds and Ultra-Sounds of the Bottle-Nosed Dolphin* (Folkways FW06132, 1973). Understanding the close connection between sound and geographical region, he would have been curious to hear environmental sounds from areas he had never visited, such as the Southwest (*Sounds of the American Southwest*, Folkways FW06122, 1959). And Thoreau, who had once vibrated ecstatically in a vernal pool filled with copulating toads, would have been thrilled by Charles Bogert's scientific recordings of frogs, *Sounds of North American Frogs* (Folkways FW45060, 1958).

The folk music revival gave us the idea of musical and cultural equity: that all groups of people have the right to express, maintain, and develop their musical and cultural traditions. I believe that a related principle, sound equity, should be extended to all creatures. I argue in my blog, *Sustainable Music*, for a commonwealth of sound, a sound commons for all living beings. A commons, or *res communes*, according to Roman law, was a thing (*res*) that by its nature is incapable of being "captured" and thereby possessed. A commons, then, is not owned by any individual; it is shared. Roman law, which is the basis of Euro-American law, gave as its usual examples of *res communes* the air mantle and the ocean. I submit that the same is true of the soundscape: it belongs to the birds and the crickets as much as to you and me.

### Note

1. Later, these would become primarily computer-generated sounds.

# 10

# THE NATURE OF ECOMUSICOLOGY

*About ten years ago, a small group of musicologists, ethnomusicologists, composers, acousticians, ecological scientists, and environmental activists formed a new academic field, ecomusicology. Although related to zoomusicology, bioacoustics, acoustic ecology, and soundscape ecology, ecomusicology's academic roots are in ecocriticism, musicology, ethnomusicology, music composition, cultural studies, and ecological science and its related fields. Ecomusicologists are interested in music, sound, nature, culture, and the environment; many of us support environmental activism.*

*A serendipitous convergence of annual conferences of my academic societies occurred in New Orleans in the fall of 2012: the Society for Ethnomusicology and the American Folklore Society were meeting there one week apart. In the week sandwiched between, ecomusicologists gathered for their second conference. I attended and presented a new paper on Thoreau and sound (later published as Titon 2016). An invitation to keynote the Brazilian Society for Ethnomusicology's annual conference in 2013 resulted in "The Nature of Ecomusicology," for which I began to think about a relational epistemology as expressed in a sound ecology, relying on my understanding of ecological science and indigenous ecological knowledges. In this address I sought to bring into ecomusicology and the environmental humanities the paradigm shift in ecological science from balance of nature to disturbance and change. I emphasized ecology's relational epistemology while contrasting the sustainability of an ecological rationality with the unsustainability of an economic rationality. In this address, I also put forth a descriptive definition of ecomusicology, as the study of music, sound, nature, culture, and the environment in a time of environmental crisis.*

By my title, the nature of ecomusicology, I mean two things: (1) its nature—that is, how ecomusicologists are constructing this new field and the kind of work they are doing in it; and (2) ecomusicology's idea of nature—that is, what ecomusicology brings both to nature and to ongoing issues concerning music and sustainability. The new field of ecomusicology is the study of music, culture, sound, and nature in a period of environmental crisis. To date, most ecomusicologists have accepted nature as real, external, and objectively knowable. However, critical theory, the so-called science wars, and a changed paradigm within ecology have posed serious challenges to scientific realism, balanced ecosystems, and to the economic rationality, which has caused environmental degradation. Going forward, ecomusicologists can meet these challenges by relying on an ecological construction of nature based in a relational epistemology of diversity, interconnectedness, and copresence. In that way, ecomusicology can work meaningfully toward sustaining music within the soundscape of life on planet Earth.

The problem of music and sustainability is not only a problem of politics but also of knowledge. It is an epistemological problem. In the last few years, I have become increasingly convinced that the proper frame is sound and sustainability; music is too narrowing. We should open our ears to all sound, music included. We think of sustainability as a discourse in environmentalism and economics and as a problem of ethics, technology, and policy. We would also do well to examine how ideas of nature are embedded in culture, how science constructs nature, and how economic rationality constructs the environment.

Ecomusicology is defined by Aaron Allen (2013) as "the study of music, culture and nature in all the complexities of these terms." It is the study of music, sound, nature, culture, and the environment at a time of environmental crisis. Ecomusicology is still a child, only about six years old as a named academic field. It combines literary ecocriticism with musicology (including ethnomusicology).

Literary ecocriticism arose in the late 1980s and offered readings of literary works that emphasized the literary author's treatment of nature, particularly wild nature but also pastoral representations of nature. Ecomusicology began similarly, offering interpretations of musical works that emphasized the composer's treatment of nature. Environmentalism, ecology, and a sense of the ongoing environmental crisis inform these interpretations. In the 1990s, the scope of literary ecocriticism broadened to emphasize "place" more generally, including suburbia, cities, and the literature of the built environment. Following the lead of acoustic ecologists, ecomusicologists pay attention to all soundscapes, including those in urban environments.

Allen is careful to define ecomusicology not as an academic discipline with consensus over its subject and method but as a field with related subjects and varying assumptions, approaches, and methods. Sustainability is one of the main concerns of contemporary ecomusicologists; indeed, within environmental discourse, sustainability is prominent. For that reason, ecomusicology holds promise for music and sustainability studies.

My plan in this essay is as follows. First, I will claim that thus far most ecomusicologists have conceived of nature from the standpoint of scientific realism, and I will suggest that sooner or later ecomusicology must confront a more problematized nature. This more problematized nature reflects epistemological difficulties that result chiefly from the impact of economic rationality on the environment, the most obvious of which are global warming, income inequality, and social injustice. Second, in a brief review of the so-called science wars and of the response of ecological science to critical theory, I will outline some of the further difficulties that a problematized nature presents to the field of ecomusicology. Third, I will suggest how a holistic relational epistemology of interconnectedness, based in a holistic ecology and fundamentally different from that arising from scientific reductionism and economic rationality, offers an epistemological pathway to a more sustainable concept of nature, music, and the environment. Even if human music turns out to be auditory cheesecake, in Steven Pinker's (1997, 534) formulation it would be hard to deny the importance of sound to animal communication (humans included) and, therefore, to life on planet Earth (Titon 2012c). Relational epistemology offers a counterforce to globalization and neoliberalism, which to my mind, present the greatest threats to music, sustainability, and the environment.

I define sustainability this way: A sustainable system is one in which the goal is permanence achieved through the utilization of renewable resources. This goal is not the permanence we associate with something that never changes. Rather, it is dynamic. The elements in the system, their proportions, structures, relations, and functions will vary; however, the integrity of the system is maintained (sometimes through restoration) for the foreseeable future, though not for eternity. The usual example of this kind of sustainable system is a forest, but we may also think of such examples as a university, an economic system, and a music community.

Insofar as ecomusicology is involved with nature, it would do well to consider the two most powerful sustainability discourses, those in environmentalism and in economics. Of course, we also have a manifestation of these discourses in the popular culture, usually taking the form of living a "green" or sustainable life, by conserving energy in one's home, recycling, eating local food, riding a bicycle, and reducing one's personal carbon use. My university has a sustainability initiative titled "Brown Is Green," which consists chiefly of recycling; however, considering its energy use, I would call Brown's current environmental impact more brown than green.[1]

Because ecomusicology is so new and presents a moving target, I think the best way to pursue its nature is not to look to definitions but rather to consider what research ecomusicologists are doing, what their subjects and assumptions are. The work presented at the most recent international ecomusicology conference, which took place in November 2012, in New Orleans, offers a window on contemporary activity in the field. Having participated in the conference myself, I was struck by the variety of subjects; however, eventually patterns emerged, and I concluded that ecomusicologists approached music and nature in one or both of two ways: first, music as a representation of nature and, second, music interacting with nature. Nature most often was wild nature, but pastoral nature and the nature of the built environment also made their appearances.

Most scholars at the ecomusicology conference offered papers discussing how musical works represent nature. In doing so, they were following the lead of ecocriticism, except that they were examining musical works, not literary works. Their titles illustrate the subjects and approaches: "Theorizing the Musical Landscapes of John Luther Adams"; "Negotiating Nature and Music through Technology: Ecological Reflections in the Works of Maggi Payne and Laurie Spiegel"; "Listening to Landscape in Luc Ferrari's Petite Symphonie"; "The Natures of David Tudor's Electronic Music." Others offered papers discussing musical representations of nature in film, music festivals, and television advertising. An environmentalist agenda always was implied, if not explicit, while nature was understood to be both real and threatened.

A second ecomusicological approach to nature, apparent at the ecomusicology conference in New Orleans in the fall of 2012, considered music's direct impact on the environment, rather than how musical compositions represent the environment. Their topics included music and social action, environmental justice, and laws proposed and enacted to promote sustainability. They also included soundscape ecology, an area of particular interest to me, and one that I like to think about as the flow of sound in the environment. In all of these areas, economics is an important consideration.

The titles of some of the papers presented at the conference give an idea of these direct approaches to music and nature: "Instrument Builders as Environmental Activists," "Guitar Making, Sustainability, and Community Building in Britain and Africa," "Environmental Scientists and the Evolution of Soundscape Ecology," "Agency and Aural Rights." Political, economic, and legal aspects of music, nature, society, and the environment are important in this direct approach to music and nature, as is a willingness to think of music as an acoustic environment, which expands the idea of music to include sound of all kinds.

Of special interest to citizens of Brazil were papers addressing the sustainability of endangered species such as Pernambuco and Brazilian rosewood used to make violin bows and guitars, and thus to the sustainability of the forest ecological systems that support their growth. The Brazilian government has passed legislation governing their use and prohibiting export. I own two old guitars made of Brazilian rosewood; I was told that if I brought them into Brazil, I would be forbidden to take them back out of Brazil.

None of the ecomusicologists presenting at that conference confronted the postmodern critique of the concept "nature." Regarding nature as real and threatened, they did not pause to consider nature as a human social/cultural construct. None of them was concerned, as I am, about the fundamental difference between nature as the scientific realist conceives of it and nature as the postmodern critical theorist regards it. While most ecomusicologists were concerned with music, nature, economics, and the environment, their ideas were rooted in the epistemology of scientific realism, that nature is real, external, and increasingly knowable through objective, Western scientific procedures. None of them mentioned the so-called science wars of the 1990s in which critics questioned the basis for scientific realism and claimed that science continues to construct a failed Enlightenment grand narrative. Likewise, although the ecomusicologists presenting at the conference attacked the economic policies that have enabled environmental disasters, they did not attack the epistemological bases of economic knowledge about human beings, nature, and human nature.

I said earlier that we would be wise to consider economics and sustainability not just in terms of carbon emissions and policy but also in the very way economists think about nature. It is a truism that Euro-American economic thought has for centuries regarded nature as a resource for human use; indeed, the phrase "natural resource" implies it. Recall also that European classical economists assumed that all human beings "naturally" trade things and that the object of a good trade is material wealth. Efficient trade and the wealth of nations require a division of labor. As Adam Smith (1776, chap. 2) wrote, the human division of labor results from "a certain propensity in human nature . . . to truck, barter, and exchange." Such a trade-driven creature has come to be called "economic man." This assumption has directed Euro-American neoclassical economic theory since the Enlightenment and is the basis for contemporary neoliberalism. It is expressed today in what is called rational choice theory, which states that "economic man" weighs predicted benefits against costs and always attempts to maximize this ratio when making an economic choice. As does Andre Gorz (1989), I call this way of thinking "economic rationality." Economic rationality is premised on commodity exchanges in the marketplace, transactions that are subject to legal contracts. The advantage of the legal contract, as economists have pointed out, is that it is impersonal. Subject to certainty and the law, it frees the buyer and seller to accumulate wealth unencumbered from what might otherwise be a tangle of social obligations of the sort that would obtain in a gift exchange.

"Sustainable development" is a quintessential expression of economic rationality. Sustainable development entered public discourse in 1987 when a United Nations agency, the Brundtland Commission, defined it as "development that meets the needs of the present without compromising the ability of future generations to meet their own needs" (Brundtland World Commission on Environment and Development 1987; UN Documents n.d.).

The ecological economist Herman E. Daly (1993) has argued that "economic man" theory is incompatible with sustainable development; rather, economic activity must always take environmental limits and constraints into account. In the 1990s, Daly believed that the concept of sustainable development was salvageable. Twenty years later, I believe "sustainable development" is an oxymoron and has become a stalking horse for sustainable growth. Certainly, when corporations such as Exxon and Monsanto proclaim that they are "green" capitalists enabling sustainable development on an international scale, it is plain from their "greenwashing" that they have co-opted the phrase "sustainable development" for their own unsustainable ends (Titon 2009a, 9).

Let us turn back from economics to ecomusicology. The 2012 ecomusicology conference began with a sound walk. On a sound walk, as many of you know, one does not talk but instead pays careful attention to and contemplates the acoustic environments encountered as one walks along. No one tells you what to listen for or interprets the sounds for you. Instead, you are encouraged to develop your own acoustic epistemology.

Like most guided sound walks, this one took place in an urban environment, and although we occasionally heard nature directly in birdsongs, most of the sounds we heard were mechanical and the result of human economic activity: airplanes, the sounds of air passing through large HVAC ventilators in the buildings, the sounds of automobile traffic, the sounds of a humanly constructed waterfall sculpture inside a restaurant, and so forth. It was an instance of the way ecomusicologists take a direct rather than representational approach to music, in this case environmental sounds.

As I mentioned, the ecomusicologists at the conference adopted the epistemological standpoint of scientific realism. Its philosophical position is familiar: Experimental science gradually reveals the nature of the universe, its patterns, and the natural laws that govern it. Scientific truth differs from mere belief in that it is inductive and subject to independent verification. Scientific experiments are replicable, hypotheses are tested, conclusions are either confirmed or, if they are not verified, they are discarded as false and replaced with better ones. Science therefore gradually progresses to offer us an increasingly accurate portrait of what nature is and how nature works.

In the last half of the twentieth century, critical theorists such as Foucault, Rorty, and Harding attacked scientific realism and its claims to universal truth. As is well known to academic humanists, this was a major part of the poststructuralist, deconstructive, and postmodern critique of modernity. Modern science, they argued, was peculiar to its time and place: western Europe and the developed world since the Enlightenment. Bruno Latour's later work on scientific laboratory culture underlined Foucault's claim that knowledge did not progress toward greater understanding but instead was captive to a social consensus among an interpretive community of qualified scientists. Scientists in turn were beholden to the political and economic needs of the developed world and subject to the general prejudices prevalent in society. Far from emancipating humankind from superstition, the critics wrote, science enslaved human beings by providing a scientific basis for false claims of racial, gender, and cultural superiority, and providing a rationale for Western colonization and empire.

Some scientists, especially physicists, fought back against this critique, and the ensuing debate came to be known as the "science wars." Of course, most scientists ignored the critique and went about their business, but environmentalists and some ecologists engaged in the debate. Understanding their activities in response to this powerful critique of scientific realism and economic rationality is crucial for the ecomusicologist seeking a more nuanced epistemology of nature and the environment, and so I summarize the impact of the science wars on environmentalism and scientific ecology, an impact that began to be felt about forty years ago and is still with us.

Environmentalists argued that the misuse of Western science in the service of economic rationality had resulted in environmental destruction. A few radical environmentalists then gave up on science altogether. But most environmentalists called for a wiser science to manage an increasingly complex environment for sustainability. They looked to ecology to inform and to help guide their conservation efforts. What did they find? How did ecological science fight the science wars?

The ecologists did not respond in a consistent way. A minority did become caught up in the environmental movement and sought to apply ecological principles to the conservation of endangered species. Led by ecologist Michael Soulé, they called themselves conservation biologists and came to be known also as conservation ecologists (Soulé 1985). Soulé himself responded to the science critics by editing a volume titled *Reinventing Nature*. In the introduction, he wrote,

> The so-called deconstructionist view ... asserts that all we can ever perceive about the world are shadows, and that we can never escape our particular biases and fixed historical-cultural positions. Moreover, some in the deconstructionist movement boldly assert that the natural world as described by scientists and conservationists, if it exists, is a human artifact produced by our economic activities, and as such it is grist for further material reshaping.... The opposing view, defended to varying degrees by the authors, assumes that the world, including its living components, really does exist apart from humanity's perceptions and beliefs about it. Most of the authors [in this volume] agree that we can gain dependable, scientific knowledge about this independent, natural world, in spite of differences among us in class, gender, culture, and historical perspective.... [We] agree that certain forms of intellectual and social relativism can be just as destructive to nature as bulldozers and chain saws. (Soulé 1995, xvi)

Soulé writes that although the postmodern assault on science was offered in the name of opposing Western hegemony, on the contrary it strengthened Western hegemony by discrediting conservation efforts.

Although conservation ecologists like Soulé engaged with the postmodern challenge to scientific realism, most ecologists did not. Instead, they were focused on a battle within their own ranks, a paradigm shift that ecology underwent in the latter decades of the twentieth century. Until then, ecology operated under the optimistic paradigm of nature's economy. To the natural historians of the Enlightenment, nature's economy meant that nature was the greatest economist, working most efficiently to take care of its own household. Nature was a patterned, interlocking whole, with its parts functioning for the greater good in a great chain of being, all overseen by God. Although the rise of modern science and the triumph of Darwin's evolutionary theory in the nineteenth century put an end to God's oversight, pattern and interlocking chains remained, coming to be expressed in the holistic concept of natural succession and the ecosystem, concepts offered between the twentieth century's two world wars by Frederick Clements and Arthur Tansley. The ecosystem paradigm came to its zenith in the mid-twentieth-century work of Eugene P. Odum, beginning in 1953 with the first edition of his highly influential textbook, *Fundamentals of Ecology*. In its most recent edition (Odum and Barrett 2005, 18) he defines the ecosystem as "any unit that includes all the organisms (the biotic community) in a given area interacting with the physical environment so that that a flow of energy leads to clearly defined biotic structures and cycling of materials between living and nonliving components." Ecosystems characterize the entire planet, whether as small as a lake or as large as a tropical rain forest. As the ecohistorian Donald Worster (1994b, 160) points out, for Odum

> what all these ecosystems have in common is a "strategy of development," a kind of game plan that gives nature an overall direction. In Odum's words, it is "directed toward achieving as large and diverse an organic structure as is possible within the limits set by the ... prevailing physical conditions of existence." Every single ecosystem, he believed is either moving toward or has already achieved that goal. It is a clear, coherent, and easily observable strategy, [and it leads to a state of dynamic equilibrium] to a world of mutualism and cooperation among the organisms inhabiting the area. From an early stage of competing against one another, they evolve toward a more symbiotic relationship ... until at last they have the power to protect themselves from its stressful cycles of drought and flood, ... cold and heat.

But beginning in the 1960s, ecologists began to challenge Odum's ecosystem paradigm. One study after another found that particular ecosystems did not move teleologically in the direction of mutualism, cooperation, and equilibrium; rather, the evidence they gathered showed that over time, particularly geological time, change, disorder, and the struggle for existence among species was the normal state of nature, not balance. Instead of order, the new normal involved frequent disturbance, human-made and otherwise: invasions of foreign species, fire and other natural accidents, and longer-term ecosystem alterations such as gradual climate change. The environmental historian Worster (1994b, 167) attributes this paradigm shift to the discovery of chaos theory: "Nature, now [in the 1990s] is seen as fundamentally erratic, discontinuous, and unpredictable. It is full of seemingly random events that elude our models.... If the ultimate test of any body of scientific knowledge is its ability to predict events, then all the sciences ... fail the test regularly." Today, ecosystem ecologists remain in retreat, while the field itself becomes increasingly specialized. Ecosystems are discussed nowadays not in terms of a balance of nature or tendencies toward equilibria but rather in terms of the "ecosystem services" (resources) they provide. Rather than a balance of nature or nature's economy, the discourse is about resilience to disturbance and resistance to change.

While environmentalists and conservation biologists resisted the paradigm change in scientific ecology, environmental humanists welcomed it.

Human history had, after all, worked many changes on the environment, transforming wilderness into farms, and agricultural areas into urban areas; forests had been cut down and logged; mining had altered many landscapes; roads, bridges, railroads, and factories all contributed to a built modern environment. For the environmental humanist, the built environment was at least as important, if not more important, than wild nature. In elevating change and disturbance, the ecological paradigm had also diminished the role of a balanced, wild nature as an ideal condition (Coates 2004, 408–416).

Ecomusicologists have not yet problematized nature. They adopt the same modernist perspective that environmentalists do—that is, nature is real and endangered. Yet it was modern science combined with economic rationality that got us into our environmental crisis in the first place. A few ecomusicologists, however, are aware of this paradox. A proposal for the first book to survey work in ecomusicology, titled *Current Directions in Ecomusicology*, coedited by Kevin Dawe and Aaron Allen, whose definition of ecomusicology is the one I quoted earlier, recognizes these complications by distinguishing between nature and "nature." In this formulation, nature without the scare quotes stands for scientific realism, while within the scare quotes nature stands for something that has no external reality but rather is humanly and socially constructed. It remains, then, to be seen how ecomusicologists may work out the complications of a problematized nature.

For music and sustainability, a relational epistemology offers an interesting and, I believe, promising alternative to economic rationality and scientific reductionism regarding nature. I do not claim originality for this concept, only perhaps for its application to ecomusicology. Relational epistemologies of various kinds have been with us for a long time, far longer than economic rationality. One version was called animism, the term used by Edward Tylor, usually regarded as the founder of modern anthropology. Postmodern anthropologists have reconfigured animism in a more positive way, not as bad science but as perspectivism, a metaphorical alternative to a science gone bad. The sociologist Karl Polanyi may have been the first to apply this relational insight globally, writing about the transformation to market capitalism from an earlier European idea of trade. Polanyi (1944) claims that prior to market capitalism, the greater significance of a trade exchange lay not in any accumulation of material wealth but in the subsequent adjustment of social relationships. A sociology that emphasizes networks of human relationships rather than economic rationality, social capital rather than economic capital, is another manifestation. It includes the work of cybernetics and systems analysis, and the late work of polymaths such as Gregory Bateson (1979). And it links to the environment in the emerging field of political ecology, which according to Enrique Leff (2013) "explores the power relations between society and nature embedded in social interests, institutions, knowledge and imaginaries that weave the life-worlds of the people . . . in environmental rationality . . . [and] decolonizing knowledge [to] open alternative ways of understanding reality, nature, human life, and social relations."

Ecology exemplifies a relational epistemology. Ecological science, after all, is the study of the relationships among living and nonliving things, growing out of natural history and the idea of nature's economy. Ecology when holistic has been uneasy with scientific reductionism, insisting on emergent, relational properties of systems that manifest only at higher levels and disappear when the whole is reduced to the sum of its parts. And while relational thinking is most powerful in ecology's older balance-of-nature paradigm, it remains in the contemporary reductionist paradigm involving disturbance and patch dynamics, for relations among living and nonliving things remain the focus.

What the ecological study of nature and the postmodern critique of nature have in common is a reliance on connectedness, on interdependence, and on relationships. That is, instead of Enlightenment individuality, we have postmodern and ecological collectivity, the web of relations. Foucault's sociological writings are not merely directed at power but power relationships. Postcolonial anthropology and ethnomusicology begins with a critique of colonial as well as scholarly authority and asymmetrical power relationships. For deconstructionists, that web is the intertextuality (ideology) that constructs the subject. Derrida himself "described his own brand of reading as aiming at 'a certain relationship, unperceived by the writer, between what he commands and what he does not command of the schemata of the language that he uses'" (Jefferson 2013, 10).

For a final example of holism in a postmodern deconstructive critique of nature, I turn to Timothy Merton's arrestingly titled book, *Ecology without Nature*. As the book title implies, Merton (2007) deconstructs "nature" as either an impossible romantic fancy or as an impossible object of scientific realism. But what can ecology be absent "nature"? Merton's (2010) next book, *The Ecological Thought*, provided his answer: what was left to ecology after the disappearance of "nature" was interconnectedness, interdependent relationships. In short, what is left is relational epistemology involving persons, networks, and intersubjective reality. Even when deconstruction erases nature, it does not erase relational epistemology.

An ecomusicological construction of nature worth having, it seems to me, will be based in this relational epistemology. Ethnomusicology has a contribution to make here. On the one hand, musical ethnographies, particularly those of indigenous peoples, have revealed indigenous peoples' worldviews involving sound, music, and the physical environment in relational epistemologies. To cite the classic example, Steven Feld's work with the Kaluli constructed a relational epistemology involving birds, myth, sound, and weeping; he calls this sound-based epistemology "acoustemology." There are at least a half dozen other such explicit musical ethnographies, and even more could be read implicitly in this way. On the other hand, ethnomusicology's belated turn to the study of world popular music confirms insights from cultural studies, that music industry behavior is an expression of economic man. Even movements to conserve or safeguard intangible cultural heritage are couched in terms of the prevailing economic rationality when they argue that heritage tourism fuels the local economy and that arts education stimulates the creativity needed for innovation that will help corporations compete globally. The UNESCO-sponsored World Intellectual Property Organization also embodies economic rationality in regarding cultural heritage as group intellectual property, to be subject to international law. To think that a music worth sustaining will grow out of cultural policies based in economic rationality is badly misguided, I believe (see Titon 2008–).

Relational epistemology, on the other hand, holds promise for sustainability, and it may be observed in musical communities, not just those such as the Kaluli or the Africans whom Turnbull (1961) thought sang to the forest to wake it up so it would take care of its people. We find the same relational epistemology in musical communities based in social rather than economic capital, particularly when there is little or no financial gain to speak of, and people come together to make music for the love of it, as Wayne Booth (1999) describes it in his important book on musical amateurism. Such amateur music making has been characteristic in Western societies all along, whether in the family consorts of viols during the Renaissance and Baroque periods, amateur string quartet playing today, or musical revivals all over the world, for fun, sometimes for truth, but seldom for money. Monographs on the Cajun musical revival by Mark DeWitt (2008) and of the Balkan musical revival by Mirjana Lausevic (2007) are just two examples by card-carrying ethnomusicologists. In these communities and others like them, musical exchanges may be understood more as gifts than commodities. Their importance lies not because they are expressions of economic man wanting to maximize wealth but rather of living beings seeking social relationships as well as pleasure. To Steven Pinker, music is no more than auditory cheesecake, a pleasant diversion but not an evolutionary advantage. Yet when ecomusicology opens music to nature and we think not narrowly of music but of the flow of all sound in the environment (music included), it appears advantaged in many ways. Sound turns space into sacred place; it enables communication among animals, including humans; and it puts beings into copresence with one another and their environments. Surely, sounding is not just an evolutionary advantage but a necessity for sustaining life on planet Earth.

## Note

1. [Author's note 2020: Since this article was written in 2015, Brown has done much more. It established the Institute at Brown for Environment and Society, while it set a goal to cut greenhouse gas emissions 75% by 2025 and become carbon neutral by 2040.]

# 11

## THOREAU'S EAR

*I'd read* Walden *and selections from Thoreau's journals in college,* course assignments for my teacher Leo Marx, a pioneering ecocritic. Later, he directed my undergraduate honors thesis. Marx emphasized Thoreau's ambivalent feelings about the Industrial Revolution and made much of Thoreau's chapter in Walden on "Sounds," where the shrieking sound of the Fitchburg railroad interrupts his pastoral sojourn daily. Thoreau's attention to the soundscape—I did not have that word for it then—intrigued me. In 1980, I bought an old cottage in rural Maine, and when I wasn't doing fieldwork in summers, I used it as a retreat for writing, also taking daily walks in the forest in back of my house and sometimes alongshore at the ocean a short distance away. Gradually I became attuned to those soundscapes, purchased the Dover two-volume reprint of Thoreau's journals, and compared what I saw and heard on my walks in the woods on a given day of the year with what Thoreau had recorded for that day in his journals, for he was a close observer of natural history. In the last century, this was a personal interest; I had no intention of integrating it with my scholarship until I began to think about music, culture, nature, the environment, and especially sound in terms of sustainability. "Thoreau's Ear" was the last in a series of essays and public lectures since 2012 on Thoreau and sound. Thoreau's writings, especially his journals, helped me to understand the possibilities of a sound ecology.

Henry David Thoreau (1818–1862) is well known as the canonical nineteenth-century American author of *Walden* and other works of literary pastoral; as the writer whose essay "Civil Disobedience" influenced Gandhi, King, and the nonviolent resistance movement; and as a natural historian, environmentalist, and proto-ecologist. Not so well known is that this nineteenth-century polymath paid unusual attention to environmental sound. His writings are of interest for sound studies, particularly in the areas of acoustic and soundscape ecology, the anthropology of the senses, and animal sound communication.

Attentive to ambient sound and the way sounds are transmitted and changed by different media such as air, water, and wood, his most ecstatic experiences occurred in response to sound vibrations. Early on a transcendentalist disciple of Ralph Waldo Emerson, Thoreau's thinking gradually moved away from spiritual correspondences and toward scientific truths experienced as patterns in nature. Unusually oriented to sensory experience, his close listening in the presence of nature became an important means toward this knowledge.

Why should sound studies scholars pay attention to Thoreau? First, he regarded human music as a manifestation of the more inclusive and significant category, sound. To him, music was chiefly a human echoing of environmental sounds. Although a musician, in his writings he paid far more attention to the sounds of insects, animals, wind, rain, bells, echoes, and other ambient sounds than he did to human music. His writing turns our attention to the relations among sounds in a given environment—that is, to soundscape ecology. Second, Thoreau helps us understand that sound waves vibrate living beings into bodily experience of the presence of other beings. When that experience and awareness is mutual, sounds vibrate beings into copresence with one another. Sounds vibrate living beings into a way of knowing that proceeds by interconnection, a community of relations: a relational epistemology. And third, Thoreau's writings aid in understanding how sound's enabling of copresence and a relational, subjective epistemology sets up an ecomusicology in opposition to the dominant subject-object economy that many view as the underlying cause of our current environmental crisis. Economic man, the cornerstone of classical, neoclassical, and neoliberal economics, desires to accumulate, possess, and control as many objects as feasible, thinking that in this material possession consists wealth. Thinking with Thoreau helps us construct an alternative economics: one that proceeds through sound toward an ecological world of interconnectedness, reciprocity, and respect. It is a world in which humans are in nature and nature is in humans as in all living beings. It is no longer the human-centered economy of economic man; it is instead is an ecological world of earth's household, of nature's economy. Thoreau's underlying epistemology is thus relational and phenomenological, a worldview of interdependence based in the experience of presence and copresence. He was led to these ideas, as others have been, through resonance (Erlmann 2010). Sound enables humans to construct a world worth wanting and keeping.

Thoreau's early experiences with music and sound enabled him to experience the ecstasy of the natural sublime and write about it imaginatively, understanding natural facts as metaphors of spiritual truths as any proper transcendentalist would do. "The fact will one day flower out into a truth," Thoreau wrote in his journal at the age of eighteen on December 16, 1837.[1] Drawing on ideas from Coleridge, Wordsworth, and especially Swedenborg's correspondence theory, Emerson had written in *Nature* that words were signs of natural facts and that particular natural facts were symbols of particular spiritual facts (or truths); thus, nature was to be understood as the symbol of spirit (Emerson 1849, 5). Emerson famously pictured himself communing with Nature as if he had become a "transparent eyeball," the poet seeing and then naming the spiritual facts found in the natural ones. Thoreau certainly used his eyes, but far more than any of his contemporaries, he used his ears. If we think of Emerson as a transparent eyeball, we might think of Thoreau as a vibrating body. He vibrated in resonance with the cries of crickets, frogs, and birds; the tolling of bells and the cries of children at play; and the sounds of rain and wind, especially moving air as it vibrated telegraph wires and gained amplification through the poles, turning it into what he called his aeolian telegraph harp.[2]

Literary and cultural critics seldom have discussed the significance of sound and music in Thoreau's writing. If they notice Thoreau's attentiveness to sounds, most are content merely to report that he was a good listener (e.g., Cavicchi 2011, 55–56). The few who go beyond listening present sound in Thoreau either as a means of expressing transcendental correspondence between the factual and spiritual, or as a means toward fashioning cultural symbols. (Instead, I will claim that sound in Thoreau serves as fact for his natural history, as a means toward ecstasy, and especially as evidence for his developing acoustemology.) F. O. Matthiessen (1941, 84) wrote that for Thoreau music represented "a close correspondence, an organic harmony between body and spirit." Sherman Paul's (1949, 511) essay on "Sound as the Agency of Correspondence in Thoreau" claims that sound represented an area of "controllable insight" between "nature as fact" and "nature as merger." For Paul, Thoreau's frequent references to the sounds of crickets, wood thrushes, and the telegraph harp are chiefly symbolic and "carry the weight of his cumulative experience with nature" (520). Unsympathetic with Thoreau's frequent scientific observations of sound in the natural world, Paul initiated a line of criticism that viewed Thoreau's increasing preoccupation with natural history as a diminution of his poetic powers. The early ecocritic Leo Marx (1964, 250–253) agreed with Paul's assessment of Thoreau's turn toward science but made a passage from the "Sounds" chapter of *Walden* into a symbol of Thoreau's ambivalence toward the Industrial Revolution. Of the Fitchburg Railroad, Thoreau (1985, 414–415) wrote, "The whistle of the locomotive penetrates my

[Walden Pond] woods summer and winter, sounding like the scream of a hawk sailing over some farmer's yard. . . . When I hear the iron horse make the hills echo with his snort like thunder, shaking the earth with his feet, and breathing fire and smoke from his nostrils, (what kind of winged horse or fiery dragon they will put into the new Mythology I don't know)." Here the train (a sign of progress) is likened to a bird of prey and then to a dragon as the machine intrudes into his pastoral garden. Marx, like Lionel Trilling and Henry Nash Smith before him, believed that the greatest American authors were those whose works expressed, in symbolic terms, the major tensions and contradictions of American culture and society in their times. Thoreau was skilled with tools and technology; after all, he earned his living as a land surveyor, devised natural history experiments, constructed everything from aeolian harps to gardens and buildings for Emerson, and had invented an improved manufacturing technique using graphite for lead pencils that enabled his father's pencil factory to prosper. Thoreau nevertheless refused to join the family business. He was not ambivalent about American industrial progress; he despised it, as a reading of this locomotive passage within the context of *Walden*'s indictment of his townspeople's economic materialism makes plain, like numerous comments and observations throughout his other writings. Later ecocritics, such as Buell, take a more positive view of Thoreau's scientific turn but ignore Thoreau's ear. Buell (1995, 171–172), a Thoreau specialist and one of the leading ecocritics of his generation, wrote perceptively of Thoreau's interest in natural history:

> The idea that natural phenomena had spiritual as well as material significance had a lifelong appeal to Thoreau, although he increasingly took an empirical and "scientific" approach to nature after 1850. . . . Thoreau became increasingly interested in defining nature's structure, both spiritual and material, for its own sake, as against how nature might subserve humanity, which was Emerson's primary consideration. . . . [To do this, Thoreau] had to overcome not only his classical education and his early Transcendentalist idealism, but also an intense preoccupation with himself. . . . This narcissism he surmounted by defining as an essential part of his individuality the intensity of his interest in and caring for physical nature itself.

This is well said, but it overlooks the way in which Thoreau's listening body integrated self and nature. It was not so much a surmounting of narcissism as an understanding of the relations between self and environment by means of listening and copresence.

Thoreau's interests in music attracted notice from his biographers, chiefly Bradford Torrey and Walter Harding, but the most direct assessment came from the American literary and cultural historian Perry Miller, who disparaged of Thoreau's musical education, taste, and abilities. "Thoreau had an insatiable hunger for music," Miller wrote. "His untutored flute-playing has become a legend. He could invoke Beethoven, but he knew little about music, had virtually no chance to learn.... [His writing] is pathetic in its revelation of musical illiteracy. [But] what he could learn of music, aside from his little 'music box' and Emerson's aeolian harp, was only what he might hear through the windows of some burgher's house wherein a daughter of respectability was practicing her piano lessons" (P. Miller 1958, 156).

Poor Thoreau. Was he truly limited to music boxes, aeolian harps, and listening through a window to some respectable young neighbor lady practicing the piano? Over and over again on some battle piece? What exactly was Thoreau's musical background? Born in 1817, he spent most of his youth in rural Concord, Massachusetts. He played the flute, loved to sing popular and folksongs, and enjoyed dancing (his mother had sent him to dancing school as a boy). In fact, his father played the flute; and according to Harding, Thoreau's father, John Thoreau, took great pleasure in it, playing it in his church parish choir. His sister Sophia was said to have played piano well, and his sister Helen gave piano lessons in Concord. In short, Thoreau was raised in a musical family, and it is almost inconceivable that in this setting he would not have at least learned musical rudiments and treble clef notation for the flute. He was renowned for his unusually keen ear; he could discriminate among different birds singing simultaneously and had a knowledge of each one's song (that is, he could sing it back) and invented a mnemonic language for recording and remembering it (Harding 1982, 354–354, 265, 195). His flute playing may have been free—he preferred what he called unplanned music—but it had likely been tutored in his family. He did most of his flute playing outdoors, taking it along on his daily and nightly walks and when boating on lakes and ponds. In his journal, he writes that he plays it in a meditative, improvisatory way: "My music was a tinkling stream which meandered with the river, and fell from note to note as a brook from rock to rock. Unpremeditated music is the true gauge which measures the current of our thoughts, the very undertow of our life's stream" (*Journal*, August 18, 1841).

As a young man, Thoreau went to dances and other entertainments (Harding 1982, 73). He did not study music at Concord Academy or Harvard University, but as far as I can tell, formal education in music was not available to him then in either institution. In his journal, Thoreau confided his puzzlement upon being given a book about the history of music: "Most lecturers preface their discourses on music with a history of music, but [they might] as well introduce an essay on virtue with a history of virtue. As if the possible combinations of sound, the last wind that sighed, or melody that waked the wood, had any history other than a perceptive ear might hear in the least and latest sound of nature!" (*Journal*, March 8, 1842). Thoreau was familiar with the theory, attributed to Pythagoras, that as the heavenly bodies rotated, they made music based on their astronomical ratios. It was said that only Pythagoras could hear the music of the spheres, but Thoreau believed that anyone could hear it in the sounds of the natural world (Thoreau 1985, 141–143). "Music," he wrote in his journal, "is the sound of circulation in Nature's veins" (*Journal*, April 24, 1841). Miller's condescending comments about Thoreau's musical education are perhaps best understood as barbs directed at bourgeois Victorian musical taste; however, as Thoreau had a much broader concept of music, Miller's critique is somewhat beside the point. Thoreau's idea of music has more in common with contemporary composers who work in the medium of ambient and environmental sound art.

Thoreau did not write in his journal about the many soirées in the family home when he played flute and his sisters played the piano, or the many social occasions when he was called on to sing popular songs and ballads. We have the reports of others to go on, and they say his singing was well regarded. His writings do not chronicle his Concord town social life. He did write about times when he and his companions, boating on rivers and lakes, broke into songs of camaraderie; and he offered some of the lyrics. We recognize these as occupational folksongs of the sort that folklorists later collected from sailors and loggers. And he also wrote about those times when adrift in a boat on a lake or pond he played his flute in a meditative way, the scene usually compared to pastoral. Seldom does he comment about concertgoing, although we know he did go to concerts in Boston. He mentions Beethoven and other Western art music composers very occasionally and usually in a complimentary way. But most of his writing about music concerns the sounds he hears in the natural world: frogs, crickets, birds, the sounds of the wind and rain, and also the ambient sounds of children playing, church bells tolling, and people chopping wood and surveyors halloing through the woods to mark their location. His hearing was acutely sensitive, and until the last years of his life he could recognize very soft sounds over long distances.

Thoreau's pastoral symphony was not, like Beethoven's, a representation of pastoral; it was pastoral. After all, Thoreau did not merely write about pastoral but had lived it in his cabin at Walden Pond. Thus, Thoreau's pastoral symphony was the music of the whole of the environment, humans included, with which he vibrated sympathetically. As Charles Ives (1920) wrote, "Thoreau's susceptibility to natural sounds was probably greater than that of many practical musicians. . . . Thoreau was a great musician, not because he played the flute but because he did not have to go to Boston to hear 'the Symphony.'"

Saint Francis, it is said, spoke to the birds as he fed them. Did they sing back to him? What could Thoreau hear in the sounds of the natural world? Could he sing back?[3] Obviously, sounds presented the environment to Thoreau's consciousness; but through that presence, was there the possibility of knowledge? Toward what epistemology does sound lead? The question fascinated Thoreau. His answer was found in presence and copresence. Presence is in experience. It is something felt or sensed.[4] The concept of presence is key in phenomenology. As Don Ihde (2007, 25) puts it, phenomenology aims "to isolate, describe, and discern the structures of immediacy or of fulfillable experiential presence." For Erving Goffman (1963, 13–22), who introduced the term "copresence" in 1963, copresence was face-to-face communication in which humans were "accessible, available, and subject to one another." Today, though, postmodern communications theorists use copresence to mean the "sense of being together" at a distance—that is, a combination of presence and absence—particularly with other people in a shared virtual environment (Zhao 2003; Lombard and Ditton 1997). Thoreau, of course, would extend copresence to all living things in the environment, including animals, trees, and stones. Rather than regard him as an animist, it is more useful to think of him as developing relational epistemologies (Titon 2013, 14–17).

Relational epistemologies are, literally, mediated; and Thoreau was, predictably, interested in sound media and their interactions with sound vibrations. He was struck by the speed and amplification of sound traveling through the solid pole of his aeolian telegraph harp, and he paid particular attention to sounds traveling through air and "conversing with every leaf and needle of the woods," as he put it:

> I hear Lincoln bell tolling for church. At first I thought of the telegraph harp. Heard at a distance, the sound of a bell acquires a certain vibratory hum, as it were from the air through which it passes, like a harp. All music is a harp music at length, as if the atmosphere were full of strings vibrating to this music. It is not the mere sound of the bell, but the humming in the air, that enchants me. . . . There comes to me a melody which the air has strained, which has conversed with every leaf and needle of the woods. It is by no means the sound of the bell as heard near at hand, and which at this distance I can plainly distinguish, but its vibrating echoes, that portion of the sound which the elements take up and modulate,—a sound which is very much modified, sifted, and refined before it reaches my ear. The echo is to some extent an independent sound, and therein

is the magic and charm of it. It is not merely a repetition of my voice, but it is in some measure the voice of the wood. (*Journal*, October 12, 1851)

Here Thoreau is developing a proto-theory of ambient sound, one that was not lost on John Cage, who beginning in 1967 read Thoreau and was delighted to find his own ideas about sound already there: "Reading Thoreau's *Journal* I discover any idea I've ever had worth its salt" (Cage [1973] 2010, 18).

Thoreau wrote frequently about birdsong and how it affected him, but toward the end of his life, he became preoccupied with that relationship: "What is the relation between a bird and the ear that appreciates its melody? . . . Certainly they are intimately related, and the one was made for the other. It is a natural fact. If I were to discover that a certain kind of stone by the pond-shore was affected, say partially disintegrated, by a particular natural sound, as of a bird or insect, I see that one could not be completely described without describing the other. I am that rock by the pond-side" (*Journal*, February 20, 1857). The relationship Thoreau is describing here is one of copresence in which the one (the bird, or the water medium) cannot be fully described without the other (the ear, or the stone). In this copresence, each is incomplete without the other: they are complementary. When he writes, "I am that rock," he means that he is like that rock—that his ear is to the bird melody as the rock is to the water that changes its shape. But he also implies that one completes the other and that therefore in a sense they are fused into a larger being.

As Thoreau came closer to the end of his life, he intensified his observations of the natural world and concentrated his thoughts on emergent patterns within nature. Among his last completed projects was a scientific paper on the succession of forest trees. He concluded that the dispersal of seeds by wind, water, and animals enabled particular plant species to arise in places where they had not been before. For Thoreau, nature's economy proceeded through interdependence and interrelationship—in this case, between the seeds and the wind, water, and animals that carried them. He quotes an English book on planting walnut trees: "The seed should be laid in a rot heap, as soon as gathered, with the husk on; and the heap should be turned over frequently in the course of the winter," and concludes that the authors "appear not to have discovered that it was discovered before, and that they are merely adopting the method of Nature. . . . So, when we experiment in planting forests, we find ourselves at last doing as Nature does. Would it not be well to consult with Nature in the outset?" (Thoreau 2001, 436, 438).

Copresence is key not only in human sound communication but also in sound signaling throughout the animal kingdom. Thoreau's curiosity about cricket sounds led him to explore predator-prey relations and interspecies acoustic communication, including false signals and honesty guarantees, a topic of special interest to moral philosophers as well as animal communication biologists (Bradbury and Vehrencamp 2011, 19–112). "I hear a cricket in the Depot Field, walk a rod or two, and find the note proceeds from near a rock," Thoreau wrote:

> Partly under a rock, between it and the roots of the grass, he lies concealed,—for I pull away the withered grass with my hands,—uttering his night-like creak, with a vibratory motion of his wings, and flattering himself that it is night, because he has shut out the day. He was a black fellow nearly an inch long, with two long, slender feelers. . . . They are remarkably secret and unobserved, considering how much noise they make. Every milkman has heard them all his life; it is the sound that fills his ears as he drives along. But what one has ever got off his cart to go in search of one? I see smaller ones moving stealthily about, whose note I do not know. Who ever distinguished their various notes, which fill the crevices in each other's song? It would be a curious ear, indeed, that distinguished the species of the crickets which it heard, and traced even the earth-song home, each part to its particular performer. Those nearest me continually cease their song as I walk, so that the singers are always a rod distant, and I cannot easily detect one. It is difficult, moreover, to judge correctly whence the sound proceeds. Perhaps this wariness is necessary to save them from insectivorous birds, which would otherwise speedily find out so loud a singer. (*Journal*, August 20, 1850)

Thoreau understood that copresence of living beings results from sound communication in what soundscape ecologists today call acoustic niches, based on frequency, pitch contour, timing, timbre, and so forth. The acoustic niche hypothesis suggests that species are adapted to communicate with one another in their particular acoustic niches so as not to interfere with one another (Pijanowski et al. 2011, 203–216). In his journal, Thoreau records just such an observation:

> Just before sundown [we] took our seats before the owl's nest & sat perfectly still & awaited her appearance. We sat about 1/2 an hour, and it was surprising what various distinct sounds we heard from there deep in the wood—as if the vistas[,] aisles of the wood were so many ear trumpets—the cawing of crows—the peeping of hylas—in the swamp—& perhaps the croaking of a tree-toad—the oven bird—the yorrick of Wilson's thrush—a distant stake driver—the night warbler—& black & white creeper—the lowing of cows—the late supper horn—the voices of boys—the singing of girls—not all together but separately & distinctly & musically from where the Partridge—& the red tailed hawk & the screech owl sit on their nests. (*Journal*, May 12, 1855)

Copresence in the soundscape, with each species communicating freely in its acoustic niche, describes a soundscape commons, which is to say a shared acoustic resource.[5] Roman law, from which English and American law derives, recognized as *res communes* those resources that by their very nature could not be "captured" or owned; the air mantle and the oceans were the usual examples. On the other hand, of course, "earth's productions" could be captured, and when they were, they were to be considered res privatae (Rose 2003, 89–110). Thoreau was well aware of commons, particularly in the economic arena. With what was left of the commons under siege from the business mentality prevalent in Thoreau's time and place, the environment and human life were being degraded by the same process. In one of his last essays, he wrote,

> Among the Indians, the earth and its productions generally were common and free to all the tribe, like the air or water, but among us who have supplanted the Indians, the public retain only a small yard or common in the middle of the village.... What sort of country is that where the huckleberry fields are private property? When I pass such fields on the highway, my heart sinks within me.... I cannot think of it ever after but as the place where fair and palatable berries are converted into money, where the huckleberry is desecrated.... As long as the berries are free to all comers they are beautiful, but tell me that this is a blueberry swamp which somebody has hired [and we] commit the berries to the wrong hands, that is to the hands of those who cannot appreciate them. This is proved by the fact that if we do not pay them some money, they will cease to pick them. They have no other interest in the berries but a pecuniary one. Such is the constitution of our society that we make a compromise and permit the berries to be degraded, to be enslaved, as it were. (Thoreau 2001a, 493–494)

Thoreau here contrasts nature's economy, where resources are "free to all comers," with his townspeople's economy, based solely in a pecuniary interest. His comparison of degradation to enslavement during this Civil War period took on a particular poignancy. He understood better than most that environmental destruction was the result of an economic system erected on the ideas of Adam Smith, John Stuart Mill, and Jeremy Bentham, particularly the assumption that human beings by nature act out of self-interest and engage in trade in order to accumulate material wealth (Reder 1999, 110–115, 236–237).[6] Thoreau suggests an alternative economy to "economic man," one based in a managed commons, open to all, that includes earth's productions like berries as well as acoustic niches enabling interference-free communication.

In the soundscape Thoreau had described, each species was communicating in its acoustic niche "separately and distinctly and musically." Sound interference blocks those communications channels; contemporary soundscape ecologists have made recordings before and after airplane flyovers, for example, showing the degradation and recovery times (Krause 2012, 179–180). The same kind of interference, or noise pollution, whether in the oceans from vessels or naval sonar, or in built environments from industry, police sirens, and so forth has been a live issue for acoustic ecologists, particularly in Europe, since the mid-twentieth century. Of course, noise pollution is part of the ongoing environmental health crisis (Office of the Scientific Assistant 1981). A recent appeal for treatment of the soundscape as a managed and sustainable ecological commons for all living creatures was based partly on Thoreau's insights (Titon 2012c).

Thoreau's major contributions to sound studies lie in the areas of acoustic and soundscape ecology, the anthropology—and science—of the senses, animal communication, and phenomenology. Thoreau "anticipates Bergson and Merleau-Ponty in his attention to the dynamics of the embodied mind, and shares with Peirce and James a concern for problems of knowledge as they arise within the horizon of practical experience. Ever so gradually, contemporary philosophers are discovering how much Thoreau has to teach—especially, in the areas of knowledge and perception, and in ethical debates about the value of land and life. His affinities with the pragmatic and phenomenological traditions, and the enormous resources he offers for environmental philosophy, have also started to receive more attention" (Furtak 2017).

Steven Feld ([1982] 2012) found what he called an acoustemology (acoustically grounded epistemology) among the Kaluli of Papua New Guinea. Colin Turnbull (1961) reported on one among the African Mbuti in the mid-1900s. Experience-based acoustemologies are more common than one might expect. Thoreau fashioned one in Concord, Massachusetts, in the mid-1800s. He was well aware of the transformative possibilities of a sound-based epistemology: "It is remarkable that our institutions can stand before music, it is so revolutionary," he wrote in 1857 as he was coming to understand that his goal had been an experience-based, ecological epistemology all along (*Journal*, October 17, 1857). When he died of tuberculosis at the age of forty-three, he left unpublished journals of more than four million words and an equal amount of notes and drafts from his extensive reading. He died before he could achieve the synthesis that he intended, his great Kalendar of natural history. Yet his pioneering contributions to sound studies make him a worthy ancestor here as elsewhere, one whose work repays study and increases in relevance, inspiration, and influence decade by decade.

## Notes

1. Because there are numerous published editions of Thoreau's journals, and because no complete, authoritative set of them has yet been made available, it is most useful to refer to their contents by Thoreau's date of entry. Thoreau's *Journal* ([1906] 1961) is the original fourteen-volume published set of journals edited by Torrey, reduced to two large volumes. Now out of copyright, the Torrey set is also available for free in PDF format at https://www.walden.org/collection/journals/. Princeton University Press in 1981 began issuing a more complete and authoritative set in sixteen projected volumes, but to date only eight have been published. Transcripts of the unpublished volumes may be viewed in PDF format at http://thoreau.library.ucsb.edu/writings_journals.html.

2. In his journal entry for September 12, 1851, Thoreau wrote that while walking near Walden Pond near the newly constructed telegraph line, he heard a loud humming. Realizing that the blowing wind was sounding the wires, as if the telegraph line were a giant aeolian harp, he ran to it and pressed his ear and the side of his body to a telegraph pole, which was amplifying the vibrations. He wrote that day in his journal that the experience thrilled him, and he wrote about returning to listen and vibrate ecstatically with the telegraph harp in thirty subsequent journal entries.

3. After Thoreau died, acquaintances recalled that when they were children, adult Thoreau amused them by taking them into the woods, showing them how to forage, how to find animals, and how to sing with birds (Harding 1982, 190–195).

4. Presence is also a key concept in theater and performance studies (see, e.g., Giannachi and Kaye 2011, 1–25).

5. Commons has received an enormous amount of attention in the past twenty-five years, whether historically (European agricultural commons and enclosure movements), or in contemporary life, as on the internet (a digital information commons), or as a cultural commons (threatened by enclosure through intellectual copyright law). See Hyde (2010), Rose (2003), Titon (2008–, 2012c).

6. See Reeder (1999, 110–115, 236–237).

# 12

## THE SOUND OF CLIMATE CHANGE

*I*N MARCH 2014, IN ASHEVILLE ON THE EVE *of the third ecomusicology conference, Denise Von Glahn asked Aaron Allen, Mark Pedelty, and me a provocative question: What does climate change sound like? In October of that same year, a snow- and windstorm wreaked havoc on the Maine coast island where I live. As the storm roared, I stepped outside the house to experience it more closely and was startled by a loud crack as a huge spruce tree snapped in two not a hundred yards from where I was standing. Soon other spruce, poplar, birch, and apple trees broke or toppled over entirely, and in the howling wind and falling trees I thought I could hear the sound of climate change. I'd agreed, several months earlier, to contribute an essay to the environmental magazine* Whole Terrain, *for an issue broadly themed on "trust." The combination of Denise's question, the answer in the storm, and the opportunity to write about it for a popular audience led me to ponder the significance of these sounds. It came to me that we might hear them as nature's alarm calls, a warning of the more frequent and intense and damaging storms to come as a result of climate change. I'd been learning about animal sound communication and that the behavioral ecologists who studied it from the standpoint of evolutionary biology distinguished between trustworthy animal alarm calls and ones meant to deceive the listener. Had I been eavesdropping on nature's alarm call in the sounds of the storm, or was I simply indulging in a poetic fancy, a version of the pathetic fallacy? The essay poured out of me in a single sitting in early December 2014, which is unusual in my writing practice. The following April, Denise, Aaron, and I spoke at a symposium at the University of Minnesota on the Music of Climate Change, and I made this essay the center of my presentation. After its publication in 2016 in* Whole Terrain, *editor Cherice Bock interviewed me about the essay and my sound ecology project (Bock 2017).*

Soundscape ecologists say sounds tell us how healthy an ecosystem is. But you don't have to be a soundscape ecologist to know that a loud buzzing, honking, croaking, singing patch of forest is a healthy one or that a silent spring is not. The global community is adjusting to reports such as the *Fifth Assessment Report* of the United Nations–sponsored Intergovernmental Panel on Climate Change (2014), confirming climate change and its effects: global warming, more extreme weather events, and the unjust distribution of risks to disadvantaged populations. We see these changes occurring; we feel the temperature change. Can we also hear climate change? If we listen to the sounds of climate change, what else might we learn about nature and about survival? Scientists tell us that creatures communicate in order to maximize fitness: the individual's ability to thrive, survive, and pass along its genes to the next generation. These communications serve as signals—honest when the creatures communicating hold a shared goal, dishonest when one seeks to manipulate another such as a predator-prey relationship. Are other creatures sending us honest signals because they share our goal of survival? What are these signals and how do we interpret them?

I live on an island on the Maine coast, back a ways in the woods, mostly white spruce and poplar with gray birch, cedar, and black alder in the wet areas—a typical down east island forest. An unusual early November storm was shaking the coast when I heard the sound of climate change for myself: fast-falling, heavy, wet snow combined with winds of forty knots. The ground was already wet and loose from the October rains. I stood out on the porch in the middle of the snowstorm, taking it all in, whistles, whooshes, scrapes, roars—eavesdropping on the forest's grand aeolian harp. The big branches of the tall, slender spruce trees moved back and forth in the gale, needles piling up with wet snow, looking like so many Shivas waving their arms about.

I heard a loud crack and knew at once it was a spruce trunk snapping in two. I saw it go, a big one, at the edge of a field a hundred yards away, two-thirds of it broken off and crashing down across the path into the woods. The next day, I counted thirty-five snapped trees, their trunks strewn across my trail through the forest. Others had toppled over, their trunks now horizontal and roots vertical, shoulder height, with heaps of soil clinging to root and rock. Craters in the earth marked where they had once fed.

The carnage included a few apple trees that were young during the Panic of 1893. Then, a bloated economy fell victim to unsound financing. People did not understand, as ecological economists do now, how economic growth is constrained by environmental limits. Today the environment lays claim to our incurred debt through the currency of climate change. In the presence of nature, I heard the sound of climate change and experienced its solemn, terrifying beauty. I felt the slow panic of the twenty-first-century ecosublime, nature's market adjustment writ large.

The storm passed. The fallen trunks and branches downed electric and phone wires. In the new silence, I heard only crows cawing. Though power returned with its familiar house sounds, I couldn't stop thinking about the storm's rushing wind and the sharp cracks and thunderous crashes of the white spruce. I thought about it yesterday when, with the help of Aaron Eaton, a neighbor, I pushed an apple tree back upright, a Stayman Winesap that I'd planted thirty years ago. Eaton, a woodcutter descended from seven generations of island woodsmen, said of the storm that he'd never seen anything quite like it. Nor had I. The 2014 US Government National Climate Assessment reported that, due to climate change, "extreme" storms increased in the Northeast by more than 70 percent over the past six decades (National Climate Assessment 2014). Climatologist Michael Mann predicts storms will grow stronger as the Arctic air masses collide with the ever-warming ocean air (Mann 2018).[1] The extreme storm I witnessed lies directly on one of those collision points: the down east coast where I live.

Now it's December; the trees echo a softer sound. The ground is frozen, and the forest birds are fewer. Nuthatches, juncos, goldfinches, and chickadees break the stillness, along with the ubiquitous crows. I know that as the climate grows warmer, the forest habitat will change. Permanent residents, such as crows and mourning doves, will expand their ranges. Migrating birds' ranges will compress to the thin latitudinal band where the temperature still matches their ecological niche, where they can find favored foods, breed, raise their young, and sing in the spring and summer months. More Canadians will hear loons laughing on their lakes, but by the end of this century, Minnesota will have lost its state bird. Audubon identifies ten state birds in the United States whose songs will no longer be heard inside their borders by 2100: Baltimore oriole (MD), loon (MN), brown pelican (LA), California gull (UT), hermit thrush (VT), mountain bluebird (ID and NV), ruffed grouse (PA), purple finch (NH), and wood thrush (DC). And if climate change accelerates, there will be more.

A different bird chorus will sound in this down east spruce forest. Some might keenly await the newcomers, but in my mind's ear I hear the ghosts, their songs soon gone from this place forever. Their absence, too, is the sound of climate change. The crashing spruces vibrate my body; the songs of last summer's hermit thrushes (fig. 12.1) ring in my ears. Sound signals the presence of nature; sounds connect me within it. I hear those sounds of climate

Figure 12.1. Hermit thrush. The species possesses one of the most complex songs among North American birds. Source: Wikimedia Commons.

change as nature's alarm calls. Am I jumping to conclusions because climate is on my mind? Or are these sounds what animal scientists call honest signals, trustworthy indicators of the changing environment?

An honest signal is a true indicator of an animal's behavior, identity, or of its environment, while dishonest signals are false indicators. In the 1970s, Richard Dawkins popularized this idea, which fit well with his "selfish gene" reading of evolution: animals' communication repertoires included dishonest as well as honest signals, all to manipulate the behavior of others and increase fitness (Dawkins and Krebs 1978).

A false or misleading signal is more likely to be given when the interests of sender and receiver differ. When competing over territory, potential mates, or a limited food source, a weaker bird may try to bluff the stronger by means of an elaborate song. The honest signal, on the other hand, is given when the interests of the sender and receiver coincide, as for example in a bird singing to its mate or fledglings crying out in anticipation of food.

I've been speaking and writing on music, sound, and sustainability for nearly a decade now, my path marked with stops in conservation biology, ecological economics, ecomusicology, and lately, animal behavior, particularly animal sound communication. While the dichotomy of honest and dishonest signals makes good sense within the context of animal communication, are we making a category mistake by hearing these sounds of storms, crashing trees, and the changing dawn bird chorus as communications for, or about, us?

Of course, animals *do* communicate about us. I approach a red squirrel resting in a white spruce; it notices me, moves about, and begins its rapid cackling chirp. The squirrel is sending an alarm call, one of the common types of animal communication. These alarm sounds indicate the presence of danger—in this instance, me. Sometimes the alarm sound is specific to the kind of danger; experiments with vervet monkeys revealed different sounds depending on the predator species (Seyfarth, Cheney, and Marler 1980). Most alarm calls are honest signals. False alarms turn out to be uncommon, for in giving a false alarm, an animal too often puts itself in the position of the boy who cried wolf.

If some alarm calls are *about* us, might we also understand that others could function *for* us? In other words, is there precedent for animals of one species to take alarm at sounds meant to warn other species? Ecologists now know that certain bird species are sentinels for other species. Their alarm calls offer honest warning signals. Squirrels listen in on blue jay vocalizations to gauge how near these potential predators are to their young. Indeed, interspecies communication is so frequent among animals that scientists term these other species eavesdroppers or bystanders whose behavior is influenced accordingly. We can think of ourselves as human animals eavesdropping on alarm calls of climate change—among them the sounding presence of intensifying storms and falling trees, and the changing mix of songs in the dawn bird chorus.

Listening to the hermits, I again experience the ecosublime: their splendid songs have become for me solemn sentinels, portents of climate change.[2] The National Audubon Society predicts their songs will be gone to the north within twenty years. Because of the unusual construction of its syrinx, a hermit thrush can sound two tones at once. Shy birds, these hermits hide in the spruce, but in spring and summer their songs are strong and prominent, especially just after sunset. One bird seemingly repeats variations on the melody where the other leaves off, the second bird consistently just a note or two lower or higher than the first. They continue, one bird and then another. More than two birds, and the songs overlap. Are these song duels, males bluffing each other? Or are they duets, trios, and quartets in a down east forest symphony? Whether honest or dishonest signals to one another, I hear their songs as trustworthy signals of climate change. I will listen for them each spring, perhaps a little earlier than last year, until someday they are gone.

A mutation of thrushes is the collective noun by which a group of them is known; how fitting. After they leave, we will be left with the sounds of a bevy of mourning doves and a murder of crows.

## Notes

1. [Author's note, 2020: Mann repeated his 2014 observation in 2018 based on further data.]
2. [Author's note, 2020: To see and hear hermit thrushes singing, visit Elliott (n.d.)]

# 13

# SUSTAINABILITY AND A SOUND ECOLOGY

*T*HIS PREVIOUSLY UNPUBLISHED ESSAY IS THE LATEST SUMMARY *of the sound ecology project that has occupied my mind since 2011. Its seed is in my essay "Knowing Fieldwork" (reprinted in this volume) and its earlier formulations, where I asked how musical being-in-the-world is experienced and how that kind of experience is different from locating one's orientation to words and objects. Reckoning with Thoreau and sound helped integrate my interests in sound, environmental activism, and ecology and helped me to develop the ideas of the sound connection, presence, and copresence. I've spoken about this project as it has been developing in numerous keynote addresses and public lectures and in an expanded version (the Basler Lectures at East Tennessee State University, when in 2016 I held the Basler Chair of Excellence in the Arts, Rhetoric and Science). An early version was published (Titon 2015c). Since then, the project has evolved: I've developed the parts on sound community and sound economy, and I've modified my views on evolutionary biology, while also writing about what a phenomenological approach to animal sound making will yield about a sound ecology. A longer version of the "Sound Economics" section will appear as "A Sound Economy" in* Transforming Ethnomusicology, *edited by Beverley Diamond and Salwa El-Shawan, forthcoming from Oxford University Press. I hope to finish a book manuscript of the full project in the not-too-distant future.*

The problem of sustainability is not only a problem of resources, technology, science, and engineering. It is also a matter for ethics and is ultimately a problem of knowledge. Unless we place an ethical value on something, we will not sustain it. Ecologist Paul Sears ([1935] 1949, 176) wrote that conservation "is not a subject . . . [rather it] is a moral attitude." What we value depends on who we think we are, what we know, and how we can know it. Normally we orient ourselves through our sensations of smell, hearing, taste, touch, sight, and sound—what Wilfrid Sellars (1962, 6, 20) called the manifest image of the world we encounter daily, as differentiated from the scientific image theorized from such things as subatomic particles, electromagnetic fields, sound, and light waves and their interactions of which we normally are unaware. Most of the time, humans feel ourselves as sensual subjects touching, smelling, listening, and, above all, looking out into a world of others, whether people, animals, plants, or objects like tools and tables and stones and soil. In this essay, I ask, What happens in those moments when we are in the world and know the world chiefly through sounds? What if we gave pride of place to sound worlds rather than object worlds, social group worlds, or text worlds? To put it yet another way, what happens in those moments of sound ontology when we feel our sensations, our being, and knowing centered in sounds? If we privilege how we feel and what we come to know in those reoriented moments, how might we re-form our communities, economies, and ecologies, and how would these differ from those as humans conceive of them at present? Is it possible by means of a thought experiment based in a sound connection to erect a just alternative to the alienated communities, neoliberal political economies, and behaviorist ecologies that drive humans toward injustice, and the planet toward extinction? To do so is to put us on a path of sound ecological rationality, which I believe will lead every being to a more sustainable world. This sound ecological rationality contrasts with and stands in opposition to the now-dominant instrumental economic rationality.

Atoms within molecules constantly vibrate; vibrations sound through every being composed of atoms and molecules—you and me and everyone and everything else. A sound signal is sent through a medium from one vibrating being to another, and with that the two beings are connected, vibrating together. Sound connects. This physical, visceral connection where the scientific meets the manifest has ontological and epistemological implications. In sound, humans may perceive a connection among beings, a direct connection in sounding vibrations. Sound also connects metaphorically. Resonance, sound, and sympathetic vibration are both physical facts and metaphors for solidarity. When I write about a sound experience, a sound community, a sound economy, and a sound ecology, I write both literally and metaphorically. A sound community is a community connected by sound, and it is also a healthy community.

In our posthuman Anthropocene, distinctions blur between culture and nature, between music and sound, and between humans and nonhuman beings. Plants, we are learning, generate and respond to sound waves (Gagliano 2016, 24–25). Whales, we now know thanks to research by Roger and Katy Payne and others, vocalize in patterns that vary over time and space, and there is a lively cross-disciplinary conversation over what extent whale song is like human music and human language (Gray et al. 2001). Scientists have found language recursiveness in the sounds of certain species of whales and songbirds (Dartnell 2001; Suzuki 2006). Humans have long thought that birds sing; ethnomusicologists tell us of cultures like the Kaluli where birdsong plays a central part in a metaphorical acoustic epistemology (Feld 2012; Watkins 2018). Further, Emory University neurobiologists Sarah Earp and Donna Maney (2012) found that female birds, on hearing the song of their mates, released dopamine, a pleasure chemical, in the brain, just as humans do when hearing music they enjoy. It is not surprising to learn that in response to sonic stimuli, songbirds and humans engage the same neuroaffective mechanisms; evolution is, after all, a continuum. What it tells us, as musicians and music scholars, is that we must consider the music of nature in asking about the nature of music (Gray et al. 2001).

In this essay, I claim that a sound connection leads to sound experience and knowledge that may enable humans to construct sound communities, economies, and a sound ecology. Therefore, my essay has four parts. In part one, I discuss sound and how beings experience it. In part two, sound community, I discuss the connective tissue of sound, copresence, and communities brought into being and maintained by sound exchanges. In part three, sound economy, I consider the nature of sound and unsound economic exchanges in the realm of goods and services. In part four, I outline a sound ecology in which I critique ecologies based in genetic determinism and economic rationality and suggest instead an ecological rationality based on sound connectivity and a social genome.

## Sound Experience

In elementary physics we learn that sound, resulting from atoms and molecules in vibratory motion, requires a medium, such as air, water, or solids (such as the Earth), to propagate or travel through. Sounds travel through media in longitudinal waves—that is, along the same direction of the wave. Humans and many nonhuman animals have ears with membranes that vibrate in response to the vibrating sound waves that strike it periodically. Human brains experience these vibrations as sounds. All animals experience sound vibrations in their bodies. Sound is tactile.

Sound connects two objects quite literally, because when one vibrating body sets another body in motion, the two bodies move together. Due to their physical construction, bodies possess what is called a natural vibrating frequency at which they will resonate. One kind of resonance appears in the world

Figure 13.1. Bumblebee pollinating arbutus flower by means of sonication. Source: Wikimedia Commons.

of insects and flowers, when bees and other buzzing and humming insects shake pollen loose by a vibration process called sonication (fig. 13.1). Blueberries and vegetables in the nightshade family are pollinated by sonication—this also includes potatoes, tomatoes, peppers, and eggplant. Sonication is an example of biological mutualism by means of sound communication between insects and plants (Cardinal, Buchmann, and Russell 2018). Some twenty thousand plant species are pollinated by sonication (Gagliano 2016, 24).

In making its vibratory connection, sound announces presence. Sound signals "Here I am." Presence is the experience of being. Presence is the felt awareness of someone or something, the "here-ness" of someone or something as it presents itself to one's awareness. One is present to oneself as well as to another. Absence is the lack of presence, the not-here-ness of someone or something, the sense that something or someone is missing. Initially, sound calls attention to the presence of the signal and signaler.

Sound has its distinguishing peculiarities. Whereas light waves are blocked by objects, for example, sound travels through objects and over distance, thereby bringing even the far distant and out-of-sight present. Presence is in experience. As Don Ihde (2007, 25) puts it, phenomenology aims "to isolate, describe, and discern the structures of immediacy or of fulfillable experiential presence." Sound has directionality and reveals the not only the presence but also the location of others. Sound's directionality is paradoxical because while it may present itself as coming from one place, it may also present itself as omnidirectional and "fill" the listening body, as music sometimes does at loud volume. The echo connects. Beyond location, the quality of the echoing sound may reveal the sounder's shape, extension (solid or hollow), attitude, or mood. Experiencing sound correlates importantly with humans' experience of time. Sounds exhibit continuity but also are marked in time by silence at either end; they are experienced as swelling, pulsating, fading; they are experienced as coming into sounding from silence, then sounding, and then passing out of sounding into silence. In Husserl's phenomenology, the experience of sound as a passing time event enables our awareness to break free from the confines of the right now, or the present, and to become a consciousness that conceives of a past and future (Larrabee 1989). The clock tower bell rings twice to signal two o'clock to a person who understands the sign. The bell signals its presence at a distance, and that presence is felt as time passing.

Presence is a cornerstone of the metaphysics of being. Indigenous ecological knowledges imbue beings with presence or personality. Religious people speak of sensing a spiritual presence, as for example the presence of Christ in the Eucharist. Communicating with others on the internet, we may feel a virtual presence. Fieldwork privileges presence; anthropologists, sociologists, ethnomusicologists, as well as botanists and other biological scientists understand the importance of being there, the in-person observation, witnessing, and experiencing that enables knowing, interpreting, and understanding. In privileging presence, we privilege experience, for presence must be felt or experienced. Of course, experience may at times be deceptive, but that is nowhere near reason to abandon an experiential approach to knowing. I have considered Jacques Derrida's critique of the metaphysics of presence elsewhere, concluding that his elevation of writing over sounding is beside the point of my project, which concerns sounding and communication not only among humans but all beings (Titon 2015c). Only humans write.

## Sound Community

As sound announces presence, copresence in sound vibrates two or more beings and in connecting them forms the basis for organic solidarity and, possibly, community. The term "copresence" was introduced to sociocultural analysis by Erving Goffman. Two people who present themselves to each other are said to be copresent with each other (Goffman 1967). Sounding is but one aspect of copresence, but it is enough to establish a presentation of one being to another. I extend the term "copresence" to include not only humans but all beings: nonhuman animals, plants, landforms, and spiritual beings. Ice can make a booming sound as it expands; such sounds were noted by Thoreau in winter at Walden Pond, for example, while the sounds of glaciers communicate copresence and more to indigenous peoples of the Far North (Cruikshank 2005).

Copresence is a prerequisite for community, but communities may be of different kinds: horizontal and more or less egalitarian, or vertical and more or less hierarchical. For the ecologist, a community is a group of populations made up of one or more species. For the sociologist, a community is a group of individuals making up a population with at least one thing in common. Since the late twentieth century, virtual communities on the internet have become increasingly important to the extent that some scholars have extended the term "copresence" to cover virtual connections (Zhao 2003). Earlier, ecological scientists viewed communities as cohesive, tightly integrated entities consisting of populations of interdependent species. But for the past half century, the dominant idea is that communities instead comprise loosely grouped populations that co-occur according to the individual responses of each species to variable environmental conditions. To use a venerable but still useful (if oversimplified) distinction, sociologists have viewed communities along a spectrum from well integrated (gemeinschaft) to loosely grouped and individualistic (gesellschaft), with the latter increasingly prevalent after the Industrial Revolution.[1] Fundamental to community, and to economy and ecology as well, is exchange between two beings. This may be exchange of information; it may be an exchange of behavior in which the behavior of one being influences the behavior of another; it may be an exchange of goods or services, as in an economic exchange; and it can be all of these and more in ecological exchanges. Gemeinschaft relationships and social exchanges are characterized by cooperation, interdependence, reciprocity, solidarity, mutual rights and obligations, tradition, and kinship; think of the social cohesion among families, relatives, and friends in the close-knit neighborhood, village, and also in musical communities, particularly amateur ones. These exchanges are characteristic of a sound ecology and an ecological rationality. On the other hand, gesellschaft social relations and exchanges result from individuals acting in their immediate self-interest with exchanges among individuals, actions that either are unrestrained or are ruled principally by laws and contracts rather than regulated by personal relationships within a community. These exchanges are characteristic of an unsound ecology and an instrumental, economic rationality. Mid-twentieth-century sociologists applied this distinction to contrast well-integrated communities versus mass society. Again, these are broad generalizations. Social cohesion is present in communities to varying degrees; it is not something that a community either has or does not have. Among humans, sound communication, performance, and community lie along a spectrum from the integrated copresent group to the loose collection of individuals. Sound (heard as noise) may also be disintegrative, as for example the sounds of weapons, sounds that control and disperse crowds, and sounds that torture prisoners. This sound of domination undermines copresence and traumatizes the individual, thereby destroying the possibility of a copresent community.

In participatory sound-making communities, such as social groups that perform music, sounding is chiefly intersubjective and involves exchange of information, behavior, social solidarity, and at peak moments, exchanges not only of expression but also emotion and feelings of flow (Schutz 1951, 76). In many instances, participation extends beyond the music makers to an "audience" of dancers and listeners who, in processing the sounds, feel as though they are exchanging intersubjectivities with the music makers and one another. The proper metaphor here is empathy, based in physical covibration. We may say that this idea resonates with another, and we say that we resonate with someone's feelings. Communicative resonance, regarded as a metaphor for interconnectedness, enables communities, economies, and ecologies. Thus, participatory sound communities offer a model for solidarity and participatory political communities (Titon 2001, 10), but they also offer a model for participatory communities in general.

A sound community embraces a sound commons. A commons is a resource that is not owned but rather one that is shared, respected, and managed by all those who make use of the resource and behave as though everything and everyone is related. Animals such as birds, caribou, and humans share a sound commons in which they communicate (Titon 2012c). Many indigenous communities regard certain repertoires of music and sound to be common possessions of the group, while others belong to individuals. Old Regular Baptists are another of many sound communities that share a music commons (Titon 2005). Old-time string band musicians, Irish traditional musicians, bluegrass musicians, jazz musicians—each group has its tunes commons, part of its shared music culture, involving not only repertoires but also ideas about music and the right way to make it.

A sound community, then, is a participatory, cooperative, cohesive group whose social exchanges based on a sound presence establish solidarity, affirm identity and maintain unity. Social justice is more likely in a sound community than in an unsound one. And human justice will not occur without environmental justice, which means justice for all living beings threatened by human-induced habitat change. Aldo Leopold (1947) declared that humans were members of the Earth community with the responsibilities that follow from membership. The sound connection instantiates tangible proof of that community membership. As Leopold suggested, it is time we erected our communities, economies, and ecologies on the basis of the implications, social, political, economic, and ethical, of that interconnected interdependence, embodied in the copresence characteristic of a sound community. I will return to Leopold's idea of a "land ethic" near the close of this essay.

## Sound Economy

A sound, well-integrated community will also enjoy a sound economy. Western mainstream economics today is governed by what economists call rational choice theory, the assumption that human beings make economic exchanges in their individual self-interest in order to maximize personal wealth. Rational choice theory is congruent with "economic rationality," the idea that the world consists of economic resources or assets: human, material, cultural, natural, and environmental. Economic rationality is the economic realization of instrumental reason, a concept originally developed by foundational sociologist Max Weber and one of the bugbears of critical theory. Economic rationality is fundamental to mainstream Western economic theory and its neoliberal expression today. Economic rationality is unsound, and it has led to an unsound economy.

Suppose one looks more closely at mainstream economics by considering how it is taught. A college textbook that went through seven editions from 1986 through 2006 claims that economics "is the study of how individuals, experiencing virtually limitless wants, choose to allocate scarce resources to best satisfy their wants" (Ekelund and Tollison 2000, 4). The authors state that "we are never satisfied with what we have," implying that greed is human nature. The authors go on to explain that economics comes down to rational choices made by individuals. "Economists focus on a particular view of human behavior—that of homo economicus." Homo economicus (Latin for economic man) is said to be guided by rational self-interest when deciding how to allocate limited resources to satisfy wants. Sellers always attempt to maximize profit, while buyers try to obtain goods at minimal cost. Indeed, modern, neoclassical economic theory postulates that individuals perform a cost-versus-benefit analysis on every economic decision they make, whether in purchasing a home, selling a musical instrument, buying groceries, "networking" for career opportunities, and sometimes in choosing a life partner.

Economic man is not new. It may be traced to the Enlightenment and found in the writings of Adam Smith ([1789] 1904, 15, 16), who famously claimed that in a market economy, human beings have a "natural propensity" to "truck, barter, and exchange" and that "it is not from the benevolence of the butcher, the brewer, or the baker that we expect our dinner, but with regard to their self-interest." John Stuart Mill (1967, 321) wrote that economics was that subject concerned with man "solely as a being who desires to possess wealth, and who is capable of judging the comparative efficacy of means for obtaining that end." The growth of trade; the increasing need for money, banking, and credit; the accumulation of capital and the growth of business organizations—these, fueled by the growing conviction that material wealth was a sign of divine favor, combined in what Max Weber nearly a hundred years ago called the spirit of capitalism, responsible for the development of the Western economy since the Reformation. Weber's contemporary Werner Sombart claimed that this new spirit "was dominated by the principle of pursuit of gain or acquisition, which formed the central core of economic rationalism" (Baldwin 1959, 6).

Today, critiques of capitalism and economic rationality appear with such regularity in scholarly books, journals, the *New York Times*, and the *Washington Post* that their readers may get the incorrect impression that neoclassical economics no longer rules economic policy in the West.[2] Among the critics, feminist economists claim that economic man is not universal but rather is characteristic of male gender behavior, ruthless and competitive (Waring 1988; see also the journal *Feminist Economics*). Behavioral economists point out that sometimes individual economic choices are impulsive; otherwise, why do most contemporary advertisers target consumer desire, not rational choice?[3] Besides, as individuals together constitute the public, so individual self-interest is also served by economic choices made for public benefit: recycling waste, bicycling to work, installing a solar or wind energy system, and volunteering for civic organizations. If greed were human nature, then US attempts to transform agriculture and alleviate poverty in third world countries by incentivizing individual farmers would have had more success. However, faced with the choice between investing outside aid monies in their farms or giving it to their relatives in need, most African farmers chose the latter (Munk 2013). In short, homo economicus is a cultural value; it is not human nature.

A sound economy starts from the premise of the soundly connected community rather than the atomized individual. Instead of presuming that individuals always behave selfishly, let us assume that individuals behave according to cultural principles within their social groups. It is rational for an African farmer to benefit his cousin, not his farm. This behavior is not selfish, yet it is self-rewarding insofar as personal relations are strengthened and the entire community, including the individual, benefits.

Rather than assuming economic rationality and homo economicus, sound economic theory begins by looking at the types of social groups in which economic exchanges take place, and attempts to understand how and why these exchanges are made. Participatory social groups found in local economies are largely integrated because of personal relationships. Hierarchical social groups found in national and international economies are individuated and governed by contracts and law. Homo economicus may be constrained in local groups whereas it is facilitated by formal legal instruments. A minimally regulated market economic system based on competition and economic rationality functions best within societies that value individualism and free choice; it functions best when goods are regarded as commodities, bought and sold in the marketplace, wherein each exchange (including music, for example) has its price, or economic value; and it functions best where trade is protected by rule of law, not custom or tradition. A sound economy, on the contrary, exhibits a commonwealth of reciprocal exchanges. In its original usage, "commonwealth" is a translation of the Latin res publicae, or public things. The *Oxford English Dictionary* dates its first use to ca. 1470, when it meant the public welfare or common good. In this formulation, public good, or res publicae, increases not in proportion to the rise in the gross domestic product but in proportion to the rise in public well-being, which resists quantification. There are such things as well-being and cultural values that are beyond price.

A sound economy rests in interdependence, both embodied and represented in sound vibration, presence, copresence, communication, and community. In contrast with homo economicus, therefore, I suggest a different model, homo reciprocans, or reciprocating human, in which cooperation and reciprocity behavior among community members is paramount (Fehr and Gächter 1998). Here the common good is not the added sum of private goods but rather the emergent good of the social group and its environment as a whole.

Figure 13.2. Homo reciprocans. Photo by Hassanelsayadd—Own work, CC BY-SA 4.0.

This requires balancing individual wants with group goods, and at times, it requires that individuals refrain from adding to their personal wealth in order that the common wealth may increase. Homo reciprocans (fig. 13.2) is the characteristic economic expression of participatory social groups. Homo reciprocans economic activity is characteristic of gift economies such as music-making groups in which a commons of musical resources is shared; however, it also applies to commodity exchanges when, for example, the participatory group is a cooperative unit, as in a food or business co-op. A sound economy is a just economy. Homo reciprocans asks what is in the interest of the community as well as the individuals within it. Cooperative economic communities offer a better chance for individuals, social groups, and the environment as a whole. Here, rather than self-interest and competition among individuals, group interest and cooperation among individuals predominates.

## Sound Ecology

By a sound ecology, I refer to an ecological rationality erected on a sound ontology and epistemology—that is, an ecological way of being, knowing, and doing that grows out of the copresence of living beings connected through sound. Copresence fosters cooperation. This ecological rationality grows out of an acknowledgment of relations among beings with one another and their environment,[4] and from assent to the kinship of all beings with one another and with the environment on account of our relations. Opposed to an economic rationality, which fosters competition, an ecological rationality values beings and the environment for who and what we are, not for what we can be used for. Just as a sound community is a healthy community and a sound economy is a healthy economy, so a sound ecology is a healthy ecology—one that is based on sound ecological principles that foster well-being.

While humanists in this century have been rethinking the human, scientists have been rethinking the animal. Yet a sound ecology aspires to be a universal condition. If an ecological rationality is to be universal, its principles must apply deeply across the human, animal, and plant kingdoms, as well as in the physical (abiotic) environment. Certainly, animals and, we are now learning, plants as well are copresent to one another in sound as cooperative social beings (Wohlleben 2016). However, the current scientific model of animal sound making in particular, and ethology (the science of animal behavior) in general, places sound in the service of an economic rather than an ecological rationality. Working from the perspective of evolutionary biology, ethologists consider animal sound communication one means among many in a competitive game of life. Animal (and plant) life is viewed as a survival game in which the individual accumulates and utilizes resources that are finite or scarce, while avoiding or overcoming predators. The best-adapted individuals succeed by mating and spreading their genetic inheritance in a struggle for existence whose outcome is natural selection and improvement of the phenotype—that is, the physical characteristics and traits of individuals in a species—through successive generations of offspring.

This combination of Darwin's theory of natural selection with modern genetics is popularly called selfish gene theory, a biological counterpart to homo economicus, which in its original, strong version proposed that the behavior of an individual organism was determined by its genotype (genetic program), rather like a computer program. Genetic determinism coupled with natural selection provided a simple, elegant explanation for animal behavior. This evolutionary biology of the late twentieth century proposed that organisms respond to stimuli (including sound stimuli) according to algorithms or sets of instructions in their genotype in service to fitness (Dawkins [1976] 2016).[5] Like a chess-playing computer, their "moves" are said to be automatic; they need not possess minds or know what they are doing. In Daniel Dennett's (2017, 84–101) memorable phrase, they possess competence without comprehension.

If the natural condition of life is competition, struggle, and fitness, then an economic rationality prevails. Yet just as homo economicus appears, in light of feminist and behavioral economics, to be an oversimplified model for economic behavior, so selfish gene theory appears inadequate in light of further developments in genetics. Today's evolutionary biologists also consider coevolution of the genome, culture, and environment, as well as emergent, cooperative group behavior that game theory is unable to predict very well by means of the rules derived for the behavior of competitive individuals.[6] Life, in short, is increasingly viewed as a complex system in which competition, adaptation, and cooperation exist on various levels from the cellular to the ecological community or ecosystem (Kaneko 2006, 3–36). A sounder ecology may prevail, moreover, when plants and animals utilize resources so abundant that competition is minimal or not required. A contemporary example in human cultural ecology is pertinent. The continued production and use of fossil fuels, a scarce resource, exemplifies an economic rationality, harms the environment, and accelerates climate change. On the other hand, the same investment in solar energy, an abundant and renewable resource, stands as an example of ecological rationality. An ecological rationality may also prevail when self-interest aligns with group interest. Sound, and in particular the sounding that animals make, provides an arena in which to examine the contemporary challenges to selfish gene theory that offer hope for an ecological rationality.[7] Among those challenges, I will discuss the debate over animal minds and agency, and also contemporary pressures on genetic determinism.

Taking songbirds as a paradigm case, ornithologists have long distinguished alarm calls that warn of predators; songs that attract mates; territorial calls that maintain spaces for a mating pair to nest and raise offspring; flight calls that keep the flock together; aggressive calls that maintain order within the community; calls associated with nesting, nurturing, and feeding; and so on. Behavioral ecologists (that is, the evolutionary biologists who study animal behavior) assume that birds and other nonhuman animals possess awareness but not intentionality or reflective self-consciousness as they respond to stimuli in their surrounding environments. Animal sounds are assumed to occur in response to stimuli, and these sounds become stimuli that may cause other responses in turn. Animal sounds are said to be signals rather than symbols, functional without providing aesthetic and pleasurable experience. Animal sound communication is thus said to consist of a range of rule-governed, predictable sound signals and responses depending on particular situations and environments.[8]

Behavioral ecologists overturned the alternative animal communication model, which assumed that animal signals, including sounds, contained information from the sender, which like language, required decoding by the receiver. Concepts such as information and metaphors like animal language were thought to be unnecessary and misleading.[9] Instead of influencing other animals by way of transmitting information, which left open the possibility that animals think and make decisions, behavioral ecologists such as Richard Dawkins and John Krebs argued on the basis of a strict stimulus-response model that senders' communications manipulated rather than influenced signal receivers' behavior (Dawkins and Krebs 1978). Senders' signals may be "honest," such as a flight call, or "deceptive," such as the grouse's broken wing flutter; in both cases, they are manipulative. The male bird who sings loudest and longest risks greater exposure to predators but also advertises himself as the biggest, most powerful bird to all potential mates. When the payoff is the female bird with the best-adapted genes, to the successive generations the benefit is worth the cost. In this way, behavioral ecologists adopt the metaphors of homo economicus, rational choice, and the cost-benefit analysis of game theory to explain animal behavior in terms of evolutionary fitness (Bradbury and Vehrencamp 2011). Altruism, for example, is not real but only apparent. An alarm call that results in the death of the individual caller may save the group nearby, which on account of kinship is likely to contain much of the individual's genetic inheritance. This apparent altruism, called kin selection or inclusive fitness, appears to confirm that "selfishness" or self-interest is as it were baked into the genes, which by means of relatives and offspring survive the death of individual organisms. In proclaiming that nature too is selfish, animal behaviorists reify homo economicus as the state of nature, while neoclassical economists assume that because nature is selfish, self-interest must be natural for humans as well.

This radical portrait of the selfish gene appears to have gone too far. "Information" in animal communication has made a comeback (Stegmann 2013). When an animal is said to undertake a "cost-benefit analysis," the possibility of animal minds, thought, and agency reenters by means of a metaphorical back door. Indeed, our folk psychology does attribute minds and emotions to the higher vertebrates, and in response to the reenergized animal rights movement, an increasing number of scientists are performing experiments revealing that animal brains do have percepts of emotions such as pain and pleasure. Inasmuch as folk psychology sometimes does predict animal behavior—for example, my dog is barking because she "wants" to go outside—it is not uncommon to find articles in science journals today testing hypotheses about whether animals have minds and undergo conscious experiences (Griffin and Speck 2004; Lurz 2010). Dennett (2017, 93–97), while maintaining that animals are competent but do not comprehend, has also maintained for decades that folk psychology is useful when it enables us to predict their behavior as though they were thinking and feeling beings. While it is true that much animal behavior can be accounted for without assuming consciousness, defined by Dennett as a complex of talents and cognitive abilities realized in the medium of neural interactions, nevertheless some animal species when faced with novel problems are capable of solving them by utilizing those talents and abilities; thus, they appear able, in their own ways of being, to think, learn, and adapt.[10]

The possibilities that some animals do have language is a promising area of contemporary research. Songbirds, for example, are not predestined to sing their species song. When raised apart from conspecifics—that is, apart from members of their own species—they sing the song of their foster parents. Experiments with songs of certain bird species, such as the chickadee, also reveal recursiveness—that is, animals combining small sound units in different ways, as if forming words and sentences, with different meanings depending on the combinations (S. Smith 1992). Animal play is another research area, where play need not be considered just rehearsal practice for the game of life (hunting, fighting, companionship, and so forth) but also for pleasure.[11] Understanding animal behavior is a hard problem, however, because it seems impossible for a human to experience what it is like to be a chickadee or a whale or a bat. Nonetheless, recent neurological research suggests biological similarities between processes in human and nonhuman animal brains, which along with mirror neuron research gives reason to think that folk psychology may yet find scientific confirmation in some respects (Ferrari and Rizzolatti 2014).

For those and other reasons, it makes sense to regard animal sounds not as genetically predetermined expressions of competent automatons in response to stimuli but rather as part of complex, nonhuman language systems based on an animal's talents, cognitive abilities, and *umwelt* (environment or perceptual field enabling the animal to express its particular being). In other words, animals express themselves (in sounds, movements, and in other ways) by means of the possibilities offered to their embodied beings, their perceptions and the affordances of their environments.[12] Considering animal sounding in this way elevates it from the instrumentality of communication and allows for the possibility of affective and aesthetic expression in a species- and even an individual-specific manner. Many nonhuman animals have more powerful abilities than humans: they can see farther, hear higher and lower frequencies, and smell better. It makes more sense to think of animal minds and agency on a multidimensional spectrum, with talents, abilities, and mental processes in the brain becoming increasingly sophisticated as the animal adapts and evolves in its environment.

Contemporary geneticists now agree that behavior is no longer predetermined by an animal's genes but rather results from responses of the animal's genome to variable and changing environmental conditions. The idea that individual genes program an organism's behavior and drive evolution solely by means of fitness has been replaced with the idea that the organism's genome works in concert with the environment and with other organisms to enable a range of behaviors that influence fitness. Moreover, culture-driven adaptations can affect biological fitness; this is called genetic assimilation. Contemporary genetics has shown that fitness is driven not by individual, selfish genes but rather by a social genome, one in which genes connect and work in concert with one another and with the environment. As Nathaniel Comfort (2015, 184–185) puts it in a review of the second volume of Dawkins's autobiography, "Today's genome is much more than a script; it is a dynamic, three-dimensional structure, highly responsive to its environment . . . [and containing] a universe of regulatory and modulatory elements. . . . Genes cooperate, evolving together as units to produce traits. Many researchers continue to find selfish DNA a productive idea, but taking the longer view, the selfish gene per se is looking increasingly like a twentieth-century construct."

In short, evolution can no longer be fully and properly explained by the genetic determinism of selfish gene theory. For humans, it is more accurate to think in terms of the coevolution of genes, environment, and culture: "Culture often leads the gene-coevolution process. Cultural evolution creates novel environments and those novel environments exert selection pressures on genes" (Richerson 2012). Coevolution of genes, environment, and culture is an important area of contemporary research in animal sound communication also (fig. 13.3). In their migrations, some bird species avoid highways because traffic noise interferes with their sound signals (McClure et al., 2013). Recall that songbirds learn their songs from their parents. Coevolution appears responsible for the observed phenomenon that songbird populations whose habitat includes interstate highways have evolved to sing longer, more complex, or higher pitched songs than their forest relatives to avoid interference from traffic noise (e.g., Gentry, McKenna, and Luther 2017). In urban habitats, one bird species was observed to have evolved to sing louder or

Figure 13.3. Conference poster, Culture-Gene Interactions. Courtesy of the Center for Academic Research and Training in Anthropogeny at University of California San Diego, carta.anthropogeny.org.

longer but not to have the flexibility to change pitch register (Rios-Chelén et al., 2018).

Evolutionary biologist Jean Roughgarden has mounted a vigorous critique of selfish gene theory, proposing that evolutionary fitness is the result of social selection among individuals, which takes cooperation rather than competition to be the most important contributor to evolutionary success within both an animal social system and in a gene pool. For example, a female animal does not always choose the biggest and baddest mate and may instead prefer the one whose potential for cooperative behavior would enable the two of them to be a better pair for companionship, nest building, parenting, and so on (Roughgarden 2010).

Social selection relates to another challenge to selfish gene theory—namely, the origins and development of sociality. Sociality measures the extent to which individuals in animal populations and communities associate in groups to form cooperative societies. Selfish gene proponents argue that the higher animals are naturally competitive and social only when cooperation benefits the survival of the individual's gene pool. Nonetheless, ethologists Robert Sussman and Paul Garber, after reviewing the growing evidence on primate social interactions, concluded that most are affiliative, not competitive. "Aggression and affiliation are necessary consequences of social life.... If an individual's survival is enhanced by the collective advantages of living in a cohesive and socially integrated behavioral unit, then an understanding of the ability to maintain affiliative and coordinated behaviors and to minimize [ant]agonistic and eccentric behaviors is likely to provide critical insight into the evolution of sociality and group living in primates" (Sussman and Garber 2004, 178). Sussman explained further that "the selfish gene hypothesis is inadequate.... We believe that instead of being genetically predisposed to competition and aggression, humans—and perhaps other animals as well—have a biological foundation for unselfish social interaction" (quoted in McClain 2004). An eminent scientist who previously had been an ardent proponent of selfish gene theory, the sociobiologist E. O. Wilson, forswore it by arguing that kin selection or inclusive fitness is insufficient to explain intraspecies cooperation among the social insects, such as bees and ants, which are Wilson's special areas of inquiry. Cooperative behavior, particularly among individuals who are not kin, must be understood in terms of what Wilson calls eusociality, literally "true social condition" (E. Wilson, Nowak, and Tarnita 2010) (fig. 13.4). Contemporary evolutionary biologists regard both Dawkins's and Wilson's positions as extreme. Natural selection appears to be multileveled, though it operates chiefly on the individual level,

Figure 13.4. Interspecies cooperation between white-breasted nuthatch and black-capped chickadee. In winter, nuthatches and chickadees flock together. Photo by John Pizniur.

not the group or genetic level. In addition, inclusive fitness appears to explain many instances of group selection.

In short, animal sound communication can no longer be explained entirely by twentieth-century behavioral ecology's reliance on competition, fitness, selfish genes, cost-benefit analyses, and manipulation. True social condition is supported instead by the sound connection that establishes visceral copresence. From connection follows *relation*, for a sound ecology has a relational ontology and epistemology. Relation means exchange, whether sound exchanges in copresence, economic exchanges among individuals, social exchanges within communities, or the genome exchanging expression in response to other organisms and the environment.

Of course, copresence of sound vibrations need not be benign. It can lead to predation and destruction. Noise happens. Noise affects human and, presumably, nonhuman physiology and psychology. Before the Reagan administration put a stop to this work, US Environmental Protection Agency scientists found negative effects of noise pollution on heart and pulse rate, blood pressure, irritability, mood, and other health measures (Office of the

Scientific Assistant 1981). Critical theorists have proposed a politics of fear and control based on sonic vibrations or subliminal noise. Loud sounds are part of the torture arsenal that the United States employs with those detained as alleged terrorists (Cusick 2008). Steve Goodman (2009) asserts that vibrational force is characteristic of sonic manipulation and crowd control in a modern nation-state.

On the other hand, in a world of vibrating molecules, each vibrating body in the world may be understood to be reciprocally copresent with the others. A recent line of philosophical inquiry emphasizes the vital culture of material things, resisting the distinction between human subjects and inanimate objects. Indeed, from a physics standpoint, the molecules in material objects are constantly in vibratory motion, whether these objects are animate or inanimate. Jane Bennett's (2004) work in "vital materialism" suggests the possibility of a rapprochement with indigenous thought about nature. For Native Americans and First Nations peoples, it is not enough simply to assert that everything is connected, nor is it quite right to conclude that for indigenous peoples everything is alive or filled with spirit. That is the mistaken attribution of animism. A closer approximation to indigenous ecological knowledges may be had in the idea that humans are kin to nonhuman beings, which include animals, plants, and landforms.[13] Thus, rather than think merely in terms of interdependence, humans and nonhuman persons are present to each other in the same social and moral community, with reciprocal rights and obligations. In this essay, I've proposed that connection is relation, which implies relational being, knowing, and acting.

This same insight, a sound ecology built on right relation, is found in what the ecological scientist Aldo Leopold called the land ethic. In *A Sand County Almanac*, Leopold proposed that we enlarge the scope of ethics from humans to Earth as a whole. He wrote,

> The land ethic simply enlarges the boundaries of the community to include soils, waters, plants, and animals, or collectively: the land. . . . [A] land ethic changes the role of Homo sapiens from conqueror of the land-community to plain member and citizen of it. It implies respect for his fellow-members, and also respect for the community as such. (Leopold [1949] 1989, 204)

Leopold here critiques human domination over nature and like Thoreau (2001c, 201) proposes that humans view themselves as "inhabitants, part and parcel" of it, not superior to it. Wendell Berry, a latter-day advocate of respect for the land community, has found Leopold's idea of membership especially useful in constructing his fictional world of Port William, Kentucky. Later in "The Land Ethic," Leopold promotes an ecological instead of economic rationality:

> Quit thinking about decent land-use solely as an economic problem. Examine each question in terms of what is ethically and esthetically right, as well as what is economically expedient. A thing is right when it tends to preserve the integrity, stability, and beauty of the biotic community. It is wrong when it tends otherwise. (Leopold [1949] 1989, 224–225)

Ecological science at the ecosystem level is a hierarchy of complex systems. The hierarchy goes from individuals in a species to a population of that species inhabiting a given environment. Within that environment there will inevitably be several populations interacting in various ways to compose the ecological community. In a forest, for example, tree species, animal species, fungi, and other plant species compose an ecological community. The ecological community includes what Leopold proposed in "The Land Ethic": the landscape with the human individual as a member and citizen.[14] Thomas Jefferson wrote in the Declaration of Independence that the "Laws of Nature" grant to humans "inalienable rights" to "life, liberty, and the pursuit of happiness." Natural rights are universal, and unlike legal rights, they don't depend on the laws or customs of any particular nation or government. If one grants that these inalienable human rights derive ultimately from laws of nature, then nature has those same rights. And so, perhaps surprisingly, inclusive fitness and kin selection has its place in our new ecological rationality. If we take the land ethic and natural rights seriously, then all life forms are related—and humans in the West may yet learn, before it is too late, that it is in our rational self-interest to treat everyone and everything as kin. This is not a declaration of independence but one of mutual dependence.

Music is the corporeal expression of a sound connection as a vibrational exchange. It is also an information exchange, a behavioral exchange, a social exchange, an economic exchange, and an ecological exchange. For human beings, nothing represents the sound connection and the sound and just community, economy, and ecology better than music. Yet all beings are in the world of vibrations and sound experience. This, I suggest in conclusion, is a sound way of knowing that is worth pondering and building on in hope of changing our unsound and unbalanced world to a world worth having.

## Notes

1. The terms "gemeinschaft" and "gesellschaft" were introduced by Ferdinand Tönnies, the nineteenth-century German scholar whose ideas were foundational in sociology and greatly influenced Durkheim, Weber, and later sociologists, economists, and anthropologists.

2. See Collier (2019), a review of five recently published books declaring the death of Economic Man.

3. Behavioral economists Daniel Kahneman and Robert J. Shiller received the Nobel Prize in Economic Sciences in 2002 and 2013, respectively.

4. Ernst Haeckel coined the term and invented the science of ecology, defining it in 1866 as the relations of organisms with each other and with their environment.

5. Of course, genes cannot be selfish because they have no agency. As Darwin before him with his phrase "struggle for existence," Dawkins has repeatedly had to explain that "selfish gene" is only an inexact metaphor.

6. However, game theory predicts cooperative behavior in some simulations, such as the now-classic problem of the Prisoner's Dilemma. Philosopher David Gauthier (1987, 167) showed how cooperative behavior (that is, if both prisoners confessed to the police) would enable a lesser overall prison sentence.

7. On account of our ethics and agency, humans are capable of making moral choices in the direction of an ecological rationality. If that weren't so, how could I write this essay?

8. Bradbury and Vehrencamp (2011), *Principles of Animal Communication*, is the best overview of the subject, with several chapters on sound communication. Other books on animal behavior include summaries of sound communication, while there are numerous studies on animal communication in particular species. All hew to the neo-Darwinian behavioral ecology paradigm pioneered by Dawkins and Krebs in the 1970s.

9. Information in the ordinary sense of the term, rather than the specialized sense in which the term is used in computer science.

10. Could a superior being from a different solar system, upon observing human behavior on Earth without being able to understand human language, determine that humans had free will, or at least thought they did? Or would that superior being assume that humans were genetically programmed to respond to stimuli and behave in predetermined ways?

11. Thoreau ([1854] 1985, 510) wrote about a loon that "played" with him on Walden Pond. The loon let Thoreau approach him in his boat, then dived underwater and emerged some distance away, emitting its characteristic laugh. When Thoreau moved close again, the loon repeated its motions:

> While he was thinking one thing in his brain, I was endeavoring to divine his thought in mine. It was a pretty game, played on the small surface of the pond, a man against a loon. Suddenly your adversary's checker disappears beneath the board, and the problem is to place yours nearest to where his will appear again. Sometimes he would come up unexpectedly on the opposite side of me, having apparently passed directly under the boat. So long-winded was he and so unweariable, that when he had swum farthest he would immediately plunge again, nevertheless; and then no wit could divine where in the deep pond, beneath the smooth surface, he might be speeding his way. . . .

12. Here I borrow from Jakob von Uexküll's concept of *umwelt*, Merleau-Ponty's ideas about animal embodiment, and James J. Gibson's notion of affordances. See Titon (forthcoming).

13. Anthropological perspectivism fruitfully explores human-animal relations among North American indigenous peoples. See de Castro (2008).

14. An ecological community plus the nonliving or abiotic parts of the environment compose an ecosystem.

# REFERENCES

Abrahams, Roger, ed. 1970. *A Singer and Her Songs*. Baton Rouge: Louisiana State University Press.
Aikawa, Noriko. 2001. "The 1989 Recommendation on the Safeguarding of Traditional Culture and Folklore: Actions Undertaken by UNESCO for Its Implementation." In *Safeguarding Traditional Cultures: Global Assessment*, edited by Paul Seitel, 13–19. Washington, DC: Smithsonian Office of Folklife and Cultural Heritage.
Allen, Aaron S. 2012. "'Fatto di Fiemme': Stradivari's Violins and the Musical Trees of the Paneveggio." In *Invaluable Trees: Cultures of Nature, 1660–1830*, edited by Laura Auricchio, Elizabeth Heckendorn Cook, and Giulia Pacini, 301–315. Oxford: Voltaire Foundation.
———. 2013. s.v. "Ecomusicology." *Grove Dictionary of American Music*. 2nd ed.
Allen, Aaron S., and Kevin Dawe, eds. 2016. *Current Directions in Ecomusicology: Music, Nature, Environment*. New York: Routledge.
Allen, T. F. H, A. J. Zellmer, and C. J. Wuennenberg. 2005. "The Loss of Narrative." In *Ecological Paradigms Lost*, edited by Kim Cuddington and Beatrix Beisner, 333–370. Burlington, MA: Elsevier.
American Folklife Center. n.d. "About the American Folklife Center." Library of Congress. Accessed December 30, 2019. https://www.loc.gov/folklife/aboutafc.html.
Appalshop. 2007. "The Singing of the Old Regular Baptists." Community Correspondence Corps. Podcast hosted by Josh Noah. Whitesburg, KY: Appalshop. https://www.appalshop.org/ccc/?p=75. Link no longer available. A digital copy of this podcast is in possession of the author.
Barclay, Robert. 2004. *The Preservation and Use of Historic Musical Instruments*. London: Earthscan.
———. 2013. "Ecomusicology." In *Grove Dictionary of American Music*, edited by Charles Hiroshi Garrett. 2nd ed. New York: Oxford University Press.
Baldwin, John W. 1959. "The Medieval Theories of the Just Price." *Transactions of the American Philosophical Society*, n.s., 49 (4): 1–92.
Baron, Robert, and Nick Spitzer, eds. 2007. *Public Folklore*. Oxford: University Press of Mississippi.
Barry, Phillips. 1939. *The Maine Woods Songster*. Cambridge, MA: Powell Printing.
Barthes, Roland. 1975. *The Pleasure of the Text*. Translated by Richard Miller. New York: Hill and Wang.
Bartók, Béla. [1976] 1992. "Why and How Do We Collect Folk Music." In *Béla Bartók, Essays*, edited by Benjamin Suchoff, 9–24. Lincoln: University of Nebraska Press.
Barton, Gregory. 2002. *Empire Forestry and the Origins of Environmentalism*. Cambridge: Cambridge University Press.
Barz, Gregory, and Timothy J. Cooley, eds. [1997] 2008. *Shadows in the Field: New Perspectives for Fieldwork in Ethnomusicology*. 2nd ed. New York: Oxford University Press.
Bateson, Gregory. 1979. *Mind and Nature: A Necessary Unity*. New York: Hampton.
Baum, Willa K. 1977. *Transcribing and Editing Oral History*. Nashville, TN: American Association for State and Local History.

Bauman, Richard. 1977. *Verbal Art as Performance.* Prospect Heights, IL: Waveland.
Bauman, Richard, and Patricia Sawin. [1991] 2012. "The Politics of Participation in Folklife Festivals." In *Exhibiting Cultures*, edited by Ivan Karp and Steven D. Lavine, 288–313. Washington, DC: Smithsonian Institution Press.
Bauman, Richard, Patricia Sawin, and Inta Gale Carpenter. 1992. *Reflections on the Folklife Festival: An Ethnography of Participant Experience.* Bloomington: Folklore Institute, Indiana University.
Bealle, John. 1997. *Public Worship, Private Faith: Sacred Harp and American Folksong.* Athens: University of Georgia Press.
Bean, Wayne Reuel, ed. 1973. *Me and Fannie. Northeast Folklore* 14.
Becker, Howard. 1986. *Doing Things Together: Selected Papers.* Evanston, IL: Northwestern University Press.
Ben-Amos, Dan. 1972. "Toward a Definition of Folklore in Context." In *Toward New Perspectives in Folklore*, edited by Americo Paredes and Richard Bauman, 3–15. Austin: University of Texas Press.
Bennett, Jane. 2004. "The Force of Things: Steps toward an Ecology of Matter." *Political Theory* 32 (3): 347–372.
Berger, Peter L., and Thomas Luckmann. 1966. *The Social Construction of Reality.* New York: Anchor Books.
Berliner, Paul. 1978. *The Soul of Mbira.* Chicago: University of Chicago Press.
Billups, Edward W. 1854. *The Sweet Songster: A Collection of the Most Popular Songs, Hymns and Ballads.* Wayne, WV: Arrowood Bros.
Boas, Franz. 1888. "On Certain Songs and Dances of the Kwakiutl of British Columbia." *Journal of American Folklore* 1 (1): 49–64.
Bock, Cherice. 2017. "Trust Author Profile: Jeff Todd Titon." *Whole Terrain*, October 26, 2017. http://www.wholeterrain.com/201704trust-author-profile-jeff-todd-titon/.
Bolter, Jay David, Michael Joyce, and John B. Smith. 1993. *Getting Started with Storyspace.* Cambridge, MA: Eastgate Systems.
Booth, Wayne C. 1999. *For the Love of It.* Chicago: University of Chicago Press.
Bradbury, Jack W., and Sandra L. Vehrencamp. 2011. *Principles of Animal Communication.* 2nd ed. Sunderland, MA: Sinauer Associates.
Brăiloiu, Constantin. [1931] 1984a. "Musicology and Ethnomusicology Today." In Constantin Brăiloiu, *Problems of Ethnomusicology*, edited and translated by A. L. Lloyd, 86–101. Cambridge: Cambridge University Press.
———. [1931] 1984b. "Outline of a Method of Musical Folklore." In Constantin Brăiloiu, *Problems of Ethnomusicology*, edited and translated by A. L. Lloyd, 59–85. Cambridge: Cambridge University Press.
———. 1984c. *World Collection of Recorded Folk Music.* Established by Constantin Brăiloiu. Recordings, 1913–1953. 6 LP recordings, notes. Geneva: VDE-Gallo.
Brewer, Richard. 1994 *The Science of Ecology.* 2nd ed. New York: Harcourt Brace Saunders College Publishing.
Brewster, Paul G., ed. 1940. *Ballads and Songs of Indiana.* Bloomington: Indiana University Press.
Brundtland World Commission on Environment and Development. 1987. *Our Common Future.* Oxford: Oxford University Press.
Buell, Lawrence. 1995. "Thoreau and the Natural Environment." In *The Cambridge Companion to Henry David Thoreau*, edited by Joel Myerson, 171–193. New York: Cambridge University Press.
Burroway, Janet. 1987. *Writing Fiction.* 2nd ed. Boston: Little, Brown.

Cage, John. [1973] 2010. *M: Writings 1969–1972*. Middletown, CT: Wesleyan University Press.
Cantwell, Robert. 1991. "Conjuring Culture: Ideology and Magic in the Festival of American Folklife." *Journal of American Folklore* 104 (412): 148–163.
———. 1993. *Ethnomimesis: Folklife and the Representation of Culture*. Chapel Hill: University of North Carolina Press.
Cardinal, S., S. L. Buchmann, and A. L. Russell. 2018. "The Evolution of Floral Sonication, a Pollen Foraging Behavior Used by Bees." *Evolution* 73 (3): 590–600.
Carnap, Rudolph. 1966. *An Introduction to the Philosophy of Science*, edited by Martin Gardner. New York: Harper Torchbooks.
Carson, Rachel. 1962. *Silent Spring*. Boston: Houghton-Mifflin.
Casagrande, Joseph, ed. 1960. *In the Company of Man*. New York: Harper.
Castaneda, Carlos. 1968. *The Teachings of Don Juan: A Yaqui Way of Knowledge*. Berkeley: University of California Press.
Cavicchi, Daniel. 2011. *Listening and Longing: Music Lovers in the Age of Barnum*. Middletown, CT: Wesleyan University Press.
Center for Folklife Programs and Cultural Studies. 1997a. *Festival of American Folklife Participant Handbook*. Washington, DC: Smithsonian Institution.
———. 1997b. *Festival of American Folklife Presenters Guide*. Washington, DC: Smithsonian Institution.
Clark, Edie. 2006. "Ted Ames and the Recovery of Maine Fisheries: One Maine Fisherman Earns a MacArthur 'Genius Grant.'" *Yankee Magazine* 70 (9): 56–63.
Clifford, James. 1988. *The Predicament of Culture*. Cambridge, MA: Harvard University Press.
Clifford, James, and George E. Marcus, eds. [1986] 2010. *Writing Culture: The Poetics and Politics of Ethnography*. Berkeley: University of California Press.
Coates, Peter. 2004. "Emerging from the Wilderness (or, From Redwoods to Bananas): Recent Environmental History in the United States and the Rest of the Americas." *Environment and History* 10 (4): 407–438.
Code, Lorraine. 1991. *What Can She Know? Feminist Theory and the Construction of Knowledge*. Ithaca, NY: Cornell University Press.
Cohen, John. 1960. *Mountain Music of Kentucky*. 12" LP recording. New York: Folkways Records 2317.
Cohen, Ronald D., ed. 2010. *Alan Lomax, Assistant in Charge: The Library of Congress Letters, 1935–1945*. Jackson: University Press of Mississippi.
Coles, Robert. 1967. *Children of Crisis*. Boston: Little, Brown.
Collier, Paul. 2019. "Greed Is Dead." *Times Literary Supplement*, no. 6088 (December 6), 4–6.
Collingwood, R. G. 1948. *The Idea of History*. Oxford: Clarendon.
Comfort, Nathaniel. 2015. "Dawkins, Redux." *Nature* 525 (7568): 184–185.
Cooley, Timothy. 2003. "Theorizing Fieldwork Impact: Malinowski, Peasant-Love, and Friendship." *British Journal of Ethnomusicology* 12 (1): 3–17.
———, ed. 2019. *Cultural Sustainabilities: Music, Media, Language, Advocacy*. Urbana: University of Illinois Press.
Cooper, James Fenimore. 1823. *The Pioneers*. New York: Wiley.
Coover, Robert. 1993. "Hyperfiction: Novels for the Computer." *New York Times Book Review*, August 29, 3, 8–12.
Cornell Lab. n.d. "How and Why Birds Sing." Bird Academy. Accessed December 22, 2019. https://academy.allaboutbirds.org/birdsong/.
Cornett, Elwood. 1990. Elwood Cornett, interviewed by Jeff Todd Titon, Blackey, KY. Recording and transcript in possession of the author.

Cornett, Elwood, Jeff Todd Titon, and John Wallhausser. 1997. *Old Regular Baptists: Lined-Out Hymnody from Southeastern Kentucky*. CD recording, with booklet. Washington, DC: Smithsonian Folkways SF CD 40106.

———. 2003. *Songs of the Old Regular Baptists: Lined-Out Hymnody from Southeastern Kentucky*. Vol. 2. CD recording, with booklet. Washington, DC: Smithsonian Folkways 50001.

Cox, John Harrington, ed. 1925. *Folk-Songs of the South*. Cambridge, MA: Harvard University Press.

Cross, Ian. 2009. "The Evolutionary Nature of Musical Meaning." *Musicae Scientae* 13 (2 suppl.): 179–200.

Cruikshank, Julie. 2005. *Do Glaciers Listen? Local Knowledge, Colonial Encounters, and Social Imagination*. Vancouver: University of British Columbia Press.

Culler, Jonathan. 1975. *Structuralist Poetics*. Ithaca, NY: Cornell University Press.

———. 1982. *On Deconstruction*. Ithaca, NY: Cornell University Press.

Cusick, Susan. 2008. "You Are in a Place That Is Out of the World. . . . Music in the Detention Camps of the 'Global War on Terror.'" *Journal of the Society for American Music* 2 (1): 1–26.

Dallmayr, Fred R., and Thomas A. McCarthy. 1977. *Understanding and Social Inquiry*. Notre Dame, IN: Notre Dame University Press.

Daly, Herman E. [1977] 1991. *Steady-State Economics*. Washington, DC: Island Press.

———. 1993. "Sustainable Growth: An Impossibility Theorem." In *Valuing the Earth*, edited by Herman E. Daly and Kenneth N. Townsend, 267–274. Cambridge, MA: MIT Press.

Danielson, Larry. 1976. "Review of *People of the Tobacco Belt*." *Folklore Forum* 9:172–173.

Dartnell, Lewis. 2001. "Is Humpback Whale Song a Language?" July 1, 2001. http://lewisdartnell.com/en-gh/2001/07/is-humpback-whale-song-a-language-2/.

Davis, Arthur Kyle. 1929. *Traditional Ballads of Virginia*. Cambridge, MA: Harvard University Press.

Davis, Cullom, Kathryn Back, and Kay MacLean. 1975. *Oral History: From Tape to Type*. Springfield, IL: Sangamon State University.

Dawkins, Richard. [1976] 2016. *The Selfish Gene*. 4th ed. New York: Oxford University Press.

Dawkins, Richard, and John R. Krebs. 1978. "Animal Signals: Information or Manipulation?" In *Behavioural Ecology: An Evolutionary Approach*, edited by J. R. Krebs and N. B. Davies, 282–309. Oxford: Blackwell Scientific.

De Castro, Eduardo Viveiros. 2008. "Cosmological Deixis and Amerindian Perspectivism." *Journal of the Royal Anthropological Institute* 4 (3): 469–488.

Degh, Linda. 1975. *People in the Tobacco Belt: Four Lives*. Ottawa: National Museum of Man, Canadian Centre for Folk Cultural Studies, Paper 13.

Dennett, Daniel. 2017. *From Bacteria to Bach and Back*. New York: Norton.

Derrida, Jacques. 1979. "Living On/Border Lines." In *Deconstruction and Criticism*, edited by Geoffrey Hartman, 75–176. New York: Continuum.

DeWitt, Mark F. 2008. *Cajun and Zydeco Dance Music in Northern California*. Oxford: University Press of Mississippi.

———. 2009. "Louisiana Creole *Bals de maison* in California and the Accumulation of Social Capital." *the world of music* 51 (1): 17–34.

Dirksen, Rebecca. 2012. "Reconsidering Theory and Practice in Ethnomusicology: Applying, Advocating, and Engaging Beyond Academia." *Ethnomusicology Review* 17. https://www.ethnomusicologyreview.ucla.edu/journal/volume/17/piece/602.

Dorgan, Howard. 1989. *The Old Regular Baptists of Central Appalachia: Brothers and Sisters in Hope*. Knoxville: University of Tennessee Press.

Dornfeld, Barry, Tom Rankin, and Jeff Todd Titon. 1989. *Powerhouse for God*. Color, VHS and 16 mm, 58 min. Watertown, MA: Documentary Educational Resources. Also available at http://www.folkstreams.net.

Dorson, Richard. 1970. "Is There a Folk in the City?" *Journal of American Folklore* 83 (328): 185–216.

———, ed. 1972a. *Folklore and Folklife*. Chicago: University of Chicago Press.

———. 1972b. "History of the Elite and History of the Folk." In Richard Dorson, *Folklore: Selected Essays*, 225–259. Bloomington: Indiana University Press.

Douglas, J. Yellowlees. 1991. "Are We Reading Yet?" In brochure notes to *Victory Garden* by Stewart Moulthrop. Cambridge, MA: Eastgate Systems.

Dyk, Walter, ed. [1938] 1967. *Son of Old Man Hat: A Navajo Autobiography, by Left Handed*. Lincoln: University of Nebraska Press.

Eagleton, Terry. 1978. *Criticism and Ideology*. London: Verso.

———. 1983. *Literary Theory: An Introduction*. Minneapolis: University of Minnesota Press.

Earp, Sarah, and Donna Maney. 2012. "Birdsong: Is It Music to Their Ears?" *Frontiers in Evolutionary Neuroscience* 4: article 14. doi: 10.3389/fnevo.

Easthope, Anthony. 1994. "Cultural Studies 1." In *The Johns Hopkins Guide to Literary Theory and Criticism*, edited by Michael Groden and Martin Kreiswirth, 176–179. Baltimore: Johns Hopkins University Press.

Ekelund, Robert Burton, and Robert D. Tollison. 2000. *Economics: Private Markets and Public Choice*. Reading, MA: Addison-Wesley.

Elliott, Lang. n.d. "Hermit Thrush—Ethereal Singer." Music of Nature. Accessed December 12, 2019. https://musicofnature.com/feature/hermit-thrush/.

Ellis, Alexander. 1885. "On the Musical Scales of Various Nations." *Journal of the Arts* 1688 (33): 485–527.

Emerson, Ralph Waldo. 1849. *Nature*. Boston: James Munroe.

Erlmann, Veit. 2010. *Reason and Resonance*. New York: Zone.

Evelyn, John. 1664. *Silva: A Discourse of Forest Trees and the Propagation of Timber in His Majesty's Dominions*. London: John Martyn for the Royal Society.

Faux, Tom. 2009. "Don Roy, Fiddle Music, and Social Sustenance in Franco New England." *the world of music* 51 (1): 35–54.

Fehr, Ernst, and Simon Gächter. 1998. "Reciprocity and Economics: The Economic Implications of *Homo Reciprocans*." *European Economic Review* 42 (3–5): 845–859.

Feintuch, Burt. 1989. "Folklorists and Cultural Conservation in the United States." Unpublished manuscript (personal copy).

Feintuch, Burt, ed. 1988. *The Conservation of Culture: Folklorists and the Public Sector*. Lexington: University Press of Kentucky.

———. 2003. *Eight Words for the Study of Expressive Culture*. Urbana: University of Illinois Press.

Feld, Steven. [1982] 2012. *Sound and Sentiment*. 3rd ed. Durham, NC: Duke University Press.

Fenn, John, ed. 2003. "Applied Ethnomusicology." Special issue, *Folklore Forum* 34 (1–2).

Ferrari, Pier F., and Giacomo Rizzolatti. 2014. "Mirror Neuron Research: The Past and the Future." *Philosophical Transactions: Biological Sciences* 369 (1644): 1–4.

Festival of American Folklife. 1973. *Program Book*. Washington, DC: Smithsonian Institution.

Fields, Grethel [Dosh]. 1997. "The Baptists Go to Washington." Unpublished typescript in possession of the author.

Fischer, Michael M. J., and George Marcus. 1986. *Anthropology as Cultural Critique*. Chicago: University of Chicago Press.

Fish, Stanley. 1980. *Is There a Text in This Class? The Authority of Interpretive Communities*. Cambridge, MA: Harvard University Press.

Frank, Gelya. 1979. "Finding the Common Denominator: A Phenomenological Critique of the Life History Method." *Ethos* 7 (1): 68–94.

Franklin, C. L. 1989. *Give Me This Mountain: Life History and Selected Sermons of the Rev. C. L. Franklin*. Edited by Jeff Todd Titon. Urbana: University of Illinois Press.

Furtak, Rick Anthony. 2017. "Henry David Thoreau." In *Stanford Encyclopedia of Philosophy*. Last modified March 3, 2017. http://plato.stanford.edu/entries/thoreau/.

Gadamer, Hans-Georg. [1975] 1992. *Truth and Method*. 2nd rev. ed. New York: Crossroad.

Gagliano, Monica. 2016. "Seeing Green." In *The Green Thread: Dialogues with the Vegetal World*, edited by Patricia Vieira, Monica Gagliano, and John Ryan, 19–35. New York: Rowman and Littlefield.

Gardner, Emelyn Elizabeth, ed. 1939. *Ballads and Songs of Southern Michigan*. Ann Arbor: University of Michigan Press.

Gauthier, David. 1987. *Morals by Agreement*. Oxford: Clarendon.

Geertz, Clifford. 1973. *The Interpretation of Cultures*. New York: Basic Books.

———. 1977. "From the Native's Point of View: On the Nature of Anthropological Understanding." In *Symbolic Anthropology*, edited by Janet Dolgin, David Kemnitzer, and David Schneider, 480–492. New York: Columbia University Press.

———. 1980. "Blurred Genres." *American Scholar* 49 (2): 165–179.

———. 1988. *Works and Lives*. Stanford, CA: Stanford University Press.

Gentry, Katherine, Megan F. McKenna, and David A. Luther. 2017. "Evidence of Suboscine Song Plasticity in Response to Traffic Noise Fluctuations and Temporary Road Closures." *Bioacoustics* 27 (2): 165–181.

Giannachi, Gabriella, and Nick Kaye. 2011. *Performing Presence*. Manchester, UK: Manchester University Press.

Gittings, Robert. 1978. *The Nature of Biography*. Seattle: University of Washington Press.

Glassie, Henry. 1968. *Pattern in the Material Folk Culture of the Eastern United States*. Philadelphia: University of Pennsylvania Press.

———. 1975a. *All Silver and No Brass*. Bloomington: Indiana University Press.

———. 1975b. *Folk Housing in Middle Virginia*. Knoxville: University of Tennessee Press.

———. 1982. *Passing the Time in Ballymenone: Culture and History of an Ulster Community*. Philadelphia: University of Pennsylvania Press.

Goffman, Erving. 1959. *The Presentation of Self in Everyday Life*. New York: Anchor Books.

———. 1963. *Behavior in Public Places*. Glencoe, IL: Free Press.

Goodman, Steve. 2009. *Sonic Warfare: Sound, Affect, and the Ecology of Fear*. Cambridge, MA: MIT Press.

Gorz, Andre. 1989. *Critique of Economic Reason*. Translated by Gillian Handyside and Chris Turner. London: Verso.

Gourlay, Kenneth A. 1978. "Towards a Reassessment of the Ethnomusicologist's Role in Research." *Ethnomusicology* 22 (1): 1–35.

———. 1982. "Towards a Humanizing Ethnomusicology." *Ethnomusicology* 26 (3): 411–420.

Gray, Patricia M., Bernie Krause, Jelle Atema, Roger Payne, Carol Krumhansl, and Luis Baptista. 2001. "The Music of Nature and the Nature of Music." *Science*, n.s., 291 (5501): 52–54.

Griffin, D. R., and G. Speck. 2004. "New Evidence of Animal Consciousness." *Animal Cognition* 7 (1): 5–18.

Grindal, Bruce, and Frank Salamone, eds. 1995. *Bridge to Humanity: Narratives on Anthropology and Friendship*. Prospect Heights, IL: Waveland.

Guilbault, Jocylene. 1993. *Zouk: World Music in the West Indies*. Chicago: University of Chicago Press.

Gunderson, Lance H., Craig R. Allen, and C. S. Holling. 2009. *Foundations of Ecological Resilience*. Washington, DC: Island Press.

Harding, Walter. 1982. *The Days of Henry Thoreau: A Biography*. New York: Dover.

Harner, Michael J. 1972. *The Jivaro*. Garden City, NY: Doubleday.

Harrison, Frank L. 1973. *Time, Place, and Music*. Amsterdam: Frits Knuf.

Harrison, Klisala. 2017. "Why Applied Ethnomusicology?" COLLeGIUM 21:1–17. http://www.helsinki.fi/collegium/journal/volumes/volume_21/index_21.htm.

Harrison, Klisala, Elizabeth Mackinlay, and Svanibor Pettan, eds. 2010. *Applied Ethnomusicology: Historical and Contemporary Approaches*. Newcastle-upon-Tyne: Cambridge Scholars Press.

Hawes, Bess Lomax. 1992. "Practice Makes Perfect: Lessons in Active Ethnomusicology." *Ethnomusicology* 36 (3): 337–343.

Hawken, Paul. 1994. *The Ecology of Commerce: A Declaration of Sustainability*. New York: HarperBusiness.

Haydon, Glen. 1941. *Introduction to Musicology*. New York: Prentice-Hall.

Hellier-Tinoco, Ruth. 2003. "Experiencing People: Relationships, Responsibility, Reciprocity." *British Journal of Ethnomusicology* 12 (1): 19–34.

Henry, Mellinger Edward, ed. 1938. *Folk-Songs from the Southern Highlands*. New York: J. J. Augustin.

Herndon, Marcia, and Norma McLeod. 1980. *Music as Culture*. Norwood, PA: Norwood Editions.

Herzog, George. 1936. "Primitive Music." *Bulletin of the American Musicological Society* 1:2–3.

Holbrand, Martin, and Moren Axel Petersen. 2017. *The Ontological Turn: An Anthropological Exposition*. Cambridge, UK: Cambridge University Press.

Holman, Hugh, ed. 1972. *A Handbook to Literature*. 3rd ed. Indianapolis: Bobbs-Merrill.

Hood, Mantle. 1960. "The Challenge of Bi-musicality." *Ethnomusicology* 4 (2): 55–59.

———. 1963. "Musical Significance." *Ethnomusicology* 7 (3): 187–192.

———. [1971] 1982. *The Ethnomusicologist*. Kent, OH: Kent State University Press.

Hood, Mantle, Frank L. Harrison, and Claude V. Palisca. 1963. *Musicology*. Englewood Cliffs, NJ: Prentice-Hall.

Hornbostel, Erich M. von. 1963. *The Demonstration Collection of E. M. von Hornbostel*. 12" LP recordings, notes. New York: Folkways Records FE 4165.

———. [1905] 1975. "The Problems of Comparative Musicology." In *Hornbostel Opera Omnia*, edited by Klaus P. Wachsmann, Dieter Christensen, and Hans-Peter Reinecke, 249–270. The Hague: M. Nijhoff.

Hudson, Arthur Palmer. 1936. *Folksongs of Mississippi and Their Background*. Chapel Hill: University of North Carolina Press.

Hufford, Mary, ed. 1994. *Conserving Culture: A New Discourse on Heritage*. Urbana: University of Illinois Press.

Hutchinson, Patrick. 1994. "The Work and Words of Piping." MA paper, Brown University.

———. 1997. "A Life in the Making: Chris Langan, Uilleann Piper." PhD diss., Brown University.

Hyde, Lewis. 2010. *Common as Air*. New York: Farrar, Straus and Giroux.
Hymes, Dell, ed. 1972. *Reinventing Anthropology*. New York: Pantheon.
Ihde, Don. [1977] 1986. *Experimental Phenomenology: An Introduction*. New York: Paragon Books.
———. 2007. *Listening and Voice: Phenomenologies of Sound*. 2nd ed. Albany: State University of New York Press.
Invested in Community: Ethnomusicology and Musical Advocacy. 2003. Conference on Applied Ethnomusicology, Brown University, March 8–9. Videotapes of presentations by applied ethnomusicologists and community scholars from Europe, the United States, and Native North America may be viewed at http://library.brown.edu/cds/invested_in_community/.
International Union for the Conservation of Nature and Natural Resources (IUCN). 1980. *World Conservation Strategy: Living Resource Conservation for Sustainable Development*. International Union for the Conservation of Nature and Natural Resources, Gland, Schweiz. A pdf of this book is available at https://portals.iucn.org/library/sefiles/documents/WCS-004.pdf.
Intergovernmental Panel on Climate Change. 2014. *Fifth Assessment Report*. https://www.ipcc.ch/assessment-report/ar5/.
Ives, Charles. 1920. "Thoreau." In *Essays before a Sonata*. New York: Knickerbocker Press. Accessed August 14, 2014. http://imslp.org/wiki/Essays_Before_a_Sonata_%28Ives,_Charles%29.
Ives, Edward D. 1978. *Joe Scott: The Woodsman-Songmaker*. Urbana: University of Illinois Press.
———, ed. 1976. *Argyle Boom. Northeast Folklore* 17.
Jackson, Bruce. 1969. *A Thief's Primer*. New York: Macmillan.
James, Henry. [1893] 2015. "The Real Thing." In *The Real Thing and Other Tales*. Urbana, IL: Project Gutenberg. https://www.gutenberg.org/files/2715/2715-h/2715-h.htm.
———. 1897. "The Figure in the Carpet." In *Embarrassments*, 3–83. New York: Macmillan.
Jefferson, Ann. 2013. "Review of Benoit Peeters, *Derrida: A Biography*." *Times Literary Supplement*, no. 5737 (March 15).
Jones, Loyal. 1977. "Old-Time Baptists and Mainline Christianity." In *An Appalachian Symposium*, edited by J. W. Williamson, 120–130. Boone, NC: Appalachian State University Press.
———. 1989. *Curing the Cross-Eyed Mule: Appalachian Mountain Humor*. Little Rock, AR: August House.
———. 1999. *Faith and Meaning in the Southern Uplands*. Urbana: University of Illinois Press.
Joseph, Rebecca. 1994. "Review Essay: Practicing What We Preach at the Festival." *Folklore in Use* 2 (2): 275–279.
Joyce, Michael. 1987–1990. *Afternoon*. Cambridge, MA: Eastgate Systems.
Kaneko, Kunihiko. 2006. *Life: An Introduction to Complex Systems Biology*. Berlin: Springer.
Keil, Charles. 1979. *Tiv Song*. Chicago: University of Chicago Press.
———. 1982. "Applied Ethnomusicology and a Rebirth of Music from the Spirit of Tragedy." *Ethnomusicology* 26 (3): 407–411.
———. 1998. "Applied Sociomusicology and Performance Studies." *Ethnomusicology* 42 (2): 303–312.
Keogh, Brent. 2013. "On the Limitations of Music Ecology." *Journal of Music Research Online* 4:1–10.
Kerman, Joseph. 1986. *Contemplating Music: Challenges to Musicology*. Cambridge: Harvard University Press.

Kingsbury, Henry. 1987. *Music, Talent and Performance*. Philadelphia: Temple University Press.
Kirshenblatt-Gimblett, Barbara. 1988. "Mistaken Dichotomies." *Journal of American Folklore* 101 (400): 140–155.
———. 1998. *Destination Culture: Tourism, Museums, and Heritage*. Berkeley: University of California Press.
Kisliuk, Michelle. 1988. "'A Special Kind of Courtesy': Action at a Bluegrass Festival Jam Session." *TDR* 32 (3): 141–145.
———. 1991. "Confronting the Quintessential: Singing, Dancing, and Everyday Life among Biaka Pygmies (Central African Republic)." PhD diss., New York University.
———. 1998. *Seize the Dance*. New York: Oxford University Press.
Krause, Bernie. n.d. "About Wild Sanctuary." Wild Sanctuary. Accessed December 20, 2019. http://www.wildsanctuary.com.
———. 2012. *The Great Animal Orchestra*. Boston: Little, Brown.
Kricher, John. 2009. *The Balance of Nature: Ecology's Enduring Myth*. Princeton, NJ: Princeton University Press.
Kroker, Arthur, and Michael A. Weinstein. 1994. *Data Trash: The Theory of the Virtual Class*. New York: St. Martin's.
Kunst, Jaap. 1950. *Musicologica: A Study of the Nature of Ethno-Musicology, Its Problems, Methods, and Representative Personalities*. The Hague: Martinus Nijhoff.
———. 1959. *Ethnomusicology*. 3rd ed. The Hague: Martinus Nijhoff.
Kurin, Richard. 1997. *Reflections of a Culture Broker*. Washington, DC: Smithsonian Institution.
Kurosawa, Akira. 1969. *Rashomon: A Film by Akira Kurosawa*. New York: Grove.
Lake, Philip S. 2013. "Resistance, Resilience and Restoration." *Ecological Management and Restoration* 14 (1): 20–24.
Landow, George. 1992a. *Hypertext*. Baltimore: Johns Hopkins University Press.
———. 1992b. *The In Memoriam Web*. Cambridge, MA: Eastgate Systems.
Langness, L. L. 1965. *The Life History in Anthropological Science*. New York: Holt, Rinehart and Winston.
Larrabee, Mary Jeanne. 1989. "Time and Spatial Models: Temporality in Husserl." *Philosophy and Phenomenological Research* 49 (3): 373–392.
Lausevic, Marina. 2007. *Balkan Fascination*. Cambridge, MA: Harvard University Press.
Le Guin, Ursula K. 1969. *The Left Hand of Darkness*. New York: Ace Books.
Leary, James P. 1994. "In the Field for the Field." *Folklore in Use* 2 (2): 201–212.
Leff, Enrique. 2013. "Political Ecology: A Latin American Perspective." In *UNESCO Encyclopedia of Life Support Systems [EOLSS]*. http://www.eolss.net/.
Leopold, Aldo. [1949] 1989. "The Land Ethic." In Aldo Leopold, *A Sand County Almanac and Sketches Here and There*, 201–226. New York: Oxford University Press.
Levi-Strauss, Claude. 1961. *Tristes tropiques*. Translated by John Russell. New York: Criterion Books.
———. 1974. *Tristes tropiques*. Translated by John Weightman and Doreen Weightman. New York: Atheneum.
Lobley, Noel. 2014. "Musical and Sonic Sustainability Online." *Ethnomusicology Forum* 23 (3): 463–477.
Lomax, Alan. 1950. *Mister Jelly Roll*. New York: Grossett and Dunlap.
———. 1968. *Folk Song Style and Culture*. Washington, DC: American Association for the Advancement of Science.
———. 1972a. "An Appeal for Cultural Equity." *the world of music* 14 (2): 3–17.
———. 1972b. "The Evolutionary Taxonomy of Culture." *Science* 177 (4045): 228–239.

———. 1976. *Cantometrics: A Method in Musical Anthropology*. Cassette tapes, booklet. Berkeley: University of California Extension Media Center.

———. 1977. *The Gospel Ship: Baptist Hymns and White Spirituals from the Southern Mountains*. 12" LP Recording. New World Records NW 294.

———. n.d. (ca. 1961). *White Spirituals*. 12" LP Recording. Southern Folk Heritage Series. Atlantic SD-1349.

Lombard, Matthew, and Therese Ditton. 1997. "At the Heart of It All: The Concept of Presence." *Journal of Computer-Mediated Communication* 3 (2): n.p.

Loomis, Ormond, coordinator. 1983. *Cultural Conservation: The Protection of Cultural Heritage in the United States*. Washington, DC: American Folklife Center, Library of Congress.

Lord, Albert B. 1960. *The Singer of Tales*. Cambridge, MA: Harvard University Press.

Lubbock, Percy. [1921] 1957. *The Craft of Fiction*. New York: Viking.

Lucas, William. 1971. *Lazy Bill Lucas*. Wild 12MO1. 12" LP, Buc, France.

———. 1972. *Lazy Bill and His Friends*. Lazy 12MO2. 12" LP, Buc, France.

Lurz, Robert. 2010. "Animal Minds." In *Internet Encyclopedia of Philosophy*. Accessed April 20, 2018. https://www.iep.utm.edu/ani-mind/.

Macleod, Morag. 1975. *Gaelic Psalms from Lewis*. Scottish Tradition, 6. 12" LP. Tangent TGNM 120. School of Scottish Studies, University of Edinburgh.

Mann, Michael E. "It's Not Rocket Science: Climate Change Was behind This Summer's Extreme Weather." *Washington Post*, November 2, 2018. https://www.washingtonpost.com/opinions/its-not-rocket-science-climate-change-was-behind-this-summers-extreme-weather/2018/11/02/b8852584-dea9-11e8-b3f0-62607289efee_story.html.

Marx, Leo. 1964. *The Machine in the Garden*. New York: Oxford University Press.

Matthews, Washington. 1888. "The Prayer of a Navajo Shaman." *American Anthropologist* 1 (2): 148–171.

Matthiessen, F. O. 1941. *American Renaissance*. New York: Oxford University Press.

McAllester, David P. [1949] 1971. *Peyote Music*. New York: Johnson Reprint.

———. [1954] 1973. *Enemy Way Music: A Study of Social and Aesthetic Values as Seen in Navaho Music*. New York: Kraus Reprint.

———. 1989. Guest seminar in the history of ethnomusicological thought, April 10. Brown University Department of Music. 2-hour 8 mm videotape in possession of the American Folklife Center, Library of Congress.

McClain, Terry. 2004. "Survival of the Fittest? Anthropologist Suggests the Nicest Prevail—Not Just the Selfish." *Newsroom*. Washington University in Saint Louis press release for Sussman and Garber, *The Origins and Nature of Sociality*, June 9.

McClure, C. J. W., H. E. Ware, J. Carlisle, G. Kaltenecker, and J. R. Barber. 2013. "An Experimental Investigation into the Effects of Traffic Noise on Distributions of Birds: Avoiding the Phantom Road." *Proceedings of the Royal Society B* 280 (1773): 1–9.

McDaid, John. 1993. *Uncle Buddy's Phantom Funhouse*. Cambridge, MA: Eastgate Systems.

McLean, Mervyn. 2006. *Pioneers of Ethnomusicology*. Mamaroneck, NY: Aeon Books.

Meadows, Donella, Dennis L. Meadows, Jorgen Randers, and William W. Behrens III. 1972. *The Limits to Growth*. New York: Universe Books.

Merriam, Alan P. 1963a. "Purposes of Ethnomusicology: An Anthropological View." *Ethnomusicology* 7 (3): 206–213.

———. 1963b. Review of Henry Weman, *African Music and the Church in Africa*. *Ethnomusicology* 7 (2): 135.

———. 1964. *The Anthropology of Music*. Evanston, IL: Northwestern University Press.

———. 1967. *Ethnomusicology of the Flathead Indians*. Chicago: Aldine.

———. 1977. "Definitions of 'Comparative Musicology' and 'Ethnomusicology': An Historical-Theoretical Perspective." *Ethnomusicology* 21 (2): 189–204.

Merton, Timothy. 2007. *Ecology without Nature*. Cambridge, MA: Harvard University Press.

———. 2010. *The Ecological Thought*. Cambridge, MA: Harvard University Press.

Mill, John Stuart. [1836] 1967. "On the Definition of Political Economy and on the Method of Investigation Proper to It." In *Collected Works of John Stuart Mill, Essays on Economics and Society*, vol. 4, edited by John M. Robson, 309–339. Toronto: University of Toronto Press.

Miller, Char. 2001. *Gifford Pinchot and the Making of a Modern Environmentalism*. Washington, DC: Island Press.

Miller, Kiri. 2008. *Traveling Home: Sacred Harp Singing and American Pluralism*. Urbana: University of Illinois Press.

Miller, Perry. 1958. *Consciousness in Concord: The Text of Thoreau's Hitherto "Lost Journal."* Boston: Houghton Mifflin.

Mintz, Sidney. 1960. *Worker in the Cane*. New Haven, CT: Yale University Press.

Mitchell, Frank. 1978. *Navajo Blessingway Singer*. Edited by Charlotte Frisbie and David P. McAllester. Tucson: University of Arizona Press.

Moore, James F. 1993. "Predators and Prey." *Harvard Business Review*, May–June, 75–86.

Morton, Robin. 1973. *Come Day, Go Day, God Send Sunday*. London: Routledge and Kegan Paul.

Munk, Nina. 2013. *The Idealist: Jeffrey Sachs and the Quest to End Poverty*. New York: Knopf Doubleday.

Munz, Tania. 2005. "The Bee Battles: Karl von Frisch, Adrian Wenner, and the Honey Bee Dance Language Controversy." *Journal of the History of Biology* 38 (3): 535–570.

Murdock, George P. 1969. *Ethnographic Atlas*. Pittsburgh, PA: University of Pittsburgh Press.

Myers, Helen, ed. 1992. *Ethnomusicology: An Introduction*. New York: Norton.

Myers, Norman. [1984] 1992. *Gaia: An Atlas of Planet Management*. New York: Anchor.

Nagel, Thomas. 1986. *The View from Nowhere*. New York: Oxford University Press.

National Climate Assessment. 2014. *Full Report*. Washington, DC: US Global Change Research Program. https://nca2014.globalchange.gov/report.

Nattiez, Jean-Jacques. 1990. *Music and Discourse: Toward a Semiology of Music*. Translated by Carolyn Abbate. Princeton, NJ: Princeton University Press.

Netting, Robert M. 1977. *Cultural Ecology*. Menlo Park, CA: Cummings.

Nettl, Bruno. 1956. *Music in Primitive Culture*. Cambridge, MA: Harvard University Press.

———. 1964. *Theory and Method in Ethnomusicology*. Glencoe, IL: Free Press.

———. 1983. *The Study of Ethnomusicology: Twenty-Nine Issues and Concepts*. 2nd ed. Urbana: University of Illinois Press.

———. 2002. *Encounters in Ethnomusicology: A Memoir*. Warren, MI: Harmonie Park Press.

———. 2005. *The Study of Ethnomusicology: Thirty-One Issues and Concepts*. Urbana: University of Illinois Press.

———. 2010. *Nettl's Elephant: On the History of Ethnomusicology*. Urbana: University of Illinois Press.

———. 2013. *Becoming an Ethnomusicologist: A Miscellany of Influences*. Lanham, MD: Scarecrow.

———. 2014. "Fifty Years of Changes and Challenges in the Ethnomusicological Field." Interview by Hector Fouce. *El oído pensante* 2 (1): 1–11. http://ppct.caicyt.gov.ar/index.php/oidopensante.

Nettl, Bruno, and Philip V. Bohlman, eds. 1991. *Comparative Musicology and Anthropology of Music*. Chicago: University of Chicago Press.

Newell, Wayne. 2003. "Returning Sounds to Communities." Panel discussion among Wayne Newell, Blanche Sockabasin, and Jeff Todd Titon. Invested in Community: Ethnomusicology and Advocacy Conference, Brown University, March 8–9. A video of this presentation is accessible at http://library.brown.edu/cds/invested_in_community/030803_session3.html.

Norton, Barley. 2005. *Sustainability: A Philosophy of Adaptive Ecosystem Management*. Chicago: University of Chicago Press.

Odum, Eugene P. 1971. *Fundamentals of Ecology*. 3rd edition. Philadelphia: W. B. Saunders.

Odum, Eugene P., and Gary W. Barrett. *Fundamentals of Ecology*. 5th ed. Pacific Grove, CA: Brooks/Cole.

Office of Folklife Programs. 1998. *Guidelines for the Research and Development of a Program for the Festival of American Folklife*. Washington, DC: Smithsonian Institution.

Office of the Scientific Assistant, Office of Noise Abatement and Control, US Environmental Protection Agency. 1981. *Noise Effects Handbook: A Desk Reference to Health and Welfare Effects of Noise*. Washington, DC: U.S. Environmental Protection Agency. Accessed November 7, 2013. http://www.nonoise.org/library/handbook/handbook.htm.

Olson, Charles. 1966. "Human Universe." In *Charles Olson: Selected Writings*, edited by Robert Creeley, 53–68. New York: New Directions.

———. 1970. *The Special View of History*. Edited by Ann Charters. Berkeley, CA: Oyez.

Pascal, Roy. 1960. *Design and Truth in Autobiography*. Cambridge, MA: Harvard University Press.

Paul, Sherman. 1949. "The Wise Silence: Sound as the Agency of Correspondence in Thoreau." *New England Quarterly* 22 (4): 511–527.

Pettan, Svanibor, and Jeff Todd Titon, eds. 2015. *The Oxford Handbook of Applied Ethnomusicology*. New York: Oxford University Press.

Pfadenhauer, Michaela. 2005. "Ethnography of Scenes." *Forum: Qualitative Social Research* 6 (3). http://www.qualitative-research.net/index.php/fqs/article/view/23/49.

Pickett, Steward T. A., and P. S. White. 1985. *The Ecology of Natural Disturbance and Patch Dynamics*. Orlando, FL: Academic Press.

Pijanowski, Bryan C., Luis J. Villanueva-Rivera, Sarah L. Dumyahn, Almo Farina, Bernie L. Krause, Brian M. Napoletano, Stuart H. Gage, and Nadia Pieretti. 2011. "Soundscape Ecology: The Science of Sound in the Landscape." *BioScience* 61 (3): 203–216.

Pillay, Jayendran. 1994. "Indian Music in the Indian School in South Africa: The Use of Cultural Forms as a Political Tool." *Ethnomusicology* 38 (2): 281–301.

Pinch, Trevor, and Karin Bijsterveld. 2012. *The Oxford Handbook of Sound Studies*. New York: Oxford University Press.

Pinker, Steven. 1997. *How the Mind Works*. New York: Norton.

Polanyi, Karl. 1944. *The Great Transformation*. Boston: Beacon.

Porterfield, Nolan. 2001. *Last Cavalier: The Life and Times of John Lomax*. Urbana: University of Illinois Press.

Propp, Vladimir. [1928] 1968. *Morphology of the Folktale*. Translated by Laurence Scott. Bloomington, IN: Research Center in the Language Sciences.

Pynchon, Thomas. 1966. *The Crying of Lot 49*. New York: Perennial Library.

Rajan, Tilottama. 1994. "Hermeneutics 1." In *The Johns Hopkins Guide to Literary Theory and Criticism*, edited by Michael Groden and Martin Kreiswirth, 375–379. Baltimore: Johns Hopkins University Press.

Rappaport, Roy. 1979. *Ecology, Meaning and Religion*. Berkeley, CA: North Atlantic.

Reder, Melvin. 1999. *Economics: The Culture of a Controversial Science*. Chicago: University of Chicago Press.

Redfield, Robert. 1947. "The Folk Society." *American Journal of Sociology* 52 (4): 293–308.
Rice, Timothy. 1994. *May It Fill Your Soul*. Chicago: University of Chicago Press.
———. 2014. *Ethnomusicology: A Very Short Introduction*. New York: Oxford University Press.
Richerson, Peter. 2012. "Culture-Led Gene-Culture Coevolution." Conference on Culture-Gene Interactions in Human Origins. University of California, San Diego. Posted by University of California Television. "CARTA: Culture-Gene Interactions: Peter Richerson-Culture-led Gene-culture Coevolution." YouTube. February 14, 2013. Video, 19:00. https://www.youtube.com/watch?v=GonViER8Ubo.
Ricoeur, Paul. 1981a. *Hermeneutics and the Human Sciences*. Edited and translated by John B. Thompson. Cambridge: Cambridge University Press.
———. 1981b. "The Model of the Text: Meaningful Action Considered as a Text." In *Paul Ricoeur: Hermeneutics and the Human Sciences*, edited and translated by John B. Thompson, 197–221. Cambridge: Cambridge University Press.
———. 1981c. "What Is a Text: Explanation and Understanding." In *Paul Ricoeur: Hermeneutics and the Human Sciences*, edited and translated by John B. Thompson, 145–164. Cambridge: Cambridge University Press.
Rios-Chelén, Alejandro, Cecilia Contlanquiz-Lima, Amanda Bautista, and Margarita Martinez-Gomez. 2018. "No Reliable Evidence for Immediate Noise-Induced Flexibility in a Suboscine." *Urban Ecosystems* 21 (1): 15–25.
Ritchie, Jean. 1955. *Singing Family of the Cumberlands*. New York: Oak.
———. 1959. *The Ritchie Family of Kentucky*. 12" LP recording. New York: Folkways Records FA 2316.
Rorty, Richard P. 1979. *Philosophy and the Mirror of Nature*. Princeton, NJ: Princeton University Press.
———. 1985. "Texts and Lumps." *New Literary History* 17 (1): 1–16.
———. 1991. *Objectivity, Relativism, and Truth*. Cambridge: Cambridge University Press.
Rosaldo, Renato. [1989] 1993. "Grief and a Headhunter's Rage." In Renato Rosaldo, *Culture and Truth*, 1–21. Boston: Beacon.
Rose, Carol M. 2003. "Romans, Roads, and Romantic Creators: Traditions of Public Property in the Information Age." *Law and Contemporary Problems* 66 (89): 89–110.
Rosen, Charles. 2001. "The Future of Music." *New York Review of Books*, December 20. https://www.nybooks.com/articles/2001/12/20/the-future-of-music/.
Rosengarten, Theodore. 1974. *All God's Dangers*. New York: Knopf.
Roughgarden, Jean. 2010. *The Genial Gene: Deconstructing Darwinian Selfishness*. Berkeley: University of California Press.
Sachs, Curt. 1943. *The Rise of Music in the Ancient World, East and West*. New York: Norton.
———. [1952] 1965. *The Wellsprings of Music*. New York: McGraw-Hill.
Schafer, R. Murray. 1980. *The Tuning of the World*. Philadelphia: University of Pennsylvania Press.
Schechner, Richard, and Willa Appel, eds. 1990. *By Means of Performance*. New York: Cambridge University Press.
Schippers, Huib. 2015. "Applied Ethnomusicology and Intangible Cultural Heritage." In *The Oxford Handbook of Applied Ethnomusicology*, edited by Svanibor Pettan and Jeff Todd Titon, 134–157. New York: Oxford University Press.
Scholes, Robert, Nancy R. Compley, and Gregory L. Ulmer. 1988. *Text Book: An Introduction to Literary Language*. New York: St. Martin's.
Schutz, Alfred. 1962. *Collected Papers*. The Hague: Martinus Nijhoff.
Sears, Paul. [1935] 1949. *Deserts on the March*. 2nd ed. Norman: University of Oklahoma Press.

Seeger, Anthony. 1987. *Why Suya Sing: A Musical Anthropology of an Amazonian People.* Cambridge: Cambridge University Press.
———. 1991. "Singing Other People's Songs." *Cultural Survival Quarterly* 15 (3): 36–39.
———. 1992. "Ethnomusicology and Music Law." *Ethnomusicology* 36 (3): 345–359.
———. 2006. "Lost Lineages and Neglected Peers: Ethnomusicologists outside Academia." *Ethnomusicology* 50 (2): 215–235.
Seeger, Anthony, and Paul Gebhard. 1984. "Memorial Resolution: Professor Emeritus George Herzog (1902–1983)." Bloomington Faculty Council Minutes, October 2, 1984. Indiana University. http://webapp1.dlib.indiana.edu/bfc/view?docId=B07-1985&chunk.id=d1e97&toc.id=&brand=bfc.
Seeger, Charles. 1963. "On the Tasks of Musicology." *Ethnomusicology* 7 (3): 214–215.
Seitel, Peter, ed. 2001. *Safeguarding Traditional Cultures: A Global Assessment.* Washington, DC: Center for Folklife and Cultural Heritage, Smithsonian Institution.
Sellars, Wilfrid. 1962. "Philosophy and the Scientific Image of Man." In *Frontiers of Science and Philosophy*, edited by Robert Colodny, 35–78. Pittsburgh, PA: University of Pittsburgh Press.
SEM Torture. n.d. "Position Statement on Torture." Society for Ethnomusicology. Accessed December 14, 2019. https://www.ethnomusicology.org/page/PS_Torture.
Seyfarth, Robert M., Dorothy L. Cheney, and Peter Marler. 1980. "Vervet Monkey Alarm Calls: Semantic Communication in a Free-Ranging Primate." *Science Direct* 28 (4): 1070–1094.
Shackelford, Laurel, and Bill Weinberg. 1977. *Our Appalachia: An Oral History.* New York: Hill and Wang.
Shapiro-Phim, Toni. 2006. "A Global-Local Interface." Paper presented at the Society for Ethnomusicology annual conference, Honolulu.
Sheehy, Daniel. 1992. "A Few Notions about Philosophy and Strategy in Applied Ethnomusicology." *Ethnomusicology* 36 (3): 323–336.
SIL International. n.d. "Arts and Ethnomusicology." https://www.sil.org/arts-ethnomusicology. Page no longer available.
Sillitoe, Paul. 1998. "The Development of Indigenous Knowledge: A New Applied Anthropology." *Current Anthropology* 39 (2): 223–252.
Slobin, Mark. 1993. *Subcultural Sounds: Micromusics of the West.* Middletown, CT: University Press of New England.
Smith, Adam. [1789] 1904. *An Inquiry into the Nature and Causes of the Wealth of Nations.* 5th ed. Edited by Edwin Cannan. Book 1, chap. 2. https://oll.libertyfund.org/titles/smith-an-inquiry-into-the-nature-and-causes-of-the-wealth-of-nations-cannan-ed-vol-1.
Smith, Susan M. 1992. *The Black-Capped Chickadee: Behavioral Ecology and Natural History.* Ithaca, NY: Cornell University Press.
Smithsonian Center for Folklife and Cultural Heritage. n.d. "Legacy Honorees: S. Dillon Ripley." https://folklife.si.edu/legacy-honorees/s-dillon-ripley/smithsonian.
Smithsonian National Museum of Natural History. 2014. Foreword to "Camping with the Sioux: The Fieldwork Diary of Alice Cunningham Fletcher." Online exhibit, Department of Anthropology, Smithsonian Institution. Accessed July 1, 2014. http://anthropology.si.edu/naa/exhibits/fletcher/foreword.htm. Page no longer available.
Sommers, Laurie Kay. 1994a. "Festival Imagined, Festival Invented: Producers' Constructs of Michigan on the Mall." *Folklore in Use* 2 (2): 181–200.
———. 1994b. "The Participant Experience Revisited: Fiddler Leslie Raber." *Folklore in Use* 2 (2): 233–241.

Sontag, Susan. [1963] 1994. "The Anthropologist as Hero." In Susan Sontag, *Against Interpretation*, 69–71. London: Vintage Books.
Soulé, Michael. 1985. "What Is Conservation Biology?" *Bioscience* 35 (11): 727–734.
———. 1986. *Conservation Biology: The Science of Scarcity and Diversity*. Sunderland, MA: Sinauer Associates.
———. 1995. "Preface." In *Reinventing Nature*, edited by Michael Soulé and Gary Lease, xv–xvii. Washington, DC: Island Press.
Spacks, Patricia Meyer. 1976. *Imagining a Self*. Cambridge, MA: Harvard University Press.
Spitzer, Nick. [1992] 2007. "Cultural Conversation." In *Public Folklore*, edited by Robert Baron and Nick Spitzer, 78–103. Jackson: University Press of Mississippi.
Stahl, Sandra K. D., ed. 1977. "Stories of Personal Experience." Special issue, *Journal of the Folklore Institute* 14 (1–2): 5–126.
Stegmann, Ulrich E., ed. 2013. *Animal Communication Theory: Information and Influence*. Cambridge: Cambridge University Press.
Stein, Gertrude. 1935. *Narration: Four Lectures*. Chicago: University of Chicago Press.
Stewart, David, and Algis Mickunas. 1990. *Exploring Phenomenology*. 2nd ed. Athens: Ohio University Press.
Sussman, Robert W., and Paul A. Garber. 2004. "Rethinking Sociality: Cooperation and Aggression among Primates." In *The Origins and Nature of Sociality*, edited by Robert W. Sussman and Audrey R. Chapman, 161–190. New York: Aldine de Gruyter.
Suzuki, Ryuji. 2006. "Information Entropy of Humpback Whale Songs." *Journal of the Acoustical Society of America* 119 (1849). https://doi.org/10.1121/1.2161827.
Tallmadge, William. 1975. "Baptist Monophonic and Heterophonic Hymnody in Southern Appalachia." *Yearbook for Inter-American Musical Research* 11:106–136.
———. 1984. "Folk Organum: A Study of Origins." *American Music* 2:47–65.
Tansley, A. G. 1935. "The Use and Abuse of Vegetational Concepts and Terms." *Ecology* 16 (3): 284–307.
Taylor, Daniel M. 1970. *Explanation and Meaning*. Cambridge: Cambridge University Press.
Tedlock, Barbara. 1992. *Time and the Highland Maya*. Albuquerque: University of New Mexico Press.
Tedlock, Dennis. 1972. *Finding the Center*. New York: Dial Press.
———. 1990. *Days from a Dream Almanac*. Urbana: University of Illinois Press.
Temperley, Nicholas. 1981. "The Old Way of Singing." *Journal of the American Musicological Society* 34 (3): 511–544.
Terkel, Studs. 1967. *Division Street America*. New York: Random House.
Terrill, Tom, and Jerrold Hirsch, eds. 1978. *Such as Us: Southern Voices of the Thirties*. Chapel Hill: University of North Carolina Press.
Thomas, E. D. 1877. *Thomas Hymnal: A Choice Collection . . .* Wayne, WV: Arrowood Bros.
Thoreau, Henry David. [1906] 1961. *Journal*. Edited by Bradford Torrey, Francis Allen, and Walter G. Harding. New York: Dover.
———. [1854] 1985. *Walden*. In *A Week on the Concord and Merrimac Rivers; Walden, or Life in the Woods; The Maine Woods; Cape Cod*. Edited by Robert F. Sayre. New York: Library of America.
———. 1985. *A Week on the Concord and Merrimac Rivers; Walden; The Maine Woods; Cape Cod*. Edited by Robert F. Sayre. New York: Library of America.
———. 2001a. "Huckleberries." In *Collected Essays and Poems*, 468–501. New York: Library of America.

———. 2001b. "The Succession of Forest Trees." In *Collected Essays and Poems*, 429–443. New York: Library of America.

———. 2001c. "Walking." In *Collected Essays and Poems*, 201–255. New York: Library of America.

Throsby, David. 2010. *The Economics of Cultural Policy*. Cambridge: Cambridge University Press.

Titon, Jeff Todd. 1969. "Calling All Cows: Lazy Bill Lucas." *Blues Unlimited* 60:10–11; 61:9–10; 62:11–12; 63:9–10.

———. 1971. "Ethnomusicology of Downhome Blues Phonograph Records, 1926–1930." PhD diss., University of Minnesota.

———, ed. 1974a. *From Blues to Pop: The Autobiography of Leonard "Baby Doo" Caston*. Los Angeles: John Edwards Memorial Foundation Special Series no. 4.

———. 1974b. *Lazy Bill Lucas*. 12" LP, booklet. Philo Records 1007. North Ferrisburg, VT: Philo Records.

———. 1976. "Son House: Two Narratives." *Alcheringa: Ethnopoetics*, n.s., 2 (1): 2–6.

———. 1977. "Living Blues Interview: Son House." *Living Blues* 31:14–22.

———. 1979. "Murder at the Folk Festival." Paper read at the conference of the Society for Ethnomusicology, Northeast Chapter, Brown University, Providence, RI.

———. 1980. "The Life Story." *Journal of American Folklore* 93 (369): 276–292.

———. 1983. "Captain Tradition and the Folklore Police." Paper read at the annual conference of the Northeast Chapter of the Society for Ethnomusicology, Brown University, Providence, RI.

———. 1984. *Worlds of Music: An Introduction to the Music of the World's Peoples*. New York: Schirmer Books.

———. 1985. "Role, Stance, and Identity in Fieldwork among Folk Baptists and Pentecostals in the United States." *American Music* 3 (1): 16–24.

———. 1989. "Ethnomusicology as the Study of People Making Music." Paper delivered at the annual conference of the Northeast Chapter of the Society for Ethnomusicology, Hartford, CT.

———. 1991. *The Clyde Davenport Web*. HyperCard stack, freeware. Providence, RI: Jeff Todd Titon. A simplified version has been available online since 1993 at http://cds.library.brown.edu/projects/davenport/CLYDE_DAVENPORT.html.

———. 1992a. "Music, the Public Interest, and the Practice of Ethnomusicology." *Ethnomusicology* 36 (3): 315–322.

———. [1984] 1992b. *Worlds of Music: An Introduction to the Music of the World's Peoples*. 2nd ed. New York: Schirmer Books.

———. 1994. "Knowing People Making Music: Toward a New Epistemology for Ethnomusicology." *Etnomusikologian vuosikirja* [Yearbook of the Finnish Society for Ethnomusicology] 6. Helsinki: Suomen Etnomusikologinen seura.

———. 1995a. "Bi-musicality as Metaphor." *Journal of American Folklore* 108 (429): 287–297.

———. [1977] 1995b. *Early Downhome Blues: A Musical and Cultural Analysis*. 2nd ed. Chapel Hill: University of North Carolina Press.

———. 1995c. "Meaningful Action Considered as Music." A reply to Roger Savage. Paper presented at the annual conference of the Society for Ethnomusicology, Los Angeles, October 20–24.

———. 1999. "'The Real Thing': Tourism, Authenticity, and Pilgrimage among the Old Regular Baptists at the 1997 Smithsonian Folklife Festival." *the world of music* 41 (3): 115–139.

———. 2001. *Old-Time Kentucky Fiddle Tunes*. Lexington: University Press of Kentucky.
———. 2003a. "A Conversation with Jeff Todd Titon." Interview by John Fenn. In "Applied Ethnomusicology," edited by John Fenn. Special issue, *Folklore Forum* 34 (1–2): 119–131.
———. [1995] 2003b. "Text" (revised). In *Eight Words for the Study of Expressive Culture*, edited by Burt Feintuch, 69–98. Urbana: University of Illinois Press.
———. 2005. "'Tuned Up with the Grace of God': Music and Experience among Old Regular Baptists." In *Music in American Religious Experience*, edited by Philip V. Bohlman, Edith L. Blumhofer, and Maria M. Chow, 311–334. New York: Oxford University Press.
———. 2008–. *Sustainable Music* (blog), https://sustainablemusic.blogspot.com.
———. 2008. "The Paradox of Authenticity." *Sustainable Music* (blog), September 4, 2008. https://sustainablemusic.blogspot.com/search?q=the+paradox+of+authenticity.
———. 2009a. "Economy, Ecology and Music: An Introduction." In "Music and Sustainability," edited by Jeff Todd Titon. Special issue, *the world of music* 51 (1): 5–16.
———, ed. 2009b. "Music and Sustainability." Special issue, *the world of music* 51 (1).
———. 2009c. "Music and Sustainability: An Ecological Viewpoint." *the world of music* 51 (1): 119–138.
———. 2012a. "Authenticity and Authentication: Mike Seeger, the New Lost City Ramblers, and the Old-Time Music Revival." *Journal of Folklore Research* 49 (2): 227–245.
———. 2012b. "The Sound Commons." *Sustainable Music* (blog), December 9, 2012. http://sustainablemusic.blogspot.com/2012/12/the-sound-world-of-innu.html.
———. 2012c. "A Sound Commons for All Living Creatures." *Smithsonian Folkways Magazine* (Fall–Winter). https://folkways.si.edu/magazine-fall-winter-2012-sound-commons-living-creatures/science-and-nature-world/music/article/smithsonian.
———. 2013. "The Nature of Ecomusicology." *Música e Cultura* 8 (1): 8–18.
———. 2015a. "A Context for the Story: A Conversation with Jeff Todd Titon (Interviewed by Marcia Ostashewski)." *MUSICultures* 41 (2): 170–183.
———. 2015b. "Ethnomusicology: A Descriptive and Historical Account." In *The Oxford Handbook of Applied Ethnomusicology*, edited by Svanibor Pettan and Jeff Todd Titon, 4–28. New York: Oxford University Press.
———. 2015c. "Exhibiting Music in a Sound Community." *Ethnologies* 37 (1): 23–41.
———. 2015d. "Sustainability, Resilience, and Adaptive Management for Applied Ethnomusicology." In *The Oxford Handbook of Applied Ethnomusicology*, edited by Svanibor Pettan and Jeff Todd Titon, 157–197. New York: Oxford University Press.
———. 2016. "Why Thoreau?" In *Current Directions in Ecomusicology: Music, Nature, Environment*, edited by Aaron S. Allen and Kevin Dawe, 69–80. New York: Routledge.
———. [1988] 2018. *Powerhouse for God: Speech, Chant and Song in an Appalachian Baptist Church*. Knoxville: University of Tennessee Press.
———. 2019. "Foreword." In *Cultural Sustainabilities: Music, Media, Language, Advocacy*, edited by Timothy Cooley, xi–xx. Urbana: University of Illinois Press.
———. Forthcoming. "The Expressive Cultures of Sound Communication in Humans and Other Beings: A Phenomenological and Ecological Approach." In *The Oxford Handbook of Phenomenological Ethnomusicology*, edited by Harris M. Berger and Katie Szego. New York: Oxford University Press.
Titon, Jeff Todd, and Kenneth M. George, eds. [1982] 2014. *Powerhouse for God*. 2 CD recordings, booklet. Folkways SF60006. Washington, DC: Smithsonian Folkways Recordings.
Toelken, Barre. 1979. *The Dynamics of Folklore*. Boston: Houghton-Mifflin.

Topp Fargion, Janet. 2009. "'For My Own Research Purposes': Examining Ethnomusicological Field Methods for a Sustainable Music." *the world of music* 51 (1): 75–93.

Turino, Tom. 2009. "Four Fields of Music Making and Sustainable Living." *the world of music* 51 (1): 95–117.

Turnbull, Colin. 1961. *The Forest People*. New York: Simon and Schuster.

UN Documents. n.d. "Report of the World Commission on Environment and Development: Our Common Future." Accessed December 30, 2019. http://www.un-documents.net/wced-ocf.htm.

UNESCO. 1989. Recommendation on the Safeguarding of Traditional Culture and Folklore. http://portal.unesco.org/en/ev.php-URL_ID=13141&URL_DO=DO_TOPIC&URL_SECTION=201.html.

———. 2008a. "Guqin and Its Music." UNESCO. https://ich.unesco.org/en/RL/guqin-and-its-music-00061.

———. 2008b. "Heritage 2008—World Heritage and Sustainable Development International Conference." UNESCO. http://whc.unesco.org/en/events/431.

———. 2008c. "Royal Ballet of Cambodia." UNESCO. https://ich.unesco.org/en/RL/royal-ballet-of-cambodia-00060.

US Geological Survey. 2002. "Buffelgrass, an Invader Fueling Wildfires in the Sonoran Desert." *Science Daily*, May 20. https://www.sciencedaily.com/releases/2002/05/020517075618.htm.

Vander, Judith. 1988. *Songprints: The Musical Experience of Five Shoshone Women*. Urbana: University of Illinois Press.

van Willigen, John. 2002. *Applied Anthropology*. 3rd ed. New York: Praeger.

Veysey, Lawrence. 1979. "The 'New' Social History in the Context of American Historical Writing." *Reviews in American History* 1:1–12.

von Rosen, Franziska. 1992. "Micmac Storyteller. River of Fire—The Co-Creation of an Ethnographic Video." *Canadian Folk Music Journal* 20:40–46.

von Rosen, Franziska, and Michael William Francis. 1992. *River of Fire*. 1/2" VHS videotape. Lanark, ON: Franziska von Rosen.

Walker, Brian, and David Salt. 2006. *Resilience Thinking: Sustaining Ecosystems and People in a Changing World*. Washington, DC: Island Press.

Wallhausser, John. 1985. "I Can Almost See Heaven from Here." *Appalachian Heritage* 13 (1–2): 82–96.

Waring, Marilyn. 1988. *If Women Counted*. New York: Harper and Row.

Watkins, Holly. 2018. *Musical Vitalities: Ventures in a Biotic Aesthetic of Music*. Chicago: University of Chicago Press.

Weintraub, Andrew, and Bell Yung, eds. 2009. *Music and Cultural Rights*. Urbana: University of Illinois Press.

Wellek, Rene, and Austin Warren. 1956. *Theory of Literature*. 3rd ed. New York: Harcourt, Brace and World.

Wengle, John. 1988. *Ethnographers in the Field: The Psychology of Research*. Tuscaloosa: University of Alabama Press.

Wenner, Adrian M. 1964. "Sound Communication in Honeybees." *Scientific American* 210 (4): 116–124.

White House. 2014. *President Obama's Promise Zones Initiatives*. White House Fact Sheet. January 8, 2014. http://www.whitehouse.gov/the-press-office/2014/01/08/fact-sheet-president-obama-s-promise-zones-initiative.

Wicks, Sammie Ann. 1989. "A Belated Salute to the 'Old Way' of 'Snaking' the Voice on Its (ca.) 345th Birthday." *Popular Music* 8 (1): 59–96.

Wigginton, Eliot. 1972. *The Foxfire Book*. Garden City, NY: Doubleday.
Wilgus, D. K. 1973. "The Text Is the Thing." *Journal of American Folklore* 86 (341): 241–252.
Wilson, Edward O., Martin A. Nowak, and Corina E. Tarnita. 2010. "The Evolution of Eusociality." *Nature* 466:1057–1062.
Wilson, Joe, and Lee Udall. 1982. *Folk Festivals: A Handbook for Organization and Management*. Knoxville: University of Tennessee Press.
Wimsatt, William K. 1956. "The Intentional Fallacy." In *The Verbal Icon: Studies in the Meaning of Poetry*, 3–20. Lexington: University Press of Kentucky.
Wohlleben, Peter. 2016. *The Hidden Life of Trees*. Translated by Jane Billinghurst. Vancouver: Greystone.
Wordsworth, William. 1805. "Preface." In William Wordsworth, *Lyrical Ballads*, i–lxiv. 4th ed. London: Longman, Hurst, Rees and Orme.
Worster, Donald. [1977] 1994a. *Nature's Economy*. 2nd ed. Cambridge: Cambridge University Press.
———. 1994b. *The Wealth of Nature: Environmental History and the Ecological Imagination*. New York: Oxford University Press.
Yeats, William Butler. 1915. "Preface." In William Butler Yeats, *Reveries over Childhood and Youth*, vii. New York: Macmillan.
Yetman, Norman. [1937] 1975. *These Are Our Lives*. New York: Norton.
Yung, Bell. 2009. "Historical Legacy and the Contemporary World: UNESCO and China's Qin Music in the Twenty-first Century." In *Music and Cultural Rights*, edited by Andrew Weintraub and Bell Yung, 140–168. Urbana: University of Illinois Press.
Zhao, Shanyang. 2003. "Toward a Taxonomy of Copresence." *Presence* 12 (5): 445–455.
Zipes, Jack David. 1983. *Fairy Tales and the Art of Subversion*. New York: Wildman.
Zolli, Andrew, and Anne Marie Healy. 2012. *Resilience*. New York: Free Press.

# SELECTED LIST OF PUBLICATIONS BY JEFF TODD TITON

## Books

2019. *The Oxford Handbook of Applied Ethnomusicology*. 3 vols. Edited by Jeff Todd Titon and Svanibor Pettan. New York: Oxford University Press. First published 2015.

2018. *Powerhouse for God: Speech, Chant, and Song in an Appalachian Baptist Church*. Austin: University of Texas Press. 2nd edition, with a new afterword by the author. First published 1988 (Knoxville: University of Tennessee Press).

2017. *Worlds of Music: An Introduction to the Music of the World's Peoples*. General editor and contributor. 6th rev. ed. New York: Cengage. Translations: *I mondi della musica*, translated into Italian by Tullia Magrini, based on the 3rd edition. Bologna: Zanichelli, 2002. *Worlds of Music*, translated into Chinese by Wu Wenzhi, based on the 3rd edition. Xi'an: Shaanxi Normal University Press, 2003. First published 1984.

2001. *Old-Time Kentucky Fiddle Tunes*. Lexington: University Press of Kentucky.

2001. *American Musical Traditions*. 5 vols. Coeditor and contributor. New York: Schirmer Reference, Gale/Thompson.

1995. *Early Downhome Blues: A Musical and Cultural Analysis*. 2nd edition, with a new afterword by the author. Chapel Hill: University of North Carolina Press. First published 1977.

1991. *Downhome Blues Lyrics: An Anthology from the Post–World War II Era*. 2nd edition, revised and expanded. Urbana: University of Illinois Press. First published 1981.

1989. *Give Me This Mountain: Life History and Selected Sermons of the Rev. C. L. Franklin*, edited by Jeff Todd Titon. Foreword by Rev. Jesse Jackson. Urbana: University of Illinois Press.

1974. *From Blues to Pop: The Autobiography of Leonard "Baby Doo" Caston*. Edited by Jeff Todd Titon. Los Angeles: John Edwards Memorial Foundation, Special Series, No. 4.

## Articles

\# = included in this volume of new and selected essays

2019. "Ecojustice, Religious Folklife and a Sound Ecology." *Yale Journal of Music and Religion* 5 (2): 103–116.

2019. "Foreword." In *Cultural Sustainabilities: Music, Media, Language, Advocacy*, edited by Timothy Cooley, xi–xix. Urbana: University of Illinois Press. Autobiographical essay.

2018. "Afterword: Ecomusicology and the Problems in Ecology." *MUSICultures* 44 (2): 255–264.

2016. "Orality, Commonality, Commons, Sustainability and Resilience." *Journal of American Folklore* 129 (4): 486–497.

#2016. "The Sound of Climate Change." *Whole Terrain* 22:28–32.

2015. "A Context for the Story: A Conversation with Jeff Todd Titon (Interviewed by Marcia Ostashewski)." *MUSICultures* 41 (2): 170–183.

#2015. "Applied Ethnomusicology: A Descriptive and Historical Account." In *The Oxford Handbook of Applied Ethnomusicology*, edited by Jeff Todd Titon and Svanibor Pettan, 4–29. New York: Oxford University Press.

#2015. "Ethnomusicology as the Study of People Making Music." *Muzikoloski Zbornik/ Musicological Annual* (Slovenia) 51 (2): 175–185.

2015. "Exhibiting Music in a Sound Community." *Ethnologies* 37 (1): 23–41.

#2015. "Sustainability, Resilience, Adaptive Management, and Applied Ethnomusicology." In *The Oxford Handbook of Applied Ethnomusicology*, edited by Jeff Todd Titon and Svanibor Pettan, 157–195. New York: Oxford University Press.

#2015. "Thoreau's Ear." *Sound Studies* 1 (1): 144–154.

2015. "Why Thoreau?" In *Current Directions in Ecomusicology*, edited by Aaron S. Allen and Kevin Dawe, 69–79. London: Routledge.

2014. "Sustainability and Sound: Ecomusicology Inside and Outside the Academy." With Aaron S. Allen and Denise Von Glahn. *Music and Politics* 8 (2). http://quod.lib.umich.edu /m/mp/9460447.0008.205?view=text;rgn=main.

2013. "Music and the US War on Poverty." *ICTM Yearbook for Traditional Music* 45:74–82.

#2013. "The Nature of Ecomusicology." *Música e Cultura* 8:8–18. http://www.abet.mus.br /revista/.

#2012. "A Sound Commons for All Living Creatures." *Smithsonian Folkways Magazine* (Fall– Winter). http://www.folkways.si.edu/magazine-fall-winter-2012-sound-commons-living -creatures/science-and-nature-world/music/article/smithsonian.

2012. "Authenticity and Authentication: Mike Seeger, the New Lost City Ramblers, and the Old-Time Music Revival." *Journal of Folklore Research* 49 (2): 227–245.

2012. "Music, Mediation, Sustainability: A Case Study on the Banjo." *Folklore Forum* 42 (1). http://folkloreforum.net/2012/06/28/music-mediation-sustainability-a-case-study-on-the -banjo/.

2011. "Textual Analysis or Thick Description?" In *The Cultural Study of Music*, 2nd ed., edited by Martin Clayton, Richard Middleton, and Trevor Herbert, 75–85. London: Routledge. First published 2003.

2010. "Religious Folklife." In *The Encyclopedia of Southern Culture*, vol. 14, *Folklife*, edited by Glenn Hinson and William Ferris, 215–221. Chapel Hill: University of North Carolina Press.

2009. "Ecology, Phenomenology, and Biocultural Thinking: A Reply to Judith Becker." *Ethnomusicology* 53 (3): 502–509.

2009. "Economy, Ecology and Music: An Introduction." In "Music and Sustainability," edited by Jeff Todd Titon. Special issue, *the world of music* 51 (1): 5–16.

#2009. "Music and Sustainability: An Ecological Viewpoint." *the world of music* 51 (1): 119–138.

2009. "Sustainability without Cultural Heritage Management: Social Networking, Education and Musical Conservation among Middle Class Folk Revivalists." In *Musik im interkulturellen Dialog: Festschrift für Max Peter Baumann*, edited by Karoline Oehme and Nevzat Çiftçi, 17–26. Bamberg, Germany: University of Bamberg.

2009. "Teaching Blues and Country Music, and Leading an Old-Time String Band—at an Ivy League School." *Journal of Popular Music Studies* 21 (1): 113–124.

2005. "Bluegrass and Country Music: The Good-Old-Boy and the Long Journey Home." In *Bean Blossom to Bannerman: A Festshrift for Neil V. Rosenberg*, edited by Martin Lovelace, Peter Narvaez, and Diane Tye, 493–508. St. John's, NL: Memorial University of Newfoundland Folklore and Language Publications.

#2005. "Knowing Fieldwork." In *Shadows in the Field*, 2nd ed., edited by Gregory Barz and Timothy Cooley, 25–41. New York: Oxford University Press. First published 1996.
2005. "Tuned Up with the Grace of God: Music and Experience among Old Regular Baptists." In *Music in American Religious Experience*, edited by Philip Bohlman, Maria Chow, and Elizabeth Blumhofer, 311–333. New York: Oxford University Press.
2003. "A Conversation with Jeff Todd Titon." Interview by John Fenn. In "Applied Ethnomusicology," edited by John Fenn. Special issue, *Folklore Forum* 34 (1–2): 119–131.
#2003. "Text." In *Eight Words for the Study of Expressive Culture*, edited by Burt Feintuch, 69–98. Urbana: University of Illinois Press.
2003. "The Blues as an Historical Phenomenon." In *Such Sweet Thunder: Views on Black American Music*, edited by Mark Baszak, 44–47. Amherst: Fine Arts Center, University of Massachusetts.
2002. "Labels: Identifying Categories of Blues and Gospel." In *The Cambridge Companion to Blues and Gospel Music*, edited by Allan Moore, 13–19. Cambridge: Cambridge University Press.
2000. "Albert Collins: Poet of South Blue Hill, Maine," *Northeast Folklore* 35:383–404.
#1999. "'The Real Thing': Tourism, Authenticity, and Pilgrimage among the Old Regular Baptists at the 1997 Smithsonian Folklife Festival." *the world of music* 41 (3): 115–139.
1997. "Ethnomusicology and Values: A Reply to Henry Kingsbury." *Ethnomusicology* 41 (2): 253–257.
1995. "Bi-musicality as Metaphor." *Journal of American Folklore* 108 (429): 287–297.
1995. "Text." *Journal of American Folklore* 108 (430): 432–448.
1994. "Hypertext and Ethnomusicology." *Ethnomusicology Research Digest* 186: n.p.
1994. "Knowing People Making Music: Toward a New Epistemology for Ethnomusicology." *Etnomusikologian vuosikirja* [Yearbook of the Finnish Society for Ethnomusicology] 6:5–13. Helsinki: Suomen etnomusikologinen seura.
1993. "Reconstructing the Blues: Reflections on the 1960s Blues Revival." In *Transforming Tradition*, edited by Neil V. Rosenberg, 220–240. Urbana: University of Illinois Press, 2004.
1992. "Music, the Public Interest, and the Practice of Ethnomusicology." *Ethnomusicology* 36 (3): 315–322.
1992. "Representation and Authority in Film/Video Production." *Ethnomusicology* 36 (1): 89–94.
1992. "Style and Meaning in Contemporary Documentary Film." *Appalachian Journal* 20 (1): 44–55.
1991–1992. "Photographs of Folk Religion in the South." In "Religion in the South," edited by Tom Rankin. Special issue, *Mississippi Folklore Register*, vols. 25–26:46–50.
1990. "'Crossing Academic Disciplines,' in *What Doth It Profit? The Study of Mountain Religion*, edited by Paul Salstrom." *Appalachian Journal* 18 (1): 56–82. [Five scholars' responses to *Powerhouse for God* and my reply.]
1989. "The Experience of Tongues: Pentecostal Seekers and Exhorters at a Camp Meeting, Elkton, Virginia, 1977." In *Time and Temperature: A Centennial Publication of the American Folklore Society*, edited by Charles Camp, 58–63. Washington, DC: American Folklore Society. [Photo essay.]
1988. "Reverend C. L. Franklin and the Afro-American Folk Preaching Tradition." *Folklife Annual, 1987*, edited by James Hardin, 86–105. Washington, DC: American Folklife Center, Library of Congress.

1987. "'God'll Just Bless You All Over the Place': Hymnody in a Blue Ridge Mountain Independent Baptist Church." *Appalachian Journal* 14 (4): 348–358.
1986. "Symposium on the Life Story." *Folklife Annual, 1986*, edited by James Hardin, 154–173. Washington, DC: American Folklife Center, Library of Congress.
1985. "Role, Stance, and Identity in Fieldwork among Folk Baptists and Pentecostals in the United States." *American Music* 3 (1): 16–24.
1985. "Folklife Studies and Religion." *Mid-America Folklore* 13 (2): 4–11.
1985. "Presenting American Religious Folklife: A Panel Discussion." *Mid-America Folklore* 13 (2): 27–36.
#1980. "The Life Story." *Journal of American Folklore* 93 (369): 276–292.
1980. A Song from the Holy Spirit." *Ethnomusicology* 24 (2): 223–231.
1978. "Every Day I Have the Blues: Improvisation and Daily Life." In "Special Blues Issue," edited by Jeff Todd Titon. Special issue, *Southern Folklore Quarterly* 42 (1): 85–98.
1978. "Introduction." In "Special Blues Issue," edited by Jeff Todd Titon. Special issue, *Southern Folklore Quarterly* 42 (1): 1–7.
1978. "Some Recent Pentecostal Revivals: A Report in Words and Photographs." *The Georgia Review* 32 (3): 579–605.
1977. "Living Blues Interview: Son House." *Living Blues* 31:13–22.
1977. "Talking about Music: Analysis, Synthesis, and Song-Producing Models." *Essays in Arts and Sciences* 6 (1): 53–57.
1977. "Thematic Pattern in Downhome Blues Lyrics: The Evidence on Commercial Recordings since World War II." *Journal of American Folklore* 90 (357): 316–330.
1976. "Son House: Two Narratives." *Alcheringa: Ethnopoetics*, n.s., 2 (1): 2–9.
1976. "Downhome Blues Lyrics since the Second World War: A Selection." *Alcheringa: Ethnopoetics*, n.s., 2 (1): 10–26.
1970. "Autobiography and Blues Texts." *John Edwards Memorial Foundation Quarterly* 6:79–82.

## Articles in Press and Forthcoming

"An Ecological Approach to Folklife Studies, Expressive Culture, and Environment." In *Performing Diverse Environmentalisms*, edited by John H. McDowell. Bloomington: Indiana University Press.
"A Sound Economy." In *Transforming Ethnomusicology*, ed. Beverley Diamond and Salwa El-Shawan. New York: Oxford University Press.
"Ethnography in the Study of Congregational Music." In *Studying Congregational Music: Key Issues, Methods, and Theoretical Perspectives*, edited by Jeffers Engelhardt, Andrew Mall, and Monique Ingalls. Ashgate.
"The Expressive Cultures of Sound Communication in Humans and Other Beings: A Phenomenological and Ethnomusicological Approach." In *The Oxford Handbook of Phenomenology and Ethnomusicology*, edited by Harris M. Berger and Katie Szego. New York: Oxford University Press.

## Fiction

2015. "Flight Call." *MUSICultures* 41 (2): 162–169.
2013. *Davey*. W. Brattleboro, VT: Longhouse.
2008. "Percy." In *The Folklore Muse*, edited by Frank De Caro, 73–83. Logan: University of Utah Press. [Short fiction.]
2004. "Letter from Ole Bull to Sara Thorp." *Journal of American Folklore* 117 (465): 316–324.

## Other Formats

2014 [1982]. *Powerhouse for God*. 2 LPs, booklet. Coproduced and recorded with Kenneth M. George. Chapel Hill: University of North Carolina Press. Reissued (2 CDs, booklet) Washington, DC: Smithsonian Institution. Folkways SFS 60006.

2003. *Songs of the Old Regular Baptists: Lined-Out Hymnody from Southeastern Kentucky*. Vol. 2. CD and booklet. Washington, DC: Smithsonian Institution. Folkways SF 50001.

1997. *Songs of the Old Regular Baptists: Lined-Out Hymnody from Southeastern Kentucky*. CD and booklet. Washington, DC: Smithsonian Institution. Folkways SF 40106.

1992. *Clyde Davenport: Puncheon Camps*. 60-minute cassette, booklet. Berea, KY: Berea College Appalachian Center.

1991. *Clyde Davenport*. Hypertext/Multimedia. Original format: HyperCard. Providence, RI: Brown University Scholarly Technology Group. Accessed November 29, 2018. http://www.stg.brown.edu/projects/davenport/CLYDE_DAVENPORT.html.

1990. *Albert "Hap" Collins of Blue Hill, Maine*. VHS video recording, 58 minutes. Orono: Maine Folklife Center, University of Maine.

1989. *Powerhouse for God*. 16-mm film, 58 minutes. Coproduced, filmed, recorded, and directed with Barry Dornfeld and Tom Rankin. Documentary Educational Resources, Watertown, Massachusetts.

1974. *Lazy Bill Lucas*. 12" LP, booklet. Philo 1007. North Ferrisburg, VT.

1972. *Lazy Bill and His Friends*. 12" LP. Lazy 12MO2. Buc, France.

1971. *Lazy Bill Lucas*. 12" LP. Wild 12Mo2. Buc, France.

# INDEX

acoustemology, 234, 238, 246
acoustic ecology, 221, 223, 246
acoustic niche, 219, 221, 244–246
adaptive management, 122, 154, 172–173, 198–215; definition, 198–199; examples, 202–215; negative connotations of, 213–214. *See also* resilience; sustainability
advocacy, 3, 53, 91, 95, 108, 113–114, 116, 175, 186. *See also* ethnography; fieldwork
affordances, 268–269
Allen, Aaron S., 224, 232, 248
Alviso, Rick, 115–116
analysis, musical, 28, 34, 62, 67, 80, 99
animal intelligence, 64, 268–269, 275n11
animal sound communication. *See* sound communication
anti-instrumentalism, 25–26, 265, 268. *See also* ecological rationality
Appalachia, 2, 18, 82, 90, 124–126, 128–129, 137, 151n10, 167, 169, 177, 189, 202–203
applied ethnomusicology, 4, 6, 87–119, 171–215; and applied anthropology, 104–105, 188; definition, 88; distrust of, 105–108; as ethnomusicology in the public interest, 114–115; examples, 168–169; history of, 94–118; and personality, 94; as public ethnomusicology, 93, 114–115; vs. public sector ethnomusicology, 92–93; vs. "pure" ethnomusicology, 88–89; and sustainability, resilience, and adaptive management, 200–201
apprenticeship, musical and cultural, 58, 84, 112, 180, 196
authenticity, 16, 48, 54, 77, 104, 123–125, 136–137, 139–141, 161–162, 177, 179, 213
authority and power, 48, 81, 124, 141, 144, 146, 148–149, 151n10, 153, 194, 233; and ethnographic representation, 39, 52–57, 73, 81, 140–142; and narrative, 40, 78

Back, I. D., 130
Bakan, Michael, 115

balance of nature, 185, 199, 223; vs. disturbance and change paradigm, 199, 224, 230–231. *See also* regime change
Balfa, Dewey, 166, 191–192
Bartók, Béla, 28, 30–31, 33, 72, 98
Bauman, Richard, 140–142, 148
behavior, cooperative, 77, 187, 261, 264, 269, 271. *See also* homo reciprocans
behavioral ecology, 266–268, 272, 275n8. *See also* selfish gene theory
Bennett, Jane, 273
Berry, Wendell, 273
birdsong, 4, 221, 228, 243, 256, 266–267; aesthetic component in, 268–271; as language, 268
blues, 3–4, 9, 11, 14, 43, 66, 68–69, 75, 85, 109, 123, 136, 190–191
Bock, Cherice, 248
Bradbury, Jack, 244, 267, 275n8
Brăiloiu, Constantin, 28, 30, 32–33, 37n1, 72, 98
Burroway, Janet, 55

Cage, John, 3
Cantwell, Robert, 54, 123, 136, 139, 154
Castelo-Branco, Salwa El Shawan, 118
Clifford, James, 113
climate change, 188, 231, 248–253, 266
Clyde Davenport HyperCard Stack, 61–62, 80
Code, Lorraine, 76
coevolution, 266, 269–270
Coles, Robert, 12–13, 26n1, 26n2
collecting: vs. fieldwork, 24, 48, 52, 67, 69, 73, 77, 80; of music and folklore, 30–33, 43, 72, 96, 99–100, 111, 170, 208
Common Ground Country Fair, 5–6
commons, 3, 219–222, 245–246, 247n5, 264; definition, 260, 264, 293, 297; res communes, 222, 245. *See also* sound commons
community, social, 3–6, 9, 43, 49, 65, 68, 79, 88, 91, 116, 118, 121, 135, 137, 148, 150, 153–154, 156, 158, 177, 179, 191–192, 195–196,

303

community, social (*cont.*) 203, 206–207; ecological, 156, 231, 266, 274; economic, 262–265; moral, 273–274; musical, 6, 164–170; participatory, 263; sound, 237, 255–261, 265
comparative musicology, 27, 30–32, 71–72, 95, 98–103, 111, 118n2
complex system, 156, 171, 199, 215, 201–203, 266, 274
consciousness, 7, 44, 51, 59, 74–76, 79, 115, 258, 266–268
conservation biology. *See* conservation ecology
conservation ecology, 152, 158, 170, 188–189, 194, 196, 199, 229–230, 254
conservation: and cultural sustainability, 185–186; ethnomusicologists and, 192–193; natural, cultural, and musical, 4, 125, 154, 174, 176–186, 192–194, 200–201, 213; vs. preservation, 172–184. *See also* sustainability
Cooley, Timothy, 7, 27, 67, 85, 113
copresence, 7–8, 217, 224, 235, 237, 239, 242–245, 254, 256, 258–261, 263, 264–265, 272. *See also* presence
Cornett, Elwood, 76, 125, 129, 131–133, 140, 142–144, 146–147, 149, 167–169
Crapanzano, Vincent, 113
Cruikshank, Julie, 259
cultural conservation. *See* conservation
cultural ecology, 188, 219, 266
cultural equity, 3, 88, 97, 112, 117, 155, 157–158, 167, 179, 182, 188, 194, 222
cultural heritage, intangible, 90, 107, 121–122, 152–155, 158–164, 167, 169–170, 179–180, 183–184, 234; as an economic engine, 186; and tourism, 90, 95, 121, 123–125, 134, 140, 143–150, 153, 155, 169–170, 184, 186, 190, 196, 200, 205, 234; unintended consequences of marking as, 161–164
cultural policy, 89–91, 134, 152–170, 194–195, 197
cultural soil, 2, 158

Daly, Herman E., 187–188, 228
Darwin, Charles, 30, 185, 230, 265, 275n5, 275n8
Davis, Martha Ellen, 114, 115

de Léry, Jean, 73–74
Degh, Linda, 13, 19, 22
Dennett, Daniel C., 265, 268
Derrida, Jacques, 64, 233, 258
DeWitt, Mark, 169, 195, 234
Diamond, Beverley, 118, 254
Dilthey, William, 50–51, 57, 71
Dirksen, Rebecca, 88, 116
diversity: biological, 152, 155–159, 164, 171, 180, 185, 188–189, 194, 196, 202, 219, 224; cultural and musical, 109–111, 157, 160, 167, 177, 180, 182, 194; economic, 186–187, 215n6; and risk management, 200
Dje Dje, Jacqueline, 193
dopamine, 256
Dornfeld, Barry, 49
Dorson, Richard, 12
Dyen, Doris, 115

ecocriticism, 223–224, 226, 236, 238–239
ecological economics, 8, 187, 228, 251
ecological knowledges, traditional and Indigenous, 8, 159, 214, 223, 234, 258–260, 273
ecological rationality, 217, 223, 255–256, 259–260, 264–266, 274. *See also* economic rationality
ecology, 3–4, 152, 155, 219, 229–231, 259, 275n4; and applied anthropology, 188; and applied ethnomusicology, 194–195; confusion of with environment, 215n4; and cultural and musical sustainability, 156–158, 170, 184–189; and interconnectedness, 155, 157–158, 233, 260. *See also* acoustic ecology; behavioral ecology; conservation ecology; cultural ecology; ecological rationality; ecosystem; sound ecology; soundscape ecology
ecomusicology, 7, 27–28, 92, 217, 223–235, 237, 248, 251; definitions, 224
economic rationality, 223–225, 227–229, 232, 234, 255–256, 260–263, 265–266, 274. *See also* ecological rationality
ecosystem, 155–156, 164, 171–174, 182, 184–185, 189, 199–200, 219, 224, 230–231, 248, 266, 274; and corporations, 187–188; definition, 230–231, 275n14; music culture as an, 155–156, 172, 196–197, 200–203, 213–215. *See also* ecology

Ellis, Alexander, 35, 71, 98
embodiment, 64, 246, 275n12
endangered species, 164, 199, 204, 227, 230, 232
environment, 3–4, 8, 27, 92, 116, 156, 160, 172, 181, 184, 187–188, 198–199, 204, 211, 213, 215n2, 215n4, 217, 219–222, 224–229, 231–232, 233, 235, 237, 239, 241–242, 245–246, 249, 251, 259, 261, 263–274; confusion with ecology, 215n4
environmental humanities, 8, 223, 231–232
environmental movement, 2, 171, 173–174, 182, 185–186, 189, 205, 213, 215n2, 223, 224, 226, 229–230, 231, 236, 248, 254
epistemology, 4–5, 70–72, 76–77, 223–224, 229, 232–237, 254, 264, 272; for ethnomusicology, 67–74, 77, 80–81, 83; relational, 223–225, 232–234, 237, 242, 272–273; sound, 242, 246, 256; and sustainability, 224. *See also* relational epistemology
ethnicity, 51, 73, 110–111
ethnography, 11, 28, 34, 38–39, 47–48, 54, 66, 78–79, 102, 140–143, 194; collaborative, 95, 168–169; as fiction, 38, 53–55, 85–86; and the "knowing text," 51–59; as quest, 81, 83–85, 86n3
ethnomusicology: as the cultural study of music, 103–104; defined as the study of people making music, 4, 27–37, 67, 73, 75, 85n1, 87–88; early history of, 97–109; establishment of graduate programs in, 105–106, 110; four paradigms of, 72–73; humanistic turn in, 27, 113–114; origin of the term, 28, 99. *See also* applied ethnomusicology
evolution, 30, 67, 196, 230, 234, 248, 251, 256, 269–271; music and cultural evolution, 30–32, 182, 269; evolutionary biology, 244, 265–266
exchanges: social, 259, 272; ecological, 259, 272, 274; economic, 259, 263–264, 272. *See also* gift exchanges
expressive culture, 2, 38, 43, 46, 52, 65, 85, 112, 121, 152, 154, 157, 170–171, 178

Fargion, Janet Topp, 195
Feintuch, Burt, 38–39, 137–138, 154
Feld, Steven, 34, 36, 194, 234, 246, 256
feminism, 53, 73, 262, 266

Fenn, John, 116
Ferris, William, 190–191
Festival of American Folklife, 124–125, 132–143, 150, 176, 192; impact of participants on, 140, 147, 169, 192; impact on participants, 140–143, 146–149. *See also* virtual folk festival
fiction: ethnography as, 53–55, 58–59, 80; vs. history, 13, 22–23; hypertext fiction, 79–80; life story as, 12–13, 16, 20, 22–26
Fields, Grethel [Dosh], 143–148
fieldwork, 2, 4, 8, 10, 12, 22, 24, 38–39, 48–49, 52–59, 62, 66–86, 88, 94, 99, 108, 112, 138, 173, 193–194; the "new fieldwork" 27, 67, 73–74, 94, 113–114; and presence, 258; roles and stances, 66, 77; as transformative experience, 58. *See also* friendship
film, documentary and ethnographic, 64, 73, 78–80, 167, 226
fitness (evolutionary), 265–267, 269
Fletcher, Alice Cunningham, 96–97
flow, feelings of, 64, 67, 260
Folk Arts Division, National Endowment for the Arts, 112, 114, 150n5, 166, 177–180, 192–193
folklife, 4, 48, 49, 52, 56, 134–135, 178–181
folk psychology, 267–268
Frank, Gelya, 16, 26n4
Franklin, Rev. C. L., 49
friendship, and fieldwork, 2, 4, 11, 20, 24, 57, 69, 77, 82–85, 114, 165, 172, 193. *See also* reciprocity

Gagliano, Monica, 255, 257
Garfias, Robert, 110, 114, 193
Geertz, Clifford, 50–51, 53, 57, 72, 78–79, 113
gender, 51, 73, 229–230, 262
genome, 256, 266, 269, 272
Gerberg, Miriam, 115, 116
gift exchanges, 228, 232, 234, 263–264
Goffman, Erving, 47, 77, 242; and copresence, 258–259
Gourlay, Kenneth, 27, 74, 113
growth, limits to, 152, 157, 185
Guilbault, Jocylene, 73

Haeckel, Ernst, 31, 275n4
Harrison, Klisala, 115–117

Haskell, Erica, 115–116
Hawes, Bess Lomax, 112, 114–115, 139, 179, 192
Healy, Ann Marie, 201–203
Hellier-Tinoco, Ruth, 85
heritage. *See* cultural heritage, intangible
hermeneutics, 5, 28, 40, 47, 50, 57, 71–72;
    hermeneutic circle and participation, 57–58
Herndon, Marcia, 35
Herzog, George, 28, 98–99, 100–103, 111–112
Heth, Charlotte, 114, 193
homo economicus (economic man), 227–228, 234, 237, 245, 261–263, 267, 275n2;
    alternatives to, 237, 245, 262–264. *See also* sound economy
homo reciprocans, 262–264
Hood, Mantle, 28, 100, 108–109, 192
Hornbostel, Eric Von, 28, 30–33, 98–100
House, Eddie "Son," 14–16, 20, 43–44, 69, 190
Hufford, Mary, 154, 180–182
Hurston, Zora Neale, 97
Hutchinson, Patrick, 76, 82
Hyde, Lewis, 219, 247n5
hypertext, 5, 38–40, 60–65, 67, 73, 78–80;
    definition of, 60. *See also* fiction

identity, 11, 21, 24, 58, 73, 76–77, 84, 160, 172, 176, 180, 190, 195, 251, 261
Ihde, Don, 72, 242, 257
intangible cultural heritage. *See* cultural heritage, intangible
intersubjectivity, 5, 40, 48–49, 52, 57, 74, 76–77, 84, 233, 260
interviews, 11–26, 56, 66, 68–70, 140, 191
Ives, Edward D., 17–18

Jabbour, Alan, 192
James, Henry: "The Figure in the Carpet," 1; "The Real Thing," 124, 149–150
Jones, Loyal, 129, 151n10
justice: social, 116–117, 260; ecojustice, 92, 194, 261; environmental, 261

Kagan, Alan, 68
Keil, Charles, 34, 36, 113–115
Kirshenblatt-Gimblett, Barbara, 93, 154
Kodish, Debora, 116
Krause, Bernie, 220–221, 246
Kurin, Richard, 139, 153

land ethic, 261, 273–274
Landow, George, 61, 79
Langness, L. L., 19–20
Leadbelly [Huddie Ledbetter], 190
Leff, Enrique, 233
Leopold, Aldo, 261, 273–274
life history, 11–12, 16, 19–22, 24, 49
life story, 11–26. *See also* personal experience story
Lomax, Alan, 20, 28, 30–33, 90, 97, 111–112, 139, 157, 190, 194
Lomax, John, 20, 97
Loughran, Maureen, 115–116
Lubbock, Percy, 58–59
Lucas, William "Lazy Bill," 20, 68–69, 136, 191

Maney, Donna, 256
Marcus, George, 113
Marx, Leo, 236, 238–239
McAllester, David, 28, 33–34, 36, 67, 74, 98, 101–104, 108, 110, 192
Merleau-Ponty, Maurice, 71, 275n12
Merriam, Alan, 28, 33, 34, 36, 72–73, 99, 101–104, 106–107, 113, 118
Miller, Kiri, 206
Miller, Perry, 240–241
mirror neurons, 268
Moore, James F., 187–188
music culture, 31, 35–36, 72–73, 77–78, 81, 91, 153, 157–158, 163, 165, 170–172, 174, 176, 182, 186, 189, 193–195, 260; as an ecosystem, 4, 155–156, 172, 196–197, 200–203, 213–215
music: as biocultural resource, 158, 170, 194, 264; as endangered, 90, 97, 129, 153, 162, 174, 186, 190, 213; as an evolutionary advantage, 234–235; as means of connection, 81–82, 83, 274; as a special case of sound, 7, 235, 237; as a thing-in-itself (the "music itself"), 35–37
musical being, 3, 8, 67, 75–76, 81–83, 85, 253–255, 264. *See also* ontology
Myers, Helen, 71

Nagel, Thomas, 29–30
narrative, 8, 11–14, 19–20, 38, 43–44, 49, 54–56, 59, 62–63, 73–74, 78–81, 125, 134, 143–145, 147, 149, 227
nature, 3, 27, 70, 154, 160, 164, 174, 175, 182, 185, 189, 196–197, 199, 201, 216, 220, 221, 223–235,

237–239, 241, 243, 245, 248–251, 255–256, 267, 273–274
nature's economy, 164, 230–231, 233, 237, 243, 245; definition, 185
Nettl, Bruno, 6, 78, 86n4, 98–104, 107–108, 110, 119n3
neurobiology, 256, 268
Newell, Wayne, 176, 195
noise, 35, 92, 206, 219–221, 244, 246, 260, 269, 272–273
Norton, Barley, 198

O'Connell, Barry, 37n1
Odum, Eugene P., 230–231
Old Regular Baptists, 21, 75–76, 123–151, 167–170, 260; and adaptive management, 210–213; doctrine, 125–126; as ideal folk society, 121–122; music of, 126–129; self-documentation project, 131–132; and resilience, 202–208
Olson, Charles, 13, 26
ontology: relational, 66–67, 272; sonic, 75–76, 81–83, 85, 254–255, 264; textual, 38–48, 64. *See also* musical being
organic farming and gardening, 2, 4–6, 158, 200

participatory music, 169; and amateurism, 234; and empathy, 260
Pedelty, Mark, 248
performance, 4–5, 11, 21, 34, 39–40, 42–52, 56, 60–61, 63, 65, 72, 80, 133–134, 139–140, 260
personal experience story, 11–12, 22, 24. *See also* life story
perspectivism, 232, 275n13
Pettan, Svanibor, 89, 94, 116, 118
phenomenology, 28, 40–41, 66–67, 71–72, 74–79, 81, 237, 242, 246, 254, 257–258. *See also* musical being
Pijanowski, Bryan, 244
plant communication, 7, 255, 257, 265–266
postcolonialism, 66, 95, 114, 188
presence, 7, 12, 43, 49, 56, 75, 77, 82–83, 237, 242, 247n4, 258; Derrida on, 233, 258; sound presence, 217, 222, 249–250, 252, 254, 257–258, 263; virtual, 258. *See also* copresence

preservation, 6–7, 24, 26, 31–32, 72, 90, 92, 104, 125, 129, 132, 134, 149, 154, 160, 162, 165, 170, 172–176, 178, 180–181, 190, 192, 201; vs. conservation, 172–184; as safeguarding (UNESCO), 6, 153, 155, 158–165, 170, 172–174, 176, 182–185, 201, 203, 234. *See also* sustainability
public folklore, 54, 87, 112–114, 123, 142, 167, 173, 176, 179–180, 182, 193. *See also* applied ethnomusicology
Puryear, Mark, 115, 116

Rabinow, Paul, 113
Rankin, Tom, 49
reciprocity, 3, 48; as animal cooperative behavior, 259–260, 263–264, 266, 271–272; and fieldwork, 69, 82, 88, 113–114; and economics, 237, 263–264; and giving back, 96–97, 116, 193, 214
reductionism, 34, 232–233; vs. holism, 225
reflexivity, 29, 48, 73, 79, 95, 113, 124–125, 194
regime change, in ecosystems, 199–200, 231. *See also* balance of nature
relational epistemology. *See* epistemology
relational ontology. *See* ontology
religious folklife, 4, 49, 123–151
repatriation, of musical artifacts, 91, 95, 116, 176, 195
resilience, 3, 172–173, 197–215; characteristics of resilient systems, 201–202; definition, 198; examples, 202–213
resonance, 237–238, 255–256, 260. *See also* vibration
revitalization, musical and cultural, 165, 169–170, 195
revival, folk music, 54, 104, 111, 136, 155, 165–166, 169, 177, 179–180, 190–191, 195, 205–207, 222, 234; old-time string band, 6, 202, 208–213
Rice, Timothy, 78, 99, 116
Ricoeur, Paul, 50, 71–72, 74
Rinzler, Ralph, 166, 191–192
Ritchie, Jean, 189–190
Rorty, Richard, 5, 45–46, 64, 67, 70, 229
Rosaldo, Renato, 78
Rose, Carol, 245, 247n5
Rosengarten, Theodore, 12

sacred space, 154, 235
safeguarding. *See* preservation
Sakata, Lorraine, 193
Sawin, Patricia, 140–142, 148
Schippers, Huib, 173
Schutz, Alfred, 70–71, 260
scientific realism, 225, 229
Seeger, Anthony, 78, 97, 98, 114, 132, 193–194
Seeger, Charles, 28, 34–35, 71, 97, 100, 102–103
Seeger, Ruth Crawford, 97
selfish gene theory, 265–267, 269, 271, 275n5
Sheehy, Daniel, 73, 97–98, 112, 114, 115, 193
Sherfey, John, 11, 25
Smart, Ninian, 66
sociality, 5, 271–272
Society for Ethnomusicology (SEM), 4, 27–28, 72, 89, 95, 98, 105, 113–118, 119n6; Applied Ethnomusicology Section of, 115–117; early history of, 100–109; and political activism, 117–118; tension between anthropologists and comparative musicologists in, 100–101, 129
Sommers, Laurie Kay, 136, 138–140
sound commons, 219–222, 245; definition, 220; examples of, 260. *See also* commons
sound communication: in animals, 225, 236, 244, 248–253, 266–271, 275n8; false (deceptive, dishonest) signals, 244, 249, 251, 267; alarm calls, 248, 252; interspecies, 249, 252, 257; and language, 255–256, 268
sound community, 255–256, 258–261
sound ecology, 3, 7–8, 11, 67, 152, 223, 236–237, 248, 254, 256, 264–274; definition, 216, 259, 264–265
sound economy, 254–256, 261–264
sound equity, 219, 220, 222
sound experience, 76, 254–258, 274
sound ontology. *See* musical being
sound: ambient sound and Thoreau, 3, 7, 242–243, 247n2; as connecting beings, 2, 7–8, 255–256, 260, 272–273; as language without metaphor, 221; as signal, 221–222, 244, 249–252, 255, 257–258, 266–267, 269. *See also* vibration
soundscape ecology, 221, 223, 226, 237, 246, 248–249
Stahl, Sandra K. D., 11, 24

stewardship, 3, 95, 152, 155, 158, 169–170; vs. ownership, 158, 170
Stumpf, Carl, 32, 33, 96, 98
sustainability, 3, 5–8; in applied ethnomusicology, 189–197; arising from fieldwork and collaborative ethnography, 193; ecological principles of, 156–158, 170, 184–189; and ecomusicology, 224–225; economic vs. environmentalist interpretations, 185–189, 225–226; musical and cultural, 90–91, 121–122, 152–170, 171–215; as sustaining people making music, 194; in theory, 184–189; sustainable development, 5, 184–185, 187, 213, 228. *See also* adaptive management; conservation; preservation; resilience

Tedlock, Barbara, 26, 57–58
Tedlock, Dennis, 11, 23, 57–58, 113
Terkel, Studs, 12–13, 26n1
text, 1, 5, 8, 17, 21, 23, 28, 35, 38–65, 70, 72–73, 77–79, 195, 255; folkloric, 40, 42–45; intertextuality, 44–45, 233; "the knowing text," 38, 39, 52–59; stability and instability, 43–44, 60–61, 83; unreliable, 62. *See also* intertextuality
Thoreau, Henry David, 3–4, 7, 22, 174, 185, 221–223, 236–247, 254, 259, 273, 275n11; and birdsong, 243; and commons, 245–247; and John Cage, 3; and music, 239–242; and presence, 237, 242; and sound, 3, 236–246
torture, music used for, 118, 119n6
tourism, heritage. *See* cultural heritage, intangible
transcription, musical and textual, 23, 30, 32, 33–34, 37, 39–40, 42–44, 49, 61–62, 67, 76, 80–81, 96, 99, 101, 195
Trimillos, Ric, 193
Turner, Rory, 6
Turner, Victor, 47, 51

UNESCO, 90, 92, 107, 122, 153, 158–164, 173, 179, 180, 182–184, 234

Van Buren, Kathleen Noss, 115
Van Buren, Tom, 115

Vander, Judith, 34
Vehrencamp, Sandra, 244, 267, 275n8
Vennum, Tom, 192–193
vibration, sound, 237–238, 247, 256–257, 272–273; covibration, 260, 274; resonance, 256–257; sympathetic vibration, 256; as visceral and metaphorical, 255, 260, 272. *See also* presence
virtual folk festival, 39
virtual reality, 60, 63–64
vital materialism, 8, 273
Von Glahn, Denise, 248

Von Rosen, Franziska, 73, 76, 79
Von Uexküll, Jakob, 275n12

Wallhausser, John, 126, 129–132, 168
Watkins, Holly, 256
Weibtraub, Andrew, 107, 184
world of music, ecological meaning of, 156
Worster, Donald, 185, 189, 215n4, 231

Yung, Bell, 107, 163, 184

Zolli, Andrew, 201–203

JEFF TODD TITON is Professor of Music, Emeritus, at Brown University. He has been active professionally both in folklore and ethnomusicology for more than forty-five years, having authored numerous articles, films, recordings, and books. A list of his selected publications appears elsewhere in this volume. He is known for developing and practicing collaborative ethnographic field research based in reciprocity and friendship; for pioneering an applied ethnomusicology based in social responsibility; for his 1984 proposal that musical cultures could be understood as ecosystems; and for developing an ecological approach to cultural and musical sustainability. In 2012 he issued an appeal for a sound commons for all living creatures, part of his current project that theorizes a sound ecology.

www.ingramcontent.com/pod-product-compliance
Lightning Source LLC
Chambersburg PA
CBHW030117240426
43673CB00041B/1316